International Theological Library

HISTORY OF CHRISTIAN MISSIONS

BY

CHARLES HENRY ROBINSON, D.D

HON. CANON OF RIPON CATHEDRAL AND
EDITORIAL SECRETARY OF THE SOCIETY FOR THE PROPAGATION
OF THE GOSPEL IN FOREIGN PARTS

NEW YORK
CHARLES SCRIBNER'S SONS
1915

PREFACE

THE story of missions, which reaches back to the beginning of the Christian era, and embraces almost every country in the world, cannot be told within the limits of a single volume. The task which I have ventured to undertake is of a far less ambitious character, my object being to provide the intelligent reader with an outline sketch of Christian missions which may enable him to obtain a correct perspective, but which will need to be filled in for each several country and period of history by much careful study. This volume is not intended to serve as a dictionary nor as a commentary upon missions, but as a text-book to encourage and facilitate their study. Those who have devoted the largest amount of time to such study will be most ready to forgive its imperfections and shortcomings. A well-known authority on the subject of Foreign Missions, to whom the task of writing this book was originally assigned, but who failed to respond to the invitation, wrote to its present author, "You have an almost impossible task; I should absolutely quail at the work you are doing."

It would have been comparatively easy to fill the space allotted to me by the publishers with a discussion of the principles which have governed the activities of Christian missionaries, and it would have been still less difficult to compile a volume of statistics which would have shown, more or less accurately, the progress that has been made in bringing about the conversion of non-Christian lands, but in neither case would the object with which this volume was planned have been fulfilled. Of

missionary statistics I have tried to avoid any extensive
use, and have only given such when they appeared to be
necessary in order to elucidate the relative progress that
has been made in different sections of the mission field or
at different epochs.

In attempting to describe the work of hundreds of
missionary societies it is obvious that no single individual,
however good his opportunities for obtaining information
may be, can estimate correctly the relative importance of
that which has been done in each several country and
by individual societies. If in some instances I have
appeared to dwell at disproportionate length upon the
work of Anglican missions, this has not been due to my
ignorance of the relative insignificance of their results, if
these are calculated on a numerical basis, but is due to the
fact that I have tried to lay special emphasis upon the
beginnings of missionary enterprises, and to the fact that
in many countries, where a large amount of work is now
being carried on by other societies, missionary enterprise
was initiated by Anglican missionaries. I desire to tender
my apologies in advance to the representatives of several
American societies concerning whose work I have found
it difficult to obtain adequate information. As the series
of which this volume forms a part is published both in
Great Britain and in America, I venture to hope that
those who live on either side of the Atlantic may be
helped by its perusal to appreciate better than they have
previously done how much good work is being accomplished by those with whom they have not themselves
been brought into contact. In order to render my task a
little less "impossible" than it would otherwise have been,
I have, albeit with reluctance, omitted any account of the
conversion of Europe and of the methods which were
adopted by its early missionaries. I had hoped to have
included at least one or two chapters which would have
served as an introduction to later missionary efforts, but
the limits of my space have rendered this impossible.

The list of those who have most kindly helped me to

obtain information for the purposes of this book in Europe and America, and who have read sections of it while it was passing through the press, is too long to give, but I desire to express my special obligations to the three friends who have read the whole of the proofs and by doing so have prevented me from making a number of mistakes. These are Dr. Eugene Stock, formerly editorial secretary of the Church Missionary Society, Professor Cairns of Aberdeen University, and the Rev. B. Yeaxlee, formerly editorial secretary of the London Missionary Society, and now editor of the United Council for Missionary Education.

I have given in various footnotes references to a few of the books which I have had occasion to consult, but it has not seemed desirable to attempt any kind of bibliography in view of the fact that the Board of Study for the Preparation of Missionaries has recently issued " A Bibliography for Missionary Students," edited by Dr. Weitbrecht, which is much more complete than any which it would have been possible for me to include.

Throughout this volume I have used the expressions Roman Catholic, Anglican, and Protestant to designate respectively the Churches which are subject to the authority of the Pope, the Churches in Great Britain, America, and elsewhere which are in communion with the Church of England, and the non-Episcopal Churches. The title Catholic is sometimes claimed as its exclusive possession by the Roman Church, but as the title officially used in the decrees of the Council of Trent is " the Catholic and Apostolic Roman Church," and as the title Catholic is universally claimed by the Anglican Church and is frequently claimed by other Churches, it would have been misleading to limit its use in the way suggested. A large section of the members of the Church of England and of Churches in communion with it are proud to designate themselves as Protestants, but inasmuch as many other members regard this designation as inadequate, if not misleading, I have used the neutral word Anglican, which does not raise any controversial issue. I have avoided the use of the expression

"Free Churches" as this would not have included several of the Protestant bodies in Great Britain or any of those in America. As the word "native" is much disliked by many of those to whom it has often been applied, and as there is no justification for its employment, I have avoided its use except in the case of quotations.

In comparing the statistics issued annually by the Roman Catholic missions with those issued by Anglican and Protestant missions, it is necessary to bear in mind the custom observed by Roman Catholic missionaries of baptizing infants and others who are at the point of death. These far exceed in number all other baptisms. Thus— to quote the figures supplied in the Atlas Hierarchicus in 1913—the number of those baptized when in the act of dying in the three dioceses of North Manchuria, South-West Chihli, and East Sichuen during 1912 was 48,339, whilst the number of adults and of children of Christian parents baptized was only 10,274.

In using the statistics supplied by several of the Anglican, Protestant, and Roman societies, it is necessary to bear in mind that they relate in some instances to work which is being carried on amongst Europeans or Americans who are living in foreign lands. The English Society for the Propagation of the Gospel, the American Methodist Episcopal Church, the American Board of Commissioners for Foreign Missions and several other smaller societies devote a certain part of their annual incomes to the support of those who are engaged in ministering to the spiritual needs of European or American Christians. In dealing with the statistics supplied by the Roman Catholic organizations a similar caution is needed.

The test of the success of missionary enterprise is furnished by moral and not by numerical results, and inasmuch as these are slow to appear and difficult to appraise, the student of missions is often tempted to impatience. He needs to remember that the progress of Christian missions, if it is to be judged aright, must be measured by units which consist not of years, but of generations. In the beginning of the third century of the Christian era Dion Cassius, referring to the inhabitants of Britain, described them as an "idle, indolent, thievish, lying lot of scoundrels." As a result of Christian teaching extending over fifty generations, the proportion of the inhabitants of Britain to whom these epithets can justly be applied has perceptibly decreased. The epithets used by Dion Cassius are often applied to some of the peoples amongst whom Christian missionaries are now working, but before we institute any comparison between these peoples and ourselves to the detriment of the former, or to the disparagement of missionary efforts, we need to ascertain whether the progress which has been achieved within recent years does not compare favourably with that which occurred in our own land during any equal period of time. Few, if any, persons who have made a prolonged study of the work of Christian missions during the last two generations have failed to reach the conclusion that, as a direct result of the spread of missionary efforts, the prospects of the regeneration of the human race and of the establishment of the kingdom of God upon earth are brighter than they have been at any previous period in the world's history.

C. H. R.

CONTENTS

ABBREVIATIONS

A.B C F.M. . American Board of Commissioners for Foreign Missions.

A.B.F.M.U. or A.B.M.U. American Baptist Foreign Missionary Union.

A.M E.C . . American Methodist Episcopal Church.

A U.P.M. . . American United Presbyterian Mission.

B. & F.B.S. . British and Foreign Bible Society.

B.M S. . . . Baptist Missionary Society.

C.I.M. . . . China Inland Mission.

C E.Z.M S . . Church of England Zenana Missionary Society.

C L.S. . . . Christian Literature Society in India.

D.U.M. . . . Dublin University Mission.

E.P.M. . . . Presbyterian Church of England Mission.

F.M.S. . . . Foreign Missionary Society.

L.J S. . . . London Society for Promoting Christianity among the Jews.

L.M.S. . . . London Missionary Society.

M.E C. or A.M.E C. American Methodist Episcopal Church.

R.C. . . . . Roman Catholic.

S.A.M S. . . South American Missionary Society.

S.P.C.K. . . Society for Promoting Christian Knowledge.

S.P.G. . . . Society for the Propagation of the Gospel in Foreign
                 Parts.

S.V.M.U. . . Student Volunteer Missionary Union.

U.F.C S. or U.F.C.   United Free Church of Scotland.

U.M.C.A. . . Universities' Mission to Central Africa.

W.M.S. . . . Wesleyan Methodist Missionary Society.

Y.M.C.A. . . Young Men's Christian Association.

Y.W.C.A. . . Young Women's Christian Association.

Z.B.M. . . . Zenana Baptist Mission.

Z.M.S. . . . Zenana Bible and Medical Mission.

HISTORY OF CHRISTIAN MISSIONS

I.

INTRODUCTORY.

THE missionary activities of the Christian Church have, since the Day of Pentecost, been one of its distinguishing characteristics. Nevertheless, there are some modern critics who maintain that its world-wide propaganda, which the apostles inaugurated and which subsequent Christian missionaries developed, was not founded upon any direct commands given by our Lord and did not form part of His original plan. Over against the command contained in St. Matthew (xxviii. 19) to go into all the world and make disciples of all the nations, they set the words, recorded in the same Gospel (xv. 24), "I was not sent but unto the lost sheep of the house of Israel," and the fact that the original commission given to the Twelve contained no statement that they were to be pioneers of a world-wide mission. It is clear that the question "Did our Lord from the first intend that the religion which He taught should become a missionary religion throughout the whole world?" cannot be answered by quoting individual texts, but that the answer must be deduced from a consideration of the essential character of His mission. The words in which He Himself defined that mission were: "The Son of Man is come to seek and to save that which was lost." The title which He here applies to Himself is, as all critics admit, one which He habitually used. If the assumption of this title be regarded, as all

I

Christians have regarded it, as a claim to be the representative of the whole human race, its occurrence in this
passage implies that the scope of our Lord's mission includes
all human beings who stand in need of being saved, and
the limitation of its scope to the lost sheep of the house
of Israel must be regarded as having been merely
provisional.

In endeavouring to interpret the underlying meaning
of our Lord's teaching, it is necessary to remember that
inasmuch as it was addressed to the hearts as well as
to the minds of men, he alone is qualified to understand
its full significance in whose heart it has awakened a
sympathetic response, and whose life has become in some
degree a reflection of the life of Jesus Christ. If this
be admitted, and if, therefore, we may appeal for the
interpretation of His intention regarding the evangelization of the world from the intellectual student of
Christianity to the man to whom " to live is Christ," there
can be no doubt as to the reply that we shall receive.
It is not too much to say that the more Christlike
a man becomes the more ardent becomes his desire
to bring the whole world to his Master's feet and the
more certain does he feel that in seeking to accomplish
this object he is rightly interpreting the mind of his
Teacher. To know the mind of Christ we must appeal
not only to the Gospel records, but to the beliefs and
aspirations of the most Christlike persons in this and every
other time.

An appeal lies, moreover, not only to the subjective
but to the objective experience of mankind.

The unique claim of Christianity to be the universal religion is not grounded upon the possession of a
sacred book, nor upon the miracles which accompanied
its introduction into the world, nor upon its revelation of
a future life, nor, lastly, upon the testimony of the saints
and heroes who have accepted its teachings. Other
religions which do not attempt to appeal to all mankind
have advanced similar claims. The unique claim which

Christianity puts forward is grounded upon the fact, of which the whole history of Christian missions serves to substantiate the truth, that it alone, of all religions, is capable of satisfying the needs of every member of the human race. The Chinese who said to Bishop Boone, whom he had helped to translate the New Testament into his own language, "Whoever made that book made me; it knows all that is in my heart," was putting into language the response which the teaching of the Christian message has evoked from men of every race and of every stage of civilization or of savagery throughout the world. If we have read aright the story of Christian missions, we are justified in saying that the religion of the New Testament has been tested in every clime and amongst races of every degree of culture, and that its teachings have never been presented patiently and lovingly to any people whom they have failed to uplift and transform and whose deepest needs they have failed to supply. The Christian religion came into existence as the result of the manifestation of One who was at once the Son of God and the Son of man, and its claim to universal acceptance is founded on the fact that this divine-human Being can supply the whole world's needs.

There is no race or people to which the gospel message, when once it has been apprehended, has appealed in vain. A savage Bechuana, on hearing the story of the Cross, was deeply moved, and exclaimed, "Jesus, away from there! That is my place." The early Moravian missionaries in Greenland laboured for years to teach their hearers the principles of right and goodness, but without result. When, however, they read to them the Gospel account of the death of Christ, one of them exclaimed, "Why did you not tell us this before? Tell us it again." [1] Its repetition was speedily followed by the conversion of many of their hearers. If Christian missions have done nothing else, they have proved that the earth contains no race so degraded but that the gospel story can appeal to it.

[1] See p. 52.

In the course of our attempt to sketch the work of
Christian missionaries we shall have occasion to point out
some of the distinctive needs of the various races to which
their appeal has been made, and the response that it has
served to evoke, but before doing so it may be well to
recall three fundamental needs of which every human
being is conscious, and which Christianity can supply more
completely than any other religion.

1. Man, whether savage or civilized, needs a power
greater than any that he is conscious of possessing which
can enable him to live up to his own highest ideals.   In
studying the chief non-Christian religions we come across
rules and maxims which, if they could be translated into
action, would enable their possessors to rise high above
the level on which their lives are being lived, but we
search in vain in the sacred books of these religions for a
power or source of inspiration that can enable them so
to rise.   In Christianity, on the other hand, we have a
revelation of the highest ideals of conduct and we have at
the same time offered to us the help of One who has Himself lived the highest life and can live it over again in the
lives of those who accept His help.   The task of the
Christian missionary is not to sweep away or undermine
the teachings of non-Christian religions, but to reveal the
source of the power which can enable men to fulfil the
best teaching which these religions inculcate and to rise to
higher ideals than any to which they point.

The contrast between the helplessness of the great
Oriental religions when confronted with failure to reach
life's highest ideals and the helpfulness of Christianity is
well illustrated by an allegory told by a Chinese catechist
who was trying to explain to his fellow-countrymen the
practical difference between the way of salvation as taught
respectively by Confucius, Buddha, and Christ.   He described man as a traveller who had fallen from the narrow
path of rectitude into an abyss of evil and despair.
Presently on the narrow path above him China's great
teacher, Confucius, appears, and to him the fallen traveller

appeals for help, but only to receive the reply uttered in tones of reproach, "Here is no place for prayer." When Confucius has gone on his way Buddha is seen approaching, and in response to an agonized appeal for help he descends a few steps from the narrow path, and peering with sympathetic gaze into the abyss, he says, "If thou couldst rise a little higher, then could I deliver thee," but the weak and exhausted traveller sinks yet lower into the murky depth. Finally, the form of Jesus Christ is seen advancing along the same narrow path, and to Him is the traveller's final appeal addressed. No sooner has it been uttered than the divine Deliverer, clothed in light, descends to the bottom of the abyss, and raising the helpless traveller in His arms, carries him up to the narrow path, and having set his feet securely upon it, walks by his side supporting him ever and anon until the path emerges at last into the final light. The allegory helps us to understand how Christianity appealed to a Confucian Buddhist, and wherein the gospel message differs from the teachings of other religions.

2. The second need of which man is conscious is sympathy. If his efforts to rise to a higher moral and spiritual level than that to which he has as yet attained are not to end in despair, he needs to know that there is a Being to whom his welfare is a matter of immediate concern, and who can both rejoice and sympathize, that is, "suffer together with" him. Divine sympathy is a concept that can hardly be said to exist outside the Christian revelation, but man has no greater need than that which these words express. Bishop Selwyn of New Zealand told how the knowledge that God suffered because of man's sin transformed the character of the cannibal savages of New Zealand. He wrote in 1840:

"I am in the midst of a sinful people, who have been accustomed to sin uncontrolled from their youth. If I speak to a native on murder, infanticide, cannibalism, and adultery, they laugh in my face, and tell me I may think these acts are bad, but they are very good for a native, and they cannot conceive any harm in them. But, on the contrary, when I tell them that these and other sins brought the Son of God, the great Creator of the universe, from His eternal glory to this world, to be incarnate and to be made a curse and to die, then they open their eyes and ears and mouths, and wish to hear more, and presently they acknowledge themselves sinners, and say they will leave off their sins."[1]

3. Lastly, if a man is to be sustained in his efforts to realize the highest ideals embodied in his own religion and to rise to those which are still higher, he needs to become the possessor of a hope which reaches out beyond his present horizon. The saddest feature of the religions of ancient Greece and Rome, and of the great religions of the East, is the absence of hope. Amongst the debris of an ancient house in Salonica (the Thessalonica of St. Paul's time) were found two funeral urns of apparently the same date: one bore the inscription, "No hope"; the other, "Christ, my life." The contrast between the two is the contrast between man's destiny as interpreted by most of the chief religions of the world and man's destiny as interpreted by the message which Christian missionaries have to proclaim. According to orthodox Hinduism, we have now reached the five thousandth year of the Kali Yuga, or "evil cycle," of which there are 427,000 more years to run. There will then be three other cycles extending over 4,000,000 years before this evil cycle again recurs, which is to happen many thousands of times. The possibility that after countless re-births, extending over unnumbered millions of years, a man may at last escape from the miseries of human existence, furnishes no ground of hope that is worthy of the name.

The conviction that in Christianity alone of all the religions of the world are to be found the revelation of the power, the sympathy, and the hope which the world needs, begets the assurance that it will one day fulfil what we believe to have been the purpose of its Founder and will

[1] *Life of Bishop Selwyn*, p. 72.

become the religion of the whole world. Meanwhile, as the message carried by the Christian missionaries makes its appeal to one race after another, the fact that it continues to meet the needs of all provides cumulative evidence that the source of the message is divine. The missionary, albeit unconsciously, becomes the Christian apologist. The only certain proof that the Christian Bible is inspired is that it continues to inspire, and this proof the missionary is in a position to furnish to a unique extent. It is impossible in the brief space at our disposal to follow out this line of thought, and to show otherwise than by incidental illustrations how the gospel message has inspired men of all races to lead new lives and to aim at higher and ever higher ideals, but the story of Christian missions will have been ill told if it does not serve to demonstrate this fact.

II.

METHODS OF MISSIONARY WORK.

ONE of the chief results which the careful student may hope to attain by a study of Christian missions is an intelligent appreciation of the methods that are likely to prove most successful in the mission field to-day. The materials for study are well-nigh inexhaustible. We may venture to assert that no new method of prosecuting Christian missions has been suggested within recent years which has not been tested in practice during the eighteen centuries that lie between us and the work of the first missionaries. It is much to be desired that those who speak, or write books, on Christian missions from the theoretical standpoint would fit themselves more adequately for their task by a prolonged study of their subject carried on both in libraries at home and in the mission field. In attempting to discuss methods of missionary work, the first question that arises is, What guidance can we hope to obtain from the pages of the New Testament, and in particular, from the experience of the greatest of Christian missionaries, the Apostle St. Paul?

The task which he set himself to accomplish was to interpret, by word and action, his Master's purpose of love towards the whole world, and, supported by the belief that Jesus Christ was not only with him but in him, he transformed Christianity from a national into the universal religion, and laid the foundation of the missionary work which the Church of Christ has since accomplished. The chapters in the Acts of the Apostles which refer to his work when read in conjunction with the letters addressed to the churches which he helped to establish, help us to understand the principles which guided his missionary policy and the methods which he adopted in his endeavours to embody these principles in action.

Every one who desires to promote the success of Christian missions to-day will admit that the records which have been preserved of St. Paul's missionary labours have a significance which transcends the limitations of time and place by which his work was originally conditioned, but when he proceeds to ask how far the methods adopted by St. Paul can or ought to be copied in any part of the mission field of to-day, he is confronted with a problem which he will find it hard to solve.

Few Christians would deny that the principles on which St. Paul based his missionary methods are applicable to all times and to all lands, but any one who surveys the vast area of the modern mission field and who appreciates, as far as the limitations of his knowledge will allow, the differences which exist between the conditions which govern missionary development, say in Japan and West Africa, or in India and New Guinea, will realize that the exigencies of the modern mission field demand more numerous and more complex methods of action than any which can be deduced from the recorded experiences of St. Paul or his fellow-apostles.

There are three questions which are constantly being discussed by the representatives of missionary societies at home and by those responsible for the supervision of missionary work abroad. These concern (1) the diffusion of missionary influence over wide areas as contrasted with its concentration at strategic points; (2) the qualifications to be required of those who are to be appointed as ministers of the Christian Church in the mission field; (3) the stage in the development of a particular mission at which it is wise to attempt the establishment of an independent Christian Church or branch of the Christian Church in a non-Christian country.

St. Paul's Missionary Methods.

Before proceeding to illustrate from the history of missions the answers which have been given and are being given to these questions, let us ask how far we are justified in appealing to the experience of St. Paul in the hope of obtaining an authoritative solution to the problems which they raise. Those who have appealed to his example and experience and, on the strength of such an appeal, have condemned many of the practices of modern missionaries, have too often failed to realize how different were the conditions under which he worked from those which prevail in the greater part of the mission field to-day.

1 The first of these questions may be expressed thus: Is it wiser as a general rule to diffuse missionary effort over a wide district in the hope of reaching all who may be found willing to listen to the Gospel message, or to concentrate the missionary forces at a few important centres, in the hope that the light of the Gospel may eventually radiate throughout the surrounding districts which are for the time being perforce neglected? It is obvious that the conditions under which missionary work has been, and is being, carried on in different parts of the world differ so widely that no answer can be given to this question to which exceptions must not be admitted.

To take a single illustration, which has a special bearing upon the problem raised by the first question.

St Paul's missionary activities were largely, if not entirely, confined to towns, whereas the chief sphere of the modern missionary may be said to lie in villages. The visitor to India or China who takes an interest in missionary work is naturally impressed with the crying needs of the vast centres of population which he sees, and is apt to forget that the population contained in the towns represents but the tiniest fragment of the total population. Nearly half the human race is to be found to-day in the villages of India and China. These villages are so small and so close together that it is often possible, where the ground rises by a few feet, to count twenty or thirty at one time.

It is obvious, therefore, that the experiences of the modern missionary who tries to evangelize the villages which constitute the greater part of the modern mission fields are likely to differ widely from the experiences which St. Paul met with in his attempt to preach the Gospel in some of the great cities of the ancient world.

Even when we compare missionary work in modern cities with that carried on by St. Paul, the conditions of the two will be found to be widely dissimilar. In nearly all the cities in which St. Paul worked, Greek or Latin was understood, and a Jewish community afforded him the opportunity to appeal through Jewish converts to the wider circle with which they were in touch. In one case only did he attempt to start missionary work and to bring into existence Christian Churches in a district where the prevailing conditions approximated to those which are found in the greater part of the mission field to-day.

Bishop Mylne, who was formerly Bishop of Bombay, in his book entitled, *Missions to Hindus*, maintains (and there is much to be said for his contention) that St. Paul adopted a mistaken policy in attempting to do peregrinating evangelistic work in Galatia, and urges that his letter to the Galatians and the fact that he never again attempted similar work prove that he had realized his mistake.

"One great convincing experience," Bishop Mylne writes, " was to come to St. Paul which would serve with its disastrous shock to convince him of the falsity of his method — the great Galatian apostasy. . . . The method which had prospered elsewhere had disastrously failed among them. The withdrawal of his personal presence from converts of a barbarous race with a poor reputation for stability, far removed from civilizing influences, had proved to be a shock to their faith against which they could not stand. They fell victims to the first false teachers, who offered them a plausible Judaism in place of the Gospel of Christ." [1]

With this one exception, it would appear from the accounts of St. Paul's missionary labours which have been preserved that he never attempted to preach in villages, but concentrated his efforts upon towns, and specially upon six or seven towns where he sought to establish Christian Churches, which should serve as strategic points in view of the eventual evangelization of the surrounding districts. On the one occasion on which he and his companions thought of attempting to evangelize the scattered country districts of Bithynia, "the Spirit of Jesus suffered them not," [2] and impelled them to extend their labours to the towns of southern Europe.

It would appear, therefore, that in so far as St. Paul's experience affords any help towards the solution of the problem raised by the first question, it tells in favour of concentrated as opposed to diffused missionary work. At the same time the fact that his experience of a diffused mission appears to have been limited to a single instance, makes it impossible to regard this as affording unmistakable guidance.

The lesson which we have ventured to deduce from the example of St. Paul is endorsed by the experience of later missionaries.

Whilst examples might be obtained from many other countries, the history of Christian missions in India affords the most convincing illustrations of the comparative value of the two methods. In the judgment of Bishop Mylne, whom we have already quoted, the three greatest missionaries who have laboured in India were the Jesuit,

---

[1] Pp. 86, 124. Bishop Mylne held with Bishop Lightfoot that "Galatia" was in the extreme north of Asia Minor, but if we accept Ramsay's theory that it was in the south, and included Phrygia and Lycaonia, it would still be the case that the majority of the inhabitants of Galatia to whom St. Paul preached were less civilized than were those amongst whom the other Christian churches established by him were founded.

[2] Acts xvi. 7.

Francis Xavier, the Lutheran, Schwartz, and the Baptist, Carey. As we shall see later on,[1] Xavier adopted the "diffusive" method as completely as it was possible for any one to adopt it. His aim was to spread a knowledge of the Christian faith over the widest possible area, and in accordance with his principles of evangelization, he baptized tens of thousands of persons whose language he did not understand and whose knowledge of Christianity was limited to the verbal acceptance of a few dogmatic statements. He did this in the hope that some of them, or at any rate that some of their children, might eventually attain a fuller knowledge of the faith. His successors down to the present day have endorsed his action, and to a greater or less extent have followed in his steps. What, then, has been the result? To quote the words of Bishop Mylne:

"The result is that the conversion of the country to Christianity is no nearer than it was when he left it, for anything that his followers have done; that they form but a Christian caste, unprogressive, incapable of evangelizing, observing distinctions of caste within the body of the Christian Church; holding their own with a pathetic faithfulness among people of other creeds, but woefully low in their practice, and scandalously superstitious in their conceptions; afraid of the Hindu gods; and all but idolaters themselves in their veneration of saints and their images." [2]

The methods adopted by Schwartz, to whose work we shall have occasion to refer later on, differed in important respects from those of Xavier. He spent nearly fifty years in Southern India and was able to speak the language of the people to whom he appealed. He refused to baptize until the candidates for baptism had given clear proofs of repentance and faith. He traversed enormous areas, and at his death in 1798 his converts were reckoned by tens of thousands. When, however, several of the missions which he had founded were taken over by the S.P.G. in 1825, villages and communities which had formerly been

---

[1] See pp. 70–74.   [2] *Missions to Hindus*, p. 115 sq.

Christian were found to have lost almost all knowledge of the Christian faith and to have relapsed into Hinduism. The collapse of the greater part of Schwartz's work is apparently to be attributed to the diffused methods of evangelization which he adopted and to his "reliance on the power of the gospel to develop spiritual independence in characters quite unprepared for it."

The aim that Carey set before him was to create one "red-hot centre from which the light and influence of Christianity might radiate throughout a gradually widening circle." We shall have occasion later on to refer in greater detail to the methods adopted by Carey and to point out the lasting nature of the results which he achieved (see pp. 81—83).

It would be easy to produce evidence of a similar character from other mission fields, though in no other country has sufficient time elapsed since missionary work was inaugurated to enable the results to be seen as clearly as they are to be seen to-day in India.

2. The second problem to which we referred is raised by the question, What moral and intellectual qualifications ought to be required of those to be appointed as ministers of a newly established Christian Church in the foreign mission field? There are some who have sought to find an answer to this question by referring to the example of St. Paul, who, in certain instances after a stay of a few months or even a few weeks in a city, felt able to appoint elders to carry on the work which he had begun and to guide and organize the infant Church. They ask, If St. Paul was able to act thus, how can it be necessary that a course of preparation extending over several years should be required before ministers are appointed or ordained in countries where Christian missionary work is being carried on to-day? Before we can admit the relevance of this direct appeal to the example of St. Paul we need to know what were the moral and intellectual qualifications of the elders to whom he was accustomed to entrust the carrying on of the missionary work which he inaugurated.

Outside Galatia, it is doubtful whether St. Paul ever founded a Church in any place in which there did not already exist a Jewish synagogue and in which Jewish methods of church organization were not well understood. It is certain that in the great majority of the places in which he is reported to have preached the infant Church included Jews or Jewish proselytes who had accepted the teaching contained in the Old Testament before they became Christians, and who must have exerted a profound and lasting influence upon the converts who joined the Church from the ranks of heathenism. How widely scattered were the Jews may be inferred from the remark of Seneca, who wrote: "The customs of this most accursed race have prevailed to such an extent that they are everywhere received. The conquered have imposed their laws on the conquerors."[1] Strabo wrote: "They have now got into every city, and it is hard to find a spot on earth which . . . has not come under their control."[2] Harnack calculates that the Jews and their converts formed 7 per cent. of the population of the Roman Empire, which at the beginning of the Christian era was reckoned at 54 millions. He writes:

"In order to comprehend the propaganda and diffusion of Christianity, it is essential to understand that the religion under whose 'shadow' it made its way out into the world not merely contained elements of vital significance but had expanded till it embraced a considerable proportion of the world's population."[3]

It is hardly necessary to point out that the conditions under which Christian missionaries labour to-day are far removed from those which existed in the countries in which St. Paul established the earliest Christian Churches. It is clear, therefore, that his example affords no precedent for leaving newly established Christian Churches in charge of Christians who have had no preparation for the fulfil-

[1] *Aug. de Civ Dei*, vi p. 11.   [2] Josephus, *Ant.* xiv. 2. 7.
[3] *Expansion of Christianity*, vol. i. p. 11.

ment of their task analogous to that which the Jewish
elders had inherited and received. In the course of this
volume we shall have occasion to refer to instances in
several different lands and at different epochs in which
those in charge of missions have sought to imitate the
letter of St. Paul's example and to note the results which
ensued. Christian missions have to a large extent passed
out of the empirical stage, and one of the most certain
lessons to be deduced from their history is that attempts
to imitate literally the example of St. Paul, and to appoint
as Christian ministers the best men who may be available in a newly established Christian community, without insisting upon any long course of preparation, are
destined to retard the establishment of the Christian
Church. Many parts of the mission field contain ruins
which represent attempts that have been made to build
the Church of God by individuals who imagined that
they were following primitive or Pauline methods, but
who acted in ignorance or disregard of the lessons which
have been taught by the long experience of Christian
missionaries.

3. The third problem, which is an extension of the
second, is raised by the question, At what stage in the
evangelization of a non-Christian country ought the
foreign missionaries to retire and to leave the entire
control of the Church to the Christians of the district or
country? One of the most common charges brought
against the representatives of foreign missionary societies
is their alleged reluctance to hand over the government of
a Church which they have helped to found to the members
of that Church. Such charges are seldom if ever brought
by careful students of missionary history, for whom the
failures of the past act as a warning against the assumption
that any uniform time limit can be suggested, at the
expiration of which it can be assumed that an independent
and self-governed Church ought to be established. Most
students of missionary history will admit that the
premature withdrawal of European supervision has not

infrequently retarded the building up of a Christian community and the establishment of a Christian Church that can be considered worthy of the name. As illustrations of the lamentable results which have followed the withdrawal of adequate European supervision we may point to the experience of the C.M.S. on the Niger, of the S.P.G. in parts of Southern India and Burma, of the W.M S. in South Africa, and of the L.M.S. in British Guiana.

Before we proceed to consider the development of Christian missions in later times, it is well that we should recall what was the spiritual condition at the close of the first century of seven of the Christian Churches in Asia Minor, one at least of which had been founded by St. Paul, and all of which must have been influenced by him. Nor is there any reason to doubt the ancient tradition that they had all been superintended during a considerable number of years by the Apostle St. John. The messages transmitted by the writer of the Apocalypse to these Churches suggest that their growth in the Christian life was as interrupted and as slow as that which we observe in the missionary Churches which have been founded within recent years. The Church at Ephesus, where St. Paul had laboured long, and where, according to tradition, St. John had afterwards resided, " had left its ' first love,' " and was urged to repent on pain of having its candlestick removed. The Church at Sardis had a name to live but was in reality dead, and contained but few who had " not defiled their garments." The Church at Laodicea was lukewarm, and knew not that it was " wretched, and miserable, and poor, and blind, and naked." To two only of the Seven Churches is a message of encouragement sent unmixed with blame.

The story of these Churches, which were cared for and superintended by the apostles and their immediate successors, should serve to encourage the missionary who is tempted to-day to suppose that because the lives of the Christians amongst whom he has laboured are un-Christlike, his work cannot have been carried on upon apostolic lines.

2

Political methods of evangelization.

We pass on now to consider a method of propagating
the Christian religion which can claim no support from the
example of St. Paul, but which has exercised a large influence upon the development of Christian missions. We
refer to the use of political influences for the purpose of
facilitating conversions to the Christian faith. Under
the term political influences we include all offers of
material inducements and threats of punishments or loss,
whether made by Governments or by individuals. The
change of attitude on the part of most Christian people
towards the employment of political methods for the
spread of the Christian faith among non-Christian races
has been so gradual and at the same time so complete that
we do not easily appreciate how far we have travelled
from the standpoint of our forefathers. From the days of
Constantine down to a period well within the nineteenth
century comparatively few Christians would have rejected
the proposition that it was lawful, and in many cases
advisable, that missionaries should avail themselves of
political influences in order to facilitate the prosecution of
their work. During the Middle Ages the writings of St.
Augustine exercised a dominating influence over the
missionary policy of Christendom. He was not himself
distinguished for missionary zeal, and apparently made no
attempt to organize any missionary enterprise amongst the
heathen races in North-West Africa. His writings, however, include several passages in which he urges that the
pagans in Hippo and the surrounding district ought to be
punished with death if they persisted in their refusal to
embrace the Christian faith.[1] His interpretation, moreover,
of the words in the Parable of the Great Supper, " compel
them to come in," as affording authorization for the employment of force to compel an acknowledgment of the
Christian faith, was accepted by most of his readers.

One or two voices were raised from time to time

[1] *Epist.* 93. 2, 185. 6.

against the policy of forcible conversion, but their protests met with little response. Thus Raymond Lull, the first missionary to Mohammedans (d. 1315), wrote:

"They think they can conquer by force of arms: it seems to me that the victory can be won in no other way than as Thou, O Lord Christ, didst seek to win it, by love and prayer and self-sacrifice."

Later on, in the sixteenth century, Las Casas, the "Apostle of Mexico," in his treatise *De unico vocationis modo*, urged that men ought to be brought to Christianity only by persuasion, and where no special injury had been received, it was not lawful for Christians to carry on war against infidels merely on the ground that they were infidels.

It would be impossible to name any country in Europe apart from Great Britain and Ireland the conversion of which to Christianity was not to a large extent hastened by the employment of physical force. In the early days of Anglican and Protestant missions, whilst the employment of force was usually discouraged, it was thought to be right to make use of material inducements in order to hasten the work of conversion.

The following extract from a journal kept by Van Riebeek in 1658 at Cape Town might be paralleled in many other lands:

"*April* 17.—Began holding school for the young slaves, the chaplain being charged with the duty. To stimulate the slaves to attention while at school, and to induce them to learn the Christian prayers, they were promised each a glass of brandy and two inches of tobacco when they finish their task." [1]

During the eighteenth century several missionaries wrote in defence of the slave trade, basing their justification of this trade upon the advantages which those captured

---

[1] *A History of Christian Missions in South Africa*, by J. Du Plessis, p. 30.

and sold as slaves would eventually receive by being brought into contact with Christian masters.[1]

An example, on a large scale, of the disastrous results of employing political methods of spreading Christianity is afforded by the religious history of Ceylon. When the Dutch took over from the Portuguese the island of Ceylon in 1656, they attempted to force a Protestant form of Christianity upon its inhabitants by subjecting Buddhists, Hindus, and Romanists who were not prepared to embrace Protestantism, to heavy civil disabilities. The unsatisfactory nature of the conversions so obtained was made clear when, on the cession of the island to England in 1798, these disabilities were removed. In 1801, soon after this change took place, there were 342,000 Singalese and 136,000 Tamils who professed Protestant Christianity; but before ten years had elapsed more than half of these had declared themselves Buddhists or had become devil-worshippers, and a large proportion of the "Government religion" churches were in ruins. The far-reaching effects of the policy adopted by the Dutch for spreading Christianity may be inferred from the statement of Bishop Copleston, formerly Bishop of Colombo, who wrote a few years ago: "Not till within the last twenty years has the Buddhist-Christian element been in the main got rid of."

Although the principle of endeavouring to spread the Christian faith by the direct offer of material inducements is now rejected by nearly all other missions, it is still accepted by the representatives of many Roman Catholic missions.

To take a single illustration which has come under the notice of the writer · After the Lutheran and Anglican missions had obtained a widespread success in the Chota-Nagpur district in North-Eastern India, the Roman missionaries, who then appeared for the first time, adopted the policy of granting small loans to all who were willing to attend their churches, on the understanding that these

---

[1] See reference to pamphlet published by the Rev. T. Thompson, the first English missionary to Africa, on p. 291.

loans would not be repayable as long as those who received them continued to attend. The recipients include a large number of those who were formerly attached to the Lutheran and Anglican missions, and the system is in working order at the present time.

The country in which this principle has been most definitely adopted and in which it has produced results which have affected all Christian missions is China. In an elaborate work,[1] which has received the official sanction of the Roman Church, lately issued by the Foreign Mission Press of Hong-Kong, the writer reviews in detail the different methods that have been adopted by missionaries in China. After explaining all that can be said for and against the adoption of political methods, he arrives at the conclusion that interference by European missionaries in Chinese lawsuits is a means designed by Providence "to draw to religion the simple country people." It is significant to find that the writer who approves this policy of offering material inducements to non-Christians in China goes on to deplore the fact that the present prospect of Roman Catholic missions in that country is far from encouraging.

To Christian missionaries the two events of recent years in the Far East which will appear of greatest importance are the official announcement that the Japanese Government is prepared to recognize Christianity as one of the three religions of Japan, Shinto and Buddhism being the other two, and the appeal for prayer addressed by the Chinese Government to its Christian subjects. In both cases the change of attitude on the part of the Government concerned marks a new stage in the spread of the Christian faith over a large part of the non-Christian world, and in both cases political and religious motives appear to have been inextricably intermingled. The student of Christian missions who is familiar with the results which, in ancient, mediæval, and modern times alike, have followed the

[1] *Méthode de l'Apostolat moderne en Chine*, par R. P. L. Kervyn, Hong-Kong. Imprimerie de la Société des Missions-étrangères, 1911.

employment of political influences in support of the Christian faith, will regard with profound misgivings the possible exercise of such influences on a wide scale. Cases are to be found in all parts of the mission field in which converts have been induced to make a profession of their Christian faith in the hope that they might secure for themselves material advantages, and in some instances the responsibility for arousing this hope lies with the missionaries. The principle, however, of endeavouring to attract converts by the offer of such advantages is one which has now been abandoned by all non-Roman missionary societies. Experience shows conclusively that missionary work prospers most and that the best types of Christian character tend to be produced when the convert to the Christian faith has to face at least a mild form of persecution. The nominal spread of Christianity throughout Europe which, in the course of time, followed the Edict of Milan, ushered in the "dark ages," from which Europe as a whole can as yet hardly be said to have completely emerged. No one would desire that the future history of China or Japan should afford any parallel to the experience of Europe.

Educational Missions.

During the last seventy years educational missions have gradually taken the place of the employment of political influences in a great part of the mission field. As will be shown later on in our references to Dr. Duff and others, the provision of colleges, schools, and industrial institutions has gradually become an important factor in the situation and has greatly affected the work of the evangelistic missionary. Missionaries have not always or generally been educational experts, and it is not a matter for surprise that the success of the schools which they have established has been by no means uniform.

Moreover, in view of the fact that they are endeavouring, by means of educational missions, to appeal to races which differ in culture and mental powers as much as do the Brahmans of India and the cannibals of the Pacific, it is obvious that the educational methods which they need to adopt must admit of wide variation. Methods of teaching which would be the best possible in West Africa or in New Guinea would be worse than useless in India, China, or Japan, and *vice versa.*

But though the methods should vary, the principles which underlie them must remain the same. The object which the educational missionary needs to keep in view is to " educate "—that is, to draw out and develop the latent capacities of his pupils in order that the additional knowledge which he desires to impart to them may be correlated with their previous knowledge and with their methods of thinking. To accomplish this would be to accomplish one of the most difficult tasks which it is possible to attempt, and it is no cause for wonder that many failures have to be recorded.

It would be easy to give illustrations of the disastrous results which have followed the attempt to provide a distinctively English education for converts to Christianity who were wholly unfitted to benefit thereby. The writer of this volume was sitting one day outside a mission school in the tropics watching its pupils walking to and fro in the mission enclosure. Some of them had come from homes in which it had not been customary to wear clothes and in which cannibalism would not have been regarded with horror. These pupils of the mission school, however, wore immaculate shirt fronts and the smartest of English clothes, and carried gilt-headed walking canes and watch chains to correspond. It was with no feelings of surprise that he learnt that the principal English trading company of the district, which had for several years employed as clerks those who had been trained at this school, had recently issued an order that henceforth no one who had attended this school was to be employed in any capacity, and that Moslems or pagans were to be employed in their stead. Superficial investigators of missionary work abroad are

never tired of asserting that missionary education tends to
deprive converts of their hereditary virtues and to give
them no others in their place, and it is impossible to deny
that in the past there has been some foundation for such
criticisms. A hopeful symptom is that missionaries themselves have become the severest, and at the same time the
most intelligent, critics of the methods which have satisfied
their predecessors and which continue to satisfy some of
their contemporaries. They have come to realize that the
more anglicized in appearance and in methods of thought
and action their pupils become the more complete has been
their own failure. They have also come to realize that in
dealing with backward races it is worse than useless to try
to anticipate the results of education by allowing to their
pupils a minimum of initiative and by providing continuous
supervision. The temptation to impatience which besets
the missionary may be described in words borrowed from
Dr. Montessori, who writes :

"Little children who are undertaking something for the
first time are extremely slow. Their life is governed in
this respect by laws especially different from ours. Little
children accomplish slowly and perseveringly various complicated operations agreeable to them, such as dressing and
undressing, setting the table, eating, etc. In all this they
are extremely patient, overcoming all the difficulties presented by an organism still in process of formation. But
we, on the other hand, noticing that they are 'tiring themselves out,' or 'wasting time,' in accomplishing something
which we could do in a moment, and without the least
effort, put ourselves in the child's place and do it ourselves. . . . What would become of us if we fell into the
midst of a population of jugglers or of lightning-change
impersonators of the variety hall ? What should we do if,
as we continued to act in our usual way, we saw ourselves
assailed by these sleight-of-hand performers, hustled into
our clothes, fed so rapidly that we could scarcely swallow,
if everything we tried to do was snatched from our hands
and completed in a twinkling and we ourselves reduced to
impotence and to a humiliating inertia ? Not knowing how
else to express our confusion, we should defend ourselves

with blows and yells from these madmen; and they, having only the best will in the world to serve us, would call us haughty, rebellious, and incapable of doing anything." [1]

These words of Montessori help to explain how extra-ordinarily difficult is the problem that confronts missionaries, who are usually the first representatives of the more advanced races to attempt to impart to the members of the more backward races the education and culture which they have themselves inherited. It is not possible to attempt here any description of the various forms of educational missionary work which have been tried in different countries. For a description and criticism of the methods which have been tried in South Africa the student would do well to consult the books written by Mr. Dudley Kidd, also the striking testimony relating to the benefits resulting from missionary education contained in the report of the South African Government Commission (see p. 335).

In India more than in any other part of the mission field the time and labour of missionaries have been devoted to educational work. In connection with this work the question has often been raised both by missionaries abroad and by missionary critics at home, Is it worth while to go on spending time and labour on the support of educational institutions in India and elsewhere when the labour spent on them produces hardly any visible result, and when men and women missionaries are urgently needed to evangelize the uneducated classes who are anxious to be taught the Christian faith? To answer this question aright, we need to be endowed with long vision; we need to look beyond the immediate present and to prepare for a future which perhaps none living may see but the advent of which is certain.

During a visit to the chief centres of missionary activity in India the writer had an opportunity of seeing most of the largest colleges which are affiliated to universities in India, and which belong to many different missionary societies. In response to inquiries

[1] See *International Review of Missions*, April 1913, p. 333.

addressed to those now in charge of these colleges, he
gathered that the conversion and baptism of a student in
any one of them was an exceedingly rare event. The
Principal of one of the largest colleges in North India was
unable to tell of the occurrence of a single case during the
sixteen years of his principalship. At another college
belonging to a different society two conversions had taken
place during the last ten years ; at another belonging to
yet another society no conversion had occurred for at least
twelve years. When it is remembered that there are large
districts in India where the missionaries in charge have
had to discourage applications from the representatives of
villages which desire to abandon Hinduism and to become
Christian, on the ground that there are no Christian
teachers, European or Indian, available, it is impossible not
to sympathize with those who desire to divert from the
educational missions a few of those missionaries whose work
is attended with no visible result and whose presence elsewhere is urgently demanded. Nevertheless, we believe
that no more fatal policy can be suggested than to weaken
or circumscribe the appeal which the Church of Christ is
making to the educated classes of India by means of its
educational missions. The great need for men created by
the success of the mass movements supplies an argument
not for withdrawing men from educational work but for
holding on to and strengthening this work. For it is
certain that the day will come when Christianity, having
overcome the opposition of caste, will spread throughout
India like a flood. It will make all the difference when
this movement occurs whether or no there is then in
existence a body of experienced European educationalists
and of highly educated Indian teachers to guide and direct
the movement. We can only secure the provision of such
a body of men at the critical moment if the various
missionary societies are content for the time being to
forgo counting the visible results of their educational
work and hold on unhesitatingly to the schools and colleges
which they possess.

Our impatience at the small number of conversions which can be traced directly to the influence of missionary schools and colleges will be lessened in proportion as we realize that their primary object is not to impart information, or even to produce conversions, but to develop character. Where the education of character is concerned, we should be content to count time not by years but by generations.

It need hardly be added that the principle which is illustrated by what is happening in India applies to all other non-Christian countries in which educational work on any large scale is being attempted.

In China the results obtained in the missionary colleges (e g. in the Tientsin College under Dr. Lavington Hart) have been encouraging, and the attitude of the student class towards the preaching of Christianity has become remarkably sympathetic (see p. 201).

In dealing with the more backward races, experience has demonstrated the high value to be attached to all kinds of industrial schools. Amongst such races industrial training can best be imparted in conjunction with book learning. Thus the author of *The Story of the Lovedale Mission* writes:

"It is a fact abundantly confirmed by experience that the greatest difficulties in the teaching of trades are to be met with in the case of those who are deficient, and just in proportion as they are deficient, in school education."

Referring to the results of the training at Lovedale, which is the best known centre of industrial training in South Africa, Dr. Stewart, who was for a long period its Principal, was able to state that of 2000 who had been educated here, and whose subsequent history could be traced, from 75 to 80 per cent. had led or were leading useful and industrious lives.

We refer later on to the work of industrial missions in various parts of the mission field.

Medical Missions.

A further method by which Christian missionaries have sought to appeal to non-Christian races is represented by the establishment of medical missions.

The aim of the medical missionary is twofold : (1) To alleviate suffering and to train those who in non-Christian lands are ignorant of the art of medicine in order that they may be enabled to alleviate the sufferings of their fellow-countrymen (2) To co-operate with the Christian evangelist by interpreting the Divine compassion and breaking down the prejudices of those who would not otherwise be willing to listen to the gospel message.

Some of those who have advocated the extension of medical missions have laid exclusive emphasis upon the latter objects, but have failed to grasp the importance of the former. The charge given by Christ Himself to His first missionaries was to preach the gospel and to heal the sick, but there is nothing in the context to suggest that in places where the preaching of the gospel was welcomed they might consider themselves absolved from the obligation to heal those who were sick. It may with confidence be asserted that apart altogether from any consideration of the fact that medical missions have proved a powerful evangelistic agency, it is the duty of the whole Christian Church to establish missions which have as their object the alleviation of bodily suffering, and that it is the duty of the individual missionary who possesses a knowledge of medicine that is not shared by any of those amongst whom he works to use his knowledge with the object of alleviating human suffering, and to continue his labours with this object in view until such time as the medical practitioners of the country are in a position to carry on the work which he has inaugurated. When such a time arrives, as it has arrived in Japan and in some other parts of the mission field, the need for medical missionaries will still remain in so far as their work may subserve the purpose of a direct missionary agency.

1. Confining our attention for the moment to the first of the two objects which medical missionaries have in view, we may note the striking service which they were able to render to China on the occasion of the great outbreak of plague in Manchuria in 1910–11. The virulence of the attack may be gathered from the fact that the number of patients attacked and the resultant deaths alike numbered 43,942.[1] Had it not been for the medical missionaries, and the Chinese doctors and attendants who worked under their direction, the deaths would have been reckoned by millions. Amongst those who took part in fighting the plague should be mentioned Dr. Aspland of the Anglican mission in Peking, Dr. Dugald Christie of the United Presbyterian mission in Moukden, and Dr. A. F. Jackson, a new recruit belonging to the same mission, who himself died of the plague. On the occasion of the death of Dr. Jackson, the Chinese Viceroy, Hsi Liang, delivered a funeral oration at Moukden on February 2, 1911, in the course of which he said :

"Our sorrow is beyond all measure, our grief too deep for words. O spirit of Dr. Jackson, we pray you intercede for the 20,000,000 people in Manchuria, and ask the Lord of heaven to take away this pestilence, so that we may once more lay our heads in peace upon our pillows. In life you were brave, in death you are an exalted spirit. Noble spirit, who sacrificed your life for us, help us still and look down in kindness upon us all."

To the list of the medical missionaries who have died whilst fighting the plague, albeit in a different country, may be added the name of Dr. Alice Marval of the S.P.G., who died at Cawnpore, January 4, 1904.

By way of illustrating the efforts which medical missionaries are making to train men and women in non-

---

[1] For a description of the kind of work accomplished by medical missionaries during the outbreak of plague in Manchuria, see *The Claim of Suffering*, by E. K. Paget, pp. 79-84 ; also *The Life of Arthur Jackson*, by A. J. Costain.

Christian lands to alleviate the physical sufferings of their fellow-countrymen, we may mention the central training colleges which have recently been established in China and elsewhere.

At the triennial conference of the Medical Missionary Association held in Peking (January 1913), it was urged that combined efforts should be made to strengthen existing hospitals in which Chinese might be trained to become fully qualified medical missionaries.

One of the most successful medical training colleges is the Union Medical College in Peking, which is supported jointly by the American Board (A.B.C.F.M.), the L.M.S. and the S.P.G. This hospital, besides ministering to the needs of Chinese patients, is turning out year by year a number of qualified Chinese doctors who will carry the fame of European medicine and a sympathetic report of the Christian faith far and wide throughout the Empire of China. A hospital on similar lines has been started in Shanghai.

Another combined hospital and medical school, which is supported by missions connected with several different denominations, is the Severance hospital outside Seoul, the capital of Corea. This was started by the Presbyterian mission, but its staff includes representatives of the S.P.G., the A.M.E.C., and other societies. Thirty fully qualified Corean doctors have already been trained here. It is in fact due to the influence exerted by this hospital that vaccination has been introduced into almost every village in Corea, with the result that smallpox, which has been one of the greatest plagues of Corea, has been checked, and may ere long be exterminated

An important step towards the education of Indian women who may become medical missionaries was taken in 1894, when the North India School of Medicine for Christian Women was founded at Ludhiana in the Punjab, the two first teachers being Dr. Edith Brown and Miss Greenfield.

2. It is hardly necessary to quote instances in which the medical missionaries have, by the exercise of their art,

gained for themselves or for others the opportunity to explain and commend the Christian faith. In the case of Corea it was the work of a medical missionary which laid the foundation of Protestant missions in that land.

"Up to 1884 no mission work had been possible, the rulers and people being determined to exclude all missionaries. In the autumn of that year, however, Dr. Allen, an American medical missionary, was deputed to attempt an entry into Corea. He could only do so by becoming physician to the American Legation at Seoul. For some time no opportunity presented itself. Then one night there occurred a riot, during which the nephew of the king— Prince Min Yong Ik—was seriously wounded. Dr. Allen was summoned to attend him, and when he arrived found about thirteen of the native doctors, who were trying to staunch the bleeding wounds by filling them with wax. They gazed in amazement as the medical missionary secured the bleeding vessels, and cleansed and sutured the wounds. Dr. Allen, by this successful application of medical skill, not only occasioned a revolution in the medical treatment of that country, but also obtained a marvellous vantage-ground for carrying on missionary work. The then Government of Corea subscribed for the building of a hospital for Dr. Allen, which was established under royal patronage, and where not only the healing of the sick was carried on, but also the preaching of the gospel. Other missionaries were allowed to settle in Corea; the people showed confidence in them, and to-day this once-closed land has been the scene of some of the most splendid triumphs of the Cross, as the direct outcome of the work of medico-evangelism." [1]

One further illustration may be given of the influence which the medical missionary may exert in a non-Christian land. During the Boxer rebellion a small mission hospital was attacked by an infuriated mob crying, "Death to the foreign devils!" The doctor and evangelist went out and faced the mob, requesting that the Chinese patients in the hospital might be spared. The leader of the mob said: "I have been told you can work miracles here; if you can prove that, all your lives will be spared." A voice at

[1] *The Appeal of Medical Missions*, by R. F. Moorshead, p. 73 f.

once replied from the mob: " They can.   Six years ago I
was blind; that doctor there gave me back my sight."
The leader at once drew off his followers, and left the
mission hospital and its inmates in peace.

" Who could doubt such love, or be unwilling to trust
such a Saviour ? " was the exclamation of a poor Chinese
woman whose body had been healed and whose soul had
been won to Christ in a mission hospital.   " We have been
loved into heaven by the love and mercy of the doctors
and nurses, and we have given our souls to Christ, who
sent them here to save us," was the answer given by an
Arab mother regarding her daughter and herself, who had
formerly been Mohammedans, when asked by a Scottish
doctor why they had become Christians.

A Brahmin woman who had bitterly opposed the
work of Christian missionaries, after being treated in a
mission hospital, exclaimed, " I was against them once, but
I know now what love means."

Similar testimonies and results might be quoted from
every land where medical missionaries have worked.   The
C.M.S. mission at Srinagar in Kashmir, which is now one
of the most successful in India, was started by a medical
missionary, Dr. Elmslie, in 1865, after several unsuccessful
attempts to preach the Christian faith had been made by
other missionaries   The United Presbyterian mission at
Jeypore in Rajputana was the result of a successful treatment by a medical missionary, Dr. Valentine, of the wife
of the Maharajah

And if the results from the missionary standpoint
which have been achieved by the work of men doctors
have been great, greater far have been the results produced
by the work of women doctors.   No language can describe
the appalling needs of India's zenanas, where women die
in countless thousands or linger on in helpless misery for
lack of medical assistance.   To such, the woman missionary
doctor comes as an angel from God, and the physical
health which she brings is often the precursor of the
spiritual health which she longs equally to impart.

The results achieved by medical missionaries in all lands cannot be better described than in the words of a Brahman who addressed a meeting at Arcot which had been summoned by the American Arcot Mission:

"I have watched the missionaries, and seen what they are. What have they come to this country for? What tempts them to leave their parents, friends, and country, and come to this, to them, unhealthy clime? Is it for gain or profit they come? Some of us, country clerks in Government offices, receive larger salaries than they. Is it for an easy life? See how they work, and then tell me. Look at this missionary! He came here a few years ago, leaving all, and seeking only our good! He was met with cold looks and suspicious glances, and was shunned and maligned He sought to talk with us of what he told us was the matter of most importance in heaven and earth, but we would not listen. He was not discouraged: he opened a dispensary, and we said, 'Let the pariahs [lowest caste people] take his medicines, we won't'; but in the time of our sickness and distress and fear we were glad to go to him, and he welcomed us. We complained at first if he walked through our Brahmin streets, but ere long, when our wives and daughters were in sickness and anguish, we went and begged him to come, even into our inner apartments; and he came, and our wives and daughters now smile upon us in health! Has he made money by it? Even the cost of the medicine he has given us has not been returned to him.

"Now what is it that makes him do all this for us? *It is his Bible!* I have looked into it a good deal, at one time or another, in the different languages I chance to know—it is just the same in all languages. The Bible!—there is nothing to compare with it, in all our sacred books, for goodness, and purity, and holiness, and love, and for motives of action. Where did the English people get all their intelligence and energy, and cleverness and power? It is their Bible that gives it to them. And now they bring it to us and say, 'That is what raised us; take it and raise yourselves.' They do not force it upon us, as did the Mohammedans with their Koran, but they bring it in love, and translate it into our languages, and lay it before us, and say, 'Look at it, read it, examine it, and see if it is not good.' Of one thing I am convinced: do what we will, oppose it as we may, it

3

is the Christian's Bible that will, sooner or later, work the
regeneration of our land." [1]

The Development of Medical Missions.

Although it does not appear that the Jesuits sent out
qualified doctors to act as medical missionaries, it often
happened that some of their missionaries possessed a
serviceable knowledge of medicine which they used to good
effect. Thus Professor Okakura Yoshisaburo of Japan
writes:

"In 1568 Oda Nabunaga gave a plot of ground of about
ten acres in Kyoto to build a Christian church . . . Two
Jesuit priests who served the church, being well versed in
the practice of medicine, built wards on the premises,
where poor patients were invited and treated free of charge.
Nabunaga also gave them an area of about 1200 acres in the
province of Omi, where three thousand kinds of medical
plants were transplanted, the *artemisia vulgaris* still used in
cauterization being supposed to be one of them." [2]

We have referred elsewhere to the presence at the
court of Japan of a Christian physician during the first
part of the eighth century.

China.—The first medical missionary to China of whom
much is known was Bernard Rhodes, who was born in
1644 at Lyons. Having studied medicine and surgery, he
entered a religious Order as a lay brother, and eventually
went to China, where he lived for sixteen years and died
near Peking in 1715. He attended all ranks of Chinese,
from the Emperor downwards. Father Karenni in a letter
written from Peking in 1715 gives a graphic account of
the widespread influence that he exerted and of the
affection with which the Chinese regarded him.[3]

In 1820 Dr. Livingstone, who was in the employ of
the East India Company and was stationed at Macao,

---

[1] *Medical Missions, their Place and Power*, by J. Lowe, p. 115 f.
[2] *The Life and Thought of Japan*, 1913, p. 109.
[3] See *Lettres Édifiantes et Curieuses*, vol. xiv. p. 431.

opened a dispensary for the benefit of poor Chinese, in connection with which Dr. Morrison acted as interpreter and endeavoured to preach the gospel to the patients.

The first medical missionary in modern times to reach China was the Rev. Peter Parker, M.D., who arrived in 1835 and was supported by the American Board of Missions. His hospital at Hong-Kong attracted patients from far and near. In 1839 Dr. Lockhart of the L.M.S. started work at Macao and was joined the same year by Dr. Hobson. Dr. Lockhart eventually undertook work at Shanghai and Dr. Hobson at Hong-Kong.

Amongst the medical missionaries who reached China during the next thirty years were the Rev. Hudson Taylor (founder of the China Inland Mission), W. Gauld and James Maxwell of the Presbyterian Church of England, and F. Porter Smith of the Wesleyan Methodist Missionary Society. In 1890 the number of medical missionaries in China had risen to 125 and in 1913 to 435 (see p. 203).

The S.P.G. may perhaps claim to have been the first missionary society or organization to attempt to train or send out medical missionaries. By his will, dated February 22, 1703, General Codrington bequeathed to the S.P.G. his two plantations in Barbados, one of the conditions being that a convenient number of professors and scholars should be maintained there who should be "obliged to study and practise Phisick and Chirurgery as well as Divinity," so that they might "both endear themselves to the people and have the better opportunities of doing good to men's souls whilst they were taking care of their bodys." [1] As soon as the society obtained possession of the estates (in 1712), superintendence of "the sick and maimed negroes and servants" was undertaken by a missionary (Rev. J. Holt) skilled "in physic and surgery," "a chest of medicines to the value of £30 being supplied him." As a result of the labours of Mr. Holt and his successors, the report for 1740 records that "some

[1] See p. 396, also *Two Hundred Years of the S.P.G.*, p. 816 a.

hundreds of negroes have been brought to our Holy
Religion, and there are now not less than seventy Christian
negroes on those Plantations."

This was, however, the only organized medical missionary work undertaken by the S.P.G. during the eighteenth
century.

The first medical missionary whom this society sent
out in the nineteenth century was the Rev. (afterwards
Bishop) F. T. McDougall, F.R.C.S., who began work in
Borneo in 1848. Amongst other Anglican bishops who
have been fully qualified medical missionaries may be
mentioned Dr H. Callaway, who began work in Kaffraria
in 1855; Dr. Strachan, Bishop of Rangoon; Dr. Smyth,
Bishop of Lebombo; and Dr. Hine, Bishop of Nyasa.

The London Society for Promoting Christianity amongst
the Jews may perhaps claim to have been the first society
to send out medical missionaries with the intention that
the missionaries should devote practically their whole time
to the practice of medicine. This society sent out Dr.
George Clarke to Gibraltar in 1823, and Dr. George Dalton
in 1824 to Jerusalem.

India.—Medical missions in India, in the modern
sense of the term, date from 1783, when John Thomas,
a ship's surgeon, commenced missionary work in Bengal.
After itinerating for three years in the Malda district, and
translating part of the New Testament into Bengali, he
returned to England in 1792, and having offered his
services to the Baptist Missionary Society, was sent out
as a companion to Carey in 1793. Though he was an
eccentric person, and had to be confined for some time in
an asylum, he laboured strenuously to promote the cause
of Christian missions. He died in 1801, and had no
successor till 1838, when Mr. Archibald Ramsay began
medical work in Travancore. In 1852 the L.M.S. sent
out Dr. Leitch, who was drowned two years later, but
whose work inaugurated the large and successful medical
mission which the L.M.S. has since developed at Neyoor
in South India. About the same time the American Board

of Missions sent out Dr. John Scudder, who laboured first in Ceylon and afterwards in Madras.

In 1856 the Free Church of Scotland sent its first medical missionary, Dr. David Paterson, to Madras.

The Church of England Zenana Missionary Society sent the first woman doctor to India (Dr. Fanny Butler) in 1880.

The S.P G. began medical missionary work in 1870 at Nazareth in Tinnevelly, and Dr Strachan, its first medical missionary, afterwards became Bishop of Rangoon.

As a development of Mrs. Winter's work at Delhi, which was begun in 1863, the first hospital for women and children in India was established in connection with the S.P.G. mission to Delhi. The work grew steadily till the foundation of St. Stephen's Hospital in the central street of Delhi in 1884. In 1906 the new St. Stephen's Hospital was founded outside the walls.

The Zenana Bible and Medical Mission (1852), which is an undenominational society, supports the Victoria Hospital at Benares, the Duchess of Teck Hospital at Patna, the Kinnaird Memorial Hospital at Lucknow, and a hospital at Nasik in Western India which was presented by local Brahmans. For further details in regard to the hospitals and medical missions which are scattered throughout India, see p. 131. The total number of qualified medical missionaries in India was 140 in 1895, 281 in 1905, and 335 in 1912.

Medical Missions to Moslems.

It has been the well-nigh universal experience of missionaries who have worked amongst Moslems that the best, and often the only, way by which a successful appeal can be made is by means of medical missions. The experience of Dr. Pennell on the borders of Afghanistan, Dr. W. Miller in Northern Nigeria, and many others, is the same, namely, that the prejudices of Moslems against the Christian faith can best be combated by the practical demonstration of the love of Jesus Christ which is embodied in a medical mission.

One reason why medical missions appeal so strongly to Moslems is that in many cases their knowledge of medicine and surgery is so deficient that it can only be compared with that of heathen or pagans. Even in Moslem lands which have long been in touch with European influence and science the knowledge of medicine has lagged behind the knowledge of all other subjects.[1]

Four doctors and four nurses were sent out by the Dutch Church, twenty years ago, to the Dutch East Indies. One of the Scotch doctors who visited the scene of their work in 1912 wrote home as follows:

"I find here over 30,000 converts from Islam, all the work of four doctors and four nurses. And these men and women are living better Christian lives than the vast bulk of our Christians at home."

Women's Work in the Mission Field.

Our failure to describe in detail the share which women have taken in the work of Christian missions is due to no want of appreciation of the supremely important part which they have played in the past and are destined to play in the future in all parts of the mission field. The

[1] An illustration of this may be found in a series of questions and answers which were published by the *Lancet*, July 16, 1898. The questions to which the answers were appended had been addressed by the French Statistical Department to the Pasha of Damascus.

"Q. What is the death-rate per thousand in your principal city? A. In Damascus it is the will of Allah that all must die—some die old, some young. Q. What is the annual number of births? A. We do not know; God alone can say. Q. Are the supplies of drinking water sufficient and of good quality? A. From the remotest period no one has ever died of thirst. Q. General remarks on the hygienic conditions of your city. A. Since Allah sent us Mohammed, His prophet, to purge the world with fire and sword, there has been a vast improvement. But there still remains much to do. And now, my lamb of the West, cease your questioning, which can do no good either to you or to anyone else. Man should not bother himself about matters which concern only God. Salaam aleikum."

future status of women for many years to come in non-Christian lands will depend to a very large extent upon the ability of missionary societies to send out into the mission field an increased staff of highly qualified Christian women. The suffragist and suffragette societies at home would be amongst the strongest supporters of missionary work could they but realize that the work accomplished by these has done more towards effecting the emancipation and uplifting of women than all other societies or political organizations in the world. To two-thirds of the women now living in the world Christian missions hold out the only immediate prospect of raising their social status. No religion other than Christianity inculcates the doctrine that women are the equals of men and should be accorded equal freedom and equal opportunities of education. Their future is therefore inseparably connected with the diffusion and acceptance of the teaching of Christianity.

More than half the women now living in the British Empire are Hindus. This fact adds point to the words uttered by a well-known Brahman in India who said that among the countless divisions and sects of Hinduism the only two things on which all Hindus are agreed are the sanctity of the cow and the depravity of woman. We note with joy the isolated efforts which have so far been made by Hindus and Moslems to imitate the actions of the Christian missionaries and to agitate for the emancipation of their women, but without the support of Christian teaching and the inspiration of Christian love it is impossible that these efforts should obtain their true fruition.

To appreciate the nature of the problem which confronts those who desire to uplift India's women, we need to remind ourselves that there are 40,000,000 Indian women confined in zenanas, that there are 26,000,000 widows, 335,000 of whom are under fifteen years of age and 111,000 under ten, that not one woman in 100 in India can read, and that only one in 100 of girls of school-going age are at school. How difficult it is for the enlightened Hindus to win over their fellow-countrymen

to the institution of any radical reforms may be gathered
from the fact that the teaching of their sacred books
strongly supports the treatment of women which is at
present in vogue.   Thus their great law-giver, Manu, whose
teaching is accepted by nearly all orthodox Hindus, can be
quoted by those opposed to reform as having said : "Day
and night must women be kept in dependence by the male
members of the family ; they are never fit for independence ;
they are as impure as falsehood itself : that is a fixed
rule." [1]

The need for transforming the life of women by imparting to them the teaching of Jesus Christ is as real in
other countries as it is in India.

Few, if any, English women outside the ranks of the
missionaries have had so wide an experience of the conditions under which women in India and the Far East live
as the famous traveller, Mrs. Bishop.   Speaking of the
influence which the religions of these countries exert upon
women, she said :

"Just one or two remarks as to what these false faiths
do.   They degrade women with an infinite degradation.   I
have lived in zenanas and harems, and have seen the daily
life of the secluded women, and I can speak from bitter
experience of what their lives are—the intellect dwarfed, so
that the woman of twenty or thirty years of age is more
like a child of eight intellectually ; while all the worst
passions of human nature are stimulated and developed to
a fearful degree ; jealousy, envy, murderous hate, intrigue,
running to such an extent that in some countries I have
hardly been in a woman's house or near a woman's tent
without being asked for drugs with which to disfigure the
favourite wife, to take away her life, or to take away the
life of the favourite wife's infant son.   This request has
been made to me nearly two hundred times." [2]

The Indian zenana was first penetrated in the name of
Christ by the wife of a missionary sixty years ago when

[1] Manu, ix. 2, 3, 18.
[2] Speech at Exeter Hall, November 1, 1893.

asked to visit a Hindu woman who was dying, and who had been in secret a reader of the Christian Bible. The sequel of this visit was the establishment in London in 1852 of the Zenana Bible and Medical Mission, which supports more than 30 stations and a number of well-equipped hospitals for women (see p. 132). Miss Swain was apparently the first woman to become a qualified medical missionary (1870). The number of qualified women doctors in the mission field is now nearly 400.

Another sphere of women's work in the mission field is afforded by the demand for qualified nurses. It is encouraging to know that during the last ten years 700 nurses have joined the Nurses' Missionary League, thereby declaring their intention, if God permit, to become missionaries, and that of this number 230 are already (1914) at work abroad.

The number of unmarried women missionaries now at work is nearly 7000. Of these 2700 come from the U S.A. and about the same number from Great Britain. The remainder are connected with continental societies.

The work which women missionaries have accomplished in the mission field will be referred to again and again in the sections relating to different countries, but nothing which can be said will give the supporters of missions an adequate idea of the important part which women are playing in the spread of Christian missions and of the supreme importance of extending their work.

III.

THE DAWN OF MODERN MISSIONS[1]
(1580–1750).

DURING the two centuries preceding the Reformation hardly any attempt was made to evangelize the non-Christian world, and nearly two centuries elapsed after the Reformation before the Churches of Europe which had the open Bible in their hands realized that it was their duty to impart the knowledge of its contents to the heathen. Some of the leaders in the Reformation movements were so far from initiating missionary work abroad that they regarded all such work as useless or even wrong.

Thus *Luther* (1483–1546) in his *Table Talk* says : " The arts are growing as if there was to be a new start and the world was to become young again. . . . Another hundred years and all will be over. God's Word will disappear for want of any to preach it. . . . Asia and Africa have no gospel. In Europe, Greeks, Italians, Spaniards, Hungarians, French, English, Poles have no gospel." " The small Electorate of Saxony will not hinder the end," he replied to one who observed that when Christ came there would be no faith at all on the earth, and that the gospel was still believed in that part of Germany.

Zwingli (1484–1531), whilst admitting that the gospel must continue to spread throughout the world, makes no suggestion that it is the duty of the Church to send out

---

[1] This chapter contains a brief sketch of missionary work other than that connected with the R C. Church up to 1750. A further account of the work to which reference is made will be found under the headings of the various countries in which the work was attempted.

missionaries. It is interesting to note that he maintained that pious heathens would be saved who died without a knowledge of the gospel.

Calvin (1509–1564) held that any special agency for the conversion of the heathen is needless, for, as he wrote, "we are taught that the kingdom of Christ is neither to be advanced nor maintained by the industry of men, but this is the work of God alone."

In 1535 *Erasmus*, who was not definitely associated with the Reformation movements, had urged in the strongest language the duty of evangelizing the whole world.[1]

The first theologian connected with the Reformation movements to maintain that " the command to preach the gospel to all nations binds the Church" for all time was *Adrianus Saravia* (1531–1613), a Dutchman, who, after being a Reformed pastor at Antwerp and Brussels, and a professor at Leyden, eventually became Dean of Westminster. In his treatise "concerning the different orders of the ministry of the gospel as they were instituted by the Lord," published in 1590, he urges the duty of the Church to carry on the task of the evangelization of the world, which had been begun by the apostles, and argues that the maintenance of the episcopal office is necessary to the fulfilment of this task.

This treatise by Saravia drew from *Theodore Beza* of Geneva a reply (1592) in the course of which he disputed the interpretation of the missionary command given by Saravia and maintained that its obligation did not extend beyond the first century. Later on, *Johann Gerhard* (d. 1637) wrote, opposing the views of Saravia and maintaining that the command to preach the gospel in the whole world ceased with the apostles (*mandatum prædicandi evangelium in toto terrarum orbe cum apostolis desiit*). He gives as one reason for believing that this

---

[1] See his treatise, *Ecclesiastes, sive de ratione concionandi.* A quotation of some length is given by Dr. Geo. Smith in his *Short History of Christian Missions*, p. 116 f.

was so, that St. Paul himself declared that this command
had been already obeyed, and that the gospel had brought
forth fruit in the whole world (Rom. x. 18, Col. i. 23).
The arguments that he adduces reappear in an official
document issued by the theological Faculty of Wittenberg
which represented Lutheran orthodoxy, and which had been
elicited by an inquiry addressed to the Faculty by Count
Truchsess, who desired to have an explanation of the scope
of the missionary command recorded by St. Matthew.
The Faculty declared that the command to go into all the
world was only a personal privilege (*personale privilegium*)
of the apostles, and had already been fulfilled. They
argued that if this were not so it would be the duty of
every Christian to become a missionary—a conclusion
which was absurd. They further declared that inasmuch
as all nations once possessed the knowledge of God, He
is not bound to restore to their descendants what has
been taken away *crimine læsæ majestatis*. Lastly, they
suggested that where a Christian Government is established
in a non-Christian land it behoves the civil authorities to
build churches and establish schools for the benefit of the
" sinners " whom they have brought under their sway.

The first attempt at missionary work made by
members of the Reformed Churches was not followed by
any permanent result. In 1555 *Villegaignon*, a French
adventurer, who founded a colony in Brazil, asked Calvin
to send Christian preachers, whether to minister to the
French Protestants or to evangelize the heathen is not
certain. Richier, who was one of four clergymen sent,
wrote shortly after his arrival in Brazil that they had
purposed to win the native heathen for Christ, but that
their barbarism, their cannibalism, and their spiritual
dullness " extinguished all our hope."

It would be interesting to watch the countenances of a
missionary committee to-day which should receive a similar
pessimistic report from one of its missionaries before he
had even begun to learn the language of the country to
which he had been sent !

George Fox (1624–91), who founded the Society of Friends, and who had himself visited America, wrote: "All friends everywhere, that have Indians or blacks, you are to preach the gospel to them and other servants if you be true Christians." In 1661 three of his followers set out as missionaries to China, but did not succeed in reaching that country.

The first Lutheran to attempt definitely missionary work was an Austrian, *Baron Justinian von Weltz* (b. 1621). After writing several treatises in which he maintained the missionary obligation attaching to all Christians, he laid aside his baronial title and sailed for Dutch Guiana, where he soon afterwards died. The change of attitude in favour of the recognition of the duty of prosecuting foreign missions that took place amongst the Lutheran Christians towards the end of the seventeenth century was due in part to the writings and example of Von Weltz.

Thus *Spener* (1635–1705), who has been called the "Father of pietism," in the course of a sermon preached on the Feast of the Ascension said:

"The obligation rests on the whole Church to have care as to how the gospel shall be preached in the whole world, . . . and to this end no diligence, labour, or cost be spared in such work on behalf of the poor heathen and unbelievers. That almost no thought even has been given to this . . . is evidence how little the honour of Christ and of humanity concerns us."

At the close of the seventeenth century the cause of foreign missions found an earnest advocate in the well-known philosopher, *Baron von Leibnitz*, whose interest in them had been aroused by his conversations with Jesuit missionaries from China whom he had met in Rome. One of those whom he influenced was Francke, who was associated with the sending out of the Danish Mission to India.

In 1700 the *Royal Society of Prussia* was founded in Berlin, and in 1702 a *collegium orientale* was added in order that the society—to quote the words of the royal declaration—

"may also be a college for the propagation of the Christian faith, worship, and virtue, that upon occasion of their philosophical observations which they shall make in the northern part of Asia, they shall likewise diligently endeavour that among the barbarous people of those tracts of land as far as China, the light of the Christian faith and the purer gospel may be kindled, and even that China itself may be assisted by those Protestants who travel thither by land or sail to that country through the Northern Sea."

Dr. Jablonski, the vice-president of the Royal Society, writing to a representative of the English S.P.G. (on January 20, 1711) stated that the formation of this "oriental college" was an act of "pious emulation" on the part of those in Prussia who had heard of the proposed formation of the S.P.G.

Dutch Missions.—The Dutch East India Company, which was founded in 1602, was bound by the charter granted by the State to care for the planting of the Church and the conversion of the heathen in the countries with which it traded. At its instigation was founded in 1622, at the University of Leyden, an institution called the *Seminarium Indicum,* which for twelve years helped to provide preachers and missionaries for the Company's service. These engaged for a period of five years only, and the majority of them returned to Holland without having mastered the languages of the peoples amongst whom they lived.

The causes of the comparative failure of the Dutch missions are thus described by Dr. Warneck:[1]

"At the best the preachers mastered the language of the Malays, but the motley population of the wide archipelago has many languages, and only in the case of Ceylon and Formosa can it be pretended that they attempted to learn other languages. No doubt there was a Malay and also a Singalese translation of the Bible: so also in Formosa some

[1] *History of Protestant Missions,* p. 45 f.

books of the New Testament were translated into the
language of the country . . . with honourable exceptions
the mission work itself became very superficial. . . . The
example of Portuguese sham-Christianization worked
infectiously. Thousands were received into the Church by
baptism without heed to inward preparedness. . . . When
in 1674 one of the kings of Timor declared that he and his
people were willing to become Christians, the preacher
Rhymdyk was sent 'to see to what was necessary'—that is, to
baptize the whole people off-hand. In the state of Amboina
the chiefs simply received a command to have always at the
time of the preacher's visit a number of natives ready for
baptism; and since for everyone who was baptized the
preacher received a sum per head, it will be easily understood that he was not particular if, as often happened, he
himself was not a man full of the Holy Ghost and of faith.
. . . With such a method of conversion it can easily be
understood how at the close of the seventeenth century the
number of Christians should be given in Ceylon alone as
from 300,000 to 400,000, in Java as 100,000, in Amboina
as 40,000, and no less easily how the Christianity of these
masses was inwardly worthless, and almost vanished when,
as in Ceylon, the rule of the Dutch came to an end, or continued to exist only as a dead nominal Christianity. . . .
In Formosa alone had a better foundation been laid, but
there, after the expulsion of the Dutch by the Chinese pirates
in 1661, the nascent Christianity was forcibly extinguished."

The Danish-Halle Mission.—The Danish colonial pos-
sessions date from 1620 in the East Indies, and from
1672 in the West Indies and Gold Coast. In 1705 Dr.
Lutkens, who had been appointed as a Danish court chaplain
in the previous year, and who had lived for a time with
Spener in Berlin, was commissioned by the king, Frederick
IV., to seek out missionaries who might be sent to the
Danish colonies. Having failed to find suitable men in
Denmark, he applied to Francke at Halle in Germany, and
through his assistance the first two missionaries, Bartholomew
Ziegenbalg and Henry Plutschau, were sent forth from
Copenhagen by the Bishop of Zealand on November 29, 1705.
Whilst staying at the Cape of Good Hope, on their way
out to Tranquebar, they sent home a deplorable account of

the Hottentots who were under Dutch rule.   This eventually resulted in the commencement of a Moravian mission
at the Cape.   On arriving at Tranquebar (July 9, 1706)
they experienced much hostility from the Danish officials,
who regarded their enterprise as fanatical and quixotic.
Their work, nevertheless, was soon attended by visible
results.   Ten months after their arrival they baptized five
heathen slaves of Danish masters, and five months later
they baptized nine adult Hindus.   In the following year
Ziegenbalg made a preaching tour through the kingdom of
Tanjore, and the reports of this tour, and of his public
conferences with Brahmans, were translated into English by
the Rev. A. W. Boehm, formerly chaplain to Prince George
of Denmark, and were dedicated to the S.P.G., and the 500
copies purchased and distributed by this society "proved
a motive to many charitable benefactions contributed by
well-disposed persons for advancing this mission."   The
English East India Company offered to convey the books
and letters belonging to the mission free of charge, and
the S.P.C.K. undertook to receive funds on its behalf.

In 1714 a college for promoting the spread of the
gospel was founded as a state institution at Copenhagen,
but, notwithstanding the existence of this college, the real
direction and control of the mission remained at Halle
in Germany.   Plutschau returned invalided in 1711, by
which time the New Testament had been translated into
Tamil and a Tamil dictionary was nearly completed.   When
Ziegenbalg returned in 1715, he was presented to George I.,
who wrote to him after he had returned to Tranquebar a
letter (dated August 23, 1717) expressing satisfaction
"not only because the work undertaken by you of converting the heathen to the Christian faith doth, by the
grace of God, prosper, but also because that in this our
kingdom such a laudable zeal for the promotion of the
gospel prevails."

When Ziegenbalg died in 1719, aged thirty-six, he
left 355 converts and numerous catechumens, a complete
Tamil Bible, a dictionary, a mission seminary and schools.

Francke was the chief supporter in Germany of the Danish-Halle Mission and helped to train many of its earliest missionaries.

We shall refer to this mission later on in describing missionary work in India. Meanwhile we may quote Dr. Warneck's statement :

"As to the history of the Danish-Halle Mission, . . . let it suffice to note that from Francke's institutions there have been sent out in the course of a century about sixty missionaries, amongst whom, besides conspicuous men like Ziegenbalg, Fabricius, Jänecke, Gerické, Christian Friedrich Schwartz was distinguished as a star of the first magnitude. Amid various little strifes and ample distress . . . this . . . on the whole solid and not unfruitful mission (about 15,000 Christians) maintained itself until in the last quarter of the century and afterwards rationalism at home dug up its roots. Only when the universities, having fallen completely under the sway of this withering movement, ceased to furnish theologians, was the first trial made in 1803 of a missionary who had not been a university student. Meanwhile a more living interest had been awakened in England, and so the connection which had already for some time existed with friends of missions there, and specially the alliance with the Church missionary societies, saved the Tamil Mission from ruin. Then later the Dresden-Leipsic Lutheran Missionary Society stepped into the old heritage of the fathers, after Halle had long ceased to be an active centre."[1]

The college which had been founded at Copenhagen sent out Hans Egede, a Norwegian pastor, to start work in *Greenland* in 1721. The hardships and disappointments that he and his associates encountered resulted in an order from the King of Denmark to discontinue the work (see p. 51).

Moravian Missions. — The missionary activities of no other branch of the Christian Church can compare with those of the Moravian Church. Within twenty years of the commencement of their missionary work the Moravian Brethren had started more missions than Anglicans and

[1] *History of Protestant Missions*, p. 57 f.

Protestants had started during the two preceding centuries.
Their marvellous success was largely due to the fact that from
the first they recognized that the evangelization of the world
was the most pressing of all the obligations that rested
upon the Christian Church, and that the carrying out of
this obligation was the " common affair " of the community.
Up to the present time the Moravians have sent out nearly
3000 missionaries, the proportion of missionaries to their
communicant members being 1 in 12.   Amongst English
Christians generally the proportion is said to be 1 in 2000.
To the Moravians it seemed impossible that any branch of
the Christian Church could continue to exist which failed
to recognize this common obligation.   It would be little
exaggeration to say that the continued existence and vitality
of the Moravian Church are a result of its missionary
activity.

The Moravian community or brotherhood (*Unitas
Fratrum*) dates back to 1467.   The Moravians who were
expelled from Austria in 1722 settled at Herrnhut, not far
from Dresden, where they were welcomed by Count von
Zinzendorf (1700–60), who helped to inspire them with
a zeal for foreign missions and was eventually consecrated
(1737) as a Bishop of the Moravian Church.   Their first
mission [1] was to the negro slaves in the Danish island of
St. Thomas in the West Indies.   A negro from this island,
who had been invited to Herrnhut by Count Zinzendorf,
appealed to the Brethren for help.   He said to them, " You
cannot come unless you are willing to become slaves "; and
although this forecast was not literally fulfilled, the first
missionaries who responded to this appeal were not discouraged by the terms proposed.   On August 21, 1732,
Leonard Dober, a potter, and David Nitschmann, a
carpenter, left Herrnhut for Copenhagen on their way to
the West Indies, being the advanced guard of an army of
nearly 3000 missionaries which the Moravian Church has
sent forth.

[1] For a sketch of Moravian missions see *A Short History of the Moravian
Church*, by J. E. Hutton.

On reaching St. Thomas :

"they won the hearts of the slaves and made them clap their hands for joy. They aroused the anger of the brutal slave-owners. . . . They caused the negroes to weep and pray in sugar-field and hut, and brought hundreds of converts to baptism. . . . They stood fearlessly before high officials . . . and by showing the slave-owners that they should no longer treat their slaves as beasts, prepared the way for negro emancipation."[1]

In 1734 mission work was started in the island of St. Croix, and a little later in Jamaica and Antigua.

The Mission to *Greenland*—When Count Zinzendorf visited the Danish Court at Copenhagen in 1731, he met two Eskimos, who had been baptized by the Danish missionary Egede. On hearing that it was proposed to discontinue the work in Greenland, two Moravian Brethren, *Stach* and *Boemish*, who were by occupation grave-diggers, volunteered to undertake work there, and reached Greenland in 1733.

"At first their outlook was gloomy. When they tried to earn their living by fishing, they found themselves unable to manage their boat, and had to live chiefly on seaweed. They had to learn two new languages—first, the Danish, and then through the Danish the Eskimo—and the Greenlanders took the opportunity to cheat them. . . . When the two cousins stood up to preach, the natives treated them shamefully, danced around them, mimicked them, howled, drummed, pelted them with stones. 'As long as we have a sound body,' said these greasy Greenlanders . . . 'we have enough. Your people may have diseased souls; go back to those that need you.' When the first convert, Kajarnak, came forward with his family to be baptized, a plot was formed, and his father-in-law was murdered. To add to the missionaries' troubles, the small-pox broke out and carried off from two to three thousand of the people. . . . The Moravians were hated and despised by the people: they were looked upon as the cause of the small-pox; they had to attend on two thousand ungrateful patients; they were

[1] *A Short History of the Moravian Church*, p. 152.

almost dying of hunger; and as they lay in their snow huts
at night, with the cold stars above them and the sounds of
midnight revelry in their ears, they felt indeed that only by
the strength of Christ could they win the hard-fought
battle.   At last, after years of waiting, the long night began
to break . . . and from the moment when Kajarnak, as he
listened with awe to the story of Gethsemane, came forward
with his eager question, 'What is that?   Tell me that again,'
the work began to flourish, the hope of the missionaries
swelled to faith, and the Rose of Sharon began to bloom in
the eternal snows of the 'Land of Desolation.'" [1]

In 1740 the Moravian missionaries made an important
change in the methods of presenting the gospel to the Greenlanders which they had hitherto adopted.   In the *Historical
Sketches of the Missions of the United Brethren*, [2] written by
John Holmes and published in 1818, this change is thus
described :

"A great change took place in the mode adopted by our
brethren in their endeavours to instruct the natives.   The
method hitherto pursued by them consisted principally in
speaking to the heathen of the existence, the attributes,
and perfection of God, and enforcing obedience to the divine
law, hoping by this means gradually to prepare their minds
for the reception of the sublimer and more mysterious truths
of the gospel: and it must be allowed that, abstractly considered, this method appears the most rational; but when
reduced to practice, it was found wholly ineffectual.   For
five years our missionaries had laboured in this way, and
could scarce obtain a patient hearing from the savages.
Now, therefore, they determined in the literal sense of the
word to preach Christ and Him crucified without first 'laying the foundation of repentance from dead works and faith
towards God.'   No sooner did they declare unto the Greenlanders 'the word of reconciliation' in its native simplicity
than they beheld its converting and saving power.   This
reached the hearts of the audience and produced the most
astonishing effects.   An impression was made which opened
a way to their consciences and illuminated their under-
standings.   They remained no longer the stupid and brutish,

[1] *A Short History of the Moravian Church*, p. 154 f.   [2] P. 31 f.

creatures they had once been; they felt they were sinners, and trembled at their danger, they rejoiced in the offer of a Saviour, and were rendered capable of relishing sublimer pleasures than plenty of seals and the low gratifications of sensual appetites. A sure foundation being thus laid in the knowledge of a crucified Redeemer, our missionaries soon found that this supplied their young converts with a powerful motive to the abhorrence of sin and the performance of every moral duty towards God and their neighbour. . . . In short, the happiest results have attended this practice, not only at first and in Greenland, but in every other country where our missionaries have since laboured for the conversion of the heathen."

Within the territory occupied by the Moravians the work of evangelization has long since been completed. At their General Synod in 1899 the Moravians handed over their missions in Greenland to the Danish Church and quitted Greenland in the following year.

The mission to *Labrador*, which was commenced soon after the middle of the eighteenth century, was attended by even greater difficulties than those which the missionaries had to encounter in Greenland, but these were successfully surmounted, and nearly all the population of Labrador is now Christian.

In 1738 a mission was established in *Surinam* or *Dutch Guiana*. On reaching the coast the missionaries made their way through three hundred miles of jungles and swamps and finally settled amongst the Accawois, the Warrows, the Arawaks, and the Caribs. George Dähne, one of the missionaries, lived in a lonely hut in the forest for two years, "surrounded by wild beasts and wilder men." After six years of strenuous toil, the first convert, an old woman, was baptized. As the work began to attain visible success it was bitterly opposed by the Dutch traders, and the Dutch Government issued orders forbidding the Indians to join any Moravian settlement.

In 1735 the Moravians undertook colonization in *Georgia*, and commenced missionary work amongst the American Indians. Their work, which met with a large amount of initial success, was so vehemently opposed by the other white settlers that they at length withdrew altogether.

In 1742 the Moravian missionary Rauch developed a mission at *Shekomeko* in the state of New York, but the opposition of the white settlers compelled its abandonment. A missionary settlement established in 1746 at *Gnadenhutten* prospered for ten years, but was then destroyed during one of the innumerable wars waged against the Indians.

In 1736 Huckoff, who belonged to an old Moravian family, attempted to start a school among the slaves on the *Gold Coast*.

In 1737 George Schmidt reached *Cape Town*, having been sent out by the Brethren at Herrnhut. By this time the Dutch had held Cape Town for nearly a century, but they had done nothing towards the evangelization of the Africans. Schmidt had been imprisoned for conscience' sake for six years in Bohemia before he set sail for South Africa. He worked for six years among the Hottentots at Bavianskloof, and won the hearts of many by his teaching and preaching. The Dutch Boers, who disliked and despised the Hottentots, were far from being pleased at his success. In 1742 Schmidt, having received an "act of ordination" from Zinzendorf, proceeded to baptize five Hottentots. His action gave umbrage to the regular Dutch ministers at Cape Town, and after fruitless attempts to arrive at an understanding with them he started in October 1743 on his return to Europe. He left behind 49 adherents, 5 of whom had been baptized. For nearly fifty years after his departure no attempt was made to carry on the work which he had inaugurated.

The principles and methods which characterized these early Moravian missions have been well summarized by a Moravian historian, who wrote :

"No Moravian missionary worked alone. The whole Church threw its heart into the task. All missionaries went out with full instructions, and were followed by the prayers of the whole Church. No man was to go unless his mind was fully made up; nay more, unless he could not help it. He must be a man, so ran the rules, who felt within him an irresistible call, a man who loathed the lusts of the world, who burned with love to Christ, who was approved by all his brethren, and whose face shone with the light of a divine joy, which should enlighten the black hearts of the heathen. As for the work of the missionaries, it was thorough and deep and well organized. Everything was done according to a well-considered plan. When the missionaries arrived at their post they were to announce themselves to the people as messengers sent by Jesus Christ. . . . As soon as possible after their arrival they translated portions of the gospels into the native language, and with this as their weapon spoke straight to the hearts of the people. Instead of puzzling the poor heathens' brains with shadowy notions of a great and good God, they went straight to the mark: 'Jesus Christ lived and died, and lives now, to save thee from thy sins.' . . . As they never baptized till they were perfectly sure (as far as man can be sure) that the candidate was a genuine Christian, they often seemed to work but slowly; but they found it better to do their work thoroughly than be content with a mere coating of sham religion. . . . Above all, with their teaching, they did not forget discipline. . . . But the iron hand had a silken glove . . . and by kindness and love and tenderness they won the hearts of the heathen . . . 'It will not do,' said Zinzendorf, 'to measure everything by the Herrnhut yard."[1]

The districts in which Moravian missionaries are at work to-day include Labrador, Alaska, California (amongst the Indians), Jamaica, eight of the West Indian Islands, Nicaragua, Demerara, Surinam, South Africa, East Central Africa, West Himalayas, and North Queensland. Their missionaries, who number altogether 367, include 38 theologians, 1 doctor, 26 tradesmen, 6 artisans, 6 deaconesses, 12 brethren trained in London and 6 at Tubingen. Of the whole number 142 are ordained. In addition to these the native missionaries include 48 ordained and 25 unordained brethren.

[1] *A Short History of the Moravian Church*, p. 102 f.

Anglican Missions.—Of missionary societies now connected with the Anglican Church the oldest is the *New
England Company* (formerly known as "The Corporation
for the Propagation of the Gospel in New England"), which
was founded by the Long Parliament in 1649. It was
founded at the instigation of Cromwell after a petition
had been presented to Parliament in 1641 by 70 English
and Scottish ministers. The money necessary for its
support was obtained by a collection directed by the
same Parliament to be made throughout England in all
parishes, which amounted to what was then the large
sum of nearly £12,000. The money was invested in
land, and the income forwarded from time to time
through the Governors of the United Colonies to the
Company's first missionary in New England, the Rev. John
Eliot, and afterwards to his assistants.

At the Restoration the Company was reconstituted,
and incorporated by King Charles II. in 1661. The first
Governor of the Company was the Hon. Robert Boyle [1]
(later one of the founders of the Royal Society).

The Company continued its work in New England until
the year 1775, when the War of Independence broke out.

After the Declaration of Independence the Company
transferred the scene of its labours to New Brunswick, and
the work among the Indians there was carried on from
1776 to 1822.

In 1822 the Company transferred its operations from
New Brunswick farther to the west. Since then its
missionaries have been working among the six Indian
nations on the Grand River Reserve, Ontario, which is
the largest Indian reserve in Canada. The Company has
built several churches on the reserve, and entirely maintains three clergymen, several catechists, and a trained
hospital nurse.

---

[1] Robert Boyle was for thirty years Governor of this Corporation. In
addition to his labours on behalf of the American Indians, he published at
his own expense the Gospels and the Acts of the Apostles in the Malay
language. These were printed at Oxford in 1677.

The Company has also charge of the Mohawk Church (which is the oldest church belonging to the Anglican Communion in Canada), and has built and maintains the Mohawk Institution. This institution is considered by the Indian Department of the Canadian Government to be one of the most successful industrial schools for the children (boys and girls) of Indians in the Dominion. The Mohawk Church and Institution are in Brantford, Ontario. The church is the only chapel royal in Canada, being styled by the Crown " His Majesty's Chapel of the Mohawks," and possesses silver communion plate and a Bible presented by Queen Anne to "Her Chapel of the Mohawks," in the Mohawk Valley, Albany (now U.S.A.), in the year 1712. During the war the plate and Bible were buried, but were subsequently recovered by the Indians and by them brought to Canada.

In 1901 the Company opened a new sphere of work and built (at the invitation of the bishop of New Westminster) a school for Indian boys at Lytton in British Columbia. The membership of the New England Company has since its foundation consisted entirely of laymen and is limited to 25 members.

The Company maintains its missionary work upon the annual income derived from its endowments, which have been obtained partly by the amount realized from the collection already referred to, and partly from the bequests of the Hon. Robert Boyle and Dr. Daniel Williams.

The Christian Faith Society, originally called the Society for the Conversion and Religious Instruction and Education of the Negro Slaves in the British West India Islands, was founded as a result of a bequest made in the will of Robert Boyle, dated 1691. Its first achievement was the foundation of the College of William and Mary in Virginia for the instruction of Indian children. After the War of Independence the operations of the society were diverted to the West Indies. It has an income of £2300 per annum, derived from investments, which is spent on the support of Anglican work for the benefit of the inhabitants of the West Indian Islands.

The formation of English missionary societies for the promotion of missionary work throughout the world may be said to date from the opening of the eighteenth century. In 1698, the *Society for Promoting Christian Knowledge* was formed, its chief object being to provide Christian literature and to promote Christian education both at home and abroad. When the Danish mission to South India was in danger of becoming extinct through lack of funds, the S.P.C.K. supported it financially for a hundred years. The missionaries were for the most part German Lutherans, of whom Schwartz was the most remarkable (see p. 79).

The oldest missionary society now existing in England, which was founded with the object of sending out missionaries, is the *Society for the Propagation of the Gospel in Foreign Parts.* It can claim to be the official representative of the Church of England, since it was brought into existence as the result of a resolution passed by convocation (March 13, 1700), and all the diocesan bishops in England are *ex officio* members of its standing committee.

The society was founded with the twofold aim of ministering to English settlers beyond the seas and of propagating the gospel amongst the heathen with whom the settlers might come into contact. The society recognized that it was as important to prevent English people from becoming heathen as it was to attempt the conversion of heathen to the Christian faith. One of its earliest missionaries, the Rev. Thorogood Moore, who was sent to New York in 1704 as a missionary to Indians, wrote home to the society: "To begin with the Indians is preposterous, for it is from the behaviour of the Christians that here they have had, and still have, their notion of Christianity, which, God knows, hath been generally such that it hath made the Indians to hate our religion."

Although the chief efforts of the society were directed

at first towards supplying and maintaining clergy for the colonies and dependencies of Great Britain, it soon began definite work amongst the Indians and negroes of North America.

It has sometimes been stated that the founders of the S.P.G. did not regard its work as definitely missionary in character, but this is far from being the case. In the sermon preached at the first anniversary of the formation of the society in 1702, the preacher stated that it was part of the design of the society "to proceed in the best methods they can towards the conversion of the natives," and that it included "the breeding up of persons to understand the great variety of languages of those countries in order to be able to converse with the natives and preach the gospel to them." At a meeting of the society held on April 20, 1710, the following resolutions were carried:

"1. That the design of propagating the gospel in foreign parts does chiefly and principally relate to the conversion of heathens and infidels, and therefore that branch of it ought to be prosecuted preferably to all others. 2. That, in consequence thereof, immediate care be taken to send itinerant missionaries to preach the gospel among the Six Nations of the Indians according to the primary intentions of the late King William of glorious memory."

Bishop Secker (who afterwards became Archbishop of Canterbury) said in 1741:

"In less than forty years, under many discouragements and with an income very disproportionate to the vastness of the undertaking, a great deal hath been done; though little notice may have been taken of it by persons unattentive to these things, or backward to acknowledge them . . . great multitudes upon the whole of negroes and Indians brought over to the Christian faith, many numerous congregations have been set up, which now support the worship of God at their own expense where it was not known before, and seventy persons are constantly employed at the expense of the society in the further service of the gospel."[1]

[1] See S.P.G. Anniversary Sermon, 1741, p. 11 f.

The "seventy persons" to whom reference is here
made included all those who were engaged in ministering
to English-speaking congregations.   Many of these would,
however, be in touch with the Indians, as "the instruction
of the negro and Indian slaves and (their preparation) for
conversion, baptism, and communion was a primary charge
to every missionary . . . and to all schoolmasters of the
society in America." [1]

Further references to the work undertaken by the
S P.G. for the benefit of Indians and negroes between
1701 and 1750 in North America and the West Indies
are given later on (p. 371–6).

[1] *Two Hundred Years of the S.P.G.*, p. 63.

IV.

INDIA.

BEFORE attempting to describe the beginnings of Christian missions in India it would be well to make a brief reference to the connection which, it is often maintained, exists between the Baghavad Gita and other Hindu literature and the Christian Scriptures. The conclusion which seems to be best supported by evidence may be expressed in the words of Dr. E. W. Hopkins (U.S.A.). After considering in detail the points of resemblance which have been suggested between the teaching of the Gospels, specially that of the Gospel of St. John, and the Gita and other Hindu scriptures, he writes:

"The most reasonable explanation of the data as a whole appears to me to be that the Fourth Gospel, perhaps not uninfluenced by the Gnosticism of the time, but not necessarily influenced by a Buddhistic tradition or by any Sanskrit texts, was of a mystical tone that made it peculiarly suitable to influence the Hindu divines, who transferred from it such phrases and sentiments as best fitted in with the conception of Krishna as a god of love. For it must be remembered constantly that before Krishna's advent in his new rôle those characteristics of Krishna that bring him into closest likeness with Christ are entirely lacking in the conception of any previous Hindu divinity. Buddha never pretended to forgive sin. . . . But suddenly there appears this benign man-god, who proclaims that all sins are forgiven to him who believes in Krishna, and that those who believe in him are very few in number, yet this new religion of love and faith is better than the old Brahmanic religion of works and ceremonial purity."[1]

[1] *India Old and New*, by Dr. E. W. Hopkins (New York, 1901), p. 158.

When we come down to the writings of Tulsi Das (the Ramayana) in the sixteenth century the influence of Christian teaching becomes so apparent that it is impossible to resist the conviction that his development of the doctrine of *bhakti* which was hinted at in the Bhagavad Gita was the outcome of Christian influences. Referring to this doctrine Dr. Grierson writes:

"Suddenly in India there came this great revolution of *bhakti*. Religion was no longer a matter of knowledge, it became one of emotion. *Bhakti* may be translated by 'faith' or 'devotion.' It requires a personal, not an impersonal, God I do not myself doubt that this great step forward of the Hindu soul was due to the influence of the Christians who were then settled in the country. It was not openly an adoption of Christian principles by Hindu thinkers, who had been wasting their lives on a barren search for knowledge. In such a search, even with the brother-love of Buddhism added to it, the people could find no permanent happiness. The craving for expressing love towards the Infinite which exists in every heart was there, a spark was sufficient to set it in a flame, and that vital spark came from Christianity."[1]

For a detailed discussion of the influence which Christianity has exerted upon the teachings of modern Hinduism the reader is referred to any of the standard books on Hinduism. A helpful account of the approximations of modern Hindu writers to Christian thought will be found in *The Crown of Hinduism*, by J. N. Farquhar, and in *The Renaissance in India*, by C. F. Andrews.

We pass on to consider the beginnings of actual missionary work in India.

The obscurity attaching to the first preaching of the Christian faith in Southern India is in part due to the fact that the word India was used during the early centuries of

---

[1] See "Hinduism and Early Christianity," by G. A. Grierson, *The East and The West*, April 1906, p. 142 f. As an incidental proof of the existence of intercourse between Rome and South India in the first century A.D. we may refer to the discovery in 1850 at Calicut of several hundred coins all of which were as early as the reign of Nero.

the Christian era in a number of different senses. The tradition that St. Thomas, whose tomb is shown to-day at Mylapore, a suburb of Madras, was the first to preach the gospel in Southern India is of comparatively late origin.[1] On the other hand, Origen's statement that St. Thomas went as a missionary to Parthia is probably correct. The tradition that he was sold to a Parthian chief called Gondophares has been rendered credible by the discovery that a prince of this name [2] actually existed in Parthia at the period when St. Thomas might have been there. Heracleon, a Sicilian Gnostic who wrote about A.D. 170, says that St. Thomas ended his days in peace; and St. Clement of Alexandria, who quotes this statement, does not deny it. It is by no means inconceivable that St. Thomas extended his missionary activities from Parthia into North-West India, but it seems certain that he never visited Southern India. Pantænus is said by Eusebius to have travelled from Alexandria to India about A.D. 190 in order to preach the gospel. The words of Eusebius are:

"He (Pantænus) is said to have found there among some of the inhabitants who were acquainted with Christ the Gospel of Matthew, which had reached that country before him. For Bartholomew is said to have preached to these people and to have left them a Hebrew version of Matthew's Gospel, which they had kept until the time of which I speak." [3]

It seems probable that by India is here meant either Southern Arabia or the India of Alexander the Great—that is, the valley of the Indus. One of the bishops who attended the Council of Nicæa, A.D. 325, was described as "John of Persia, in all Persia and Great India," the latter word apparently being intended to denote the country which lay between Persia and the Indus. The

---

[1] See "St. Thomas and his Tomb at Mylapore," by James Kennedy, in The East and The West, April 1907.

[2] Undaphares of Arachosia.

[3] Historia Ecclesiastica, v. 10. 3.

India visited by Frumentius early in the fourth century was apparently Abyssinia, and the India of Theophilus the Indian towards the end of the fourth century was Arabia Felix. A tradition which does not date back earlier than the seventh century assigns Calamina, or Calamita, as the site of St. Thomas' martyrdom. Possibly this may be Kerman in Eastern Persia, or Calama in Beluchistan.

The Church in Southern India, which claims to trace back its ancestry to St. Thomas, was an offshoot from the Church in Persia, which, at the time when the Church in India was established (that is, at the beginning of the sixth century), was part of the patriarchate of Babylon.

Referring to the missionary activities of this patriarchate, Dr. Neale writes:

they "pitched their tents in the camps of the wandering Tartar: the Lama of Thibet trembled at their words: they stood in the rice fields of the Panjab and taught the fishermen by the Sea of Aral: they struggled through the vast deserts of Mongolia: the memorable inscription of Singanfu attests their victories in China: in India the Zamorin (the ruler of Calicut) himself respected their spiritual and courted their temporal authority. . . . The power of the Nestorian patriarch culminated in the beginning of the eleventh century, when he had 25 metropolitans, who ruled from China to the Tigris, from Lake Baikal to Cape Comorin." [1]

The identification of the founder of Christianity in Southern India with the Apostle is probably to be explained by the local tradition which asserts that in the year 345 there landed in Malabar, under the convoy of a Jerusalem merchant, a bishop from Edessa, named Thomas, who brought with him a large following, which included several priests and deacons. We know from other sources that in 343 a severe persecution of Christians occurred in the Persian Empire.

The first definite authority for the existence of a

[1] *A History of the Holy Eastern Church*, vol. i. p. 3, 143. For a further reference to Nestorian Bishoprics in Asia, see p. 164 f.

Christian Church in Southern India is Cosmas Indi-copleustes, who, about A.D. 535, found Christian churches and clergy in Ceylon, interior India and Male (Malabar), as well as a bishop at Kaliana (Kalyan) near Bombay.

He states that the Bishop of Kaliana receives imposition of hands from Persia.

In 1547 the so-called Thomas Cross was discovered at Milapur, Madras. On it and on two other similar crosses found at Cottayam, 500 miles away, there is an inscription in ancient Persian (or Pahlavi). In the case of the cross at Madras and of one of those at Cottayam the inscription proves that the cross must have been in existence at least as early as the seventh century. In 883 King Alfred of England sent two priests, Sighelm and Athelstan, to India *via* Rome to carry the votive offerings which he had promised to St Thomas during the siege of London.

Of what befell the Christians in South India during the next four centuries we know nothing. Marco Polo, who travelled in the East from 1270 to 1295, writes:

"In the kingdom of Quilon (Travancore) dwell many Christians and Jews who still retain their own language."

By this time the connection between the Apostle Thomas and Milapur had attained general acceptance. Marco Polo says that there lies

"the body of the glorious martyr St. Thomas Apostle, who suffered martyrdom there . . . a great multitude of Christians and Saracens (Mohammedans) make pilgrimages thither."

John of Monte Corvino, who afterwards became Archbishop of Cambaluc (Peking), spent thirteen months in South India, 1292–93, on his way to China. He writes:

"At different places in that province (which contains the Church of the Apostle St. Thomas) I baptized some hundred persons."

Menentillus, a friar who visited India in 1310, writes :

" Christians and Jews there are, but they are few and of no high standing. Christians and all who have Christian names are often persecuted."

Sir John Mandeville, who visited South India early in the fourteenth century, states that round about the tomb of St. Thomas were fifteen houses inhabited by Nestorian monks, recreant Christians and schismatics. He states that the body of St. Thomas has been transported to Edessa in Syria, but had again been brought back to India. The papal nuncio John of Marignola on his way home from China spent nearly two years in India, 1348–50, but the information which he supplies adds little to our knowledge of the development of Christianity in South India.

In 1503 the Nestorian Patriarch Mar Elia IV. sent three bishops to Southern India, and a letter received by his successor which announced their arrival stated that in one of the two districts in which Christians were found there were 30,000 " families of the faith." In 1599 the Portuguese representatives in India succeeded in forcing the Syrians into obedience to the See of Rome, but half a century later, when Portuguese political influence in India began to wane, the larger part of the Church renounced its connection with the R.C. Church.

The Syrian Christians in South India are now divided into four sections :—

1. " Orthodox Syrians," or simply " Syrians." These live under their Matran, Mar Dionysius, and his four suffragans. They are Monophysite in confession, and subordinate to the Patriarch of that Church, who resides at Mardin in Chaldæa. They are often called Jacobites because they use the Liturgy of St. James, in the form employed by the Church referred to.

2. Romo-Syrians. These of late years have been ruled by Indian bishops, guided by Roman Catholic fathers of the Jesuit and Carmelite orders. While Roman

Catholic in confession, they use their own rite, which is an expurgated and amended version of the Liturgy of SS. Adai and Mari, though not identical with the version of the same liturgy used by the Chaldæans of Mosul.

3. Reformed Syrians, called by themselves the "Christians of St. Thomas." This is an independent Church, an offshoot from the Monophysite Syrians, having their own bishop, Mar Titus Thomas, with two suffragans. Their formal separation from the "Syrians" dates only from about the year 1880. The Church is in close accord with the English C.M.S. missionaries but is in no way under their control, and it uses an expurgated and amended version of the Liturgy of St. James, in the Malayalam language.

4. The Syro-Chaldæans. This body, which is the smallest of the four, is an off-shoot from the Romo-Syrians, from whom they separated in 1880. In theory they are Nestorian, and their bishop, Mar Timotheus, was consecrated by the Nestorian Patriarch in 1907, but in practice they bear considerable traces of long subjection to Roman Catholic influences, and would better be described as "Old Catholics." The real reason for their separation was apparently the refusal of the Vatican to allow native bishops to the Romo-Syrian Church; but though that concession has been made since their departure, it has not brought about their reconciliation. They use the same liturgy as the Romo-Syrians.

(For the number of Christians belonging to each of these bodies see p. 121 f.)

In 1816 the C.M.S. sent four clergy to try to revive the Syrian Church and to translate the Scriptures into the vernacular. This "mission of help" continued for twenty years, after which the C.M.S. undertook independent missionary work amongst non-Christians.

The Syrian Christians during the long centuries of their history have never been inspired with missionary enthusiasm and have constituted a select community which corresponded closely to an Indian caste. During the last few years, however, there has been a revival amongst them, and the " Reformed Christians " have sent four missionaries of their own race to work in connection with the National Missionary Society at Karwar in the Bombay Presidency.

The only contemporary reference to Christianity in India during the fifteenth century is the statement of the Venetian Nicolo de Conti, who on his return to Rome stated that the body of St. Thomas "reposes honourably in a large and beautiful church, close to which dwell a number of Nestorian Christians, who are also found disseminated all over India, just as Jews are found in Europe." We should greatly like to penetrate the darkness which conceals the fortunes and condition of these tiny Christian communities during this long period, but there seems little hope that we shall ever be enabled to do so.

On May 9, 1498, Vasco da Gama landed at Calicut after sailing round the Cape of Good Hope. His arrival in India inaugurated the establishment of missions, supported by the kings of Portugal. The expedition under Cabral, which sailed in 1500, included several monks who were intended for missionary work, and their numbers were rapidly augmented. In 1534 Goa was constituted a bishopric, and in 1557 an archbishopric. The missionaries belonged to the Franciscan and Dominican Orders. The Portuguese encouraged their soldiers and sailors to take native Indian wives, and as the offspring of these unions, which were often of a temporary nature, were baptized, the moral character of the Christian community tended to become more and more deplorable. During the first forty years of the sixteenth century the missionaries do not appear to have made any considerable number of converts, but before the middle of the century India was to receive a missionary whose arrival forms a landmark in the history of Christian missions in the East.

In 1523—that is, eleven years before the institution of the " Company of Jesus "—*Ignatius Loyola* had himself left Spain with the avowed object of converting the Mohammedans of Palestine to the Christian faith and of reconciling the Greek Church to the See of Rome. Sailing from Barcelona to Gaeta, he visited Rome and thence begged his way by land to Venice. From here he sailed to Cyprus and eventually to Jaffa. On September 4, 1523, in company with other pilgrims, he set foot inside the Holy City. Here, had he been allowed to do so, he would have spent the rest of his life. The Superior of the Franciscan convent in Jerusalem, who had been given by the Pope control over Christian pilgrims, refused, however, to allow him to stay, and when he lingered behind the pilgrim caravan he was forcibly conducted to Jaffa. Had he been able to carry out his purpose, there is little doubt that the Society of Jesus would not have been formed and that he would himself have met his death at the hands of the fanatical Moslems of Jerusalem. Despite the failure of his efforts in Jerusalem, he deserves to be remembered as one of the earliest missionaries who made a definite attempt to convert Mohammedans otherwise than by the sword.

By his personal activities and by his teaching Loyola was largely instrumental in arousing the whole Roman Church to a sense of missionary obligation. His society sent missionaries to India, Brazil, and North America, and his zeal was the indirect cause of the missions of the Dominicans to China, of the Franciscans to Tartary, of the Theatins to Armenia, Persia, and Sumatra, and of the Sulpicians in Montreal. He founded at Rome the first Jews' Society, the first Magdalene Asylum, and the first Orphan House on record.

In the year that Columbus died (1506) *Francis Xavier* was born. The youngest of a large family in which all the other boys became soldiers, he entered the University of Paris at the age of eighteen, and became a teacher of philosophy in this university when he was little more than twenty. His conversion from a life of carelessness and selfishness to one of self-denial and devotion was the result of five years' close intercourse with Ignatius Loyola, who began by being his pupil, but whom he soon learned

to regard as his master. On the Feast of the Assumption
in the year 1534, Loyola and six companions, of whom
Xavier was one, repaired to the subterranean chapel of
Montmartre, and amid the darkness, at dead of night,
dedicated themselves by solemn vows to become missionaries
of the Church and to preach the gospel to every man
whom they might meet. Two years later the members of
the new Order placed themselves unreservedly at the disposal of the Pope, to be sent by him as missionaries to any
part of the world. The seven years which passed before
a definite plan was elaborated were spent by Xavier in
visiting hospitals and tending the sick in some of the
principal towns in Italy and in preaching to the poor
wherever he could obtain an audience. After abstaining
from interviewing his widowed mother and his much-loved
sister, lest he should be tempted to 'draw back from his
high call, he embarked, with a smiling face, on his thirty-
fifth birthday, in a ship sailing for India. His first year
there was spent in preaching, catechizing, and visiting the
sick. At the time of his arrival a missionary college was
in course of erection at Government expense to accommodate
100 Indians who were to be trained as Christian
missionaries. The Franciscan Principal ere long gave
place to a member of the Jesuit Order, and the college
became one of the chief centres of its work in India.
Prior to the arrival of Xavier, 85 deputies had come to
Goa to implore help on behalf of a community of low caste
pearl-fishers (Paravas) who lived between Cape Comorin
and Ramnad on the east coast and were oppressed
by Mohammedan pirates. They offered, as the price of
assistance, to become Christians and to acknowledge the
sovereignty of Portugal, and as an earnest of the genuineness
of their offer they all allowed themselves to be baptized in
Goa. A fleet was dispatched to their aid, which drove off
their enemies. The whole community, 20,000 in number,
were baptized in the course of a few weeks, no teacher,
however, being left behind to teach them the meaning of
Christian baptism.

After Xavier had laboured for a year in Goa he spent fifteen months with these Paravas, living on rice and water and associating with them as one of themselves. After returning to Goa and obtaining the assistance of some of the students in the missionary college there, he returned to the Paravas and endeavoured to minister both to their material and spiritual wants. During this period he is said by his biographer to have spent twenty-one and a half hours each day in prayer and labour on their behalf, and his zeal begat a corresponding zeal in his companions.

To those who are familiar with modern missionary methods, it may seem almost incredible that during the whole of Xavier's missionary activities in India and in the Far East he made no attempt to learn any language understood by those to whom he preached and was dependent entirely upon interpreters. How unsatisfactory were the efforts of his interpreters may be gathered from his own words:

"It is a difficult situation to find oneself in the midst of a people of strange language, without an interpreter. Rodriquez tries, it is true, to act in that capacity, but he understands very little Portuguese. So you can imagine the life I lead here, and what my sermons are like, when neither the people can understand the interpreter nor the interpreter the preacher—to wit, myself."

Again he writes:

"We could not understand one another, as I spoke Castilian and they Malabar, so I picked out the most intelligent and well-read of them and then sought out with the greatest diligence men who knew both languages. We held meetings for several days, and by our joint efforts and with infinite difficulty we translated the Catechism into the Malabar tongue. This I learnt by heart, and then I began to go through all the villages of the Malabar country, calling around me by the sound of a bell as many as I could, children and men. I assembled them twice a day and taught them the Christian doctrine, and thus in the space of a month the children had it well by heart.

"Every Sunday I collected them all, men and women,

boys and girls, in the church. They came with great readiness and with a great desire for instruction. Then, in the hearing of all, I began by calling on the name of the most Holy Trinity, Father, Son, and Holy Ghost, and I recited aloud the Lord's Prayer and the Creed in the language of the country, and they all followed me in the same words, and delighted at it wonderfully. Then I repeated the Creed by myself, dwelling upon each article singly . . . and asking them after each article whether they believed it. . . . After explaining the Creed I go on to the Commandments, teaching them that the Christian law is contained in these ten precepts, and that everyone who observes them all faithfully is a good and true Christian. After this I recite our principal prayers, such as the Our Father and the Hail Mary, and they say them after me. Then we go back to the Creed, adding the Our Father after each article with a short hymn; for as soon as I have recited the first article I sing in their language: ' Jesus, Son of the living God, grant us the grace to believe firmly this first article of Your faith, and that we may obtain this from You we offer You the prayer taught us by Yourself.' We do the same after all the other articles.

"We teach them the Commandments in the following way. After we have sung the first, which enjoins the love of God, we pray thus: ' Jesus, Son of the living God, grant us the grace to love Thee above all things '; and then we say for this intention the Lord's Prayer. So we go on through the other nine, changing the words of our little invocation as occasion requires. Thus I accustom them to ask for these graces with the ordinary prayers of the Church, and I tell them at the same time that if they obtain them they will have all other things that they can wish for more abundantly than they would be able to ask for them.

"I make them all, and especially those who are to be baptized, repeat the form of general confession. These last I question, after each article of the Creed as it is recited, whether they believe it, and after they have answered ' Yes,' I give them an instruction in their own language, explaining the chief heads of the Christian religion and other duties necessary to salvation. Last of all I admit them, thus prepared, to baptism.

"As to the number who become Christians, you may understand from this that it often happens to me to be hardly able to use my hands from the fatigue of baptizing; often in a single day I have baptized whole villages. Sometimes I have lost my voice and strength altogether with repeating again and again the Creed and the other forms."

In a letter relating to a missionary tour which he had made through Travancore, he speaks of having baptized all the fishermen (Machhas) whom he could possibly meet with, but does not say whether these baptisms were preceded by any kind of instruction.

In forming an opinion on the methods adopted by Xavier, it is only fair to him to remember that he was himself profoundly dissatisfied with the results which his labours produced. In a letter addressed to Ignatius Loyola in January 1549 he writes:

"The natives [of India] are so terribly wicked that they can never be expected to embrace Christianity. It is so repellent to them in every way that they have not even patience to listen when we address them on the subject; in fact, one might just as well invite them to allow themselves to be put to death as to become Christians. We must now therefore limit ourselves to retaining those who are already Christians."

From first to last Xavier did not scruple to invoke the aid of the secular powers in order to further his missionary projects. He obtained authority from the King of Portugal authorizing him to punish by death the makers of idols, and in 1543 he urged the Portuguese Viceroy in India to support the claims of a brother of the King of Jaffna, who offered to be baptized as a Christian if the Portuguese would establish him on his brother's throne. With reference to this proposal Xavier wrote:

"In Jaffna and on the opposite coast I shall easily gain 100,000 adherents for the Church of Christ"

Two years later, in the course of a letter addressed to the King of Portugal, he wrote:

"I have discovered a unique, but, as I assuredly believe, a sure means . . . by which the number of Christians in this land may without doubt be greatly increased. . . . I demand that your Majesty shall swear a solemn oath affirming that every Governor who shall neglect to disseminate the knowledge of our most holy faith shall be punished on his return to Portugal by a long term of imprisonment and by confiscation of his goods. . . . I will content myself with assuring you that if every Viceroy or Governor were convinced of the full seriousness of such an oath, the whole of Ceylon, many kings on the Malabar coast, and the whole of the Cape Comorin district would embrace Christianity within a year. As long, however, as the Viceroys and Governors are not forced by fear of disfavour to gain adherents to Christianity, your Majesty need not expect that any considerable success will attend the preaching of the gospel in India, or that many baptisms will take place."

After the departure of Xavier the Jesuit missions continued to make rapid progress on the lines on which he had started them. So unsatisfactory have been the results that Bishop Caldwell, who spent a long lifetime in South India, and knew the people as few Europeans have learned to know them, could write concerning the converts connected with the Roman missions in Tinnevelly: "In intellect and morals they do not differ from the heathen in the smallest degree." As the Jesuit missions spread they came into conflict with the Syrian Church in Travancore, the metropolitan of which they burnt in 1654.

There is no Christian missionary other than Xavier in whose case it is more necessary to separate his life and character from his methods of work, if we are to do justice to the former. Of his self-devotion, his prayerfulness, and his capacity for inspiring others with his own spirit it is hardly possible to speak too highly. The record of his life has sent many to the mission field, and has helped to sustain their faith there, and to support them in times of despondency and trouble. But whilst we thank God for the many virtues which he possessed and which have placed his name high in the roll of missionary heroes, we cannot blind our eyes to the fact that his work was so marred by the methods of missionary enterprise which were recognized by his contemporaries, and which he adopted as his own, that it is at least open to question whether the final conversion of India to the Christian faith has not been retarded by the work done by himself and by those who followed in his steps.

In 1567 the Governor of Goa, at the suggestion of the Jesuit missionaries, issued a decree ordering that in those districts of Goa which yet remained heathen, the pagodas and mosques should be pulled down and that orphans under fourteen years of age should be baptized. Similar action was taken in the other Portuguese settlements in India. Dr. Richter estimates the number of R.C. missionaries in India in 1590 as 500, and the number of converts connected with these missions as 254,000; these representing the result of ninety years' work. He compares these results with those obtained up to 1870 by about the same number of Anglican and Protestant missionaries, after eighty years' work; the number of converts connected with these missions being then 224,000. It is apparently true to say that the numerical results obtained by Anglican and Protestant missionaries in the face of frequent opposition on the part of Government authorities were approximately equal to those which the R.C. missionaries obtained when backed by the material forces of the Portuguese Government.

The next great missionary to India was *Robert di Nobili*, an Italian, who reached India in 1605. His work is deserving of special attention inasmuch as the principle which he adopted of recognizing and accepting the Indian caste system has been accepted to a greater or less extent by nearly all the R.C. missionaries who have since laboured in India. He started his work at Madura,[1] which was outside the region in which Portuguese political influence prevailed. Having determined to make himself an Indian, in order that he might win the Indians, he adopted the dress and the sacred thread of a Brahman, and painted the sandal-wood sign on his forehead. He

[1] See *Lettres Edifiantes*, vol. x. pp. 46, 62.

called himself a Rajah from Rome, and eventually produced a new Veda, which he had himself forged, in support of his own teaching. He kept aloof from men belonging to the lower castes and only allowed Brahmans, or men of high caste, to have access to him. The principle which underlay his action was sanctioned by a Papal Bull in 1623 which declared that "out of compassion for human weakness, Nobili's converts are permitted to retain the plait of hair, the Brahmanical thread, the sandal-wood sign on the forehead, and the customary ablutions of their caste." The hair and thread were, however, first to be sprinkled with holy water. After more than fifty years' work, Nobili died at Milapur in 1656. After his death the Jesuit missions in South India were carried on on the lines which he had inaugurated, and the missionaries who worked amongst the higher castes refrained from any intercourse with those who worked amongst the lower castes. In the eighteenth century, when it was found impossible to provide Jesuit missionaries for the lower castes, those who worked amongst the Brahmans were accustomed to administer the sacraments at dead of night outside the doors of the higher caste churches.

From 1690 to 1750 the missionaries and converts were subject to constant persecutions, and one at least of the Jesuit missionaries suffered martyrdom. At the time of Nobili's death the Christians connected with this mission were reckoned at 100,000, but by 1815, according to Dubois, himself a Jesuit, these numbers had decreased to 33,000.

In 1703 Pope Clement XI. commissioned Tournon, the Patriarch of Antioch, to visit and report upon the methods which had been adopted by the Jesuits in this mission. On his suggestion the Pope published a decree which condemned several of the practices introduced by the Jesuits and contained the statement: "In future, refusal of the Holy Sacrament to Pariahs who may be sick will no longer be permitted."

Unfortunately this decree, which was confirmed later

on by several other decrees, failed to effect any fundamental change in the methods which had been adopted
and which are still to a large extent followed. The writer
of this volume has himself seen three R.C. churches in a
village not far from Madura which are used by Christians
from three different castes.

In considering the work accomplished, or attempted,
by Robert di Nobili, we need, as in the case of Xavier, to
distinguish between the man and the methods which he
adopted. Of the missionaries who have laboured in India,
few have lived lives of such continuous self-denial, or have
been inspired with a more ardent passion to effect the
conversion of the Indians. Whilst we deplore the superficial character of the results which his work produced, and
the methods to which these results were due and which he
bequeathed to his successors, we cannot withhold our admiration and respect for the Christ-like enthusiasm which
was the motive power of his life.

At the time that Nobili was living in Madura, the
Jesuit missionaries at the Court of Akbar in North India
were prosecuting their labours with a large amount of
success. In 1610 three princes of the royal blood received
baptism in Lahore at the hands of *Geronimo Xavier*, a
nephew of St. Francis Xavier. Akbar himself reverenced
"the images of Jesus Christ and the Virgin when they
were shown to him by the missionaries, and solicited
permission, reluctantly accorded, to retain them in his
palace for a single night."[1]

Another name deserving of special mention is that of
Juan de Brito, the son of a Viceroy of Brazil, and for a
time one of the royal pages at Lisbon. He arrived in
India in 1673, and in the course of a few years baptized
with his own hands many thousands of converts, who had,
however, received a far more careful preparation than many
of those who had been baptized by his predecessors. On

---

[1] Elphinstone's *History of India*, vol. ii. p. 328. Many thousands were
baptized, and it seemed for a time as though Christianity were about to
supplant Islam and Hinduism in North India.

several occasions he was imprisoned and tortured, and at length, on February 3, 1693, he suffered death as a martyr.

Another member of the Society of Jesus who was martyred a few years later, *Xavier Borghese*, when bidden by his heathen judge to refrain from mentioning the Holy Name, replied, "Think you that I left my country and all that was dear to me on earth, and came here to preach the law of the true God, which I have preached for so many years, only to keep silence now? I declare to you that, so far from obeying your command, I will employ all that remains to me of life and power to make new disciples to the God of heaven."[1] "We will see," said the judge, "whether your disciples have as much courage as yourself," and then he ordered his soldiers to break the bones of one of his catechists. When the catechist heard the command which had been given, he exclaimed, "Now I begin to be truly your disciple. Do not fear, my father, that I shall do anything unworthy of a Christian."

Another R.C. missionary whose name is deserving of mention is the Abbé *Dubois*, who went to India on the outbreak of the French Revolution and remained there for thirty-two years, living a simple and self-denying life. He laboured amongst the R.C. Christians in South India, whom he describes in pessimistic language. "I must confess," he wrote, "with shame and humiliation, that there was not a single member of them of whom it could be said that he had accepted Christianity save for some objectionable secondary consideration." He returned to France in 1823, expressing the belief that missionary work in South India had been and was likely to be a complete failure. The book which he published on the manners and customs of India is a standard work of reference.

Anglican and Protestant Missions.

Long before the advent of the first Anglican or Protestant missionaries Anglican chaplains were sent out

[1] *Lettres Edifiantes*, vol. x. p. 210.

by the East India Company, and especially in the early
years were allowed or even encouraged by the Company
to take an interest in the religious welfare of the Indians
with whom they were brought into contact. Between
1667 and 1700 eighteen chaplains were provided by the
Company, the first being sent to Madras in 1667.

The first Indian to become a Christian as a result of
the missionary efforts of a representative of the Anglican
Church was, perhaps, an Indian from Bengal, who was
baptized in 1616. According to a minute contained in
the Court Minute Book of the East India Company at
Masulipatam, which is dated August 19, 1614, Captain
Best took home a young Indian who was instructed by
Mr. Patrick Copland, or Copeland, the preacher, one of
the first chaplains to travel in the Company's ships to
Masulipatam. On December 22, 1616, the lad was
baptized, after consultation with the Archbishop of Canterbury, in the presence of some members of the Privy
Council, Lord Mayor and Aldermen, and also the members
of the East India Company, and the sister company of
Virginia. He received the name of Peter, chosen by the
King (James I.). Some Latin letters exist written by the
lad signed "Peter Papa." He seems to have gone with
Mr. Copeland to Virginia. It is not possible to determine
the actual place of his birth, but it is certain that he
came from the Bay of Bengal, that he was taught by
a visiting chaplain to Masulipatam, and that he was taken
home at the Company's expense.

1750–1820.

We have already referred to the work of the Danish
and Moravian missions to India down to 1750. On
July 16 of this year *Christian Friedrich Schwartz*
landed at Cuddalore and continued to work in South
India till his death in 1798 (aged seventy-two). After
working at Tranquebar for ten years he moved to Trichinopoly, where he laboured for sixteen years (1762–78),

Trichinopoly then belonged to the Mohammedan Nawab of Arcot, who was an ally of the English. It contained an English garrison, and in 1767 Schwartz ceased to be connected with the Danish Mission and became an English chaplain and was in part supported by the S.P.C.K. He was a Lutheran and did not receive Anglican Orders. In 1763 he visited Tanjore and, at the request of its Rajah, settled there in 1778 and made this the centre of his work till his death His reputation for probity spread throughout South India and became a distinct asset to the English Government. Thus Colonel Fullerton, the Commander of the British army in South India, wrote in 1783 : " The knowledge and integrity of this irreproachable missionary have retrieved the character of Europeans from imputations of general depravity." The Rajah of Tanjore before his death in 1787 desired to appoint Schwartz as the guardian of his heir and Regent of his kingdom. Two years after his death Schwartz was appointed to both these posts by the English authorities. He entrusted the care of the young Rajah to his colleague Gerické at Madras till his accession to the throne in 1796. The important political offices which Schwartz filled naturally affected his work as a missionary, and many accepted Christianity under the influence of the " royal priest of Tanjore " who were not Christians at heart. He travelled extensively throughout South India and established a considerable number of schools, and at the time of his death, in 1798, the total number of Christian adherents connected with the Danish Mission was about 20,000.   Between 1706 and 1846, 57 missionaries connected with this mission went out to India, of whom 20 died at Tranquebar, the chief educational centre of the mission.   When the Tanjore Mission was handed over to the S.P.G. in 1825, there were about 2000 persons in the congregations and 700 children in the schools During the ten years which followed the adherents increased to 4300.

It is interesting to note that Schwartz, together with

his adopted son, J. C. Kohlhoff, and his son, J. B. V Kohlhoff of Tranquebar, worked in South India for an aggregate period of 156 years.

The permanent results of Schwartz's work were disappointing, but when we consider the conditions under which it was carried on, it is hard to see how a better foundation for subsequent work could have been laid. He deliberately refrained from using the political influence which he possessed as prime minister of the Rajah of Tanjore in order to increase the number of baptisms, and those whom he baptized had for the most part an intelligent knowledge of their new faith; but the wide area over which his activities were spread, and the difficulty of sending efficient teachers to carry on the various mission centres which he created, gave to his work a superficial character which he would have been the first to deplore.

Six years before his death there had landed in Bengal one who may be regarded as one of the greatest missionaries who have set foot in India, *William Carey*, a cobbler who was sent out by the newly formed Baptist Missionary Society. He was so far from possessing the material and political support which Xavier enjoyed, and which in a lesser degree Schwartz obtained, that the East India Company refused him permission to work anywhere within the sphere of its influence, and he was compelled to retire to Serampore, a mission station which had been occupied but abandoned by Moravian missionaries, and which belonged to the kingdom of Denmark. Carey's first companions were Marshman, who had been a ragged-school teacher, and Ward, a printer—a trio of missionary heroes and geniuses to which it would be impossible to suggest a parallel. By the beginning of 1800 Carey had translated the whole of the New Testament into Bengali. The style of Bengali writing which he created in doing this, and which was specially distinguished by his efforts to enrich its vocabulary by a liberal borrowing of Sanskrit words, has affected all Bengali prose literature which has since been published. In 1801 he was appointed by Lord Wellesley master of

6

the new college in Calcutta which had been erected for the
training of Anglo-Indian officials, and he subsequently filled
the posts of Professor of Bengali, Sanskrit, and Marathi.

Amongst many books which he published were a
Sanskrit grammar and dictionary. He also edited three
volumes of the Ramayana and other Sanskrit works, and
before his death in 1834 he had translated the whole
Bible into Bengali, Hindi, Marathi, and Sanskrit. These
translations were imperfect, and were eventually replaced
by completely new versions, but their production testifies
to the marvellous enthusiasm and industry of their author.

The Serampore Brotherhood sent out missionaries or
missionary agents to places as far distant as Benares, Agra,
Delhi, and Bombay in the one direction, and to Burma, the
Moluccas, and Java in the opposite direction. They also
started work at Barisal, Dacca, Chitagong, Dinajpur, and
Katwa in Bengal, and among the Khasia tribes in Assam.
Many of these stations were eventually handed over to
other missionary societies. In 1816 the missionaries at
Serampore separated from the Baptist Missionary Society,
but on their death the greater part of their work passed
into the hands of this society. In 1818 they commenced
the foundation of a college which was intended to expand
into a university with a view to the education and training of
Indian missionaries   To this college the King of Denmark
granted the right to confer degrees.

After the death of the three missionary founders the
college was carried on with decreasing effectiveness till
1883, when it came to an end. After this date it became
a Baptist seminary for preachers and teachers in Bengal,
and has recently been reorganized as an arts college with
a theological faculty on an undenominational basis.

The distinguishing characteristic of Carey's work was
his adoption of the principle of concentration. It is true
that he sent agents to distribute his translations of the
Bible and to attempt to found mission stations in places
far distant from Serampore, but his life-work was the
establishment of the training college at Serampore and of

the group of schools in its neighbourhood. To a far greater extent than any of his predecessors he realized the comparative futility of diffused missions and the impossibility of converting India by means of European evangelists. By concentrating the greater part of his activities within a narrow circle, and by spending his time upon the education and training of Indian teachers, he inaugurated a new method of missionary work the importance of which it is impossible to exaggerate.

Dr. Mylne, formerly Bishop of Bombay, writes:

"If ever a heaven-sent genius wrought a conquest over obstacles and disabilities it was . . . this humbly-born Englishman. Not only was he born in low station . . . but he received hardly any education. . . . And this man before he died took part in translating the Bible into some forty languages or dialects, Chinese among the number! He started in life as a cobbler—would never let anyone claim for him the more dignified title of shoemaker—he died a professor of Sanskrit, the honoured friend and adviser of the Government whose earliest greeting, when he landed on the shores of the country, had been to prohibit him from preaching. He founded a notable college (Serampore) for the training of native missionaries. . . . But the one grand merit of Carey, without which his marvellous qualities had been lost like those of his predecessors, was that he, with the intuition of genius, set to work instinctively from the first on the lines of the concentrated mission. There was no diffusion of his energies over impossible tracts of country and impracticable numbers of converts. A few really Christianized people, with the means of future extension—this he seems to have set before him as his object. He left no great body of converts, but he laid a solid foundation, to be built on by those who should succeed him. . . . I should hardly be saying too much did I lay down that subsequent missions have proved to be successful, or the opposite, in a proportion fairly exact to their adoption of Carey's methods."[1]

In 1797 the S.P.C.K. sent the Rev. W. T. *Ringeltaube* as a missionary to Calcutta. He returned after two years, and was then sent out by the L.M.S. to Travancore. Between 1806 and 1815 he was stationed at Myladi,

[1] *Missions to Hindus*, p. 129 f.

where his work resulted in the conversion of more than
1000 of the Shans. Of these, 677 were admitted to
Holy Communion in 1812.

Of the *Anglican chaplains* who did much to promote
a missionary spirit in Calcutta in the early part of
the nineteenth century the Rev. David Brown and the
Rev. Claudius Buchanan deserve special mention. The
Rev. T. Thomason and the Rev. Daniel Corrie, who
acted as chaplains up the country, also contributed much
to create interest in missions both at home and in
India. Yet another chaplain whose name is still more
widely known was the Rev. *Henry Martyn* (1781–
1812). Landing in Calcutta in 1806, he commenced
the study of Hindustani, Hindi, Persian, and Arabic, and
within five years he had translated the New Testament
and the Book of Common Prayer into the first of these
languages. In 1811 he proceeded to Persia. After
spending ten months in Shiraz, where he translated the
greater part of the New Testament into Persian, he set out
on his return to Europe *via* Asia Minor. Worn out by
mental and physical strain, he died at Tokat at the age
of thirty-one. Although he apparently made but one
convert, and his translations needed much revision,
his life and death did much to inaugurate a new
interest in missionary work both in India and elsewhere. The romance connected with his scholarship—
he had graduated at Cambridge as senior wrangler—and
with his early death, far from the help of friends, helped
to attract the attention of many who had taken no interest
in missions to the cause to which he had given his life,
and the ardent faith and piety which are reflected in the
letters that were subsequently published inspired many
who read them to become missionaries in their turn. His
only convert, Abdul Masih, was ordained by Bishop Heber
in 1826 and was the second Indian to receive Anglican
Orders. The first was a Ceylon catechist, Christian David,
who was ordained by Bishop Heber in 1824.

The year 1813, in which the Charter of the East

India Company was renewed and modified by Parliament, was a critical year in the history of Indian missions. A clause was then inserted in the Charter the effect of which would be to authorize and encourage the sending out of Christian missionaries. A similar clause had been suggested twenty years before, but was then vehemently opposed by some of the Directors, one of whom, Mr. Bensley, speaking at an assembly of the General Court held on May 23, 1793, at the East India House, said : " So far from approving the proposed clause or listening to it with patience, from the first moment I heard of it I considered it the most wild, extravagant, expensive, and unjustifiable project that ever was suggested by the most visionary speculator."

One of the clauses in the new Charter ordered the appointment of a bishop and three archdeacons for the oversight of work amongst Europeans in India. Bishop Middleton, who was consecrated in 1814, founded Bishops' College, Calcutta, the object of which was to train Indian Christians to become preachers, catechists, and teachers, and to serve as a centre for translation and other literary work. The college, which was established at a cost of £60,000, was placed under the supervision of the S.P.G. Its foundation-stone was laid in 1820, and the Rev. W. H. Mill, Fellow of Trinity College, Cambridge, was appointed as its first Principal. The Bishop of Calcutta reported in 1837 that "the amount of good already effected by the College was really surprising," and in 1840 it was stated that there were 1800 Christians in the Barripore and Tollygunge missions as a result of the influence exerted by the College. But despite these and other encouraging reports of a later date, it cannot be maintained that the College has so far fulfilled the hopes of its founders. When, however, the new scheme for its removal from Calcutta and its reconstitution has been carried into effect, there is good reason to hope that it may do much to help forward the work of Anglican missions not merely in Bengal but throughout India.

We have already referred to the work of Ringeltaube, which was begun in Travancore in 1806. By 1835 the total number of converts connected with his mission numbered 11,000. In certain districts of Tinnevelly not far removed from the scene of his labours the Rev. C. T. Rhenius, who was in Lutheran Orders but was employed by the C.M.S., began work in 1820, and was so successful that by 1835 there were nearly 12,000 baptized Christians living in 261 villages, and nearly 3000 children were under instruction in 107 schools.

The work in Tinnevelly, which was at first supported by the S.P.C.K. and for which the S.P.G. a little later became responsible, was started by Schwartz, who dedicated the first church in Palamcottah in 1785. There were at that time 40 baptized Christians. In 1803 the Rev. C. W. Gerické, a colleague of Schwartz, visited this mission and took part in one of the "mass movements" towards Christianity for which Tinnevelly subsequently became famous. In a single tour he baptized 1300 people who had been carefully prepared, and an Indian missionary, Satthianadhan, soon afterwards baptized 2700 more. By 1835 the total number of Christians connected with the English and Danish missions in South Travancore and Tinnevelly was about 30,000.

After the death of Schwartz, Jänicke (1795), and Gerické (1803), the work of the Danish Mission rapidly dwindled. The enthusiasm of its missionaries in the field seemed to decline, and it became increasingly difficult to provide them with successors from Europe. By 1840 the greater part of the mission stations had been transferred to the S.P.G. and nearly all were occupied by English missionaries in Anglican Orders. In 1835, Archdeacon Corrie was consecrated as the first Anglican Bishop of Madras.

Caste in the Christian Church.

We have already referred to the results produced by the recognition of caste within the Christian Church by

R.C. missionaries in South India.[1] Their recognition of caste rendered it extremely difficult for the Danish and German missionaries to do otherwise than follow their example. With few exceptions, they permitted the Sudras and Pariahs to observe their caste distinctions, to sit apart in church, and to receive the Holy Communion on separate occasions. The Rev. C. T. Rhenius was one of the earliest missionaries to make a decided stand against the observance of caste. Bishop Wilson of Calcutta, who visited South India in 1833, issued a pastoral letter in which he said, "The distinction of caste must be abandoned, decidedly, immediately, and finally." He further described caste as "eating as doth a cancer into the vitals of our infant Churches." When his pastoral letter was read in Vepery Church, Madras, the Sudra Christians rose and left the church, and for the time being renounced their membership of the Christian Church. In Tanjore the reading of the pastoral caused a similar upheaval and produced but little permanent result.

We have not space in which to discuss the significance of caste observances or the grounds on which they appear to be inconsistent with the spirit of Christianity. It is sufficient to say that an overwhelming majority of the most intelligent and the most successful missionaries who have laboured in India have agreed with the view expressed by Bishop Wilson.

Nehemiah Goreh, himself a Brahmin convert and one of the most remarkable missionaries of Indian nationality, once said, "Christianity with caste would be no Christianity at all."[2]

The General Missionary Conference which met in India in 1902 passed this resolution:

"The Conference would earnestly emphasize the deliverance of the South India Missionary Conference of 1900. namely, that caste, wherever it exists in the Church, be treated as a great evil to be discouraged and repressed. It is further of opinion that in no case should any person who

[1] See p. 76.   [2] *Life of Father Goreh,* p. 7.

breaks the law of Christ by observing caste hold any office in connection with the Church, and it earnestly appeals to all Indian Christians to use all lawful means to eradicate so unchristian a system."

Ever since the establishment of Protestant missions in South India the Lutheran missionaries, and especially those connected with the Leipzig Missionary Society, have practically condoned the observance of caste by the Christian converts. The Anglican and the other Protestant missionaries have striven with varying, but on the whole with very incomplete, success to put an end to its observance.

Alexander Duff and his work (1830–57).

Of the pioneer missionaries whose labours have left a permanent impression upon missionary work in India and to whom we have already referred, four names stand out pre-eminent—Xavier, Nobili, Schwartz, and Carey. To these we should now add that of *Alexander Duff*.[1] Dr. Duff, who landed at Calcutta in 1830, after being twice shipwrecked on his outward voyage, was the first missionary sent out by the Established Church of Scotland. He at once resolved to strike out what was then a new line of missionary policy and attempt to influence the higher castes of North India by providing schools in which, through the medium of the English language, a liberal education should be offered to all who were willing to receive Christian instruction at the hands of missionaries. In adopting the English language as the chief medium of instruction he did not desire to discountenance the use of the vernacular languages, but he was convinced that the use of these was incompatible with the imparting of a comprehensive education, and still more that they were inadequate to express the fundamental conceptions of Christian doctrines. In carrying out his scheme he obtained the assistance of Ram Mohan Roy, the founder

---

[1] See *Life of Alexander Duff*, by Geo. Smith.

of the Brahmo Samaj. The first school which he opened
in Calcutta in July 1830 proved so great a success and
seemed likely to result in the conversion of so many of
its scholars, that the Hindu newspapers announced that
anyone continuing to send his son to school would be
driven out of caste. The school thereupon emptied, but
only to fill again to the very last place before the end of
a week. With a few interruptions Duff continued his
work in Calcutta till 1863. His converts were not
numbered by thousands, or even by hundreds, but they
included a large number of high caste Hindus whose
brilliant mental gifts and whose strength of character
have exercised an immense influence upon their fellow-
countrymen in North India.

Amongst the names widely known in India are Krishna
Mohan Banerjea, Gopinath Nundy, Mohesh Chunder
Ghose, and Anando Chunder Mozumdar. Not only in
the schools started by Duff, but in other schools and
colleges which were founded as an indirect result of his
work, conversions from amongst members of the highest
and most distinguished families took place during this
period. Amongst the number of important colleges which
were founded during Duff's time in India may be mentioned
the Robert Noble College at Masulipatam (C.M.S.), 1841;
St. John's College at Agra (C.M.S.), 1853; the General
Assembly's school, afterwards known as "the Christian
College," in Madras, 1837; St. Thomas' College, Colombo
(S.P.G.), 1851; Almora College (L.M.S.), 1851; Trichinopoly
College (S.P.G.), 1863; the Forman College, Lahore
(A.U.P.M.), refounded in 1886.

A colleague of Duff, Dr. John Wilson, founded the
college in Bombay which now bears his name.

The influence which Duff exerted upon the Government
of India was at least as important as that which he
exerted upon those who were responsible for the control of
missions. The trend of its policy and the course of legislation were profoundly affected by Duff, and had he done no
direct missionary work he would still have left a permanent

impress upon the development of education throughout India. No sooner had the success of Duff's initial efforts become apparent than the Government of India—Lord Bentinck being then the Governor-General and Sir Charles Trevelyan one of his chief advisers—issued a minute (1835) in which it was stated that it was the desire of the Government to naturalize European literature and science and to foster English culture. Later on, and after consultation with Duff, the Government announced the establishment of a department of Public Instruction in each of the Presidencies, and in 1857 founded universities in Calcutta, Madras, and Bombay. These were eventually supplemented by the foundation of one at Lahore in 1882 and one at Allahabad in 1887. During this period the system of grant-in-aid was also established by which government grants could be claimed by missionary or other schools which provided a secular education up to a given standard. This system has made it possible for missionary societies to establish and carry on mission schools at little or, in some instances, at no cost to their own funds.

Indian Christians in 1851.

In 1851 the first attempt was made to count the number of Christians connected with the Anglican and Protestant missionary societies in India. The statistics obtained, though incomplete and less accurate than those which were subsequently available, enable us to form some idea of the progress of these missions up to the middle of last century. The number of Christians in 1851 was 91,092, they formed 267 congregations, and 14,661 of them were communicants. Of these, 24,613 were connected with the C.M.S. Tinnevelly Mission, 10,315 with the S.P.G. Mission in the same district, and 16,427 with the L.M.S. Mission in South Travancore. These three missions claimed 51,355 out of the 74,176 Christians in the Madras Presidency. The remaining number included those who had become converts in connection with the old Danish

missions in the Cauvery districts. In the whole of the
rest of India there were only 16,916 converts, of whom
14,177 were in Bengal. Of these, 4417 were connected
with the C.M.S., 3476 with the S.P.G., and 1600 with the
Baptist mission.

Of the 339 ordained missionaries in India at this time
the C.M.S. had 64, the L.M.S. 49, the S.P.G. 35, the
Baptists 30, the Basel Missionary Society 23, and the
American Board 22.

The advent of American missionaries.

The *American Board of Commissioners for Foreign
Missions* (A.B.C.F.M.) sent their first missionaries to India
in 1812, but, owing to the opposition of the East India
Company, they were not allowed to remain in Calcutta.
In 1813 they started work in Bombay, but little progress
was made till 1833, when they crossed over from Ceylon,
where they had been previously at work, and founded a
series of mission stations at Madura and in the surrounding
districts. Soon afterwards they began work in Madras
and in the Arcot district. In 1831 they began work in
Ahmadnagar, which subsequently developed into their
Maratha Mission.

The American *Presbyterians* started work in the United
Provinces and subsequently in the Punjab. Their first
station was opened at Ludhiana in 1834. Later on they
opened stations at Allahabad (1836) and Fatehgarh
(1838), and in the Punjab at Jullundur (1846), Ambala
(1848), and Lahore (1849). They were the first Protestant
missionaries to work in the Punjab.

The American *Baptists* started their Telugu Mission
in 1840 and their mission to Assam in 1841. For
a long time neither of these societies made any great
progress.

The American *United Presbyterians* started work at
Sialkot in 1855.

Lutheran Missionary Societies.

We have already referred to the work of the German missionaries who went out to India in connection with the Danish-Halle missions.   The *Basel Missionary Society*, which was founded in 1815, began work at Mangalore on the south-west coast in 1834, and a little later at Dharwar (1837) and Hubli (1839) in the South Maratha country.

The *Leipzig Missionary Society*, which was founded in 1836, took over the work amongst the Tamils in 1840 which had been carried on by the Danish-Halle mission.

Pastor *Gossner*, after severing his connection with the Berlin Missionary Society in 1836, sent out missionaries, who commenced work at Hadjipore (1839), and other places on the river Ganges.   Later on, in 1845, he began the work amongst the Kols of Chota Nagpur which was to develop into one of the most successful missions in North India   For a further reference to Lutheran societies in India, see pp. 121, 124.

The Mutiny (1857).

Exactly a century after the battle of Plassey, which gave India to England, North India was convulsed with war and massacre and many Indian Christians were murdered on the ground of their supposed sympathy with the English.   On the capture of Delhi (May 11) by the mutineers, every missionary was killed Their number included the Rev. A. R. Hubbard and two catechists, Sandys and Koch, of the S.P.G., the English chaplain, and Mr. J. Mackay of the Baptist mission, also an Indian Baptist preacher, Wilayat Ali.   At Cawnpore were killed the Rev. W. H. Haycock and the Rev. H. E. Cockey of the S.P.G., and the Revs. J. E. Freeman, D. E. Campbell, A. D. Johnson, and R. M. M'Mullen from the American Presbyterian mission at Fatehgarh.   At Sialkot the Scotch Presbyterian missionary and his family were massacred. Including English chaplains and their families, about 36 connected with missionary work were murdered and 15 leading Indian Christians. Ghokal Parshad, the headmaster of the American Presbyterian mission at Farrukhabad, on being offered life and freedom for himself and his family if he would abjure his faith, replied, "What is my life that I should deny my Saviour? I have never done that since the day I first believed on Him, and I never will."

Throughout the Mutiny the Indian Christians remained loyal, and they assisted materially in holding the fort at Agra.

The Mutiny helped Englishmen to realize the obligation which rested upon them to spread the knowledge of their faith throughout India, and the years which immediately followed it witnessed a great expansion of missionary effort, more especially in the north-west. This development of missionary work was greatly aided by the whole-hearted support accorded by some of the officials who were responsible for the government of the north-west. Amongst these were Sir John Lawrence (Viceroy, 1864–69), Sir Robert Montgomery and Sir Donald M'Leod, Lieutenant-Governors of the Punjab; Sir Herbert Edwardes, General Reynell Taylor, and Sir Bartle Frere, Governor of Bombay. Without infringing the policy of religious neutrality, which was enunciated in the Queen's proclamation that followed the suppression of the Mutiny, they made no secret of their personal faith, and contributed largely out of their private incomes towards the establishment of new mission stations, especially those which were supported and controlled by the C.M.S. Amongst the important centres occupied in succession by this society in the Punjab were Amritsar (1852) and Peshawar (1854), Multan (1856), Lahore (1867), Dera Ismail Khan (1868), and Srinagar, the capital of Kashmir (1863). In Oudh it established centres of work at Lucknow (1858) and Fyzabad (1862).

A few months before the Mutiny, the first representa-

tive of the *Methodist Episcopal Church of North America*
(A.M.E.C.), Dr. Butler, had landed in India. Immediately
after the Mutiny this society started work at a number of
centres in Oudh, and later on in the United Provinces, and
it soon established single stations in almost every part of
India. It has been the policy of this society to spread
its operations over the widest possible area, rather than
to establish a series of centres in any one province or
district. During the first ten years of its operations in
India, it devoted its attention (except in the United
Provinces) to work amongst Europeans and Eurasians, but
later on it developed its missionary activities in all the
districts in which it was represented. Bishop Thoburn
and his sister, Isabella Thoburn, exercised a large influence
upon the development of its work.

The distribution of mission workers.

In order to gain some idea of the present condition of
missionary enterprise in India, we will try to make a brief
survey of the field from south to north. In this survey
only the work of the larger societies can be mentioned.
The total number of the societies at work exceeds a
hundred. The distribution of the workers belonging to
the R.C. missions will be referred to later on.

In *the Tamil-speaking country*, which forms the eastern
portion of South India to the south of Madras, the Anglican
missions, *i.e.* the C.M.S. and the S.P.G., which latter took
over many of the converts belonging to the old Lutheran
missions, have about 100,000 converts. The bishop
resides at Palamcottah, which is the chief centre of the
C.M.S. mission. At Nazareth, which is the most important
centre of the S.P.G. mission, there is a medical and an
industrial mission. The mission workers include 13
European and 80 Indian clergy. Amongst the missionaries who have worked in these missions should be mentioned Edward *Sargent* (C.M.S.) and Robert *Caldwell*
(S.P.G.), both of whom afterwards became bishops. Many

thousands of Indian Christians belonging to the Anglican missions in Tinnevelly have become Roman Catholics in order to avoid having to abandon their caste customs and ceremonial. In the district of Madura the American Board and the Leipzig Missionary Society are represented.

Travancore.

We have already referred to the work of the L.M.S. missionary, Ringeltaube. The work which he began in South Travancore has developed till the number of converts is now over 80,000, the greater part of whom are ministered to by Indian teachers and pastors. The mission staff includes 16 Europeans, 17 ordained Indians, and over 600 preachers and teachers.

The C.M.S. began work amongst the Syrian Christians who were independent of Rome in 1816, in the hope of creating a revival amongst the members of this ancient Church. During the first twenty years encouraging results were attained; but when this work was brought to a standstill by the opposition of the metropolitan, the C.M.S. began to develop work amongst the Hindus. This mission has steadily developed. It is superintended by the Anglican Bishop of Travancore, but is largely self-supporting. Connected with the Anglican Church in Travancore there are 12 European and 40 Indian clergy. The bishop lives at Kottayam, where the C.M.S. has a college which is affiliated to the University of Madras. Part of the C.M.S. mission is in the State of Cochin, where missionary work is carried on amongst the Arayer, a hill tribe which had not become Hindus. The chief stations in Cochin are Trichur and Kunnankulam.

The members of the ancient Syrian Church[1] under the Jacobite Patriarch of Antioch number 225,190, and those of the Reformed, or St. Thomas Syrian, Church under its own metropolitan about 75,000. Those owing

---

[1] The following figures include the members of the Syrian Church in Cochin and in other parts of South India.

allegiance to the Church of Rome number, according to the Syrian or the Latin rite, 413,142. Those under the East Syrian Patriarch (the Catholicos of the East) number about 13,780. These Churches are supervised by 11 Indians, 1 Chaldean, and 3 European bishops (see p. 66 f).

Madras and the Telugu country.

In the districts which include Trichinopoly and Tanjore, the chief agencies at work are the S.P.G., the Leipzig Mission, and the Wesleyans. The Trichinopoly college (S.P.G.) and schools attached to it have about 1600 pupils. The college is affiliated to the University of Madras.

In the city of Madras the best-known missionary institution is the Christian College (1837), belonging to the Scotch *U.F.C.M.*, of which Dr. Miller was for many years Principal. As a direct missionary agency the college has attained little success, but it has helped to raise the ideals of education in Madras and throughout South India. One of the aims of the college is "to influence and mould the corporate thought of Hinduism," and to be a constant witness to the close bond that exists between Christian faith and modern thought. Those who have been educated at the college and who now hold posts of responsibility throughout South India are to be numbered by thousands. There are 800 students at the college, 200 of whom live in hostels and 800 in the school attached to the college. The Anglican diocese of Madras includes the whole Presidency, with the exception of Tinnevelly and Madura, and the bishop also superintends the Anglican clergy in the native states of Hyderabad, Mysore, and the province of Coorg. In the area included in the diocese there are 38 European and 110 Indian clergy.

To the west of Madras the Reformed Dutch Church of America has a mission, including about 30 stations and about 10,000 Christians. Eight sons and two grandsons of the founder of this mission, Dr. Scudder, who died in 1855, have worked in its service.

The principal societies which are at work in the Telugu districts to the north of Madura are the C.M.S., the S.P.G., the L.M.S., and the American Baptists (A.B.M.U.). In these districts there has been within recent years a series of mass movements towards Christianity. If these should continue, as seems likely to be the case, there is every prospect that within the lifetime of this generation the greater part of the 20,000,000 people speaking the Telugu language who inhabit these districts will have become Christians. Up to the present the movements have been almost entirely confined to what is called the outcaste population, but applications for Christian instruction have recently been received from communities belonging to the Sudra class. The conversion of any large number of Sudras would pave the way to the acceptance of the Christian faith by the caste population throughout the whole of India.

The L.M.S. began work in the Telugu country in 1805, in which year they sent two missionaries to Vizagapatam, but it was not till 1835 that their first converts were made. They opened a station at Cuddapah in 1822. By 1870 they had 23 stations, which five years later had increased to 80. After the famine of 1877 they, like the other societies working in this district, were wholly unable to cope with the applications which were received for Christian teachers. Their converts and adherents, which include a considerable number of Sudras, number about 25,000. The society has an important medical mission at Jammalamadugu.

The American Baptists began work in 1835. One of their first missionaries, Sewett, who was invalided home after twelve years of apparently unsuccessful work, when informed by his society that they wished to abandon this mission, said, "I know not what you will do, but for myself, if the Lord gives me my health, I will go back to live, and if need be to die, among the Telugu." "Then," was the answer, "we must surely send a man to give you a Christian burial." In 1869, at a new centre which had

7

been opened at Ongole, the number of converts began rapidly to increase, and by 1879 they numbered over 10,000. The number at the present time exceeds 60,000. The mission supports five hospitals, three high schools (at Ongole, Nellore, and Kurnool), and a training school for teachers.

The territory occupied by the C.M.S. mission lies between the rivers Krishna and Godavery, and stretches from the coast about 100 miles inland. Work was commenced in 1841, when R. T. Noble and H. W. Fox were sent to Masulipatam. From the high caste school which Noble started a number of Brahmin converts were obtained, especially during its early years. On the staff of the college there were in 1911 four Brahmin converts and five sons of Brahmin converts. A mission at Nellore was opened in 1854 and at Bezwada in 1858. In 1859, after eighteen years' work, the converts connected with the mission numbered about 200. In this year a remarkable man named Pagolu Venkayya was converted, and with his conversion the whole aspect of the mission changed. He belonged to the Mala caste, and had been the leader of a band of violent men. At the age of forty-seven, having been told by a companion that a Christian missionary had declared that idols were incapable of helping their worshippers, he then and there determined to renounce the worship of idols. His friend also told him that the missionary had spoken of one only God. From that time he began to use these words as a form of prayer: "O Great God, who art Thou? Where art Thou? Show Thyself to me." Later on he came across a Christian tract which referred to God as the Saviour of the world. Thenceforth he prayed, "O great God, the Saviour, show Thyself to me." For three years he continued to pray. In 1859, whilst attending a Hindu bathing festival at Bezwada, he met a Christian missionary, and having heard and eagerly accepted the Christian faith, he became a preacher of Christianity amongst his fellow-countrymen. Conversions soon followed, and when Venkayya died in 1891 the converts connected with the C.M.S. mission, who had

numbered 200 at the time of his baptism, had increased to
10,000. At the present time they number over 32,000.
There are 28 Indian clergy connected with this mission.
Hopeful work is also being carried on amongst the members
of the Sudra caste.

The territory occupied by the S.P.G. lies to the west
of the C.M.S. mission, and comprises the collectorates of
Cuddapah and Kurnool. In 1842 several of the L.M.S.
missionaries, amongst whom was Dr. Caldwell, afterwards
Bishop of Tinnevelly, became members of the Anglican
Church. In 1854, in response to repeated requests, the
S.P.G. undertook to support the Anglican mission at
Cuddapah, which had been carried on by the Rev. V.
Davies and by the Rev. J. Clay, who had been previously
supported by the Additional Clergy Society. In 1855
the centre of this mission was moved to Mutyalapad. By
1859 the mission included 13 congregations, 619 baptized
Christians, and 527 persons under instruction for baptism.
A station which was opened at Kalasapad in 1861 soon
became the centre of a large number of other stations.

The S.P.G. Telugu Mission has from the start been
greatly undermanned, with the result that its representatives
have had to refuse a long succession of pressing requests
from villages which asked, but asked in vain, to receive
Christian instruction. Despite the fact that there had
never been half a dozen European missionaries in the field,
by 1879 the number of congregations had increased to 76,
and the baptized Christians to 2377. Ten years later
they had increased to 115 congregations and 5562
baptized Christians. In 1913 the number of congregations was 230, and of baptized Christians 13,541. The important factor in this mission has been the 300 or more
Christian teachers, most of whom have been trained at
Nandyal, and who in most cases have had to act not
only as teachers of village schools but as catechists or
preachers. The general rule, in the case of the S.P.G. and
C.M.S. missions, has been that when an application for
Christian instruction has been received from a Hindu

village, the inhabitants of the village have been asked to provide evidence of their sincerity by building a school and a house for a teacher, and by guaranteeing to supply him with food. Where these conditions have been fulfilled, and it has proved possible to supply a teacher, the teacher has taught the children of the village, and given daily religious instruction, and conducted daily worship for the inhabitants of the village for perhaps two years. The village has, meanwhile, been periodically visited by an Indian catechist, and at rarer intervals by a European missionary. After three, or in some cases four or five, years' continuous instruction, a third, or perhaps half of those who have become candidates for baptism, are baptized. A more or less similar course of procedure has been followed by the other missionary societies represented in the Telugu country. Experience has shown that a long course of instruction and period of probation is necessary if due precautions are to be taken to guard against moral relapses. In 1913 the Bishop of Dornakal ordained 16 Telugu Christians, 10 of whom belonged to the S.P.G. and 6 to the C.M.S. mission. In addition to the large number of day schools connected with its mission, the S.P.G. has 5 boarding schools, one at each of its principal centres of work. A beginning has been made of work amongst women, but there is urgent need of further development.

In the district which comprises the estuary of the rivers Krishna and Godavery the Canadian Baptists and the American Lutherans have missions which have achieved considerable success.

Before we leave the Telugu-speaking country, reference should be made to a small but specially interesting mission which was founded and is maintained entirely by Indian Christians. At a meeting of Indian Christians connected with the Anglican Church which was held at Palamcottah in Tinnevelly in 1903, it was resolved to form the Indian Missionary Society of Tinnevelly. In 1904 this society sent two Indian Christians to open a mission at Dornakal, 600 miles from Palamcottah, between Bezwada and Hyderabad, in Hyderabad State. In 1906 the staff had grown to 3, in addition to 4 local workers. In that year the Bishop of Madras baptized 23 converts who had been won by this mission. The work, which is rapidly spreading, is carried on in over thirty villages. In 1912 the Rev. Vedanayakam Azariah was consecrated as Bishop of Dornakal and the surrounding district, and as an assistant bishop to the Bishop of Madras.

The fact that this mission is entirely self-supporting, and that it has as its head the first Indian bishop in communion with the Anglican Church, will appeal to all who desire to see Indian churches self-supporting and governed by men of their own race.

Farther north, in the *Hyderabad State*, the American Episcopal Methodists, the American Baptists, and the English Wesleyans have a considerable number of mission stations.

Malabar.

In *Malabar*, which lies to the north of Travancore and Cochin on the west coast, several societies are represented by one or two mission stations. The Basel Mission Society has a series of stations reaching from here north-wards to the South Mahratta country in the Bombay Presidency. A chief characteristic of this mission is its development of industrial training, especially of weaving, brick-making, and carpentry. These industries were started in order to give employment to those who had been left orphans by famine, and Indian Christians who had been deprived of any means of livelihood by their conversion to Christianity. These are carried on by an industrial committee in Basel, which is not connected financially with the Basel Missionary Society.

From a commercial standpoint this mission has been a great success:

"There are dangers in such work, chiefly lest the mingling of business and evangelism shall hamper the

spiritual influence of the mission, and lest the tendency
shall be to induce individuals to profess Christianity for
the sake of securing a lucrative position. Even those who
for these reasons believe that only necessity will justify the
starting of mission industries, have to admit, however,
that this Basel work has made a real contribution to
economic progress and to the dignifying of labour as worthy
of a Christian." [1]

Mysore.

In the native state of *Mysore* work is carried on by the
L.M.S. from Bellary as a centre. The English Wesleyans
have also been at work since 1838. The A.M.E. Church
has mission stations at Bangalore and Kolar. The L.M.S.
has an extensive mission of which Bangalore is the centre.
This is also the site of an important United Missionary
College.

From the missionary standpoint, the educational policy
which has been adopted by the native Hindu Government
of Mysore is of special interest, as it may perhaps forecast
what will be eventually adopted in other parts of India.

The *Times* correspondent in Mysore, writing on
October 3, 1908, said :

"The tendency of the present system is purely secular
in character and has not been satisfactory. For various
reasons the homes of the pupils have ceased to impart
religious education, and the influence of religious teachers
and places of worship has almost disappeared. Irreverence
and disrespect for authority have been on the increase;
modesty, self-restraint, and good sense have been largely
at a discount, while presumption, vanity, and unrestrained
aggressiveness appear to be increasing. In the circumstances, the Maharajah's Government has decided that the
readiest way of remedying this state of affairs is by imparting religious and moral instruction as a systematic part of
education."

In view of the widespread interest which was aroused
by the regulations issued by the Mysore Government and
the possibility that they may create a precedent in other

[1] *Sociological Progress in Mission Lands*, by E. W. Capen, p. 66 f.

parts of India, it will be well to quote the actual wording of the regulations :

"The time to be given to religious and moral instruction will be limited to five periods a week, the first thirty minutes after roll-call being devoted thereto. There will be a moral discourse on Mondays, Wednesdays, and Fridays, and religious instruction on Tuesdays and Thursdays. The moral discourse will be common to pupils of all persuasions, and be based on a text taken from some religious, moral, historical, or literary book. In addition, there will be specific religious teaching from books like the Sanatana Dharma Advanced Text-Book, the Koran and approved commentaries and essays on the Mohammedan religion, and the Bible. The question of extending the scheme to aided schools not under Government management is reserved for future consideration.

"As Mysore is a Hindu State and the bulk of the population is Hindu, provision for imparting teaching in the Hindu religion will be made in all Government institutions other than those intended purely for the education of particular classes of non-Hindus—as, for instance, Hindustani schools. The classes will be open for Hindus of all denominations, but attendance will be optional in the case of other pupils. It will at the same time be laid down for the present that, when in any Government institution the number of Mohammedan or Christian pupils is not less than twenty, arrangements should be made, as far as may be possible, for imparting instruction to them in their respective religions. If, however, any private persons or bodies interested in either of these religions wish to make special arrangements at their own cost for teaching their respective religions in Government institutions, where the number of pupils of such religions is below twenty, every facility should be given for this being done."

In the Native States of Mysore, Baroda, and Travancore, primary education is now compulsory.

Bombay District.

In the Mahrathi-speaking country which lies to the north of the Kanara country the societies represented by the largest number of Christians are the American Board, the

S.P.G., and the United Free Church of Scotland.   In Ahmadnagar and the neighbouring districts the S.P.G. has several hundreds of village schools and a large amount of work amongst women.   There are also signs of special interest which may develop into a mass movement amongst some of the Sudra villages.   In Poona the C.M.S. is represented, and there is also a strong mission which has been worked by the Cowley Fathers since 1870.   Closely associated with this mission, which also maintains work in Bombay, are the Wantage and All Saints' sisterhoods, which carry on work amongst Indian women.   Khedgaon, near Poona, is also the centre of the remarkable work amongst high caste Indian orphans which has been carried on by Pandita Ramabai since 1899.

Industrial work is being carried on by a large number of missionary societies and by several independent industrial associations, e.g. the Scottish Mission Industries, which works in connection with the U.F.C. of Scotland at Ajmer and Poona, and the Industrial Mission Aid Society, which has a large carpet-weaving establishment at Ahmadnagar in connection with the A.B.C.F.M.

In the city of *Bombay* a number of missionary societies —including the A.B.C.F.M., the C.M.S., the S.P.G., the U.F.C.S., and the A.M.E.C.—are at work, but the visible results have been small.   The Wilson College connected with the U.F.C.S. is doing good work.

In *Gujerat* the Irish Presbyterians have been working since 1841.   In the province of *Sindh*, where the majority of the population is Mohammedan, the C.M.S. and American Episcopal Methodists have a few stations.

The A.M.E. Church has resident missionaries at Ajmer and Phalera.

The Punjab.

We have already referred to the starting of missionary work in the Punjab (see pp. 91, 93).   Of the population of the Punjab 10,955,721, *i.e.* rather more than half, are Moslems. The Sikhs in the Punjab number 2,093,804; in the whole of India they number 3,014,466.

Reference has been made to the rapid development of missionary work in the Punjab by the C.M.S. which followed the Mutiny, and to the active support given to this work by leading Government officials. It was alleged at the time, and the statement has frequently been made since, that for Government officials to display sympathy with Christian missions was to render the task of governing Hindus and Moslems more difficult than it would otherwise be. This suggestion has been refuted again and again by the history of the missions which have been established in the North-West Provinces. Dr. Richter, quoting one of many instances, writes:

" No town was so notorious for its fanaticism as Peshawar, near the Khyber Pass. An English Commissioner had declared that so long as he had anything to say in the matter, no missionary should cross the Indus. A short time afterwards this individual was stabbed by an Afghan on the veranda of his house. His successor, Sir Herbert Edwardes (in 1853), began his official activity in the very house, the veranda pillars of which were still splashed with the dead man's blood, by founding an evangelical mission for the town, and he established peace and quiet in the place."[1]

The chief centres of the C.M.S. work in the Punjab are Lahore, Amritsar, and Multan. At Clarkabad, and by other missions at other centres, attempts have been made to establish villages to be inhabited by Christian converts, but great difficulties have been experienced in regard to their organization and control. On one occasion 200 nominal Christians, who imagined that they had a grievance, suddenly announced their conversion to Islam. Successful attempts have been made by the C.M.S. to create a series of representative church councils with a view to encourage self-government and self-support amongst the Christian converts.

[1] *History of Indian Missions*, p. 210 f.

Lahore is also an important centre of the American Presbyterian Mission, and its college, the Forman College, which has over 500 students, is one of the most important colleges in North India. The A.M.E.C. has mission stations in several parts of the Punjab, but the greater portion of its work is in the Patiala state, and specially in Patiala city.

During the last few years the Central Punjab has been the scene of several movements towards Christianity similar to the "mass movements" that have taken place in South India. These have occurred in the American United Presbyterian missions and in the C.M.S. missions. There are over 60,000 Christians connected with the former.

The great increase in the number of Christians in the Punjab may be seen from the fact that whereas thirty years ago their number was about 4000, in 1901 they had increased to 37,000 and in 1911 to 163,000. In the C.M.S. missions in the Chenab colony there were in 1913 about 10,000 Christians, and the number is rapidly increasing. Both the C.M.S. and the A.U.P.M. are very inadequately staffed in view of the large number of Indians, mostly Chuhras, who are desirous of receiving instruction. The Bishop of Madras, who has had experience of the "mass movements" in the Telugu country, after visiting (in 1913) the missions in the Punjab wrote:

"One result of the scarcity of workers in the Punjab is that their whole system of education is far behind ours . . . but the fact that they have such an inadequate organization and such a great dearth of workers has obliged them to stimulate the Christians to take a larger share in the management of their own affairs than is the case in the South. Many congregations of the United Presbyterian Mission — the strongest and in many ways the best organized mission among the outcastes of the Punjab—are self-supporting and self-governing. One feature of the work in the Punjab which impressed me very much was their system of agricultural colonies and settlements. As

I passed through the Chenab colony I visited five of these, each with a population of 1000 to 1500 Christians. . . . There are two classes of Christian villages and agricultural settlements in the Punjab. In one class the mission holds the land as the property of the Mission, and the Indian Christians are the tenants of the Mission. In the other class of Christian villages the people own their own land and are independent. It is an interesting fact that the first class of villages are nearly all a failure, and the other class, where the people are independent, are so far a success."

The total number of Christians in the Punjab at the end of 1912 was reckoned at 167,413. Their rapid increase in number has been in part due to the policy adopted by certain missionary societies of baptizing those who desired to receive baptism without demanding any period of probation or any intelligent knowledge of the Christian faith. Most of the missionary societies which are at work in the Telugu country, where mass movements on a large scale have taken place, have found by experience that it is necessary to keep groups of inquirers under instruction for three or even four years before admitting them to Christian baptism. A contrary policy has been adopted in the Punjab by the American Methodist Episcopal Church, the American Presbyterian missions, and the Salvation Army, which are working among the Chuhras, who occupy a position similar to that of the Lal Begis in the United Provinces, at the very bottom of the social scale.

Professor Griswold of the Forman (Presbyterian) College in Lahore, in defending the policy of these missions, writes:

"The conditions laid down for baptism are not the same in all the missions. Earnestness of purpose is required by all. Sometimes considerable numbers are baptized with no other qualification than an apparently sincere desire to become Christians. But usually something is given in the way of instruction, e.g. at least the name of the Saviour, and the fact that He gave His life for sinners and that salvation is only through Him, and frequently the Lord's Prayer, Ten Commandments, and Apostles' Creed, either the whole or in part." [1]

Replying to the objection that as a result of this policy the Christian Church will be crowded with those who are practically heathen, he urges that though this may be true as long as the adult members are concerned, there is hope that "their children may become very much better than their parents, and really enter the promised land of spiritual renovation." The same experiment has been made and the same argument has been urged in other parts of the mission field and in different periods of Christian history; but few who have made a careful study of Christian missions from the earliest times down to the present day would venture to say that in any single case have the final results justified the adoption of the policy of "speedy baptism" for which Professor Griswold pleads.

Amongst the C.M.S. stations on the North-West Frontier are Srinagar in Kashmir, Peshawar, Bannu, Dera Ismail Khan, and Dera Ghasi Khan. At Srinagar, where the work was started by Dr. Elmslie (see p. 32), there is a large mission hospital under Drs. A. and E. Neve, and a boys' school under the Rev. C. Tyndale Biscoe. This school, which is chiefly attended by high caste Hindus and Moslems, is one of the most remarkable in India. By his personal influence and example the Principal has inspired his pupils with the desire to display many Christian virtues which are but seldom practised by those who are nominally Christians. The visitor to this school may see high caste boys engaged in rowing on the lake low caste women and other patients who are convalescents at the Srinagar Hospital, and performing, for the benefit of suffering people and animals, tasks which the ordinary high caste Hindu would regard as defiling. Although few of the scholars or ex-scholars

[1] See article " The Mass Movement in the Punjab," by H. D. Griswold, *The East and The West*, January 1915.

have as yet been baptized, the Christian influence exerted by this school has been felt throughout a large part of North-West India.

Delhi, the capital of India, is an imperial enclave within the Punjab province. We have already referred to the S.P.G. and Baptist missions which were established there prior to the Mutiny (see p. 92). As soon as the S.P.G. received the news of the massacre of its missionaries, it issued an appeal for fresh workers, which met with an immediate response. Before the arrival of the new workers, amongst whom the Rev. T. Skelton, Fellow of Queens' College, Cambridge, and the Rev. R. Winter deserve special mention, Ram Chunder and another Indian had recommenced the mission school, which by the end of 1859 contained 300 boys. During the years that followed, the educational work carried on by this mission developed to a large extent.

In 1877 the Cambridge University Mission was formed, its object being to co-operate with the S.P.G. in developing its educational and evangelistic work in Delhi. The Rev. E. Bickersteth, who afterwards became a Bishop in Japan, was the first Head. The next Head of this mission was the Rev. G. A. Lefroy, who afterwards became Bishop of Lahore (1899), and subsequently Bishop of Calcutta and Metropolitan of India (1913). St. Stephen's College, which is affiliated to the University of Lahore and has over 200 students, has an Indian Principal, Professor Rudra, who is assisted by a staff of English University graduates. The college, which is now being rebuilt in the new city of Delhi on a site granted by the Government of India, has recently increased its staff of professors and has the prospect of a wide sphere of usefulness in the future.

The S.P.G. also supports a large mission hospital for women and educational, industrial, and zenana work. The S.P.G. and Baptist missions work in complete harmony and have been able to co-operate in some of the educational work which they carry on.

On the Indian border of Tibet to the north of the Punjab the Moravians have carried on a mission for over fifty years, and have translated the Bible into the Tibetan language.

Central Provinces and Rajputana.

The C.M.S. has mission stations at Jubbulpore and in the country of the Gonds in the Central Provinces, and at Bharatpur and in the Bhil country in the eastern part of Rajputana. The Scotch Episcopal Church has a mission to the Gonds at Chanda. The C.E.Z.M.S. has also work in these Provinces. The U.F.C. of Scotland has work at Nagpur, the Swedish Fatherland Institution at Sagar, and the German Evangelical Synod of North America at Bisrampur. The A.M.E.C., the Friends Foreign Missionary Association, and several other Bodies have also a number of mission stations in Rajputana. The A.M.E.C. has resident missionaries at Nagpur, Jubbulpore, Gondia, Raipur, Khandwa, and Jagdalpur.

United Provinces.

The United Provinces, i.e. Agra and Oudh, include the important towns of Agra, Cawnpore, Lucknow, Allahabad, and Benares The Anglican Bishop of Lucknow, in whose diocese these provinces lie, resides at Allahabad.

We have already referred to the development of missionary work in these provinces up to the time of the Mutiny, and to the missionaries who were killed in *Cawnpore* on the outbreak of the Mutiny. After the Mutiny the Government handed over the church which had been built for the use of Europeans, and which was not destroyed by the mutineers, to the S.P.G., which has made it the centre of its work in Cawnpore. It is interesting to record that the son of the man who was the direct instigator of the massacre at Cawnpore eventually became a catechist in the S.P.G. Mission. In 1889 George and Foss Westcott (who are now Bishops of

Lucknow and Chota Nagpur) started a Brotherhood in connection with the S.P.G. Mission which has been the means of developing educational, industrial, and evangelistic work in the city and the surrounding country.

The college which the Brotherhood helped to establish at Cawnpore is affiliated to the Allahabad University.

Amongst the Indian clergy who have done good work in connection with the S.P.G. Mission should be mentioned Sita Ram, a Brahman convert, who died in 1878.

In 1899 St. Catherine's Mission Hospital for Women was opened. One of its doctors, Alice Marval, and four of the hospital workers died as a result of nursing plague patients in 1904. Offshoots of the S.P.G. Cawnpore Mission have been established at Roorkee (1861) and Banda (1873).

Other missionary societies represented in Cawnpore are the A.M E.C.,[1] the American Presbyterian Mission, and the Women's Union Missionary Society of America. The A.M.E.C. Mission dates from 1871. Here as in many other places in India its representatives work not only amongst the Indians but amongst the Europeans and Eurasians.

Agra.—St. John's College, which is supported by the C.M.S., was established in 1853 and is now affiliated to the University of Allahabad. The daily attendance at the college and its branch schools in the city is over 1200. The Queen Victoria Girls' High School (1904) has about 100 Christian scholars and exercises a large influence amongst the Christian community throughout the province.

Other missions represented in Agra are the A.M.E.C., the English Baptist Missionary Society, and the Edinburgh Medical Missionary Society.

The C.M.S. and the A.M.E.C. began their work in *Lucknow* in 1858. The A.M.E.C. supports the Reid Christian College for Boys and the Isabella Thoburn

[1] For a reference to the rapid development of the work of the American Methodist Episcopal Mission in the United Provinces, see pp. 124, 138.

College for Girls.   It also supports work at several stations in the Sitapur and Philibhit districts.

In *Allahabad* the C.M.S. began work in 1813, when it placed there Abdul Masih, who was the first Indian to receive Anglican Orders.   The American Presbyterians have an important college which is affiliated to the Allahabad University, and the C.M.S. has a hostel for students attending the University.   The A.M.E.C. and the Z.B.M. are also represented.

In *Benares*, which is in a sense the religious capital of India, work was begun by the C.M.S. in 1817, by the L.M.S. in 1820, by the Baptists in 1827, and later on by the Wesleyan Missionary Society and by the Zenana Bible and Medical Mission.   This latter society supports a strong medical mission and hospital.   The L M.S. and the C.M.S. have large high and elementary schools.

Chota Nagpur.

Work amongst the aboriginal tribes in Chota Nagpur was inaugurated by the Rev. J. E. Gossner, a German who had received priest's Orders in the R.C. Church, and having separated from its Communion prepared and sent out evangelists to India.   Four of these, who were sent to India in 1844, were instructed to start work in some district in which there were no other workers.   Their attention was directed to Ranchi in Chota Nagpur by coming across some of the inhabitants of that district who were working as coolies in the streets of Calcutta and whom they followed to their homes.   After they had laboured at Ranchi for four years, four men came to them asking that they might be allowed to see Jesus, and when told that this was impossible, they went away disappointed, believing that the missionaries had refused their request because they were not high caste people.   As the result, however, of watching the missionaries at their devotions, they became the first converts to Christianity in that district.

By 1851 thirty-one baptisms had taken place, and by

the time of the Mutiny the converts had increased to
900. At the close of the Mutiny Gossner proposed to
transfer the mission and his funds to the C.M.S. This
offer was refused, though the C.M.S. made a grant of
£1000 to the mission in 1858. On the death of Gossner
in this year a committee was formed in Berlin to carry on
the mission. When in 1868 this committee proposed to
alter the constitution of the mission, the older Lutheran
missionaries found themselves unable to accept the orders
of the Home Committee, and were obliged to quit the
churches and mission buildings which they had erected.
At this time the number of Christian Kols was about
9000. Application was made by the missionaries to
Bishop Milman of Calcutta to receive them and their
converts into the Anglican Church. The Bishop for a
long time refused to take action and did his utmost to
promote a reconciliation between the older Lutheran
missionaries and the Berlin Committee. When it at
length became apparent that no reconciliation could be
effected, he applied to the S.P.G., and having received a
promise of support from this society, he formally received
7000 Kols into the Anglican Church and conferred
Anglican Orders upon their three pastors. On the same
occasion he ordained an Indian catechist, Daud Singh.

It is scarcely necessary to point out that for one
society to invite converts who had previously been attached
to another society to join its mission would be wholly incompatible with the principles of Christian comity and
would be altogether deplorable. In this case, however, the
Anglican Bishop had refused to recommend the S.P.G. to
undertake work in Chota Nagpur till the representatives
of the Lutheran Mission had declared that their separation
from the Berlin Committee was irrevocable. The mission
supported by the Berlin Committee was carried on with
undiminished enthusiasm and increasing success. Satisfactory relations, moreover, were soon established with the
S.P.G., and the two missions have since worked harmoniously
side by side.

8

In 1890 the Rev. S. C. Whitley was consecrated as the first Bishop of Chota Nagpur.

Seventy miles to the north of Ranchi a Dublin University Mission was established at Hazaribagh in 1891. This mission maintains a college, several schools, and a hospital, and has done much to further the higher education of the people of Chota Nagpur. It has a number of women associates, who form part of the mission staff.

Missionaries belonging to the R.C. Church first appeared in Chota Nagpur in 1880, when the Lutheran and S.P.G. missions had already attained a large amount of success. In order to win the confidence of the people, the new missionaries started an extensive system of agricultural loans, offering to those whose wages did not exceed 2d. or 3d. a day a loan of two or three rupees, which was not to be repayable as long as the borrowers continued to be "good Catholics." As the Lutheran and S.P.G. missionaries did not consider it to be right to offer similar advantages, the result was that a large number of the converts who had been baptized by them joined the Roman Church. This method of conversion was not adopted on the initiative of individual missionaries, but was definitely sanctioned by the R.C. Jesuit authorities on the ground that to rely upon religious motives would be to forgo the possibility of extending their work. Thus the editor of the Government Census for 1911 writes: "A well-known R.C. missionary in Chota Nagpur writes to me as follows concerning the inducements to conversion :—

"'As a general rule religious motives are out of the question. They want protection against *zamindars* (farmers) and police extortions, and assistance in the endless litigation forced on them by *zamindars*. . . . Personally, I know of some cases where individuals came over from religious motives. But these cases are rare.'"[1]

The Belgian Jesuit missionaries in Chota Nagpur have acted from the highest motives, and they have

---

[1] *Census Report*, vol. i. pt. i. p. 137.

themselves lived self-denying and laborious lives, but it is much to be deplored that in Chota Nagpur, as in many other districts in India, the R.C. missionaries should have thought it to be their duty to proselytize those who were already Christians rather than to begin new work amongst non-Christians.

So great was the success attained by the Jesuit missionaries in the districts round Ranchi that they were able to baptize, or re-baptize, 10,000 converts within the course of a few years. Their best work has been the establishment of village schools where a large number of children are in course of being educated. Moreover, as their work has extended they have gathered in many who had not been touched by other missions. In the Jashpur native state, which lies to the west of Chota Nagpur in the state of Berar, they had in 1911 33,000 adherents, chiefly aboriginal Oraons, nearly all of whom had been won since 1901. A considerable number were won from the ranks of the Lutheran Christians, who number about 10,000.

Bengal.

The Indian Christian community in Bengal [1] numbered 43,784 in 1911. Of the total number of Christians in Bengal 35 per cent. are Roman Catholics, 27 per cent. Baptists, and 22 per cent. Anglicans. Nearly two-fifths of the Roman Catholics are found in the district of Dacca. The Baptists have obtained their greatest success amongst the Namasudras of Eastern Bengal, and half their converts are in the Dacca division. The great majority of the Indian members of the Anglican Communion are found in Nadia, the twenty-four Parganas, and Calcutta. [2]

A large number of missionary societies are represented in Calcutta, amongst which are the C.M.S., the S.P.G.,

---

[1] These statistics relate to "Bengal proper." In Behar, Orissa, and Chota Nagpur—which were also included in the Bengal census—the Indian Christians numbered 19,893, 7110, and 197,168 respectively.

[2] See *Census Report*, 1911, vol. i. pt. i. p. 134.

the Oxford University Mission, the Scotch Established and the U.F. Churches, and the Baptist and Wesleyan Missions.

In Calcutta itself (as in the case of Bombay and Madras), the progress of missionary work has been slow and unsatisfactory compared with the progress achieved in some other parts of India. This is partly due to the very unsatisfactory moral atmosphere which prevails in these cities, and partly to the mixed and changing character of their populations.

The work of the Oxford Mission to Calcutta amongst students attending the Calcutta University has been carried on for thirty-five years with a self-denying devotion which has never been excelled in the history of modern missions, but the visible results are as yet insignificant.

The largest missionary college in Calcutta is that belonging to the Church of Scotland and the U.F.C., which has over 1000 students. The L.M.S. and the S.P.G. have also colleges, and the C.M.S. has a college and two high schools for boys, and a boarding school for girls.

Throughout the greater part of Bengal, missionary work is being carried on, but a large proportion of the inhabitants are still unreached. The Anglican, Scottish, London, Baptist, and Wesleyan societies are all represented. At Barisal, east of Calcutta, the Oxford University Mission and the English Baptists are strongly represented. The C.M.S. has many stations in the Krishnagar or Nadia district north of Calcutta. In this district there occurred a mass movement towards Christianity about sixty years ago, but the results were not altogether satisfactory.

The C.M.S. began work at Taljhari in Western Bengal among the *Santals*, one of the aboriginal races which have not embraced Hinduism, in 1860, and soon covered the Santal districts with a network of mission stations. In 1913 there were 24 European and 25 Indian clergy, and 389 Christian lay agents connected with this mission; the total number of Christians being about 6000. The Indian Home Mission, founded by two Scandinavians in 1867, has also a considerable amount of work amongst the Santals, its chief station being Ebenezer.

The U.F.C. of Scotland also began work amongst the Santals in 1871, and has several mission stations.

The Church of Scotland has excellent work in the neighbourhood of Darjeeling and Kalimpong amongst the hill tribes of the Lepcha, Gurkha, and Bhutia.

Assam.

The Assamese people have for the most part become Hindus, but there are several hill tribes (Garos, Nagas, Khasis, Lushais, and Kacharis) which are still pagan. The largest number of converts have been won by the Welsh Calvinistic Methodists, who started work in 1841. Their chief work lies in the Khasi and Jaintia hills, their principal station being Shillong. The mission has also branches in Cachar, Sylhet, and the Lushai hills. In the latter district rapid progress has been attained. The heir to the throne of a small independent kingdom in the Khasi mountains who embraced Christianity when offered the choice of renouncing his new faith or of abandoning his claim to the throne, chose the latter alternative. During the decade the converts connected with the W.C. Mission have nearly doubled. They numbered 31,000 in 1911.

The American Baptists, who started work in 1836, number over 21,000. The Christians connected with this mission are chiefly found in the Brahmaputra valley and in the Garo and Naga hills. This mission has also some work amongst the Assamese.

Anglican Mission in Assam.—In 1850, Captain Gordon, who was stationed at Tezpur, began a mission at this place, which was taken over by the S.P.G. in 1862. In 1851 the S.P.G. started work at Dibrugarh, and later on opened several stations amongst the Kachari in the neighbourhood of Dibrugarh and Attabari. In this district there are about 3000 converts. Quite recently a R.C. mission has been started amongst the people to whom the S.P.G. is ministering.

Apart from the work which is being done amongst the hill tribes and the Assamese, the S.P.G. and the German Lutherans minister to the needs of a large number of Christian Kols and Santals (numbering about 8000), who have come as immigrants to labour on the tea and other plantations.

The recent creation of a diocese of Assam will probably lead to a considerable expansion of Anglican missions in this province.

The total Christian population of Assam (apart from Europeans) is about 64,000 (1911).

Indian Census Returns.

Greater facilities exist for gaining a bird's-eye view of the progress of missions over a wide area and during a considerable number of years in India than in any other non-Christian country. These facilities are afforded by a careful study of the returns issued by the Indian Census Commissioners at intervals of ten years since 1871. The student of missions is warned that great care is needed in making comparisons supplied for the different decades, as the limits of the Indian Empire have undergone several important changes. Moreover, the returns do not include the Portuguese and French territories in India, in which a large proportion of the Christians attached to the R.C. Church reside. Many of the tables, moreover, which are contained in the returns include European and Eurasian Christians. It is obvious that the number of these must in every case be subtracted before any trustworthy estimate of the progress of Christian missions can be gained.

During the decade 1901–11 the population of India as a whole increased by 6·4 per cent., or, if we include the gain due to the addition of new areas, 7·1. The Indian Christians have increased during the same period from

2,664,313 to 3,574,770—that is, 34·2 per cent., or five times as fast as the whole population (included in both the returns) has increased.

The rate of increase of Indian Christians during the last four decades has been 22 per cent., 33·9 per cent., 30 8 per cent., and 34·2 per cent. Roughly speaking, it may be stated that the Indian Christians in the Indian Empire numbered 1 in 143 in 1891, 1 in 111 in 1901, and 1 in 86 in 1911.

Those interested in the spread of Christianity in India have sometimes tried to forecast the future and to estimate the length of time which may be expected to elapse before India becomes a Christian country. Those who regard the future from a more hopeful standpoint are influenced by a consideration of the mass movements which are now in progress and by the anticipation that the caste system which is the chief obstacle to the spread of Christianity will probably ere long disappear as by a landslide. The fact that 24,000 Moslems in the Dutch East Indies have become Christians within recent years forbids them to despair of the conversion of the Indian Moslems, when they come to be surrounded by a Christian population of the same race and speaking the same languages as themselves.

On the other hand, those who take a less hopeful view point to the comparatively small number of conversions which are taking place at the present time amongst the high caste peoples and the Mohammedans, and contemplate the possibility that the present conditions may long continue to operate. It is obviously unwise to rely upon statistics relating to progress in the past in order to prognosticate what the future has in store, but this at least may be said: should the increase which has been taking place during the last 30 years be maintained, in 50 years' time the Christians will number 1 in 21 of the population, in 100 years they will number 1 in 5, and in 160 years the whole population of India will be Christian. If the relative rate at which the Roman and non-Roman

missions are expanding be also maintained, in 160 years the
Christians in India connected with the R.C. Church will
form about 1 in 30 of the whole Christian community.

The following table shows the number of Christians of
Indian nationality according to the last three census
returns :—

Provinces.	1891.	1901.	1911.
Madras	825,424	983,888	1,150,379
Travancore and Cochin . .	713,403	892,054	1,149,495
Bengal and Assam . . .	167,304	258,305	367,079
Bombay	127,575	171,214	191,973
United Provinces . . .	23,406	68,341	136,469
Punjab	19,639	37,695	163,220
Burma	101,303	129,191	185,542
Mysore	27,981	39,585	46,554
Total for all India [1] . .	2,036,590	2,664,000	3,574,770

As will be seen from the above table, the rate of
increase has varied considerably in different parts of India.
The most striking increase has been in the Punjab, where
the rate has been 333 per cent. This has been due
to the mass movements among the Chuhras, which have
resulted from the work of the American Presbyterian and
C.M.S. missions. More than half the Indian Christians in
the Punjab are connected with the A.U.P.M. (see p. 106).
The Salvation Army converts in the Punjab have increased
during the decade from a few hundreds to 18,000. "A
special feature of the activities of the Salvation Army is
the attention which they pay to the criminal tribes and
depressed classes generally. In several provinces they have
entered into special arrangements with Government for
the reclamation of tribes whose criminal proclivities it has
been found impossible to curb by means of police surveil-
lance. They endeavour to improve the moral and material

[1] These totals include the Christians in the Provinces as given above
together with the Christians in the native states.

condition of these people by sympathetic supervision and by teaching them various industries which will enable them to earn an honest livelihood." [1]

In the Central Provinces and Central Provinces States the general increase of the population has been 18 per cent. while the Christian increase has been 162 per cent.

The population of the Madras Presidency, including the Travancore and Cochin States, has increased by 3 per cent., whilst the Christians have increased by 16·9 per cent. In the case of Burma, the statistics revealed by the Government Census are much more encouraging than missionaries had anticipated. During the last ten years there has been an increase of 56,000 Christians, the ratio of increase being 44 per cent.

The following table shows the comparative progress of Roman and Anglican missions, and of the largest of the Protestant denominations during the decade 1901–11 :—

	Total Number of Indian Christians.		Actual Increase.	Increase Per Cent.	Number per 1000 Indian Christians.
	In 1911.	In 1901.			
Roman Catholics, excluding Romo-Syrians	1,393,720	1,122,508	271,212	24	390
Romo-Syrians . .	413,134	322,583	90,551	28	116
Anglicans . . .	332,807	213,273 [1]	119,534	56·2	98
Baptists . . .	332,171	216,915	115,256	53·1	98
SyrianChristians(Jacobite, Reformed, Chaldæan) .	315,157	248,737	66,420	26·7	88
Lutherans . . .	216,842	153,768	63,074	41	61
Presbyterians . .	164,069	42,799	121,270	283·3 [2]	46
Methodists . . .	162,367	68,489	93,878	137	45
Congregationalists . .	134,240	37,313	96,927	259·7 [3]	38
Salvationists . .	52,199	18,847	33,352	177	15

[1] Omitting the 92,644 unclassified "Protestants" which were added to the Anglican totals in 1901, but which were omitted in 1911.

[2] The greater part of this increase has been in the Punjab, where a mass movement has occurred. See p. 106.

[3] In 1901 nearly 60,000 Christians in Travancore connected with Congregationalist missions were classified as Protestant or un-sectarian. If these be added to the 1901 figures, the rate of increase would appear to have been about 88 per cent.

[1] See *Census of India Report*, vol. i. pt. i. p. 133.

The preceding table affords information which will enable us to appreciate the present strength and the rates of increase of the chief Churches or religious organizations in India.

The *Romo-Syrians* who are found in Travancore acknowledge the authority of the Pope, but their services are in the Syrian language and they follow in part the Syrian ritual. If they are included in the R.C. returns, it appears that slightly over half the Indian Christians were connected with the R.C. Church when the census was taken in 1911. The rate of increase for the decade in the case of the *Roman Catholic* missions was only 25 per cent. as compared with 45 per cent. for the Anglican and Protestant missions taken together. If we suppose that the proportionate rates of increase have been maintained, the converts connected with the R.C. Church within the Indian Empire will now (1915) number about 1,980,000 as against rather more than 2,000,000 converts connected with non-Roman missions. In addition to the R.C. Indian Christians within the Indian Empire there are, according to a return made by R.C. missionaries six months after the census was taken, 25,918 in French and 296,148 in Portuguese territory within the Indian Peninsula. Their rate of increase is probably less than that of the R.C. Christians within the Indian Empire. In the province of Madras, where the Roman Catholics are most numerous, they have increased only by 8 per cent., the rate of increase being slightly in excess of that of the general population. In Behar and Orissa (chiefly in the Ranchi district and the state of Gangpur) they have gained 68 per cent., in Burma 62 per cent., in Bombay 35 per cent., and in Bengal 19 per cent. Their greatest progress has been attained in Jashpur State in the Central Provinces and Berar, where they have now 33,000 adherents, chiefly aboriginal Oraons, practically all of whom "have been gathered into the fold" since 1901.

The rate of increase of the R.C. Church in the Indian Empire taken as a whole is slower than that of any other large body of Christians in India.

Anglican Missions.—In interpreting the figures which are given for Christians connected with the Anglican Church it should be noted that in 1901 and in the earlier returns all Indians who called themselves Protestants, and did not claim to belong to any particular Church or body, were returned as Anglicans. In this way, 92,644 Christians were added to the Anglican total in 1901. In the census for 1911 all Protestants who did not claim to belong to any particular Church were entered in a separate column by themselves. In order, therefore, to compare the number of Christians connected with Anglican missions to-day with those which existed in 1901, we must deduct from the returns for 1901 92,644. We then discover that the number of these Christians has increased during the past ten years from 213,273 to 332,807—that is, an increase of 56·2 per cent.

The editor of the Government Census for 1901, referring to the 92,644 Christians who returned themselves as belonging to no denomination and were wrongly added to the Anglican totals, says: "Of these 59,810 were returned in Travancore, where the majority were probably members of the London Mission."[1]

The Anglican Church in India comes next in point of numbers to the R.C. Church, but it includes only one-eleventh of the Indian Christians.

The principal centre of the *Baptists* is in the Madras Presidency, where about two-fifths of their converts are found, chiefly in the districts of Guntur, Nellore, Kurnool, and Kistna. In Burma, where there are 120,000 converts, they have nearly doubled their number, but, according to the Census Report, " the increase is probably less than would appear from the figures, as in 1901 many failed to return their sect, and were thus not shown as Baptists." In Burma the Baptists have by far the largest number of Christians : thus the Baptists have 120,549, the Roman Catholics 50,770, and the Anglicans 9999. In

[1] Vol. i. pt. i. p. 387, note.

Assam, where their numbers are much smaller, the proportional increase has been greater.

The *Syrians* (excluding Romo-Syrians) show an increase of 66,420, or 26·7 per cent. By far the largest number of Syrian Christians are in the Travancore State. Most of the rest are in Cochin. Madras contains over 20,000 (see p. 66 f).

The *Lutherans*, whose actual increase in the decade has been 63,074 Indians, have increased at the rate of 41 per cent.; 104,074 out of a total of 216,842 are in the Madras Presidency. Here their increase has been at the rate of 35 per cent. In the province of Bihar and Orissa, where their numbers are nearly 88,000, they have increased at the rate of 43 per cent.

The *Presbyterians* show an actual increase of 121,270 Indians, which is larger than any other Protestant denomination. Their numbers for 1901 have been multiplied three and five-sixth times in the course of the decade. The most remarkable progress has been made in the Punjab, which now contains 95,000 Presbyterians, against only 5000 in 1901; in the two districts of Sialkot and Gujranwala alone there are now 52,000, whereas in 1901 there were only 500. Most of the converts belong to the Chuhra, Chamar, and other depressed castes. In the United Provinces there are 14,000 Presbyterians, or nearly three times as many as in 1901.

In Assam there are 31,000 converts, chiefly connected with the Welsh Calvinistic Mission in the Khasi and Jaintia hills, where their number has risen from 16,000 to 28,000.

The *Methodists* (most of whom are connected with the A.M.E.C. missions) have doubled their numbers in the United Provinces in the course of the decade, and have a large absolute majority of Christians of all races taken together in these Provinces—104,148 out of a total of 177,949. Three-fifths of the present strength of the Methodists are in the United Provinces. Their rate of increase has been higher in the Punjab, where they now number 11,582 Indians: in Bombay 11,609, Baroda 4833, and Hyderabad 8121. Their total of Indian Christians (162,367) is two and one-third times as large as in 1901. Their total increase of Indian Christians in the decade has been 93,878.

The *Congregationalists*, according to the census figures, have gained 96,927, though in 1901 their numbers were only 37,313, an increase at the rate of 259·7 per cent. This increase, however, is largely artificial, due mainly to Congregationalists in 1901 being put down as Protestant or Unsectarian. If (as is suggested by the editor of the Census returns) the figure 59,810 was added to 37,313, the actual increase in the decade would be reduced to 37,117, or 38 per cent. The Congregationalists number 134,240 Indian Christians. Of these 81,499 are in Travancore, 36,565 in Madras, 11,519 in Bombay, and 2336 in Bengal.

The *Salvationists* have grown from 18,847 to 52,199, at the rate of 176·4 per cent. In the Punjab they have now 17,970, as against a few hundreds in 1901. In Travancore their present strength of 16,759 is five times what it was ten years ago. In Bombay they number 9924 Indians, in Madras 4876, in Baroda 1540.

Of the effect of conversion on the Indian Christians themselves, Mr. Blunt (one of the Provincial Superintendents of the Census), writes:

"The missionaries all these years have been providing the *corpus sanum* (if one thing is noticeable about Indian Christians it is their greater cleanliness in dress and habits), and now they are being rewarded by the appearance of the *mens sana*. The new convert, maybe, is no better than his predecessors; but a new generation of converts is now growing up. If the missionaries could and can get little out of that first generation, the second generation is in their hands from their earliest years. The children of the converts born in Christianity are very different from their parents; their grandchildren will be better still. It is this which provides the other side to the black picture so often drawn of the inefficiency of Christian conversion. And this generation is now beginning to make its influence felt. The Hindu fellows of these converts have now to acknowledge not only that they are in many material ways better off than themselves, but that they are also better men."

The Census Superintendent of the Mysore State, himself a Hindu, says that the missionaries work mainly among the backward classes, and that

" the enlightening influence of Christianity is patent in the higher standard of comfort of the converts, and their sober, disciplined, and busy lives. To take education, for instance: we find that among Indian Christians no less than 11,523 persons, or 25 per cent., are returned as literate, while for the total population of the State the percentage is only 6. . . . The success in gaining converts is not now so marked as the spread of a knowledge of Christian tenets and standards of morality."

The figures of the Indian census returns which we have been considering, whilst they afford mathematical demonstration that the number of Christians is increasing in India, are but a skeleton outline. They need to be clothed with flesh and blood in order that their significance may be appreciated. It is instructive to learn that India is becoming Christian at a rate unprecedented in the history of the world, but to realize what this means one needs to go out to India and to walk through the districts where the Christian faith is being taught, and to note the changes which are taking place. A visitor will not need to ask as he enters any particular village whether its inhabitants are Christians. A glance at their faces, or even at the faces of their children, will show whether the spirit of fear, engendered by the debased form of Hinduism which is professed in the average Hindu village, has been exorcised, and whether Christian hope and freedom have taken its place. He may find many who call themselves Christians, but whose lives are unworthy of their profession; but the proportion will not be as large as he will have been prepared to discover if he is acquainted with the history of

Europe during the centuries which succeeded its nominal conversion to Christianity, nor will the superficial Christianity of a few greatly lessen the impression which will be produced upon him as he comes to understand the marvellous transformation which is taking place in the experience alike of individuals and communities.

It is easy to criticize the mass movements which have taken place in South India and are beginning to take place in the north, and to call in question the motives which, in some instances, lie behind these movements. The nominal acceptance of Christianity on the part of a community is, obviously, no substitute for the conversion of heart and character which can alone enable individuals or communities to lead a Christian life, but in many instances the nominal and to some extent superficial conversion of a community may be regarded as the almost indispensable preparation for the conversion of its individual members. The atmosphere which caste has generated is so unwholesome, and so completely destroys the recognition of individual responsibility, that until this atmosphere can be dispelled it is well-nigh impossible for individuals to appreciate the liberty wherewith Christ would set them free. The nominal conversion of a whole village may not be accompanied by many signs of spiritual life, but it brings every individual in the village within the reach of spiritual influences and renders possible the growth of the Christian character. It is not difficult for the critic of Christian missions to discover instances in which the desire for Christian instruction on the part of a village community has been strengthened, if not created, by the hope of material advancement, but the student of missions, who is familiar with the many unworthy motives which hastened the nominal conversion to Christianity of the peoples in Northern Europe, will not be unduly disheartened when he realizes that in the history of the evangelization of non-Christian countries to-day a limited number of cases are to be found which recall what might almost be termed the normal occurrences of the past.

Missionary Education.

The Government has come to realize that if elementary education is to be spread throughout India and is to bring any moral gain to its peoples, its efforts must be largely helped and supplemented by the missionaries. These alone are in a position to supply trained Indian teachers and to superintend the teaching if it is to be supplied on any large scale. In the province of Chota Nagpur, which is chiefly inhabited by races that have not embraced Hinduism, the Government has offered to place the whole school system of the province under the direction of the three missionary societies which are at work there, *i.e.* the S.P.G., the R.C. Mission, which is manned by Belgian Jesuits, and the German Gossner Mission. Here, and in many other parts of India, an unlimited opportunity is offered to the representatives of Christian missionary societies to exercise a decisive influence upon the whole moral and religious future of its peoples.

Missionary Colleges.—The Anglican and Protestant missionary societies have 38 colleges, of which 23 prepare for the B.A. degree, the other 15 having only a two years' course and finishing with the First Arts qualification. In these colleges there were (in 1912) 5447 students, including 61 women. Of these students 4481 were Hindus, 530 Mohammedans, and 436 Christians. All the students receive daily instruction in the Christian Scriptures, and of those attending mission schools throughout India 92 per cent. are non-Christians. There is a Christian college for women at Lucknow and one has recently been organized at Madras. This latter has received support from eleven British and American missionary societies. In South India at least 1000 Christians are university graduates.

There are 1163 boarding and high schools belonging to missionary societies with 110,763 students.

In the Christian elementary schools there are about 450,000 pupils, of whom 146,000 are girls and 170,000 are Christians. The 160 industrial schools have 9125 pupils.

The colleges connected with the *Anglican Church* include St. Stephen's College, Delhi (S.P.G.); St. John's College, Agra (C.M.S.); Christ Church College, Cawnpore (S.P.G.); Hazaribagh College, Chota Nagpur (D.U.M.); Trichinopoly College (S.P.G.); the C.M.S. colleges, at Madras, Peshawar, Amritsar, Masulipatam, and Kottayam.

Those connected with the *Church of Scotland* include the General Assembly's Institution, Calcutta, and the college at Sialkot. The principal colleges supported by the United Free Church of Scotland are the Christian College, Madras, the Wilson College, Bombay, and Nagpur College.

Those connected with the *L.M.S.* include the Ramsay College at Almora in the United Provinces, a college in Calcutta, and colleges at Bellary and Nagercoil in South India.

Those connected with the *American Presbyterian* missions include Forman College, Lahore, and the Ewing Christian College, Allahabad.

Those connected with the *American Methodist Episcopal Church* include the colleges at Lucknow (for men and women) and Allahabad.

Amongst other colleges which deserve special notice may be mentioned the *Canadian Presbyterian* college at Indore, the *Wesleyan* colleges at Bankura and Manargudi, and the *American Baptist* college at Ongole.

The total number of students attending colleges of university standing in India is about 25,000, and of these about 5500 are at missionary colleges. During recent years the Government of India has realized that the provision of university education to all who desired it has been anything but an unmixed blessing to its recipients, and that the moral atmosphere of many of the university towns was injuriously affecting the characters of a large number of university students. They have in consequence adopted the policy of contributing largely towards the cost

9

of establishing residentiary hostels in which students may live under sympathetic supervision. By far the greater number of these hostels are in the hands of the missionary societies. At the two new universities of Patna and Dacca the Government desire that the majority of the students should live in such hostels. How great is the need of establishing university colleges or hostels may be gathered from a statement made by the Rev. W. E. S. Holland of Calcutta, who writes :

"Seven thousand Bengali students congregate in Calcutta under conditions that are nothing less than appalling. The circumstance that determines everything else is their extreme poverty. A mere handful are in properly supervised hostels. A good many live at home. The remainder are huddled together in the cheapest lodgings they can find ; so that the slums and student quarter are almost interchangeable terms. Fancy Oxford transferred to lodgings in the slums of Whitechapel ; and picture an England with its leading classes educated thus ! The moral and sanitary environment is deplorable . . . 80 per cent. [of the students] join no college societies, 90 per cent. play no games ; their only recreation a slack stroll up and down College Street, their only pabulum the gutter-press of Calcutta."

At Dacca and Patna hostels to accommodate 200 students are being built almost entirely at Government expense which are to be under the direction of the Oxford University Mission in the one case and of the C.M.S. in the other.

Interest in education has been steadily increasing throughout India during recent years. According to the Government Quinquennial Review published in 1914, the number of boys in attendance at secondary schools in which English is taught went up from 473,000 to 667,000 between 1907 and 1912. During the same period the number attending primary schools went up from 3,986,000 to 4,998,000. Of these about a quarter were attending missionary schools. During the year 1912–13 the total increase of pupils attending all kinds of schools was nearly 400,000.

The backward condition of female education may be inferred from the fact that whilst nearly 30 per cent. of boys of school-going age were at school, the proportion of girls was only 5 per cent. During the period 1907–12 the number of girls in primary schools increased from 645,028 to 952,911.

Seminaries.—Of Anglican seminaries for the training of Indian clergy the S.P.G. and C.M.S. each have one in Madras; the S.P.G. has also Bishop's College, Calcutta (which is being re-organized); the C.M.S. has also divinity schools at Lahore, Allahabad, Calcutta, Poona, and Kottayam. The American Board (A.B.C.F.M.) has seminaries at Madura and Ahmadnagar, the A.M.E.C. at Bareilly, the Lutheran Mission at Tranquebar, the A.P.M. at Saharampur, the A.U.P.M. at Rawal Pindi, and the Baptists have the theological college at Serampore, which has the standing of a university. In 1910 a United Theological College was established at Bangalore which is supported by the L.M.S., W.M.S., A.B.C.F.M., the American Reformed Church, and the U.F.C. of Scotland. The largest theological seminary in the Indian Empire is that at Insein in Burma, which is supported by the A.B.M. and has 160 students.

Medical Missions.

Anglican.—The C.M.S. has hospitals at Srinagar in Kashmir, Peshawar, Bannu, Quetta, Dera Ismail Khan, all on the North-West Frontier; and at Amritsar and Multan in the Punjab. The S.P.G. has hospitals at Delhi, Cawnpore, Hazaribagh (D.U.M.), Murhu in Chota Nagpur, and at Nazareth and Ramnad in South India. The Church of England Zenana Missionary Society works to a large extent in conjunction with the C.M.S. and maintains hospitals at Peshawar, Quetta, Tarn Taran, Dera Ismail Khan, Amritsar, Bangalore, etc.

The *U.F.C. of Scotland* maintains hospitals at Ajmer, Udaipur, Jodhpur, Nasirabad, Poona, Nagpur, Bhandara, and Wardha. In the Santal country it has three medical missions and in the Madras Presidency it has hospitals for women at Royapuram and Conjeveram. It also supports a medical mission at Aden in Arabia. The Church of Scotland has medical missions for women at Poona, Gujerat, and at Sholinghur in Madras.

The *Canadian Presbyterians* maintain hospitals for women at Neemuch, Indore, and Dhar, and have several other general hospitals. The A.U.P.M. has hospitals for women at Jhelum and Sialkot.

The *A. Presbyterian Church* has a large medical mission at Miraj in the South Maratha country. It has also stations at Kolhapur, Vengurla, and Kodoli in the same district, and at Sabathu, Ambala, Ferozepore, Kasur, Allahabad, and Fategarh. The *Irish Presbyterians* have a hospital at Anand in Gujerat.

The *L.M.S.* has a large medical mission at Neyoor in Travancore. It has also hospitals at Jammalamadugu in the Telugu country, and at Kachwa, Almora, and Jiaganj in North India.

The *A.B.C.F.M.* has medical missions in the Marathi country, at Madura and in Ceylon.

The *A. Baptist F.M.S.* has medical missions in Burma, Assam, and in the Telugu country.

The *W.M.S.* carries on medical work chiefly amongst women in South India. It supports hospitals at Mysore, Hassan, Ikkadu, Medak, Nizamabad, Nagari, and Madras.

The *A.M.E.C.* has hospitals at Bareilly, Bhot, Brindabun, Baroda, Kolar, and Bidar.

The *Zenana Bible and Medical Mission* has hospitals at Benares, Patna, Lucknow, and Nasik.

The *Basel Mission* has medical stations at Calicut and Betgeri-Gadag.

The *Salvation Army* has hospitals at Nagercoil, Anand, Moradabad, and Ani.

In addition to these there are a large number of hospitals and medical missionaries connected with smaller missionary societies. In 1910 there were in mission hospitals about 50,000 in-patients, more than 1,000,000 out-patients, and over 56,000 surgical operations. Training institutions for Indian doctors and nurses have been founded at Ludhiana and Agra.

The greatness of the need to which medical missionaries minister may be gathered from a recent statement made by the Inspector-General of Civil Hospitals in Bengal, to the effect that in order to supply the rural districts with dispensaries sufficient to bring the supply of medical aid up to the lowest standard that is considered necessary in England, the agencies would have to be multiplied by 40.

Work amongst Indian Moslems.

The first missionary to work amongst Moslems in India was Geronimo Xavier, who came to Lahore from Goa in 1596. He wrote three books—a Life of Christ, a Life of St. Peter, and a disquisition on the religion of Islam. It is known that he baptized several converts (see p 77). Amongst those who worked amongst Indian Moslems in the nineteenth century should be mentioned Dr. C. G. Pfander, Bishop French, Robert Clark, Rev. T. P. Hughes, Rev. R. Bateman, Dr. Imad-ud-din, and Safdar Ali. In 1856 the Harris school, which is under the charge of the C.M.S., was opened in Madras. The C.M.S. has also some work amongst Moslems in Hyderabad and Alleppey. The Church of England Zenana Missionary Society supports schools for Moslem girls in Madras, Bangalore, Mysore city, Ellore, Bezwada, Masulipatam, and Khammamett, the last four being in the Telugu country.

The S.P.G. works amongst Moslems in Delhi, where a large proportion of the students attending St. Stephen's College are Moslems.

The A.M.E.C. Mission has work at Hyderabad and Kolar.

The U.F.C.S. has a mission at Conjeveram in the Tamil country, and the L.M.S. has a station at Trivandrum in the Malayalam country.

One or two small associations have work amongst Moslems in the Tamil and Telugu country. Industrial schools have been established in Madras, Bangalore, and Guntur to provide employment for destitute Mohammedan women. Most of the larger missionary societies carry on indirect mission work amongst Moslems in connection with their missions to Hindus.

Missionary Societies in India.

Of the 117 foreign and 19 indigenous missionary societies working in India and Ceylon, 41 are British, 41 American, 12 from the continent of Europe, 8 from Australia, and 3 are international. The three societies which support the largest number of missionaries are the C.M.S., which supports (1913) 142 European clergy; the American Baptists, who support 136, and the A.M.E.C., which supports 124 American clergy. The tendency of the British and American societies is to leave the administration of affairs and the initiative to those in India, whilst the tendency of the continental missionary societies is to retain a larger measure of control in the hands of the home committees.

The following is a brief summary of the work of some of the chief missionary societies in India and Ceylon, with the date at which they began work.

I. *Anglican.* — The C.M.S. (1816) and the S.P.G. (1818) are at work in all the provinces of India. The total number of Indian Christians in India connected with the Anglican missions in 1914 was about 350,000. These include the converts connected with the C.M.S., the S.P.G., the Church of England Zenana Mission (1851), and several smaller Anglican societies or associations.

In 1913 the C.M.S. had 142 European and 206 Indian clergy and 196,000 baptized Christians; the S.P.G. had 104 European and 139 Indian clergy and 113,000 baptized Christians.

The Church of England Zenana Missionary Society (C.E.Z.M.S.) is an offshoot formed in 1880 from the Indian Female Normal School and Instruction Society, an undenominational body which began work in Bengal in 1851. It supports medical and evangelistic work among women in Bengal, the Central Provinces, the Punjab, Sindh, and in several parts of South India. This society works in close association with the C.M.S., and occasionally the two societies interchange workers. (For a list of hospitals supported by the C.E.Z.M.S. see p. 131).

The total number of missionaries supported by this society in India in 1913 was 145 Europeans and 256 Indians.

Of the twelve bishops in India who superintend the Anglican missions, seven are appointed by the English Government—namely, those of Calcutta, Madras, Bombay, Lahore, Rangoon, Lucknow, and Nagpur. These occupy a somewhat anomalous position, as they are at once Government officials and in charge of the Government chaplains, and superintend the Anglican missions which have been established in their dioceses. The Bishops of Travancore, Tinnevelly, Chota Nagpur and Assam, are not appointed or paid by Government and are simply missionary bishops. The Bishop of Dornakal, who was appointed by the Bishop of Madras, has a small diocese of his own in the state of Hyderabad. He also acts as an assistant bishop in the diocese of Madras.

As long as there is an English army in India and a large European population it will be necessary to have English chaplains and English bishops. It would, however, be an undoubted advantage from a missionary standpoint if the bishops who are responsible for the supervision and development of missionary work in India were no longer supported or appointed by the Government.

II. *Baptist Missionary Societies.*—The English *B.M.S.* (1792) works chiefly in Bengal, Bihar, the United Provinces, and the Punjab. Its "church members" number about 11,000 and its adherents 30,000. It has hostels for students at Calcutta and Dacca, and a university college at Serampore. In Ceylon, where it began work in

1812, it has 1057 "members." The *Baptist Zenana Mission* has 70 missionaries and 100 girls' schools.

The *A.B.M.U.* (1813) has 140 European and 425 Indian clergy and 135,000 baptized adherents. Nearly half these are in Burma. In Assam it has 60 missionaries (including men and women) and about 11,000 communicant members. It has also work in Bengal and the Telugu country. The total number of Baptists in India in 1911 was 332,000.

III. *The Lutheran Missions.* — Next to the Anglican and Baptist missions come, in point of numbers, the Lutheran missions, the largest of which are (1) the *Gossner Mission* of Berlin (1841), which has 71,000 baptized adherents in Chota Nagpur, and a staff of 50 European and 44 Indian missionaries and 400 Indian lay-workers (see p. 112). (2) The *Evangelical National Missionary Society of Stockholm* (1877) has 1500 baptized Christians and 23 European (men) missionaries in connection with its work in the Central Provinces. (3) The *Schleswig - Holstein Evangelical Lutheran Mission* (1883) works among the Telugus in the Vizagapatam district and amongst the Uriyas of the Jeypore Agency. The Christian community numbers about 15,000 and is ministered to by 24 European missionaries.

The *Basel Mission* (founded in 1815) started work on the west coast of India in 1834. It has 26 principal stations in the districts of Kanara, Malabar, Coorg, the Nilgiris, and South Maratha. It has 60 European and 26 Indian clergy, and its baptized Christians number 20,000. Its constitution is Presbyterian in character. Industrial work forms a chief feature of the mission.

The industrial mission work of this society has been criticized by many of the supporters of Indian missions, and not altogether without justification. A member of the Basel Mission, the Rev. A. Scheuer of Tellicherry, writes:

"This system is not without its disadvantages. Most Christians look to the mission for everything; the temporal and the spiritual are too closely allied, and therefore often confounded. The factories attracted undesirable converts. In the minds of the people mission work became associated with providing a living. Well-to-do Hindus may not seldom have stood aloof from the Church because they needed no material help. . . . There can be no doubt that these industrials have been very helpful factors in building up a few strong congregations in the most caste-ridden parts of India. But it remains doubtful if without them a smaller and more efficient Church, better distributed, would not in the long-run have amply compensated for speedier numerical success."[1]

There are also two *American Lutheran Missions*, the General Synod (1842) with its headquarters at Guntur, and the General Council with its headquarters at Rajahmundry. The former has over 40,000 adherents, which include over 1000 Sudra converts; the latter, which started in 1869, has about 17,000 adherents.

The *Danish Evangelical Lutheran Missionary Society* (1867) has 29 European missionaries, 5 Indian pastors, and about 1600 members connected with its work at Pattambakam in South Arcot. The total number of Christians connected with the Lutheran missions in 1911 was 216,000.

IV. *Presbyterian Missions.*—(1) The *Foreign Missions Committee of the Church of Scotland*, which sent out Alexander Duff as its first missionary (1829), works in Calcutta, the Eastern Himalayas, the Punjab, Poona, and Madras. It has 77 European agents (32 men and 45 women) and 16,000 baptized Christians.

(2) The *United Free Church of Scotland* (U.F.C.S.) includes three missions which existed before the time of the Disruption in Western India (1823), Calcutta (1829), and Madras (1837). Its other missions are in Rajputana, Santalia, and in the Central Provinces. The European workers which it supports include 56 ordained and 32 unordained men and 117 women. Its Indian workers include 18 ordained men. There are about 12,000

[1] *Year-Book of Indian Missions* (1912), p. 507.

persons "in fellowship with the Church." It supports
16 medical stations. The Women's Foreign Mission
in connection with the U.F.C. of Scotland supports 275
schools with 15,000 scholars. The Christian College at
Madras founded by this society also receives support from
the C.M.S., the W.M.S., and the Church of Scotland
Mission.

(3) *American Presbyterian Missions.*—The chief centres
of work are in the Punjab (1846), Allahabad (1836), and
in the state of Kolhapur (1852), which lies about 150
miles south of Bombay. It supports university colleges
at Lahore and Allahabad (see p. 91).

(4) The *Canadian Presbyterian Mission* (1877) has
eleven chief stations, mostly in Central India. It has an
important college at Indore. It supports a good deal of
medical work, including three hospitals for women.

The total number of Indian Christians connected with
Presbyterian missions in 1911 was 164,000.

V. *Methodist Missions.*—(1) The largest Methodist mission is that of the A.M.E.C., which works in many different
parts of India. This society has done excellent educational, medical, and industrial work. In the carrying out
of its evangelistic work it has been content to accept a
lower standard as a qualification for baptism than that
accepted by other societies, and complaints, which have
often been well grounded, have been made against its
representatives that the society has established itself in
areas already occupied by other societies, and has baptized
large numbers of converts who were in course of being
prepared for baptism by other missions. It is greatly to
be hoped that those who are responsible for the direction of
its policy will fall into line with that adopted by all other
great societies with the exception of the representatives of
the R.C. Church and of the Salvation Army.

The A.M.E.C. also works to a considerable extent
amongst Europeans and Eurasians in India. It has 112
American and 264 Indian ministers.

(2) The *Wesleyan Methodist Missionary Society* (W.M.S.)

supports work in Ceylon (1814), Madras, Negapatam
Hyderabad, and Mysore, and in North India in Bengal,
Lucknow, Bombay, and Burma. A large part of its work
is amongst Europeans and Eurasians.

The total number of Indian Christians connected with
Methodist missions in 1911 was 162,000. (In 1912 the
A.M.E.C. claimed to have 185,000 " baptized adherents.")

VI. *Congregationalist Missions.*—(1) The *London Mis-
sionary Society* (L.M.S.) occupies 10 centres in North
India, 12 in South India, and 6 in Travancore. In connec-
tion with its missions in North India it has about 4000, in
South India about 33,000, and in Travancore about 81,000
Christians. Its staff consists of 70 European men, 50
European women, and 41 Indian clergy.

(2) The missions of the American Board support
29 American and 83 Indian clergy attached to three
principal centres—Ahmadnagar, the Jaffna peninsula in
Ceylon, and the Madura district. It has about 40,000
Christian adherents. It supports 6 mission hospitals

The total number of Christians connected with
Congregational missions in 1911 was 134,000.

VII. *The Salvation Army* employs 207 European and
2285 Indian officers and teachers. Its work is carried on
in 13 different districts and in 12 languages, its general
headquarters being at Simla. The contributions raised in
India and Ceylon equal in amount those sent from
England. It supports 3 hospitals, 21 industrial boarding
schools, 6 farm colonies, 17 weaving schools, and 11 settlements for criminal tribes accommodating 2300 persons
(see p. 125).

The Indian National Missionary Society.—One of the
most hopeful developments of missionary work in India
during recent years has been the formation of the National
Missionary Society of India, which was first organized on
Christmas Day, 1905, and began its missionary operations
in 1907. Mr. K. T. Paul, the Secretary, writes:

"The society is strictly denominational in the evangelistic work done in its fields. Each field is worked in a

particular connection exclusively of others. For instance, the Punjab field is Anglican, to which only those candidates who are of that connection are sent. The first missionary to that field was ordained by the Bishop of Lahore in 1911. The field in the United Provinces is Presbyterian, to which only those candidates who are of that connection are sent. One of the workers there was ordained by the Presbytery of Ludhiana (in 1912). And so with the other fields, one of which is in connection with the ancient Syrian Church." [1]

The " five fields of labour " which have so far been selected are the Montgomery district in the Punjab; the Nakkar *tahsil* of the Saharanpur district in the United Provinces; the Omaher *taluk* in the Salem district, Madras; the district of North Kanara in the south of the Bombay Presidency; and the Karjat-Karmala *taluks* near Ahmadnagar. In 1914 there were 26 agents employed by the society, of whom 12 had received a college education and of whom 2 were doctors. The converts numbered about 1000.

Had we space, we should like to refer to some of the movements which owe their origin to the Christian ideals which missionaries have inculcated in India, such as the *Society of the Servants of India,* founded in 1906 by Mr. Gokhale; the *Seva Sadan or Sisters of India Society,* founded in Bombay in 1908 by the Parsee philanthropist Mr. Malabari; or the *Ramakrishna Home of Service,* in Benares. The Seva Sadan Society seeks to train Indian women for educational, medical, social, and philanthropic work. These and many others are supported by those who do not call themselves Christians but whose lives have been influenced by the spirit of Christ.

Bible Societies.—An important missionary agency is the British and Foreign Bible Society, which employs many hundreds of Biblewomen and colporteurs to read and distribute the Bible. Since its foundation (1804) it has issued in the languages of India nearly 20,000,000

---

[1] *Year-Book of Indian Missions,* p. 481.

portions of Scripture. The American Bible Society (1817) does similar work on a smaller scale. The National Bible Society of Scotland (1861) maintains 223 colporteurs in India and Ceylon, who sold in 1910 239,000 copies of the Scriptures.

Roman Catholic Missions in India.

We have already referred to the early missions of the R.C. Church in India and to the work which it is carrying on in special districts. In 1886 India and Ceylon were placed under a regularly constituted hierarchy with eight arch-bishoprics (Goa, Calcutta, Madras, Bombay, Pondicherry, Verapoly, Agra, and Colombo). The total number of bishops and priests (1912) is 2653, of whom 1700 are indigenous to the country and 953 are Europeans. "Of these European missionaries a small percentage are of Irish and a still smaller percentage of English descent. The rest are members of various religious Orders from Italy, Spain, France, Holland, Belgium, and Germany, while the prelates, in every case except one, belong to these continental nationalities."[1]

R.C. Colleges and Schools.—The R.C. Church has 23 seminaries containing 700 candidates for the priesthood, of which the most important are situated at Kandy in Ceylon, Shembaganur near Trichinopoly, Ranchi, and Kurseong near Darjeeling. It has 11 colleges which prepare for university degrees with 1300 students, 65 high schools, 248 middle schools, and 2438 elementary schools with 98,000 pupils. It has also 47 industrial and 74 boarding schools with 5917 pupils, and 97 orphanages. For girls it has 59 high schools, 240 middle class schools, and 672 elementary schools. The total number of pupils (1912) in R.C. schools is 143,000 boys and 73,000 girls, out of whom about 12,000 are orphans. The boys' schools are for the most part managed by members of religious Orders and the schools for girls by professed Sisters.

[1] See article by Father E. R. Hull in *The Year-Book of Missions in India*, p. 160.

Of, the university colleges the most important are St. Xavier's College, Calcutta, under Belgian Jesuits (276 students); St. Xavier's College, Bombay, under German Jesuits (350 students); St. Joseph's College, Trichinopoly, under French Jesuits (420 students).

The educational establishments are to a large extent supported by Government grants-in-aid. They are in part maintained by the two European societies, the Association for the Propagation of the Faith and the Society for the Holy Childhood.

Religious Unity in South India.

In 1908 five separate missions in South India were organized as one body under the name of the South India United Church—namely, the United Free Church of Scotland in and about Madras, the Arcot Mission of the Reformed Church of America, the American Madura Mission, and two London Missionary Society missions— the Travancore Mission and the South Indian District Committee Mission. Its affairs are managed by a small committee elected by the General Assembly which meets once in two years. The Basel Evangelical Mission and one or two other missions are considering the possibility of joining the South India United Church.

Proposals have also been made to incorporate in a "Federation of Christian Churches in India" all churches and societies that "accept the Word of God as contained in the Scriptures as the supreme rule of faith and practice, and whose teaching in regard to God, sin, and salvation is in general agreement with the great body of Christian truth and fundamental doctrines of the Christian faith."

In December 1911 a Presbyterian Alliance was organized in Allahabad. As a result the General Assemblies of the Church of Scotland, the U.F.C. of Scotland, the Presbyterian Church in America, and the Canadian and Irish Presbyterian Churches approved the scheme and voted to allow their Indian Churches to join the Union.

The number of missionaries in India.

In 1912 there were 5200 Anglican and Protestant missionaries in India (compare China, 4299). Of the 1442 ordained missionaries, 620 were from Great Britain, 559 from the U.S.A., and 222 from the continent of Europe. There were 118 men and 217 women doctors. Of the total number of missionaries, 2076 were men and 3124 women; of these latter, 1800 were unmarried women. Of Indian men and women there are about 40,000 who devote their whole time to missionary work; of these, 1665 are ordained. Amongst the Indian workers there are about 250 university graduates, most of whom are teachers. Of the 40,000 Indian workers about 10,000 are women.

The difficulty of developing an educated ministry supported entirely by Indian contributions will be realized when it is remembered that the average income *per capita* of the people of India is £2 per annum. At the present time the average contribution towards the support of his Church made by each member of the Indian Christian Churches is 4s. per annum.

The Young Men's Christian Association, which works chiefly amongst students in the larger towns, exercises a widespread influence. The Christian Literature Society (C.L.S.) translates and produces in various Indian languages books bearing directly or indirectly upon the Christian faith, and thereby furnishes invaluable aid to the missionary societies.

Philanthropic Work.

Some idea may be obtained of the organized philanthropic work, apart from that of medical missions, which is being done by missionary societies in India from the following statement. The figures in brackets denote the number of inmates in the various institutions. There are now in India in connection with missionary societies: orphanages, 181 (13,400); leper hospitals and asylums, 59 (4815); institutions for blind and deaf mutes, 8 (340); rescue homes, 8 (360); industrial homes, 19 (1134); houses for widows, 15 (410).

V.

CEYLON.

Soon after the arrival of the Portuguese, who effected a settlement in Ceylon early in the sixteenth century, some Franciscan monks reached Ceylon, and a bishopric of Colombo was established. In 1544 St. Francis Xavier preached among the Tamil fishermen of Manaar in the kingdom of Jaffna and baptized over 500 of them. These were massacred by the Rajah of Jaffna, whose kingdom was conquered by the Portuguese in 1548. The Portuguese used forcible methods of conversion, and a large proportion of the people, including the Brahmans, were baptized. In the south of the island less violent means were adopted, but even here " many became Christians for the sake of Portuguese gold." When the Dutch expelled the Portuguese in the middle of the seventeenth century, they strove hard to induce the Singalese to adopt the Reformed faith. The R.C. priests were banished, R.C. rites were forbidden on pain of death, and the people were ordered to become Protestants. No unbaptized person was allowed to hold any office or to possess land. Before the end of the Dutch occupation it had been realized that the conversion of the people was merely nominal, and when pressure was relaxed the number of the Christians rapidly fell. When the English gained possession of the island in 1798, 300,000 persons registered themselves as members of the Dutch Church. Of these a few were intelligent members, a large number were Roman Catholics, but the majority were Buddhists or Hindus. The English Government proclaimed religious toleration, but did nothing to teach or evangelize the people. As a result of the religious liberty which they established, a number of the Singalese declared themselves to be Roman Catholics and a larger number claimed to be Hindus or Buddhists.[1]

The first Protestant missionary to establish work in Ceylon in the nineteenth century was James Chater of the *Baptist M.S.* After spending six years in Burma, he reached Colombo in 1812, where he laboured for sixteen years. His successor, the Rev. E. Daniel, did much to spread Christianity in the villages near Colombo. The B.M.S. has now 4 European missionaries and 1057 baptized Christians, its chief centres of work being Colombo, Kandy, and Ratnapura.

In 1814 five *Wesleyan missionaries* arrived and started work at Jaffna and Batticaloa for the Tamils, and at Matara and Galle for the Singalese. The mission proved discouraging in its early years, but afterwards maintained a steady growth. In 1842 work was started among the savage Veddahs. The W.M.S. has training colleges at Colombo and Galle and a large number of day and boarding schools in various parts of Ceylon. In 1913 the number of European missionaries was 26 and of communicants 6186.

In 1816 four missionaries belonging to the *A.B.C.F.M.* arrived, and in the following year started work at Jaffna. The work of this society, which has since been developed, has been concentrated in this district. A special feature of the mission, especially in its earlier days, has been the establishment of missionary schools. The greater part of its work has been handed over to Singalese, and but little evangelistic work is now being done. In 1912 it had a staff of 3 American missionaries, and its communicants numbered 2170.

In 1818 four missionaries sent by the *C.M.S.* landed in Ceylon and, like their predecessors, received a warm welcome from the Governor, Sir Robert Brownrigg. They

[1] For a further reference to the relapse of the Protestant Christians in Ceylon, see p 20.

began work among the Tamils at Jaffna and among the
Singalese at Kandy. The mission to the Tamil coolies in
the north has for many years received a large amount of
financial support from the English planters, who have
learnt to appreciate its value. The college at Kandy, of
which the Rev. A. G. Fraser is the Principal, is a "red-
hot centre" of missionary life and enthusiasm, and seems
likely to exercise a far-reaching influence upon the prospects
of Christianity in Ceylon. Another important college belonging to the mission is situated at Jaffna. In 1913 it
had 20 European missionaries and 5097 communicants.

The first missionary supported by the *S.P.G.* was
stationed at Colombo in 1840, and was transferred to
Matara in the south in the following year. A large part
of the work which this society has helped to develop has
been done in close conjunction with Government chaplains
or with the diocesan clergy. The centre of its educational
work is St. Thomas' College, Colombo, which has recently
been rebuilt on a new site. It is one of the leading
educational institutions in Ceylon.

In 1845 the first Anglican Bishop of Colombo (Dr.
Chapman) was appointed.

The words which one of the C.M.S. missionaries wrote
in 1868, on the occasion of the jubilee commemoration of
the C.M.S. Mission in Ceylon, apply to the work of all the
existing societies. He wrote:

"A more arduous task, a more trying field of labour, it
would be difficult to imagine. . . . Pure Buddhists and
Hindus are tenfold more accessible than are the thousands
of relapsed and false professors of Christianity. . . . The
tradition preserved in native families of the fact that their
forefathers were once Christians and afterwards returned to
Buddhism is naturally regarded by them as a proof of the
superiority of the latter religion; whilst the sight of churches,
built by the Dutch but now gone to ruin, adds strength to
the belief that Christianity is an upstart religion which has
no vitality, and which, if unsupported by the ruling powers,
cannot stand before their own venerated system."[1]

[1] *History of the C.M.S.*, i, 218.

During the years which have elapsed since these words were written, Christianity has made considerable progress, but the missionaries have not yet got rid of the handicap created by the religious history of the past centuries.

Other societies at work in Ceylon are the Salvation Army, which commenced work in 1882, and the Friends' Foreign Mission Association, which began in 1896.

There are five *R.C. dioceses in Ceylon*—Colombo, Kandy, Galle, Trincomalee, and Jaffna. The missions in the dioceses of Colombo and Jaffna are conducted by the Oblates of the Blessed Virgin Mary, those in Galle and Trincomalee by the Jesuits, and those in Kandy by the Silvestrine Benedictines. The staff includes 173 European and 67 native priests. The European priests are also engaged in ministering to European residents. The number of R.C. Christians, according to the latest R.C. returns, is 345,628. These figures include about 1300 Europeans and 12,500 Burghers (*i.e.* Dutch half-castes).

The Jesuits are in charge of the seminary at Kandy, which was established in 1893 for the training of native priests.

The population of Ceylon (excluding the military), according to the census of 1911, is 4,105,535. The following table gives the religious profession of the inhabitants as shown by the last four census returns :—

TOTAL POPULATION (INCLUDING EUROPEANS).

	1881.	1891.	1901.	1911.
Christians . .	267,977	302,127	349,239	409,168
Buddhists . .	1,698,070	1,877,043	2,141,404	2,474,270
Hindus . . .	593,630	615,932	826,826	932,696
Mohammedans .	197,775	211,995	246,118	283,582

Of the total Christian population of 409,000, 239,000 were low-country Singalese, 6000 Kandyan Singalese,

86,000 Ceylon Tamils, 41,000 Indian Tamils, 7470 Europeans, and 26,454 Burghers.

The Anglican Christians (who included 4983 Europeans and 7299 Burghers) numbered 41,095; the Wesleyans (who included 1977 Burghers and 310 Europeans) numbered 17,323; the Presbyterians (who included 663 Europeans and 2684 Burghers) numbered 3546; Baptists, 3306; Congregationalists, 2978; Salvation Army, 1042.

The figures belonging to the different denominations given in these census returns include adherents as well as baptized Christians.

During the decade 1901–11 the percentage of increase in the Christian population was 16·8, whilst that of the total population was 16·5. In the Christian schools in Ceylon, 54,967 scholars are in charge of Roman Catholics, 32,713 of Anglicans, and 29,192 of Wesleyans. The percentage of literates—*i.e.* of those who can read—is much higher both in Ceylon and in Burma than it is in India, and there are therefore greater opportunities for extending missionary influence by the circulation of Christian literature.

One result of the progress of Christian missions during recent years has been that the Buddhists, who include the majority of the inhabitants, have recently awakened to the fact that Christianity is a force to be feared, and therefore deserving of active opposition. In an article entitled "The Buddhist Revival in Ceylon,"[1] Mr. Ekanayake, who is himself a Singalese Christian, describes the remarkable efforts which have been made by the Buddhists in different parts of Ceylon to establish schools and to organize lectures and addresses in order to counteract the spread of Christian influences. He writes:

"Work among children, which was entirely unknown in Buddhist circles, whether in the earliest or in the latest days of Buddhism, is being vigorously carried on. Catechism, Sunday schools, religious instruction in day schools, the teaching of Buddhist stanzas to school children, and their

[1] *The East and The West*, July 1904.

processions to temples on festival days, are noteworthy features of work amongst children."

Unfortunately, it does not appear that this revival of Buddhism is accompanied by any serious effort to bring the debased form of this religion which is found in Ceylon up to its original standard or ideals.

"What is most disappointing," writes Mr. Ekanayake, "is that in spite of all this activity there is no attempt made to purify Buddhism of its corruptions . . . the worship of trees, relics, and images still takes place . . . devil worship has not been denounced, but still goes on, though it is contrary to the principles of Buddhism. Caste, which the teaching of Buddhism denounces, is strongly upheld in Buddhist circles."

From the missionary standpoint this attempt to revivify Buddhism is perhaps the most encouraging feature of the present situation. The fact that the revival itself is, so to speak, on the surface, and that it is doing little to raise the religious and moral standards of the people, suggests that it is not likely to interfere for long with the progress of Christian missions.

VI.

BURMA.

In 1603 Felipe de Brito, a Portuguese adventurer, established himself as Governor of Syriam near Rangoon. He built a church at Syriam and began to destroy the Buddhist pagodas and to force the Buddhists to become Christians. After ten years he was killed by the king of Ava, and his wife and most of the Portuguese at Syriam were taken as slaves to Ava. Their descendants constitute the bulk of the R.C. population in that part of the country to-day. In 1692, the first missionary priests of the Society of Foreign Missions at Paris reached Pegu. In the following year they were arrested by order of the king, exposed naked to the bites of mosquitoes, and then sewn up in sacks and thrown into the Pegu River. In 1721 two more priests arrived, who were followed by others.

During the next forty years a bishop and several priests were murdered, including Father Angelo, who was "a skilled doctor," but the work continued. By 1800 there were two R.C. churches in Rangoon and 3000 Christians, but in 1824, on the outbreak of the first Burmese War, the two churches were destroyed. In 1857 King Mindon helped the R.C. priests in Mandalay to build a church and a mission house. Soon after this the R.C. mission work in Burma was handed over to the Foreign Mission Society of Paris, and Father Bigandet, who had already been a missionary for fourteen years, was consecrated as bishop. He became one of the chief authorities on the language and religion of the Burmese.

The Christian Brothers started work at Moulmein in 1859 and at Rangoon in 1861. In 1867 the Milan Society for Foreign Missions took charge of the work at Toungoo and in East Burma. The Roman Catholics have virtually abandoned direct evangelistic work amongst the Burmese, the bulk of their adherents in Burma being Tamils, Pwo-Karens, and Eurasians. They have also done good work amongst the Chinese immigrants. During the decade 1901–11 their increase in Burma was at the rate of 62 per cent., and the total number of their converts in 1911 was 50,770. They have 3 bishops and over 200 European priests, monks, and nuns. The Rev. **W. C.** Purser of the S.P.G. Mission writes:

"The Roman priests have won the admiration of the European residents by the devotion of their lives. Few return to Europe after coming out to the East, and the missionary priests live right among the natives The educational and social work of the Roman Catholics is beyond praise. St. Paul's School, Rangoon, is one of the largest and best equipped boys' schools in the East, and is staffed by the 'Teaching Brothers,' who are trained lay teachers and give their labour free. It is the wonderful organization of the Roman Church, as shown by this brother-hood of teachers, that enables it to compete successfully with other Christian bodies in India, with the result that many Anglican and Nonconformist children are being educated in R.C. schools."[1]

Baptist Missions.

In 1806 five students sat beneath the shelter of a haystack in Williamstown, Massachusetts, discussing the possibility of evangelizing the world. Mills, one of their number, suddenly cried out, "We can if we will," and the cry was taken up and repeated by his four companions. Five years later Adoniram Judson joined this company, each member of which was pledged to give up all and dare all in order that they might spread the Kingdom of Christ throughout the world.

[1] *Missions in Burma*, p. 93.

In 1810 Judson, with three others, offered himself for missionary work to the General Association of the Congregational Church, and as a result the American Board for Foreign Missions was founded. After being ordained for the Congregational Church he and his companions eventually reached Calcutta in 1812, where soon afterwards he became a Baptist. The East India Company having refused him permission to work in India, he arrived on July 13, 1813, at Rangoon, where one of the Careys had already (1807) begun missionary work. When the American Baptists heard of Judson's change of views, they determined to support him, and founded the society which is now known as the American Baptist Missionary Union. Thereupon the English missionaries in Rangoon handed over their work to this society. At the end of seven years Judson had baptized 10 Burmese converts.

On the outbreak of the Burmese war with England in 1823, he and his companion, a medical missionary named Price, were thrown into prison, and for twenty-one months endured the greatest hardships. When the war was over, and after the death of his first wife (he married three times), he lived the life of a hermit, and on one occasion fasted for forty days in the jungle. In 1828 Mr. Boardman baptized the first convert among the Karens—Ko Tha Byu—who became an apostle to his fellow-countrymen.

Meanwhile Judson gave himself up to the task of translating the Bible into Burmese. He died in 1850. Judson believed in peregrinating as opposed to concentrated mission work, and was doubtful as to the value of missionary schools. His legacy to those who came after him was the inspiration of a devoted life and the translation of the Bible into Burmese.

In 1852 there were 62 missionaries, male and female, and 267 Burmese and 7750 Karen Christians belonging to the A.B.M. The number of baptized members belonging to this mission in 1911 were: Burmese, 3182; Karens, 54,799; Kachins, 371; Chins, 1011; Shans,

338, Talaings, 308; Muhsos, 9343; Tamils, 465; others, 579—making a total of 70,396. The total number of Christian adherents belonging to the mission was 120,549.

There are about 200 American missionaries (including wives) and 2200 native workers, and the contributions of the native congregations amount to over £20,000 per annum. Of the 976 churches connected with this mission, 717 are self-supporting. Two institutions connected with the mission deserve special notice:

1. The Baptist College at Rangoon, which is affiliated to Calcutta University. Its new buildings were opened in 1909 in memory of Dr. Cushing, a former Principal and the translator of the Bible into the Shan language.

2. The theological seminary at Insein, established in 1845, where Karens, Burmese, Chins, and others are trained to become evangelists. It has 150 students in residence.

The *American Methodist Episcopal Mission* has been represented in Lower Burma since 1878. For many years its missionaries confined themselves to work amongst Europeans, but they are now doing missionary work as well.

In Upper Burma the English *Wesleyan Methodists* have been at work since 1885. They help to support a home for lepers which has accommodation for 250 lepers.

The *Y.M.C.A.* has a large organization in Rangoon, but its work is chiefly amongst Europeans.

Anglican Missions.

At the close of the second Burmese war in 1853 the Anglican chaplain at Moulmein, supported by English civilians, began to organize missionary work. In 1854 the S.P.G. sent a Eurasian from Calcutta to assist him, and in 1859 they sent the Rev. A. Shears from England. In 1860, Mr. J. E. Marks (now Rev. Dr. Marks), a trained schoolmaster, arrived, who enlarged and developed the school which had been started. In 1863 Mr. Marks was ordained and transferred to Rangoon, where he started a school which was afterwards known as St. John's College, which stands in 13 acres of land and has now nearly 700 boys, 190 of whom are boarders.

In 1867 Mr. Marks visited Mandalay on the invitation of the king, and in 1869 he opened a school which had been built at the king's expense, and which included amongst its scholars nine of the royal princes. The king also built a church, to which Queen Victoria gave a font, and which was consecrated by the Bishop of Calcutta in 1873.

In 1863 difficulties arose between some of the A.B.M. missionaries amongst the Karens and their converts, and in 1870 the wife of the founder of the Karen Mission suggested handing over to the Anglican Church 6000 converts together with a number of mission schools and other property. The Rev. J. Trew, whom the Bishop of Calcutta deputed to make inquiries, advised that the offer should be refused and that the members of the A.B.M. should be left to settle the dispute among themselves. In 1873 a mission station for work amongst Burmese was opened at Toungoo. In 1875, the dispute among the members of the A.B.M. still continuing, and some of the Karen Christians having drifted back into heathenism, the Anglican Mission at Toungoo undertook the care of the Karen Christians who had finally separated themselves from the A.B.M. In 1877 the bishopric of Rangoon was constituted, and in the following year the first four Karen clergy were ordained.

On the succession of King Thibaw in 1878, the mission at Mandalay was broken up, and the church was converted into a state lottery office. In 1885 the mission was re-started, after the annexation of Upper Burma by the English Government, by the Rev. James Colbeck, a most capable missionary and a man of saintly character. He died in 1888, after fifteen years of unbroken service in Burma. In 1895 Dr. Marks was compelled to return to England after thirty-five years of strenuous work in the

cause of Burmese education.   On the resignation of Bishop
Strachan, after an episcopate of twenty years, the Rev. A.
M. Knight was consecrated as third bishop of Rangoon in
1903.   During the six years which followed, before he
was forced by ill-health to resign, he did much to
strengthen and develop the work of the Anglican missions,
and on his return to England he became the Warden of
St. Augustine's Missionary College at Canterbury.

A Missionary Brotherhood, supported by funds collected
in the diocese of Winchester, started work amongst Burmese
in Mandalay in 1904, and a community of women was
organized in 1909.   The first Head of the Brotherhood
was the Rev. R. S. Fyffe, who became Bishop of Rangoon
in 1910.

The S.P.G., besides supporting work amongst the
Burmese and Karens, carries on work amongst Tamil,
Telugu, and Chinese immigrants at Rangoon, Moulmein,
Toungoo, and Mandalay, and has a small mission amongst
the Chins.   Connected with the Anglican Mission there
are 16 ordained native missionaries, of whom 10 are
Karens, 3 Burmese, and 3 Tamils.

Its most important institutions are St. John's College
for boys, and St. Mary's High and Normal Schools for girls
in Rangoon.   It has also some work at Car Nicobar, one
of the group of islands south of the Andamans, which are
in the diocese of Rangoon.   The total number of baptized
Christians connected with the Anglican Mission is about
10,000.

Of the converts in Burma connected with all the
Christian missions, by far the largest proportion have been
won from amongst animists who had not previously
embraced Buddhism.   But although the profession of
Buddhism renders the Burmese difficult for the Christian
missionary to approach, the Burmese are far from being
consistent Buddhists.

No picture could be more ideal than that of Burmese
Buddhism depicted in the book entitled *The Soul of a
People*.   We are loth to admit the truth, which is that

the Buddhism described by Mr. Fielding Hall exists
only in the imagination of the writer. Over against the
poetical, but wholly misleading, descriptions of Mr. Hall
we have to set the matter-of-fact, but true, description by
Mr. C. Lowis in the official Census Report for India and
Burma. He speaks of

" the fact—now largely recognized—that the Buddhism
of the people is of the lips only, and that inwardly
in their hearts the bulk of them are still swayed by
the ingrained tendencies of their Shamanistic forefathers—
in a word, are, at bottom, animists pure and simple. . . .
The Burman has added to his animism just so much
of Buddhism as suits him, and with infantile inconsequence
draws solace from each of them in turn. I know of no
better definition of the religion of the great bulk of the
people of the province than that given by Mr. Eales in
his 1891 Census Report: ' a thin veneer of philosophy laid
over the main structure of Shamanistic belief.' The facts
are here exactly expressed. Animism supplies the solid
constituents that hold the faith together, Buddhism the
superficial polish. Far be it from me to underrate the
value of that philosophic veneer. It has done all that a
polish can do to smooth, to beautify, and to brighten; but
to the end of time it will never be more than a polish. In
the hour of great heart-searching it is profitless. It is then
that the Burman falls back upon his primæval beliefs. Let
but the veneer be scratched, the Burman stands forth an
animist confessed." [1]

A more hopeful view of the possible developments
of Burmese Buddhism was expressed by Dr. Tilbe, an
American missionary working in Burma. Speaking at a
recent Conference in America of the change which has
taken place during recent years in Burmese Buddhism,
he said:

"This whole country of Burma is absolutely different from
what it was not so very long ago. The people are different,
the religion is different. Twenty-five years ago the term
' Buddhism ' meant the Buddhism of the books, the Buddhism
of the priesthood. To-day, Buddhism is still a religious term,

[1] *Census Report*, 1901, vol. i. p. 85.

but the thing itself is vastly different from what it was twenty-five years ago. At that time, when I spoke of God, I had to prove the existence of God in a way that would satisfy those people. When I spoke then of man having a soul, almost every man in my congregation denied it. To-day, I preach everywhere, appealing to their own belief in God, appealing to their own belief in the human soul: and I find unanimous assent. Christian teaching, Christian tracts, Christian schools have modified the belief in Buddhism until to-day it is not the Buddhism of the books, not the Buddhism of the priesthood." [1]

One of the most remarkable of the Burmese converts to Christianity is a man named Maung Tha Dun, who lived in the forest for thirteen years the life of a Buddhist hermit. Without having received any Christian instruction, or having come into contact with a European missionary, he came to believe that much of the teaching of modern Buddhism was false and that there was a Supreme God who could be thought of as the great Father, and he began to preach this truth in the surrounding villages. He at length came into contact with the Rev. T. Ellis, an Anglican missionary at Kemmendine, and, after long and careful preparation, was baptized in 1911. Since his baptism he has lived the life of an ascetic and has occupied his time partly in meditation and partly in travelling from village to village in districts where he was previously known, in order to preach the faith of Christ to his former disciples and followers. Of these, 150 have been baptized as the result of his efforts, and the number of those who have been influenced by him, but have not yet been baptized, may be counted by thousands. Of the hermit and his followers the Rev. G. Whitehead writes:

"I am more and more struck with the self-denying life and the earnestness of the hermit, and with the beauty of character reflected in the face of him and of quite a

[1] *Students and the World-wide Expansion of Christianity.* Report of a Conference at Kansas City, 1914, p. 270.

number of his followers. The hermit himself is so patient and unselfish, humble and pure minded, earnest and devout, full of benevolence towards all men, anxious to lead his brethren into the right way, and unwearied in service, that it is a great joy to be with him."

In the discovery and the conversion of men like Maung Tha Dun lies the hope of interpreting Christ to the Burmese.

VII.

CHINA.

THE story of Christian Missions in China may be considered under five heads: 1. The influence exerted by Christian teachers upon the development of Chinese Buddhism, prior to the arrival in China of the Nestorian missionaries. 2. The Nestorian Missions of the fifth and following centuries. 3. The Franciscan Missions in the thirteenth and fourteenth centuries. 4. The Jesuit and other Roman Missions from the sixteenth to the end of the eighteenth century. 5. Modern Missions to China from the beginning of the nineteenth century.

I. The influence of Christianity on Northern Buddhism.

Any inquiry into the history of Christian Missions in China, if it is to take account of the conditions under which these missions have been carried on, must include a reference to the influence which Christian teaching may have exerted in China before the Christian faith was definitely preached there. Northern Buddhism, that is, roughly speaking, the Buddhism of China and Japan, differs so fundamentally from the southern Buddhism, which is now represented in Ceylon and Burma, that only by a stretch of language can the two be called one religion. The differences that exist between them are more fundamental than those that exist between Christianity and Islam. How then was Indian Buddhism transformed, and under what influences? One answer appears to be that northern Buddhism was indebted for part of its distinctive teaching first to Gnostic teachers of the first and second centuries, and, later on, to the teaching of Manicheism.

Before we attempt to suggest how this debt may have been incurred, it is well to recall the essential difference between northern and southern Buddhism. The latter, as represented in Ceylon, Burma (and apparently in Tibet), knows nothing of a personal God, or of salvation to be gained as a gift from God or as the result of faith in Him. It teaches that without expecting to receive divine, or external, help man should aim at securing salvation by accumulating merit. The salvation which, after countless rebirths on this earth, he may hope to secure will result in his individual life and consciousness being merged in universal life and, in so far as the expression has a definite meaning, in universal consciousness.

If by northern Buddhism we mean the Buddhism embodied in *The Awakening of Faith* and *The Lotus Scripture*,[1] which are accepted by Chinese Buddhists, and the Buddhism of the Amida sects and the Pure Land School in Japan, we may claim for northern Buddhism a belief in a personal God who is moved with love towards men, and in a salvation which includes personal immortality to be won not by the accumulation of merit but by faith in God.

The teaching of the Amida sects and the Pure Land School, which include more than half the population of Japan, go far beyond this.

---

[1] *The Awakening of Faith*, the Chinese translation of which was made by the Buddhist missionary Paramartha during the first half of the sixth century, and which is about the size of the Gospel of St. Mark, is said to rank fifth amongst the religious books of the world which have the largest number of adherents, *i.e.* after the Bible, the Koran, the Confucian Classics and the Vedas. *The Lotus Scripture*, which is the most popular of all the Buddhist scriptures in Japan, existed before A.D. 250, and was translated into Chinese about the end of the third century.

According to the doctrine accepted by the Amida and Pure Land sects, "Amida is without beginning and without end: all love, wisdom, benevolence and power. In ages incalculably remote he appeared in various forms among men, all his incarnations being to bring salvation to mankind. In his last incarnation he registered a vow that, should the perfect consummation of the Buddhahood ever be in his power, he would not accept deliverance unless such deliverance should also mean the salvation of mankind. . . . To grasp the salvation wrought out for man by Amida . . . nothing is needed but faith—no works of the law, no austerities, penances, no repentance, nothing but faith." [1]

Whilst it is impossible to maintain that this teaching, or the teaching of those Buddhists in China to whom reference has been made, is a natural development of the teaching of southern Buddhism, it is hard to suggest any source from which the distinctive doctrines of this form of Buddhism could have been derived other than Christianity or the early heretical sects which had accepted part of the Christian faith. The two sects which were in touch with Christian thought, and which might have exerted influence upon Buddhist teachers in very early times, are the Gnostics and the Manichees. A book entitled *Pistis Sophia*, which is a Gnostic Gospel and professes to give in the words of Jesus an exposition of the chief doctrines of Gnosticism, was discovered by Schwartze in 1851 among the Coptic MSS. contained in the British Museum. The original, which was apparently written in Greek, dates from the second century and may have been written by Valentinus. The resemblances which can be traced between the teaching of the *Pistis Sophia* and that of the Amida sects of Japan are so striking as to make it difficult to doubt that Egyptian Gnosticism either influenced, or was influenced by, Buddhism. The latter alternative is apparently quite inadmissible. Professor Lloyd has shown that it is far from being impossible that Gnostic

[1] *The Creed of Half Japan*, by Arthur Lloyd, pp 266–8.

teaching may have reached Japan *via* Southern India at a very early date.[1]

We cannot give even a summary of the evidence which Professor Lloyd and others have adduced in proof of the theory that Chinese Buddhism was influenced by Christianity, represented in a distorted form by early Gnostic and Manichee teachers, but no careful student can lightly disregard such evidence.

An interesting discovery was made in China in 1908 which tends to support the theory that Manicheism exerted a widespread influence in China in very early times. In 1908 there was found in a cave in Tunhuang in the province of Kansu, a large number of MSS. which have been in part deciphered by MM. Chavannes and Pelliot.[2] The cave had been sealed up for many centuries (from 1035 A.D.). One of the MSS. is a Chinese translation of two short Manichean treatises.[3] The discovery of this book affords evidence that Manichean teaching was represented in China in or about the eighth century.[4] Another MS. found in the same cave consists of a hymn addressed to the Holy Trinity entitled "A hymn by which to obtain salvation to the Three majestic Ones of the Illustrious Religion." The hymn consists of 309 words divided into eleven stanzas of four lines each, and includes a list of persons and books venerated by Christians. This recent discovery confirms and supplements the information supplied by the famous stone discovered at Hsianfu, to which we shall have occasion to refer.

[1] See "Gnosticism and Early Christianity in Egypt," by P. I. Scott-Moncrieff, *Church Quarterly Review*, October 1909 ; "Gnosticism in Japan," by A. Lloyd, in *The East and The West*, April 1910 ; and *The New Testament of Higher Buddhism*, by Timothy Richard.

[2] Cf. *Un traité manichéen retrouvé en Chine*, traduit et annoté par Chavannes et Pelliot, Paris, 1912 ; cf. also "An Ancient Chinese Christian Document," in the *Church Missionary Review* for October 1912, by A. C. Moule

[3] The actual title of the Chinese MS. is missing.

[4] In A.D. 981 the Chinese traveller Wang Yentê spoke of the existence of Manichean temples in the neighbourhood of Tourfan.

II. The Nestorian Mission.

There is no certain proof that a mission connected with any branch of the Christian Church reached China prior to the arrival of the Nestorian missionaries.

It is true that a fourteenth-century tradition mentioned by Nicholas Trigault (1615) states that St. Thomas, after preaching the gospel in South India, preached and founded Christian churches in China, but the tradition has no historic value. The earliest reference of any value to the existence of Christianity in China is that of Arnobius, who wrote about A.D. 300. He says: "The work done in India, among the Seres, Persians and Medes may be counted and come in for the purpose of reckoning."[1]

If by Seres we are to understand Chinese, the statement would show that Arnobius believed that Christian missionary work amongst Chinese was in existence there at the time when he wrote. It is difficult to say what value can be attached to this statement. We are on surer ground when we come to speak of the Nestorian Mission.

At the Council of Ephesus held in A.D. 431, Nestorius, who was then Patriarch of Constantinople, was condemned as a heretic and banished beyond the frontiers of the Roman Empire. His banishment, which was apparently the result of a serious misunderstanding of his teaching, was the immediate cause of a great extension of Christian Missions throughout the Far East. A school was founded at Edessa (the modern Ourfa) which became a centre for missionary expansion, and owing to the activity of the followers of Nestorius the Christian faith was spread over a great part of Central Asia.

Many archbishoprics or metropolitical sees were eventu-

[1] *Adversus Gentes*, Leyden, 1651, lib. ii. p. 50, quoted in the *Book of Governors*, i. p. 115, note 2. The *Book of Governors* is the *Historia Monastica* of Thomas, Bishop of Marga, written in Syriac, c. 840, printed with English translation and notes by Dr. Budge, 1893. Bishop Thomas was secretary to Mar Abraham, the Patriarch, between 832 and 840.

ally established, of which two were at Cabul and Cambaluc
(Peking). Other metropolitical sees were at Elam, Nisibis,
Bethgerma, and Carach in Persia; at Halavan or Halach
on the confines of Media; at Mara in Korassan; at Hara
in Camboya; at Dailen, Samarcand, and Maravalnabar;
and at Tanket or Tangut—the modern province of Kansu.[1]
The canon of Theodore, Bishop of Edessa in 800 A.D.,
refers to "Metropolitans of China, India, and Persia, of
the Merozites of Siam, of the Raziches, of the Harinos, of.
Samarcand, which are distant, and which by reason of the
infested mountains and turbulent sea are prevented from
attending the four-yearly convocations with the catholicos,
and who therefore are to send their reports every six
years."[2]

Our chief source of information in regard to the work
of this mission is the famous Nestorian Stone which was
inscribed at Hsianfu in the eighth century, and was
buried during the great persecution of A.D. 845, to be
rediscovered by Chinese workmen in 1625, and roofed
over by a patriotic Chinese in 1859. The inscription
refers to the work accomplished by one or more Syrian
monks who arrived at Hsianfu in A.D. 635. It throws so
much interesting light upon the work of the Nestorian
missionaries that it is worth while to describe it in some
detail. The inscription is in Chinese, the names of the
clergy being given for the most part in Chinese and Syriac.
The inscription, which is entitled, "Monument commemor-
ating the propagation of the noble law of Tach'in (the
Roman Empire) in the Middle Kingdom," states: It is
handed down by Chingching, priest of the Tach'in
monastery (called in Syriac Adam, Priest and Chorepiscopos
and Papas of China), that there is one Alaha, Three in
One, the unoriginated true Lord. Then follows the story
of creation, an account of Man, of Satan, and the rise of

[1] See Assemani, *Bibliotheca Orientalis*, vol. iii. This is a collection of
Syriac and other MSS. published in Rome, 1719-28. The complete list of
Nestorian dioceses given by Assemani (vol. iii. pt. ii.) occupies eighty
folio pages.

[2] Quoted in *The Greek and Eastern Churches*, by W. F. Adeney, p. 534 f.

idolatry. The Triune Alaha divided His Godhead, and
Messiah appeared. Angels proclaimed Him; a Virgin
bore Him in Tach'in; a bright star announced His birth;
Persians visited Him. He left twenty-seven books of a
New Testament, and baptism. His ministers turn to the
east at prayer and wear beards as a sign that they
maintain outward relationships, shaving their crowns.
They pray for the living and the dead; they have the
weekly offering; they have no slaves, no wealth, but they
promote harmony. In the days of T'ai Tsung (627–650),
Alopên brought the Scriptures and translated them into
Chinese. He built a monastery for twenty-one monks.
Religion spread through ten provinces (650–683).
Monasteries filled a hundred cities (698–699). But
Buddhists derided it. The Emperor Tai Tsung (763–780)
every year on the day of the Nativity presented divine
incense to proclaim the perfected work, and offered a royal
feast to do honour to the Christian congregation. Chien-
chung (780–784) helps us. Priest Issu restored the old
monasteries and doubled the size of the churches. Erected
(781) in the days of Henan Ishu, the Catholicos (ob.
780), by Jazedbouzid, Priest and Chorepiscopos of Kumdan
(Hsian) by the disposition of our Saviour, and preaching
of our fathers to the Kings of the Chinese.

Then follow names, Lingpao, Adam, Hsingt'ung,
Sabranishu, etc., of Kumdan and Sarag (China).[1]

As suggestive of the possible influence exerted upon
the development of Chinese Buddhism, we may note that
Chingching, the author of this inscription, helped an
Indian Buddhist missionary to translate a Buddhist sutra
into Chinese.

We have already referred to the references to the
Nestorian Mission contained in the Christian MS. found
in the cave at Tunhuang. The following references, which
occur in the writings of contemporary Chinese writers, are
deserving of special notice :—

[1] A rubbing of the stone, the lettering of which is easily decipherable,
can be seen at the S.P.G. Mission House, Westminster.

"*Allusions to the Nestorian Mission in Chinese Writings.* — In the seventh month (August 15 to September 12) of the twelfth of the Chêngkuan years (A.D. 638) a decree was made saying: Teaching has no immutable name, holy men have no unchanging method. Religions are founded to suit (respectively, different) lands, that all the masses of men may be saved. Alopén, a Persian monk, bringing the religion of the Scriptures from far, has come to offer it at the chief metropolis. The meaning of his religion has been carefully examined: it is mysterious, wonderful, calm; it fixes the essentials of life and perfection; it is the salvation of living beings, it is the wealth of men. It is right that it should spread through the Empire. Therefore let the ministers build a monastery in the Ining quarter, and let twenty-one men be duly admitted as monks.[1]

"In the ninth month (September 30 to October 29) of the fourth of the T'ienpao years (A.D. 745) a decree was made saying: It is long since (the teachers of) the religion of the Scriptures of Persia, starting from Syria, coming to preach and practise, spread through the Middle Kingdom. When they first built monasteries we gave them in consequence (of their supposed origin) the name (of Persian). In order that men may know their (real) origin, the Monasteries of Persia at the two capitals are to be changed to Monasteries of Syria. Let those (monasteries) also which are established in all the Prefectures and Districts observe this."[2]

The next decree suggests alike the widespread influence of the Nestorian Mission and the development of official government opposition to its claims:

"As to the monks and nuns who come under the head of aliens, making known the religions of other countries, we decree that over 3000 Syrians and Muhufu return to lay life and cease to confound our native customs."[3]

---

[1] *T'ang hui yao* (ed. 1884, first published A.D. 960), xlix. fol. 10. Chinese text in *Variétés Sinologiques*, No. 12, p. 376.

[2] *T'ang hui yao*, xlix. fol. 10, 11; *Hsihsits'ung*, vii. fol. 22. Text in *Variétés Sinologiques*, No. 12, p. 376; translation, p. 255. There seem to have been "Persian" if not "Syrian" monasteries of other creeds besides the Christian.

[3] *Variétés Sinologiques*, No. 12, p. 378. The words come in a decree dated A.D. 845.

"When Wu Tsung (A.D. 840–846) was on the throne, he suppressed the Buddhist religion, destroying in the Empire 4600 monasteries and 40,000 lesser establishments. Monks and nuns to the number of 265,000 were enrolled as ordinary subjects, with their slaves, 150,000; and many thousand myriad *ch'ing* of land were confiscated; Syrians (Tach'in) and Muhuyao over two thousand. In the chief metropolis and the eastern metropolis two monasteries were left in each main street, with thirty monks in each monastery. In the provinces, monks were left in (monasteries of) three grades, with a limit of twenty men (in the largest houses). . . ."[1]

"Long ago some foreigners built a monastery here (Chêngtu) for a Syrian monastery. The ten divisions of the gate-tower all had blinds made of strings of pearls and blue jade. Later it was destroyed and fell to the ground. To this day the foundations remain, and every time there is heavy rain, people (living) behind and in front (of the site) pick up quantities of pearls, *shêshê*, gold, blue jade and different things."[2]

"Among the different foreigners who have come there are the Moni (Manichees), the Tach'in (Nestorians) and the Hsienshên (Zoroastrians). All the monasteries of these three (sorts of) foreigners in the Empire are not enough to equal the number of the Buddhists in one small district."[3]

Of the subsequent development of the Nestorian Mission in China hardly anything is known.

Abou'l Faradj, writing in A.D. 987, speaks of having met a Christian who had travelled extensively in China, and who declared that there was not a Christian then left in the country and that the Church buildings had been destroyed.[4]

Apart from references to the existence of Syrian monasteries at Hsian in 1076 and at Chêngtu at about the same date, Chinese contemporary writers make hardly a single allusion to Christianity between the decree of

---

[1] *Variétés Sinologiques*, No. 12, p. 376 f.

[2] Chinese work quoted by A. C. Moule, to whom it was communicated by P. Pelliot.

[3] *Variétés Sinologiques*, No. 12, p. 394.

[4] See *Les Influences Iraniennes en Asie centrale et en extrême-orient*, par Paul Pelliot, Paris, 1912, p. 15.

845 and the coming of the Franciscan Mission in the thirteenth century. The following is a quotation from *Cathay and the Way Thither*, translated from a book written in the fourteenth century:—

"*Concerning the Schismatics or Nestorian Christians who dwell in that country.*—In the said city of Cambaluc there is a manner of schismatic Christians whom they call Nestorians. They follow the manner and fashion of the Greeks, and are not obedient to the Holy Church of Rome, but follow another sect, and bear great hate to all Catholic Christians there who do loyally obey the holy Church aforesaid. And when the Archbishop of whom we have been speaking was building those Abbeys of the Minor Friars aforesaid, these Nestorians by night went to destroy them, and did all the hurt that they were able. But they dared not do any evil to the said Archbishop, nor to his friars, nor to other faithful Christians in public or openly, for that the Emperor did love these and showed them tokens of his regard.

"These Nestorians are more than 30,000, dwelling in the said Empire of Cathay, and are passing rich people, but stand in great fear and awe of the Christians. They have very handsome and devoutly ordered churches, with crosses and images in honour of God and the saints. They hold sundry offices under the said Emperor, and have great privileges from him; so that it is believed that if they would agree and be at one with the Minor Friars and with the other good Christians who dwell in that country, they would convert the whole country and the Emperor likewise to the true faith."[1]

In 1725, what is supposed to be a relic of the Nestorian Christianity in China was discovered in the shape of a Syrian MS. which contained a large portion of the Old Testament and a collection of hymns. These were in the possession of a Chinese Mohammedan.

[1] *Cathay and the Way Thither*, vol. i. p. 238. The Latin original is not extant. The French version is found in the Bibliothèque Nationale at Paris, MSS. 7500 and 8892, and was printed in the *Journal Asiatique*, vi. pp. 57-72. Cf. *Cathay*, vol. i. pp. 189-190. Yule gives the original date as *circa* 1330. The author was John of Cora, who had served under John of Monte Corvino and was made Archbishop of Sultania in Persia in 1328. Cf. *Ency. Brit.*, 1910, vol. vi. p. 190.

III. The Franciscan Missions.

At the Council of Lyons which was held in 1245, Pope Innocent IV. appealed for a spiritual army which should be the means of converting the Mongols to Christ. In response to his appeal three Franciscan friars started on April 16, 1245, and succeeded in penetrating to the heart of the Mongol territory, but failed to reach China. A second attempt made a little later met with still less success. In 1271, Nicolo Polo and his more famous son Marco visited the Great Khan, and after his return in 1295 Marco Polo dictated the well-known story of his travels in the Far East. Meanwhile, in 1289, Pope Nicolas IV. sent forth John of Monte Corvino with letters addressed to Kublai, the ruler of Cambaluc[1] (Peking), who after many adventures in Persia and India reached Cambaluc in 1294. On his arrival he found the Nestorian Mission strongly established and bitterly opposed to his Mission. Thus he writes on January 8, 1305:

"The Nestorians, certain folk who profess the name of Christians but who deviate sadly from the Christian religion, have grown so powerful in those parts that they will not allow a Christian of another rite to have ever so small a chapel, or to proclaim any but the Nestorian doctrine."

A further extract from this letter will give in the fewest words an idea of the work accomplished by Friar John during the twelve years which followed his arrival in China:

"I, indeed, was alone in this pilgrimage and without confession for eleven years, until there came to me brother Arnold, a German of the province of Cologne, who came to me last year. In the city of Khanbalig, where the king's chief residence is, I have built a church, which I completed six years ago, and I have built a campanile to it, in which I have put three bells. I have baptized

---

[1] Cambaluc does not appear to have become the capital of Northern China before the tenth century A.D.

there up to this time as well as I can estimate about six thousand persons, and if there had not been those charges of which I have spoken above, I should have baptized more than thirty thousand; and I am still often engaged in baptizing.

"Also I have gradually bought forty boys, the children of pagan parents, between the age of seven and eleven, who up to that time had known no religion. These boys I have baptized, and have taught them Latin letters and our rite, and have written out thirty psalters for them, with hymnaries and two breviaries, by means of which eleven of the boys already know our Office, and form a choir and take their weekly turn of duty as is done in convents, whether I am there or not; and several of them are writing out the psalter and other necessary books; and the Lord Emperor delights much in their singing. I have the bells rung for all the hours, and with my congregation of babes and sucklings I fulfil the Divine Office, and we sing by ear because we have no Office book with the music. I have a competent knowledge of the language and character which is generally used by the Tartars; and I have already translated into that language and character the whole New Testament and the Psalter, which I have caused to be written out in their most beautiful script. I understand the language and read and preach, openly and publicly, in testimony of the Law of Christ."[1]

On receiving the news contained in this letter Pope Clement v. nominated John of Monte Corvino as Archbishop of Cambaluc and Primate of the Far East, and dispatched seven friars whom he had consecrated as bishops with orders to consecrate Friar John as Archbishop. Apparently four of these bishops died before reaching China. The other three arrived and performed the act of consecration in 1308. After this we have very little information in regard to the work of the Franciscan Mission. Archbishop John died soon after 1328 and his place was left unfilled for many years despite the dispatch of a message from the Great Khan himself, begging that more teachers might be sent.

[1] The original of this Latin letter is given in *Annales Minorum*, ed. Fonseca, vol. vi. p. 69, and in the *Journal* of the Royal Asiatic Society, July 1914. For an English translation see *The East and The West*, April 1904.

Mr. Marshall Broomhall writes:

"One of the grandest opportunities that the Church of Christ has ever had presented to it is connected with the lifetime of Kublai Khan. There are letters still extant, preserved in the French archives, relating the remarkable fact that Kublai Khan actually requested the Pope to send one hundred missionaries to his country, ' to prove by force of argument to idolaters and other kinds of folk that the law of Christ was best, and that all other religions were false and naught; and that if they would prove this, he and all under him would become Christians and the Church's liegemen.'

"'What might have been' is a question that cannot but rise in the hearts of those who read this extract. The death of the Pope, however, and faction among the cardinals, with the subsequent failure of the two missionaries sent—they turned back because of the hardships of the way—lost to Asia an opportunity such as the Church has seldom had."[1]

The last authentic reference to the mission mentions the sending of a mission by Pope Urban v. in 1370, but it is doubtful whether any of its members reached China. Meanwhile the tolerant Tartar dynasty had given place to the intolerant and persecuting Ming dynasty. James of Florence, fifth bishop of Zaitun, a city on the coast three weeks' journey from Peking, was martyred, together with certain of his fellow Christians, in 1362, and his martyrdom is the last fact which we know concerning the Franciscan missions in China. If the representation of Odoric on his tomb in the cathedral at Udine is true to life, it would appear that the Franciscan missionaries were accustomed to wear the dress of the people amongst whom they worked and to shave their heads in the Tartar fashion.

[1] *The Chinese Empire*, p. 8. The quotation made by Mr. Broomhall is from a summary of a letter given by Marco Polo, but Dr. George Smith, who is his authority for the statement quoted above (cf. *The Conversion of India*, p. 35), was mistaken in supposing that the letters in the French archives referred to the request made by Kublai Khan, see *The Book of Ser Marco Polo* (1903), i. p. 13.

Before going on to refer to the establishment of the Jesuit missions in China it may be well to say a few words with regard to the failure of the Nestorian and Franciscan missions to leave any permanent traces of work which was carried on for so long a period and with so many outward signs of success. Three special reasons may be suggested to account for the eventual failure of these missions.

1. In neither case was any serious attempt made to establish the missions on a democratic basis. After they had been dispatched from their home base, no financial help was sent to them, and they were therefore compelled to be self-supporting. In order to fulfil this requirement it was considered to be necessary that they should obtain support from the rulers of the countries to which they went. "They did not labour with their own hands, nor receive support as a rule from their converts, as far as we know. They went with letters of recommendation from the Pope (or some other potentate), and received support from the Emperor as forming part of his retinue in some vague sense, or as the representatives of a friendly foreign Power. This applies at least to the early Nestorians (635-845) in part and to the Franciscan Mission (1294-1350). The later Nestorians did engage in trade and agriculture, and there are Imperial decrees extant which refuse exemption from taxes to Christian monks who were so engaged."[1]

2. A second reason that may be assigned for the disappearance of the later Nestorian and Franciscan converts is to be found in their connection with the ruling dynasty, the overthrow of which involved the overthrow and persecution of the Christians. The Christians came to be regarded as foreigners and lost all power of influencing those who were not already Christians.

3. A third reason is the failure on the part of either mission to train an effective body of Chinese clergy. For the early Nestorian Period (635-845) there is no evidence

[1] A. C. Moule, *The East and The West*, October 1914.

to show whether the Nestorian missionaries included any Chinese priest, though it is at least possible that some of the seventy names on the Hsian monument are those of Chinese clergy. In the accounts of the later Nestorians, though there is no mention of the ordination of Chinese, it is probable that some were ordained. The Franciscan Mission apparently took no steps to found a Chinese ministry. There is only one case on record of a Chinese bishop, and he was a Chinese who had become a Dominican monk. Alu, subsequently called Gregory Lopez, came from the Province of Fukien. He followed the Dominican preachers to Peking and was imprisoned, and subsequently banished with them. At Manila he studied Spanish, Latin, and philosophy. In 1654 he was ordained, being the first Chinese priest of whom any record exists. In 1674 Clement x. designated him as Bishop of Basilea and Vicar Apostolic over six provinces in China. He was, however, too humble to accept the honour, and was not consecrated as a bishop till 1686, when he was over seventy. He died at Nanking in 1687. He was the author of a pamphlet of twenty pages, in which he defended the observance by Christians of the rites observed by Confucianists in the worship or commemoration of their ancestors. The Bishop is reported to have been a man of great saintliness.[1] Had either the Franciscan or Nestorian Mission succeeded in training a body of Chinese clergy, there is little doubt that their work would have continued.

In regard to the translation of the Bible and of other books in connection with these missions, it is interesting to note that of 500 books which the early Nestorian missionaries possessed 35 were translated into Chinese. One of these, the *Book of the Holy King David*, was apparently the Psalter, and another was the hymn in praise of the Holy Trinity to which we have already referred. The later, and probably the earlier, Nestorian

[1] Further particulars in regard to Bishop Alu are given in *Quétif (Echard) Scriptores Ord· Praedicatorum*, Tome ii. (1721), p. 708, and in Huc's *Christianismus*, Tome iii. ch. 3.

missions used Service books in Syriac. John of Monte
Corvino translated into the "Tartaric tongue" the Psalms
and the New Testament and part of the Missal.

The Jesuits obtained leave in 1615 to celebrate
Mass in Chinese, but there is no evidence to show that
they acted upon this permission, and it is most unlikely
that either of the earlier missions translated the Mass
into Chinese.

By the time that the Jesuit Mission reached China few
traces remained of the work of the Nestorian or Franciscan
missionaries. According to *Nicholas Trigault*,[1] who wrote
early in the seventeenth century, a Jew named Ai who
had come from Kaifengfu told Ricci that the Christians
"had been very numerous, especially in the northern
provinces, and had prospered so much both in civil and
military careers that they had made the Chinese suspect
a revolution. He thought the suspicion had been excited
by the Saracens . . . not more than sixty years before.
And it had reached such a pitch that they were afraid
that the magistrates would lay hands upon them, and all
fled in different directions and professed, from fear of
death, to be Saracens or Jews or for the most part
idolaters. Their churches were changed into idol shrines."[2]

IV. The Jesuit Mission.

It had been the special ambition of S. Francis Xavier
to preach the gospel to the Chinese. After spending
two years in Japan, he landed on the island of Shangch'uan,
near Macao, where he died of fever on December 2, 1552,
aged forty-six, without having set foot on the mainland of

[1] *De Christiana expeditione* (Rome, 1615), pp. 119, 122 ff. Nicholas
Trigault was a Jesuit who reached China just after Ricci's death and was
entrusted with the editing of the latter's commentaries.

[2] I am indebted for this reference and for much help in obtaining in-
formation concerning the Nestorian and Franciscan Missions to the Rev.
A. C. Moule, who has done much original work relating to early Christian
missions to China. See article, "The Failure of Early Christian Missions to
China," in *The East and The West* for October 1914, and article in the
Journal of the Royal Asiatic Society for July 1914.

China. Thirty years later an Italian missionary named
Ricci, who was a member of the Society of Jesus, came to
China as a member of an embassy from Macao. He had
been preceded by Michael Rogers, who had arrived three
years before. Ricci's methods, which were followed by all
subsequent Jesuit missionaries in China, differed widely
from those of Xavier. During the first seven years of his
work he dressed as a Buddhist priest. He strove to overcome the prejudice of the Chinese and to ingratiate himself
and his mission in their favour by assuring them that
the faith which he came to teach was a development of
Confucianism, and that they could embrace it without
abandoning their ancestral beliefs or customs. His knowledge of mathematics and of astronomy won their respect,
and his preaching was ere long attended by widespread
results.

A mandarin of Shanghai, who on his baptism took the
name of Paul, did much to commend the Christian faith to
the educated classes.

"His youngest daughter, Candida, was a remarkable
woman. Having been left a widow at an early age she
devoted herself to the promotion of the cause of Christianity,
and, reserving enough for her eight children, she consecrated the rest of her fortune to the founding of churches
and the printing of Christian books, for the instruction of
the surrounding heathen. Having heard that the pagans
in several of the provinces were accustomed to abandon
their children as soon as born, she established a foundling
hospital for infants, and seeing many blind people telling
idle stories in the streets for the sake of gain, she got them
instructed and sent forth to relate the different events of
Gospel history. A few years before her death the Emperor
conferred on her the title of the 'virtuous woman' and
presented her with a rich dress covered with plates of
silver, which she disposed of in order to apply the proceeds
to acts of charity."[1]

At the time of Ricci's death in 1610 it seemed likely
that Christianity, or rather an amalgamation of Christianity

---

[1] *China, its State and Prospects*, by W. H. Medhurst, 1838, p. 227 sq.

and Confucianism, would ere long become the religion of China. In 1622, Adam Schall, a German, whose policy was the same as that of Ricci, became the head of the mission in China. Reports of its success reached Europe and evoked the enthusiasm of the other great religious Orders, and in 1631 the first Dominican missionaries arrived. They were followed by the Franciscans, who re-entered China in 1633. Ere many years had elapsed the missionaries attached to these two Orders began to protest in vehement language against the methods employed by the Jesuits. The two special grounds on which they denounced the Jesuit missions were that they allowed their converts to continue " ancestor-worship " and that the words *Tien* and *Shang Ti*, which they had accepted as representing the Christian God, were inadequate and misleading.[1] For some years the three missions worked on side by side.

In 1617 the number of Christians in China was reckoned at 13,000. These had increased in 1650 to 150,000.[2] In 1669, according to a volume [3] which was published in Rome in 1671, the Dominicans had 21 churches, the Franciscans 3, and the Society of Jesus 159.

The number of baptized Christians was then 308,780, of whom 3500 had been baptized by the Franciscan missionaries.

In 1692 the Emperor Kanghsi, who had been educated by Schall, one of the Jesuit missionaries, issued a decree in which he legalized the preaching of the Christian faith throughout the Empire.[4]

[1] For a detailed account of the use of *Tien* and *Shang Ti* in Chinese literature see article by Stanley Smith in *The East and The West*, April 1913. In A.D. 1116 the latter title was given to a Taoist priest by an imperial decree.

[2] These are the figures given by Joannis Adam Schall in a book entitled *Historica relatio de ortu et progressu fidei orthodoxae in regno Chinensi* (published at Ratisbon in 1672), p. 109.

[3] See *Compendiosa narratio de statu Missionis Chinensis ab anno 1581 usque et annum 1669*, oblato Eminentissimis Cardinalibus sacrae Congregationis de propaganda fide. Romae, 1671. (Copy in the S.P.G. library.)

[4] See *Lettres édifiantes et curieuses* (published in Paris, 1781), vol. xvi. Preface, p. xiii.

12

Père Pelisson, writing from Canton on December 9, 1700, states that the Emperor of China had given to the members of the Jesuit Mission a house in the Palace enclosure and had contributed towards the building of a Christian church in Peking [1]

In 1645, Morales, a Dominican missionary, had obtained a bull from Pope Innocent x. which denounced as superstitious and abominable the rites connected with ancestor-worship which the Jesuits had approved. In 1656, however, the Jesuits induced Pope Alexander VII. to declare that they were merely political ceremonies, and that the toleration of them was both prudent and charitable. In 1665, during a temporary persecution, the missionaries belonging to the different Orders made an unsuccessful attempt to arrive at an agreement. In 1693, Maigrot, the Apostolic Vicar of Fukien, decided that *Tien* signified nothing more than the material heavens and that the rites connected with ancestral worship were idolatrous, a decision which was endorsed by a papal decree of Clement xi. in 1704. In 1707, Tournon, the papal legate who had been sent from Rome to China, promulgated this decree. The Emperor, Kanghsi, thereupon banished the legate to Macao, where he died under suspicious circumstances in 1710. The Pope sent yet another legate, who arrived in 1720, and who granted "eight permissions" in connection with the points in dispute, which were, however, afterwards disallowed at Rome.[2]

The expression *Tien Chu* is used to-day by all the Chinese connected with the Roman Missions, and the religion of these Chinese is everywhere spoken of as the *Tien Chu* religion. The same term is used by the members of the Greek Church, by the Anglican Mission in North China, and by the American Episcopal Mission in Mid-China.

Shang Ti (supreme ruler), which was the original

---

[1] *Lettres édifiantes et curieuses*, vol. xvi p. 409.

[2] See *The Jesuits in China and the Legation of Cardinal de Tournon*, by R. O. Jenkins, 1894.

Jesuit term, is used by nearly all the Missions in Central and South China. It is also adopted as the rendering for God in the Anglican Prayer Book in use in North China.

Some American missionaries have adopted the expression *Shên,* a word which is used by the Chinese for spirit and is frequently applied by them to an idol. It is recognized by all that the Chinese language does not contain any satisfactory equivalent for the word God, and that every rendering which has been suggested is open to more or less serious objection.

It is impossible for the impartial student of Missions to take sides either with the Jesuits or with the Franciscans and Dominicans in the long series of controversies which did much to discredit the work of Christian Missions in the eyes of the Chinese. Ricci and some of the earliest of the Jesuit missionaries in China honestly believed that they were following the example set by St. Paul at Athens when they tried to identify the God of the Christians with the Power or Powers held in reverence by the Chinese, and that they were further justified in putting for the time being into the background of their teaching the doctrine of the Atonement. They numbered amongst the members of their Order some of the most devoted and earnest missionaries who have ever visited China. Whilst most students of Christian Missions will agree that the methods which they adopted in China and in other non-Christian lands have been shown by the logic of history to have been unwise, if not actually wrong, they will not hastily condemn the motives that prompted the policy which the Jesuits adopted. The steady decline in the number of Chinese Christians during the eighteenth century was in part due to a decrease of missionary enthusiasm in Europe and in part to persecutions in China. In cases where Christian missionaries appeal for support to rulers of non-Christian countries, the success which they secure as the result of such an appeal is apt to be transitory. A new ruler, prompted by advisers who are not themselves Christians, is easily induced to suspect the Christians of political or revolutionary aims and to persecute them on this plea.   So it was in China, and so it has been in many other countries where Christian missionaries have attained success under the friendly auspices of a ruler who has not himself become a Christian.

Kanghsi, the Emperor who had done much for the Jesuit missionaries, died in 1721.   His successor, Yung-chêng, was persuaded by the Chinese *literati* to persecute the Christians, and in the following year 300 churches were destroyed and 300,000 Christians were left without the ministrations of their Church.   When Chienlung became Emperor in 1736 the persecution became more severe and was continued with occasional intermission for many years.   In 1773 the Jesuit Mission was further weakened by the suppression of its Order by Clement XIV. (It was re-established by Pius. VII in 1814)   In 1815 a special persecution occurred in the province of Szechwan. In 1819 the imperial censor complained of the existence of Christians, but his suggestion that the existing laws against them should be rigorously enforced was rejected by the Emperor on the ground that to do this would create a disturbance.

In Tonking, where Christian missions were carried on by the Jesuits,[1] the persecutions were exceptionally severe, and continued with little intermission from 1720 down to the time of the French occupation in 1883.

In 1840 the Vicariate Apostolic of Eastern Tonking, administered by the Spanish Dominicans, contained 40 native priests and 120,000 "catholics," whilst the Vicariate of Western Tonking, the missionaries in which belonged to the French Society of Foreign Missions, contained 80 native priests and 180,000 "catholics."[2]

According to Marchini's map of Missions presented to

---

[1] The Head of the Jesuit Mission in Tonking during the first year of his work in the province of Tonking, 1692–93, states that he and one companion had baptized 1735 persons and had given the Holy Communion to 12,122.

[2] See *Annals of the Propagation of the Faith* (published in Paris, 1840), vol. 1. p. 419.

the Bishop of Macao in 1810, the Christians in the Chinese Empire then numbered 215,000, the number of missionaries being 23 and of native agents 80. It is difficult to say what reliance can be placed upon these figures, which are at best very rough estimates. At this time the chief missionary agencies were the Propaganda and the Lazarites.

(For a further account of R.C. missions in China see p. 208.)

V. Modern Missions.

A Chinese politician who held one of the highest positions under the new republican government, in answer to the question, When did the Chinese revolutionary movement begin? replied, On the day that Robert Morrison the missionary landed in Canton. The start of Protestant missions in China, notwithstanding the fact that the earliest Protestant missionaries were wholly devoid of political aims, was, in fact, the introduction of a new factor into the political life of China, the far-reaching results of which can now be seen.

Robert Morrison[1] reached China in 1807 as the representative of the London Missionary Society.

Although he was not directly instrumental in winning many converts, his literary work and his skill and perseverance in overcoming what often seemed insuperable difficulties, justify us in regarding him as one of the greatest among Christian missionaries to China.

Robert Morrison was born near Morpeth in 1782 and his youth was spent at Newcastle, where his father was an elder of a Scotch church. After being accepted as a missionary he started for China *via* America and landed at Macao on September 7, 1807. At this time the dislike of foreigners was so strong that it was a capital offence to be found teaching Chinese to a foreigner, and in

[1] For a sketch of his life and work see *Life of Robert Morrison*, by W. J. Townsend.

order to avoid exciting suspicion he lived at first in complete retirement. In 1808 he ceased to be dependent upon the L.M.S., having accepted the post of interpreter to the East India Company. In 1813 he was joined by Mr. and Mrs. Milne, who, however, were not allowed to remain at Macao. Mr. Milne was the author of the description of the Chinese language which has been often quoted, " To acquire Chinese is a work for men with bodies of brass, lungs of steel, heads of oak, eyes of eagles, hearts of apostles, memories of angels and lives of Methusaleh."

Morrison's chief work was of a literary character. In 1813 he published the whole New Testament in a colloquial dialect, and later on he printed, at the expense of the East India Company, his Chinese dictionary, which was of immense use to subsequent missionaries and students of the language. Before his death in 1834 he had translated nearly the whole of the Bible into Chinese and had published in addition a large number of tracts and booklets. It may also be claimed for him that he introduced medical mission work into China, as he established a dispensary over which he placed a qualified Chinese practitioner. The first medical missionary sent from England to China was Dr. Lockhart, who was sent out by the L.M.S. in 1839. The first Chinese to become a Christian as the result of Protestant missions was Tsai Ako, who was baptized by Morrison in 1814 "at a spring of water, issuing from the foot of a lofty hill, by the seaside, away from human observation." During the twenty-five years which followed the arrival of Morrison in China ten baptisms took place, two of the converts being Chinese printers who had worked for Dr. Milne at the Malacca College. This college, which was started by Dr. Milne, was intended partly for the education of Chinese and partly for training European students of Chinese who desired to work in China.

For twenty-seven years, with the exception of his furlough in 1824, Morrison laboured on practically alone at Canton and in the face of almost every possible discouragement. At the time of his death there were only two Protestant missionaries in China, both of whom belonged to the American Board of Missions.

1835–1850.

We shall now refer very briefly to the new missions which were started in China during the next twenty-five years.

The Church Missionary Society sent Mr. E. B. Squire, an officer in the Navy, on a tentative mission to Singapore and Macao in 1837. In 1844 the first two missionaries belonging to this society arrived in China, namely, the Rev. G. Smith (afterwards Bishop of Victoria, Hong-Kong), and the Rev. T. M'Clatchie. The latter started missionary work at Shanghai. In 1848 the Rev. W. A. Russell (afterwards Bishop of North China) and the Rev. R. Cobbold began work in Ningpo, which eventually became one of the centres of the C.M.S. Chekiang Mission (see p. 189).

In 1845 the *English General Baptists* commenced work in Ningpo which was carried on for some years, but was eventually given up.

In 1847 the *English Presbyterian Church* sent the Rev. W. C. Burns as their first missionary to China. He spent some time in Hong-Kong and Canton, and eventually started permanent work in Amoy (see p. 195).

In 1836 the *American Southern Baptist Mission* sent the Rev. Jehu Shuck as a missionary to Macao. In 1842 their mission was moved to Hong-Kong, and during the next six years work was started at Canton and Shanghai.

In 1834 the *American Baptist Missionary Union* sent a missionary to work amongst Chinese in Siam, and in 1842, the year in which Hong-Kong was ceded to England, started work in that town.

In 1835 the *American Protestant Episcopal Church* sent two missionaries to Canton, who retired for a time to Batavia. In 1837 the Rev. W. J. Boone, M.D., joined the mission, which in 1842 was established at Amoy. In 1845, Dr. Boone, who had been consecrated as a bishop, brought out from America a party of nine workers, whereupon the mission was removed to Shanghai. The first convert, who was baptized on Easter Day 1846, was afterwards ordained and was for many years an effective missionary.

In 1842 the *American Presbyterian Mission* (North) sent a missionary to Macao, and during the following eight years opened missions at Ningpo, Amoy and Canton.

In 1847 the *American Methodist Episcopal Mission* sent their first missionary to China, who started work at Foochow.

In 1848 the *American Southern Methodist Mission* sent two missionaries to China.

In 1844 the *American Presbyterian Dutch Reformed Church* started work at Amoy, where, in 1846, a first convert was baptized.

In 1846 the *Rhenish Mission* at Barmen sent out four missionaries, two of whom belonged to the Basel Mission. They reached Hong-Kong in 1847.

It will be seen from the list of missionary societies given above that by the middle of the nineteenth century active interest had been aroused in the work of Chinese Missions in England, America and Germany. When King Frederick William of Prussia was informed by Bunsen that experienced men in England doubted the possibility of doing missionary work in China, he "wrote a letter of sixteen pages, urging Bunsen to arouse the Bishops and clergy of the Church of England to more vigorous action for the evangelization of China." [1]

By 1850 there were at least a dozen Anglican and Protestant missionary societies at work in China. In most cases these societies had but recently commenced work, and it is doubtful whether the whole number of

[1] See "Private Journal," October 11, 1850, quoted in *History of the C.M.S.*, i. 468.

Christian converts connected with these missions exceeded a hundred. Missionary work, moreover, hardly extended beyond the five treaty ports, Canton, Amoy, Shanghai, Ningpo and Foochow, which were declared open to foreigners by the Treaty of Nanking in 1842.

1850–1875.

On Good Friday, 1850, the first English bishop (Dr. George Smith) arrived at Hong-Kong accompanied by a party of C.M.S. missionaries. Work was started by the C.M.S. in the great city of Foochow in May 1850, and in 1851 the first five converts in connection with the C.M.S. were baptized, two at Ningpo and three (blind men) at Shanghai. By the end of 1855 the number of converts at Ningpo had increased to sixty. While Bishop Smith was delivering his first charge, the church at Shanghai in which he was speaking was struck by a cannon ball fired by the Taipings, the rebellion raised by whom had a direct bearing upon the progress of the missions in China.

No rebellion that has taken place for centuries has been so prolific in massacres and nameless atrocities; nevertheless, as we look back, after an interval of sixty years, we are forced to admit that General Gordon's successful repression of the Taiping rebellion, and the continuance of the Manchu dynasty which it involved and on behalf of which he fought, put back the clock of China's progress for at least several decades.

The instigator of the Taiping revolt, Hung Hsiuch'üan, came under the influence of a Christian missionary (who was probably Morrison) at Canton in 1833. In 1837 he declared that he had seen a vision in which he had received a divine command to destroy idolatry, and to put an end to the Manchu dynasty. In 1853 he and his followers stormed and captured the great city of Nanking. When the British Plenipotentiary went up to Nanking, his boat encountered "hundreds of colossal images of Buddha and various gods and goddesses, broken and defaced, floating down the river." It is not possible here to describe the course of the Taiping revolt [1] Suffice it to say that the movement, the leaders of which were at first inspired by good motives, degenerated into a rebellion which devastated the fairest provinces of China and resulted in the massacre of millions of people. The rebellion, which began in 1850, ended with the capture of Nanking in 1864.

After describing the course of the Taiping rebellion, Dr. Norris (now Bishop in North China) writes:

" It is argued with much apparent reason that Christian missions may aim at the conversion of Chinese individuals, may found little Christian communities in every province of the Empire, may perhaps in time meet with such success that those communities will be mainly self-supporting and self-governing; but that the idea of Christianity ever really permeating China, as much, for example, as it permeated Western Europe in the Middle Ages, or as it permeates European nations to-day, is a wild and impossible dream which will require the lapse of several centuries before it can approach fulfilment. . . . Surely the history of the Taiping movement has a warning for the critic, no less than a real encouragement for ourselves. Granted that it was not in the end successful, granted that it won its way by methods of which a truer Christianity would be ashamed, it remains true that a movement which took shape originally in the brain of a single man . . . which made no apparent stir for several years, ran like wildfire when once it started. Spreading from district to district, from province to province, it speedily established itself from Canton to Nanking, and from thence made a great effort, not far short of success, to reach Peking itself. . . . The Church of Christ, whatever her shortcomings, has something better to offer than the religion of the Taiping Wang . . . it may be that for the present, and for years to come, she will make no apparent stir; but at least she is justified in claiming that in the light of history it is not incredible that Christianity should one day run like wildfire over China, until the whole nation has been won for Christ." [2]

[1] For specimens of its proclamations and literature see *History of the C.M.S.*, ii. 297 ff.
[2] *China*, by F. L. Norris, pp. 48 squ.

In 1842 the total number of communicants unconnected with the Roman Missions was 6, by 1855 these had increased to 500, and by 1860 to about 1000. In 1877 [1] the number of Christian converts was reckoned at 13,000, and the total number of European missionaries at 473, of whom 228 were connected with British, and 212 with American societies. We have already mentioned the names of the societies which were represented in China prior to 1850. There are now over 100 missionary societies, large and small, at work in China. It may be well to note the dates at which some of the larger societies began their work there. The *Wesleyan Methodist Missionary Society* entered China in 1852, the *United Presbyterian Mission* (to Manchuria) in 1872, the *Church of Scotland Mission* in 1877, the *Society for the Propagation of the Gospel* sent two men to Peking in 1863, but did not commence regular work in China till 1874. The society which supports more missionaries in China than any other, i.e. *The China Inland Mission*, was founded in 1865 by the Rev. Hudson Taylor, who himself began work in China in 1853. In 1875 the C.I.M. was carrying on work in fifty stations scattered over five provinces (see p. 192).

In few other countries have the pioneer missionaries met with so many discouragements and waited so long to see visible results from their labours. This fact is specially significant, as the progress of Christianity in China during recent years bids fair to outdo the progress in any other large non-Christian country. The experience of the C.M.S. missionaries in Foochow may be quoted as typical of that which has been repeated in many other places. This society commenced work in the city of Foochow in 1850. After ten years had elapsed, " without a single conversion, or the prospect of such a thing," the committee at home discussed the desirability of withdrawing this mission. In the following year, that is after eleven years of earnest, devoted work, the first convert was baptized, who was the first-fruits of a mission which has since attained most encouraging results (see p. 189).

[1] We have not been able to secure the exact statistics for 1875.

It is impossible to sketch in detail the work of the hundred and more European and American missionary societies which are now represented in China, but it will be worth while to give a very few statistics which will show how far the various denominations are represented. The figures relate to the year 1913.

	Foreign Missionaries.	Chinese Workers.	Communicants or Full Members.
Anglican . . .	626	1,814	28,317 [5]
Presbyterian . .	898	3,831	59,884
Methodist . .	753	4,527	44,844
Baptist . . .	567	1,527	25,693
Lutheran [1] . .	503	1,551	24,419
Congregationalist [2] .	263	1,244	17,691
China Inland Mission [3]	1,076	1,551	31,243
Miscellaneous . .	500	1,834	3,212
Total .	5,186	17,879 [4]	235,303

[1] Under Lutheran are included most of the German, Swiss, Norwegian, Scandinavian and Swedish missions.
[2] Under Congregationalist are included the L.M.S. and the A.B.C.F.M.
[3] These returns include those of twelve continental societies which are affiliated to the C.I.M.
[4] These returns include school teachers as well as church workers.
[5] These statistics are for 1912.

Anglican Missions.

On April 26, 1912, the representatives of the eleven Anglican dioceses in China decided to form one united Church, the title of which should be Chung Hua Shêng Kung Hui (pronounced Joong Hwa Shung Goong Hway). Its constitution and organization correspond with those of the Nippon sei Kokwai of Japan. It is founded upon the recognition of the Lambeth quadrilateral, i.e. the historic episcopate, two sacraments, two creeds, and the acceptance of the Old and New Testaments. The first act of the synod of the new Church was to form a Board of Missions, which is to present at its next meeting, in 1915, a report proposing that the eleven united dioceses should combine to send a mission to some untouched part of China and that this mission should have a Chinese bishop as its leader.

The Anglican missions are supported by the C.M.S. in Central and Southern China, by the S.P.G. and the Canadian Church in North China, and by the Protestant Episcopal Church of America in Central China.

The dioceses in which the missions of the *Church Missionary Society* are situated are those of Victoria (Hong-Kong), Chekiang, Western China, Fukien and Hunan.

Hong-Kong (1849). Since 1900 the Chinese Christians have undertaken the entire pecuniary responsibility for the support of their pastors and the upkeep of their churches in the city of Hong-Kong. A church hostel for undergraduates at the new Hong-Kong University was opened at the same time as the university in 1912. The mission work of the Church on the mainland is carried on from Canton and Pakhoi. At Canton a training college was opened in 1912 ; at Pakhoi there are hospitals for lepers and other patients.

Chekiang, formerly part of Mid-China (1872). The missionary work centres round Ningpo, Hangchow, Taichow, Chuki and Shaohing. There is a theological college and normal school at Ningpo, an Anglo-Chinese school at Shaohing, and a girls' high school at Hangchow. The C.M.S. supports three hospitals in this diocese. Its staff includes 24 Chinese clergy.

The diocese of *Western China* (1895) is practically co-extensive with the province of Szechwan, and the work is chiefly of an evangelistic character. There is a diocesan training college at Paoning, a church hostel in connection with the new university at Chêngtu and a medical mission at Mienchu. In this diocese several of the Anglican missionaries are supported by the C.I.M. The bishop and the missionaries wear Chinese dress.

Fukien (1906). Foochow, which is the chief centre of work, was occupied in 1850, and eleven years passed before the first convert was baptized (see p. 187). The missionary institutions in Foochow include a hospital and a Union medical college and a school for the blind. The diocesan staff includes 18 Chinese clergy. Work amongst lepers is carried on at five centres. Dublin University supports a mission in this diocese in connection with the C.M.S.

Kwangsi and Hunan (1909). Work is carried on at Siangtan, Kueilinfu, Yungchow and Hengchow.

Amongst the missionaries who have worked in connection with the C.M.S. in China should specially be mentioned the Rev. George E. Moule, who went out to China in 1858 and was Bishop in Mid-China 1880–1907, and Archdeacon J. R. Wolfe, the pioneer of the Fukien Mission.

The *Society for the Propagation of the Gospel* began work in China in 1863, but its work was interrupted and was not definitely started till 1874, when the Rev. C. P. Scott and a companion were sent to Chefoo. Mr. Scott became the Bishop of *North China* in 1880 and continued as bishop till his resignation in 1913. The present bishop, Dr. Frank Norris, by the influence which he exerted over the Chinese Christians in Peking, was largely instrumental in preserving the European Legations during the Boxer revolution in 1900, till they were relieved by the allied forces. With the help of the Pan-Anglican grant a large school has been opened in Peking. The society also shares in the work of the Union medical college.

The diocese of *Shantung* (1903) includes the province of the same name. There is a college at Chefoo. Other centres are at Pingyin and Taianfu. The medical work of the university is at Chinanfu and the Arts College at Weihsien. It is proposed to remove the latter also to Chinanfu. A mission hospital has been established at Yenchowfu, near the birthplace of Confucius.

Three missionaries in connection with the S.P.G. were martyred during the Boxer outbreak, namely, S. M. W. Brooks, C. Robinson and H. V. Norman. In 1912 the Rev. Frederick Day was murdered by Chinese soldiers near Paotingfu.

The *Protestant Episcopal Church of America* supports missions in the Yangtse Valley at Shanghai, and in the district of Hankow and Wuchang. This mission has from the first afforded an instructive object-lesson of the good results to be attained by concentrating on a few strategic positions instead of attempting to spread its influence over a wide area. In 1844 the Rev. W. S. Boone was consecrated as bishop of the missionary district of Shanghai. No missionary colleges have exercised a wider influence in China than St. John's University College, which was founded by Bishop Schereschewsky in 1872 at Shanghai, and Boone University College at Wuchang, which was started (as a school) in 1871. At the latter college several of those who acted as leaders in the last Chinese revolution received their education. At Wuchang are situated also the Boone Medical and Divinity schools.

The bishoprics, or rather missionary districts, supported by this mission are those of Shanghai (1844), Hankow (1901) and Anking (1911). In the missionary district of *Shanghai*, which consists of the province of Kiangsu, the chief centres of work, apart from Shanghai, are Soochow, Wusih, Kiating, Yangchow and Zangzok. In the missionary district of *Hankow*, which includes the provinces of Hupeh and Hunan, the chief centres are Hankow and Wuchang. In the missionary district of *Anking* (formerly Wuhu), which comprises the province of Anhwei and that part of Kiangsi which lies north of lat. 28°, the chief centres of work are Wuhu and Anking in the Anhwei province, and Kiukiang and Nanchang in the province of Kiangsi.

Amongst the missionaries who have been members of this mission, the name of Bishop Schereschewsky is deserving of special mention. He was a Russian Jew who was converted in America, and after working as a missionary in Peking for some years, was eventually consecrated as Bishop of Shanghai (1877). For the last twenty-five years of his life he was paralyzed and unable to speak distinctly, and used a typewriter which he worked with two fingers. He translated the whole Bible and the Prayer Book into literary Chinese (Wenli) and the Old Testament into Mandarin. After he became paralyzed he relinquished the duties of the bishopric in 1884, but he continued to work in the cause of missions till his death in 1906.

In 1909 the Church of England in Canada undertook to support a bishop and a staff of missionaries in the province of *Honan*. The centre of the work, which is still in a pioneer stage, is at Kaifêng.

Protestant Missions.

The founder of the *China Inland Mission*, the Rev. J. Hudson Taylor, M.R.C.S., went to China in 1853 in connection with the Chinese Evangelization Society. Forced by ill-health to return in 1860, he spent several years in pleading the cause of China, and in 1865 he organized the China Inland Mission. One of its distinctive rules has been that its workers receive no fixed salaries and are not authorized to solicit funds on its behalf. In 1866 Dr. Taylor returned to China accompanied by the first fifteen members of the mission staff. For the first twenty years the work of this mission was largely of a pioneer character. In 1876 it started work in the provinces of Shansi, Shensi and Kansu, and in 1877 in Szechwan, Yunnan and Kweichow. Since then its field of operations has steadily expanded until it has now work at 227 centres situated in eighteen provinces of China and in Chinese Turkestan. In 1884 seven Cambridge graduates, who included amongst their number the captain of the cricket eleven (C. T. Studd) and the stroke of the university boat (Stanley Smith), joined the mission staff, and their departure for China helped to make known to a wide circle the needs of the Chinese and the good work which the C.I.M. had already accomplished on their behalf. In 1876 the mission began to send out unmarried women as missionaries, and by 1881 work amongst Chinese women had been started in six of the inland provinces. The income of the

mission in 1913 was £91,000, of which £51,000 was
received in England. Its European and American staff
in China is 988 (including wives), of whom 580 are
women. Its list of martyrs contains 58 names. Its
missionaries belong to various denominations, those attached
to each denomination being grouped together. In Western
China its members, who belong to the Church of England,
are superintended by Bishop Cassels.

Amongst the ranks of its workers have been many the
record of whose lives, if it could be given, would add a
new page to the story of missionary heroism. It is true
that criticisms have from time to time been made that this
society, in its anxiety to start new centres and occupy new
provinces, has sent out men and women whose chief qualification was their intense desire to become missionaries, but
who had given no evidence that they were able to act as
Christian teachers under the extremely difficult conditions
under which their work in China would have to be carried
on. These criticisms, which have sometimes been made by
those who knew China well and were anxious to promote
missions to the Chinese, are to some extent justified, but
the fact that enthusiasm has outrun knowledge and that
the methods adopted have been proved by experience to
be faulty, must not be allowed to diminish our appreciation
of the great work which has been accomplished by this
society. The mission has established training homes in
China for men and women missionaries, where newly
arrived recruits can study the Chinese language and receive
training to prepare them for their future work.

The work of the *London Missionary Society* (1807) is
carried on in North China, Central China, Shanghai and
district, Amoy and district, and in Canton province. Its
European staff includes 43 missionaries, in addition to 25
doctors who superintend twenty-six hospitals. The number
of its full church members is about 10,000. In many
cases its congregations have become entirely self-supporting
and self-governed, and carry on missionary work on their
own initiative. In Peking the L.M.S. has a large medical

college in which teaching is given by members of all the missions in that city except the Roman Catholics. Its most famous institution is the Anglo-Chinese College at Tientsin, of which Dr. S. Lavington Hart was the founder and first Principal. Its list of missionaries includes the names of Morrison, Milne, Medhurst, Lockhart, Legge, Griffith John and Gilmour. We have already referred to the work done by the first three. Dr. James Legge (1815–97) was appointed in 1840 to take charge of the Anglo-Chinese College at Malacca, which had been founded by Dr. Morrison and Dr. Milne, and was afterwards moved to Hong-Kong. In 1876 he was appointed Professor of Chinese Language and Literature at Oxford, and was the translator into English of all the Chinese Classics. Dr. Griffith John (1831–1912) spent the greater part of his life at Hankow. His writings in Chinese are known all over China. (For reference to the work of James Gilmour see p. 215.)

Its first woman missionary was appointed to China in 1868.

The *American Board of Commissioners for Foreign Missions* (1847) supports work in the city and neighbourhood of Foochow. In this city it has a theological seminary which is jointly supported by the C.M.S. and the A.M.E.C. It also helps to support a Union medical training college in conjunction with the C.M.S. and the Methodists.

In Peking it helps to support a Union men and women's medical college, a Union women's college and a Union theological college Its roll of missionaries includes the name of Dr. Peter Parker, who was the first regular medical missionary to China in modern times.

The Government officials in the province of Shansi have offered to place all the Government schools in eight counties, containing a population of 4,000,000, under the superintendence of the A.B.C.F.M. missionaries, and the society has sent additional missionaries to take charge of the schools.

The chief centres of the *Presbyterian Church of England Mission* (1847) are at Amoy, Swatow and Tainan in Formosa. The mission supports 14 hospitals, 4 theological colleges and a large number of schools. It has 50 ordained Chinese ministers and about 12,000 communicant members. Its most famous missionary was Rev. W. C. Burns (1815—68), who laboured chiefly at Amoy and Swatow. He became a good Chinese scholar, and translated *The Pilgrim's Progress* and other books into Chinese.

The *Board of Foreign Missions of the Presbyterian Church in the U.S.A.*, which began work in China in 1844, has over 300 missionaries, of whom 90 are ordained clergy and 40 are medical missionaries. It has eight chief centres situated in the provinces of Chihli, Shantung, Kiangsu, Chekiang, Anhwei, Hunan, Kwangtung and the island of Hainan. It has a staff of over 1000 Chinese preachers and teachers, 126 organized churches with more than 20,000 communicants. Its 69 hospitals and dispensaries treat about 200,000 cases each year. Its educational institutions include the Shantung Union University, the University of Nanking, the college, medical school and theological seminary in Peking and the theological seminary in Nanking, in all of which it works in co-operation with other missionary organizations.

Amongst those who have served on its staff may be mentioned the names of John G. Kerr, M.D., John L. Nevius, C. W. Mateer and W. A. P. Martin. Dr. Nevius laboured in China from 1854 to 1893 and did much useful translation work. Dr. Martin, who is the author of a number of books in Chinese, was President of the Imperial University.

The various Presbyterian missions in China have taken steps in view of constituting an independent Chinese Presbyterian Church. The Churches represented at the Council which was held at Chinanfu in 1914 in view of organizing this Church were the English, Scotch, Irish, Canadian, Dutch Reformed, Northern and Southern (U.S.A.)

Presbyterians. The converts connected with these missions number over 60,000 adult Church members.

The *Wesleyan Methodist Missionary Society* (1852) supports work in the central portion of the Kwangtung province and in the adjoining Kwangsi province. It has hospitals at Fatshan and Wuchow and a home for lepers at the latter place. Farther north in the Wuchang district it has 4 hospitals. At Wuchang itself it has a college, high school and theological institution. In the Hunan district it supports 2 hospitals and a theological school. Its roll of missionaries includes the name of the Rev. David Hill (1840–96). He worked chiefly at Hankow, and died of typhus whilst administering famine relief. He was instrumental in the conversion of Pastor Hsi, a well-known Chinese missionary connected with the C.I.M.

The *English Baptist Mission* (1859) carries on work in the provinces of Shantung, Shansi and Shensi. It has a European staff of 52 men and 52 women who work at nineteen chief stations. Its communicant members number about 6000. The mission supports 12 medical missionaries and 6 hospitals.

In Shantung the mission has started a Christian University, which is carried on partly by the B.M.S. and partly by the American Presbyterians. It consists of a theological college and normal school at Chingchoufu with 200 students, rather more than half of whom are Baptists; an arts college at Weihsien with 350 students, and a medical college and hospital in Chinanfu, which is the capital of the province. The S.P.G. has opened a hostel for its students at Weihsien who are attending the university. In the course of a revival which took place in November 1909, 100 of the students joined the Volunteer Missionary Band and have since been actively engaged in evangelistic work.

One of the missionaries belonging to the B.M.S. is Dr. Timothy Richard, who was the first Chancellor of the Imperial University established by the Chinese Government of Shansi after the Boxer rising in 1900. He has contributed more than any other missionary towards the creation of a Chinese Christian literature.

The *Baptist Foreign Mission Society* (U.S.A.) (1836) supports work in South, West and East China. In conjunction with the Southern Baptist Convention Mission it supports a large college and seminary at Shanghai. It shares in the support of the universities of Nanking and Chêngtu in West China.

Other societies which support a large amount of work in China are (the numbers in brackets represent the foreign staff)—The Irish Presbyterian Church Mission (44), The Canadian Presbyterian Mission (80), The Berlin (59), The Basel (72), and The Swedish Missionary Societies (51), The Christian and Missionary Alliance, U.S.A. (87), The Presbyterian Church, South, U.S.A. (129), and the International Y.M.C.A. (75).

Amongst missionary organizations should be mentioned the Christian Literature Society for China, which by its translations and by its books composed in Chinese has done much to spread a knowledge of Christian literature throughout China.

The Young Men's Christian Association is exerting a wide influence in many different parts of China, and several Chinese who have recently become prominent politicians have been associated with it. At its national convention held in Peking in 1912 requests were received from several provincial governors asking that branches of the Association might be formed in their provinces. The Y.M.C.A. is likely to exercise an increasing influence in the near future.

In China, as in all other non-Christian countries, the work of missions has been greatly helped by the circulation of the Scriptures by the Bible Societies of England, Scotland and America. The B. and F. B. Society alone circulated in 1913 considerably over two million portions of the Bible in various Chinese versions.

We do not propose to trace the statistical advance of the 104 missionary societies which are now working in

China, nor to illustrate by tables the gradual spread of their work throughout the different provinces. In each of its twenty-one provinces mission stations are now to be found, but in several of them the proportion of missionaries to the population is less than 1 to 200,000.

The increase in the number of Christians in China which has taken place since the beginning of this century has been proportionately more rapid than at any previous period within recent times. During the first ten years of this century the number of European missionaries (which is now 5186) increased 50 per cent., the number of Chinese missionaries still more rapidly, and the number of Christian adherents was more than doubled.

The rapid increase during recent years is undoubtedly connected with the persecutions to which the Christians have been exposed.

There are few, if any other, instances in Christian history in which an attempt to exterminate the Christians over a wide area has resulted in so immediate and large an increase in their number and in such a strengthening and expansion of the Christian Church. The movement organized by the Boxers in 1900 was directed against Europeans and against all Chinese Christians, inasmuch as these were supposed to be in sympathy with foreigners. The Chinese Christians were in many instances offered their lives if they would abjure their religion, but despite the cruel tortures to which they were subjected comparatively few recanted and about 16,000 died a martyr's death. Of Europeans there were killed 135 Anglican and Protestant missionaries and 53 children, 35 R.C. priests and 9 R.C. sisters. Had it not been for the efforts of Yüan Shihkai and some other Chinese viceroys the massacres might have spread over the whole Chinese Empire.

Statistics.

The following table will give some idea of the rapidity with which the Anglican and Protestant missions developed

during the ten years which followed the Boxer persecution :—

Year.	Ordained Missionaries	Laymen other than Doctors.	Women.[1]	Men Doctors.	Women Doctors.	Total of European Missionaries	Chinese Workers.	Adherents.
1900 . .	610	416	1518	162	79	2785	6,388	204,672
1910 . .	910	582	2347	251	114	4175	12,082	469,896

[1] Including wives of missionaries.

The number of Christian adherents, apart from those
connected with R.C. missions, were in 1860 about 1000 ; in
1877, 13,000 ; in 1890, 37,000 ; in 1900, over 200,000 ;
and in 1910, about 470,000.

At the end of 1913 the number of full members of
Christian Churches was returned as 235,303, the number
under Christian instruction as 59,106, and the "total
Christian constituency" as 356,209. The last figure does
not include those who are merely "adherents."

The following table illustrates the progress made by
Anglican and Protestant missionary societies in China
between 1876 and 1913 :—

Year.	Foreign Missionaries, including wives.	Ordained Church Pastors.	Chinese Mission-Workers (Men).	Bible-Women.	Chinese Christian School Teachers, Male and Female.	No. of Pupils in Schools, Boys and Girls	No. of Communicants or Full Members.	No. of Inquirers.
1876	473	73	511	90	290	5,686	13,035	No returns
1895	1324	252	1157	326	1333	21,353	55,093	12,495
1905	3445	345	5722 (including lay preachers)	897	2583	57,683	178,251[1]	78,528
1913	5186	650	6851	2270	6436	118,650	235,303	356,209

[1] The returns for 1905 include some baptized children.

Comparing the progress of Anglican and Protestant missions in India and China between 1900 and 1910, we note that whilst the increase in India was at the rate of 45 per cent. the increase in China was at the rate of 129 per cent. Within the memory of one or two missionaries still living the Christians connected with these missions increased from less than 200 (in 1860) to nearly half a million (1912). During the same period (1900–10) the baptized Christians connected with the Roman Catholic missions increased from about 762,000 to 1,363,000, the increase being at the rate of about 70 per cent. As far as we can appraise the prospect of Christian missions in China by the use of missionary statistics, it appears to be singularly encouraging. In the case of China, however, more than in the case of other countries, we need to remember that the evangelistic work which is being done in different parts is very unequal in character. A considerable number of the missionaries now working in China have been sent there by small local associations in America and have received no training to prepare them for their work. The result has been that European visitors to China have had occasion to point out that their methods of work would admit of great improvement, and that there was reason to fear that some of those who had been moved to go forth as missionaries had mistaken their vocation.

Nevertheless, after making all deductions in view of the inefficiency of some missionaries, and of some of the societies now working in China, there is no reasonable doubt that the Christianization of China is rapidly coming within the sphere of practical politics. The one thing certain in regard to its future is that within a very few years the greater part of its population will come under the influence of Western education. It depends upon the peoples of England and America whether the Western education, which is about to sweep the country, will tell for or against the spread of the Christian faith, and whether at the close of this century China will be mainly Christian

or mainly agnostic. The peoples of China are not instinctively religious, as are the peoples of India, and if China
does not become Christian it may long remain content
without any form of vital religion. Very few of the
Chinese Christians belong to the literary classes. This has
been largely due to the fact that their contempt for
Western knowledge has led them to despise what they
regarded as a Western religion. But, as the reception
which Dr. Mott received from tens of thousands of Chinese
students in 1913 has shown, a great change has come over
the attitude of the literary classes.[1] A unique opportunity
now exists for establishing Christian universities and for
developing higher education under Christian auspices, and
upon the use which is made of this opportunity will depend
the attitude of the learned classes towards the Christian
faith. In six years, 1905–11, the number of students in
the one province of Chihli rose from 8000 to 230,000, and
what has happened in this province is happening throughout the length and breadth of China. A recent visitor to
China saw in course of building the new normal school at
Canton, which was rising in the very same compound in
which stood the ruins of the stalls used for the old Chinese
examinations. In this new school 800 teachers are now
being trained. Yuan Shihkai, who is now President, bore
emphatic testimony to the good work done by Christian
missionaries at the time of the Boxer riots, and his sons
were educated at a missionary school in China and afterwards at a school in England.

University Colleges in China.

Boone University, which was founded at Wuchang in
1871 and was incorporated (in the U.S.A.) as a university

[1] An equally remarkable series of meetings was held by Mr. Sherwood
Eddy in 1914 for Government students and officials. In seven cities, the
meetings in which averaged an attendance of 3000, there were 7000
"enquirers," who included many Government officials and scholars. A
large number of women students have also been reached.

in 1909, had about 400 students previous to the Revolution. It and *St. John's College, Shanghai* (see p. 191), are under the control of the American Church Mission.

The *University of Nanking*, which began work in 1910, represents the union of the educational work in Nanking of the Presbyterian Mission, the A.M.E.C. and the Foreign Christian Missionary Society. It is the property of a Board of Trustees elected by these societies. Its students number about 500.

Shantung Christian University. This was formed by the English Baptist and American Presbyterian Missions. The Anglican Mission (S.P.G.) has also a representative on its teaching staff, and is building a hostel for its students in attendance at the university. The college of arts and science at Weihsien, the normal and theological college at Chingchowfu and the medical college at Chinanfu are to be united in the university buildings to be erected at Chinanfu. In the three colleges there are about 600 students.

Peking University College belongs to the A.M.E.C. and has 81 students in the "collegiate department." The Union Medical College, which is supported by several missionary societies, is uniting with this college in order to form a university of Peking.

Canton Christian College, which has about 200 students, represents the union of several American missionary agencies in the neighbourhood of Canton.

As a result of the formation of the West China Christian Educational Union there has been created the *West China Union University*, in which five missionary societies participate. A site for this university was purchased outside Chêngtu in 1908. The various societies which it represents propose to establish colleges or hostels in which their students in attendance at the university will reside.

A *Foochow Christian University* has been organized and a constitution adopted. It is supported by the following missionary societies : C.M.S., A.M.E.C., A.B.C.F.M., E.P.M. and L.M.S.

The Shansi University, which was for ten years under

foreign supervision, has not been a help to the cause of missions. Until the recent Revolution it was rendered practically impossible for Christian students to enter it.

An important step towards *Christian unity in China* was taken by the National Conference which met under the chairmanship of Dr. Mott in 1913. The following formed part of the resolutions passed by this Conference, which represented nearly all the chief Anglican and Protestant missions in China :—

A. "In order to do all that is possible to manifest the unity which already exists among all faithful Christians in China and to present ourselves in the face of the great mass of Chinese non-Christian people as one brotherhood with one common name, this Conference suggests as the most suitable name for this purpose . . . The Christian Church in China.

B. "As steps towards unity this Conference urges upon the Churches: 1. The uniting of Churches of similar ecclesiastical order planted in China by different missions. 2. The organic union of Churches which already enjoy intercommunication in any particular area, large or small. 3. Federation, local and provincial, of all Churches willing to co-operate in the extension of the Kingdom of God. 4. The formation of a National Council of the Churches."

The constitution of the Chung Hua Shêng Kung Hui (see p. 188) in 1912 by the representatives of the Anglican missions anticipated, as far as these missions were concerned, the proposal B. 1.

In no part of the great mission field have *medical missions* done so much to break down opposition and to commend the Christian faith as in China. At the end of 1913 there were 300 men and 135 women doctors connected with missionary societies. In addition to these who are Europeans or Americans, there were 94 qualified Chinese doctors and over 10,000 Chinese medical students. There are about 264 mission hospitals in China, and the number of in-patients treated in 1913 was 126,788 and of out-patients 2,129,774. (For a further reference to the development of medical missions in China see p. 199.)

Reference should be made to the *Schools for the Blind* which have been started by various missions. In Europe the proportion of blind to seeing is about 1 in 1500, in India it is about 1 in 500, and in China about 1 in 400. The total number of blind is about 1,000,000. Many of the blind have been taught to read by the system invented by the Rev. W. H. Murray of Peking, and industrial work has been taught in most of the schools.

Work amongst Women. — The various missionary societies have been gradually extending and developing their work amongst Chinese women, but there is still much to be accomplished in order to bring it up to the level of the work which has been done amongst men. The following are extracts from the "findings" of the National Conference over which Dr. Mott presided in 1913 :—

"The present conditions present an unparalleled opportunity for widespread and aggressive evangelization. . . . There are hundreds of walled cities and thousands of towns in China in which the women are absolutely unreached as yet. . . . The number of women missionaries is hopelessly inadequate. . . . We favour the speedy establishment of more and better primary schools for girls, especially in country districts. . . . We must increase our educational work in quantity, so that we can provide the teachers needed in missionary schools and respond to calls for help from non-Christian schools. We must increase it in quality, and fit our graduates for college and training schools to investigate social and industrial problems, to study religious questions and in every way to be leaders of Chinese women in the regeneration of China."

The general outlook is certainly more encouraging than it has been at any previous time. Thus a C.M.S. missionary in Mid-China writes :

"One of the changes wrought in the country by the Revolution is said to be that while in the past it has always been difficult to get any one to look after the sick, quite a number of educated women are now desirous of undertaking the work. Five women, all belonging to literary families, were under training at Foochow, and four of them did well in an examination in elementary physiology and general nursing." [1]

Early in 1914 two Chinese women received diplomas from the Union Medical College in Peking. They were the first women in North China to become qualified as doctors.

The importance of the training of China's women, to which the "findings" of the Conference bear witness, is accentuated by the past history of Christian missions in this country. The failure of the Christian Church to establish permanent Christian communities in China may be traced, at least in part, to the failure of its missionaries to influence the lives of its women. Had the Nestorians, the Franciscans or the Jesuits been able to appeal to China's women and to create Christian homes, it is inconceivable that the after results of their work, carried on during such long periods and with such apparent success, should now be so far to seek.

A Student Volunteer Movement has been started, the members of which pledge themselves to prepare to enter the Christian Ministry. They are for the most part college students who have the prospect of good secular positions with large salaries on the completion of their college course. Six hundred members have already been enrolled and 100 have already begun their theological training. In fifteen of the chief theological training schools in China there are 450 Chinese who are preparing for ordination.

The total number of Anglican and Protestant foreign missionary workers in China is about 5200. This represents one man or woman worker to each 75,000 of the Chinese.

Although Christian mission centres are widely scattered throughout China, there are still large districts in which very little work is being carried on. The provinces of Yunnan, Kwangsi, Kweichow and Kansu are largely unoccupied by representatives of any missionary society.

[1] *China Mission Year Book*, 1914, p. 193.

In the provinces and dependencies of China there are 552 centres from which missionary work over the surrounding district is organized, but in China proper, the population of the provinces and districts in which hardly any missionary work has as yet been attempted amounts to 40,000,000, and beyond these there lie Mongolia, Turkestan and Tibet. In one county in the province of Shensi, which includes 900 walled villages, the only non-Roman missionaries are one man and his wife belonging to the C.I.M.

An Appeal for Prayer.—No event has served to impress the general public with the progress attained by missionary propaganda in China more than the official request which was made by the acting Chinese Government for the prayers of its Christian subjects on Sunday, April 27, 1913. A few days prior to this date telegrams were sent to the leaders of Christian Churches asking that special prayers should be offered on behalf of the Chinese nation, and to provincial governors and other high officials directing them to attend the Christian services. The suggestion apparently originated with the Christians, of whom sixty were reported to have been members of the first Chinese parliament, and was perhaps adopted by the Government authorities partly in the hope of securing the goodwill of the nations of the West. The day of prayer was widely observed in England and in America as well as in China, and its observance helped to bring home to many the rapid progress which Christianity in China had made during recent years.

It was a happy coincidence that within a fortnight of the day appointed for prayer by the Chinese Government, the House of Commons in England was officially informed that the exportation of Indian opium to China, which had done so much to retard missionary work in China, had finally ceased

We have not space to do more than allude to the discussions which have from time to time been raised in regard to the attitude which missionaries ought to take towards what is usually described as "ancestor-worship." In deciding what attitude he ought to adopt, the missionary cannot afford to forget the lesson taught by the experience of the past. The policy adopted by the R.C. missionaries in regard to the maintenance of ancestor-worship has been fraught with disaster, and has tended more than any other action on their part to produce a superficial conversion of character which must hinder rather than hasten the true evangelization of China. On the other hand, the missionary who knows anything of the early history of his religion cannot fail to remember how helpful and inspiring memorial services for the dead have been, especially in countries where Christians have formed a small minority of the population, and how incomplete is the presentation of Christianity which does not lay emphasis upon the indissoluble connection which exists between those who are striving to live the Christ-life here and those who are with Christ in the life into which they have passed. There is no problem raised by missionary work in the Far East on which it is more difficult to formulate a definite policy and which at the same time presses so urgently for a solution.

In trying to appraise the prospect of the missionary appeal in China to-day we need to take into consideration the distinctive features of the Chinese character.

The writer of the section of the Edinburgh Conference Reports which dealt with Christian Missions in China, after summarizing the contents of the reports from missionaries in the field, writes:

" While they (the Chinese) possess certain traits which are inimical to the Gospel, those which promise most as allies to the propagation of truth are the following: love of peace and a high regard for law; absence of all caste distinctions and the prevalence of a democratic spirit; respect for superiors, whether in age, position or intellect; unusual docility and imitativeness; domination by the historic instinct to such an extent that the past is not only reverenced but is a wholesome check upon ill-considered innovations in belief and practice; a genius for labour, and

thrift in making provision for the future ; a mental capacity
and willingness to apply the mind unremittingly to study
which may one day make them the greatest students in the
world ; a perpetual emphasis of reason . . . ; a suavity and
tact that will meet any hard situation and win unexpected
victory from apparent defeat ; a talent for organization
which has made the Chinese past-masters in combinations,
guilds, and societies of all sorts ; a sense of responsibility
which is based on a high ideal of the duties of kinship ;
an economy which will one day make the most out of every
Christian resource ; and great susceptibility to the influence
of a strong personality, be it the missionary or the Master
whom he is trying to imitate. Men of such traits have
already made superb preachers and teachers, as well as
most consistent Christians."[1]

The author of a recently published work entitled
Méthode de l'Apostolat moderne en Chine, after a survey of
the difficulties which missionaries encounter who work
among the Chinese, sums up his impressions of the
Chinese character in words that partly supplement and
partly contradict the opinion which we have just quoted.
He writes :

" Les phénomènes bien caractéristiques de l'affaiblissement
de la volonté chez les Chinois : manque de caractère, besoin
de solidarité, versatilité, pusillanimité, force de l'inertie,
absence d'initiative, suggestibilité tels que nous venons de les
étudier, présentent au missionaire justement préoccupé de
la persévérance finale de ses chrétiens, un bien douloureux
problème.   Car ce que nous avons surtout à reprocher dans
nos fidéles, n'est pas un manque de sincérité dans leur foi,
mais cette absence d'énergie de volonté qui est cause que
leur conduite sera païenne ou chrétienne, exacte ou relachée
d'après les circonstances."[2]

Roman Catholic Missions in China.

Partly as a result of the suppression of the Jesuit
Order and partly as the result of the closing of religious

---

[1] *Edinburgh Conference Reports*, i. p. 85.
[2] Par R. P. Louis Kervyn de la Congrégation du cœur immaculé de Marie,
Hong-Kong, 1911, p. 359.

houses and seminaries which followed the French Revolution, the Christians of China were almost entirely left to their own resources. In many provinces "the converts left without priests drifted back into paganism, or if they kept the faith, were ill-instructed and had no sacrament but baptism. The Vincentian (Lazarist) Fathers, in the face of terrible trials, held on to Peking and a few other places, and the re-establishment of the famous Paris Seminary of Foreign Missions eventually supplied a reinforcement for other districts. The Spanish Dominicans in the south-east, and the Portuguese priests at Macao, kept the faith alive in these places." [1]

Timkowski, a Russian official who visited Peking in 1805, wrote:

"A fresh persecution was commenced against the Christians. They endeavoured to oblige them to trample upon the cross and to abjure their errors; they who refused were threatened with death. At Peking many thousand persons were discovered who had embraced the Christian religion, even among the members of the imperial family and mandarins." [2]

In 1815 Bishop Dufresse was led to execution at the head of 32 confessors. In 1818 many Christians were exiled to the wilds of Tartary. In 1816 a Franciscan Father and 4 Chinese priests were martyred in Szechwan. Nevertheless in the same province and at the same time a priest was able to report that he had baptized 1006 adults and given the Holy Communion to 79,000 persons in one year.

In the Salle des Martyrs belonging to the Paris Seminary of Missions are preserved relics of the martyrs of China and Corea. One of these is the chalice belonging to the Bishop Boric, who was tied to a stake and slowly cut to pieces in Central China. Every priest trained in this seminary who is about to leave for China is allowed to say a Mass at which he uses this chalice.

---

[1] *The Missions of China*, by A. H. Atteridge, p. 12. Published by the Catholic Truth Society.

[2] See "Roman Catholic Missions," by R. Eubank, *The East and The West*, January 1905.

14

The revival of Roman Catholic missions in China dates from 1830. These missions are now to be found in every province in China and on the borders of Tibet, and in 1850 the number of baptized Christians was estimated at 330,000. In 1881 they numbered 470,000; thirty years later, *i.e.* in 1911, these had increased to 1,363,000. (Rapid as this rate of increase has been, it has, however, been less rapid than the increase of the non-Roman missions throughout China, see p. 200.) These were grouped in 47 dioceses or vicariates. There were 1365 European and 721 Chinese priests and 1215 Chinese students for the priesthood. There were also 247 European and 86 Chinese lay-Brothers in religious houses or in "teaching congregations," and 2172 nuns, of whom 1429 were Chinese women.

According to *Die Katholischen Missionen* of June 1913, the total number of converts connected with R.C. missions in China was 1,421,258, in addition to 448,220 catechumens. The three tasks which are put forward as being most pressing are: the development of education; the securing of a more powerful political unity and influence; and the formation of strong religious organizations within the Church.

The R.C. missions have for many years supported orphanages in different parts of China for the care of destitute children. These number 260, and a considerable proportion of the baptisms which take place annually are of infant children in these homes. As a general rule the Chinese priests are members of families which have been Christian for at least three generations.

The R.C. priests for the most part live simple, self-denying lives, and live and die amongst their converts. On the other hand, their bishops claimed the rank and dignity of mandarins. This claim, and the further claim to interfere in Chinese lawsuits wherever a R.C. Christian was concerned, often gave rise to hostility and persecution on the part of Chinese officials, and was one of the causes of the Boxer insurrection in 1900.

When, in 1898, the claim to rank with a governor of a Chinese province and to travel in a green sedan chair with a retinue following was eventually allowed by the Chinese Government, the same honours were offered to the Anglican bishops, but were declined.[1] The right to assume this rank has been disallowed by the present Chinese Government.

At the close of the Boxer riots, in which 54 R.C. missionaries lost their lives, the R.C. missionaries claimed £1,500,000 from the Chinese Government as an indemnity.

The following Orders and foreign missionary societies are at work in China: Jesuits in Chihli and Kiangnan; Lazarists in Chihli, Kiangsi and Chekiang; Franciscans in Shensi, Shansi, Shantung, Hupei and Hunan; Augustinians in Hunan; Spanish Dominicans in Foochow and in Amoy; Milan F.M.S. in Honan and in Hong-Kong; Paris F.M.S. in Manchuria, Kweichow, Szechwan, Kienchang, Yünnan, Kwantung, Kwangsi and Tibet; Scheutvelt Belgian F.M.S. in Mongolia and Kansu; Rome F.M.S. in Shensi; Steyl German F.M.S. in Shantung; Parma F.M.S. in W. Honan; and Spanish Augustinians in N. Hunan.

In Tonking, where work was begun in 1678, the R.C. Church has 7 vicariates. The Christians, including Europeans, number 711,000. The work is carried on by 230 priests and is supported by the Paris F.M. Society. In Cochin China, where the work dates from 1659, there are 3 vicariates, 164 priests and 180,000 Christians. In Cambodia, where work was begun in 1850, there are 45,000 Christians and 48 priests.

The Russian Mission.

The *Chinese Mission* of the Russian Orthodox Church was the result of the capture of some Russians, one of whom was a priest, by a Chinese force at the end of the

[1] See " R. C. Mission Work in China," by Clement Allen, formerly Consul at Foochow, *The East and The West,* April 1905.

seventeenth century. In 1716 a missionary party, including 2 priests, a deacon, and 7 students, reached Peking. Though the mission has remained small, its members have translated the Bible and other Christian books into Chinese. Of the 700 Christians attached to the mission in 1900, 400 are said to have been killed during the Boxer insurrection. The work has since been resumed and has a Russian Bishop as its head.

Chinese Turkestan.

Chinese Turkestan or Sinkiang contains over 550,000 square miles, but a population of only 1,250,000. It is the meeting-point of many races, Kalmuks, Mongolians, Tangus, Tartars Manchus, Chinese and Turkis. The majority of its inhabitants are Moslems. In the extreme west the Swedish mission have centres at Kashgar and Yarkand, and at the capital, Urumchi, the C.I.M. has had a station since 1905.

Manchuria.

The *Presbyterian Church of Ireland* began work at Newchwang in 1869. In 1872 the Rev. John Ross arrived, as a pioneer of the *United Free Church of Scotland Mission*, and ten years later he and Dr. Christie established the medical mission at Moukden, which has exercised a far-reaching influence.

In 1891 the two Presbyterian missions united in order to form a native Manchurian Church.

The *Danish Lutheran Mission*, which began work in 1895, has stations at Port Arthur and in the surrounding district.

The missionaries belonging to the Scotch, Irish and Danish missions, together with the B. and F. B. S. and Y.M.C.A. representatives, number 153, including wives. These occupy 26 stations. The number of baptized Christians (1913) is 26,024 and of catechumens 7000.

Though the more visible results of the great Revival which took place in 1908 have passed away, the spiritual impetus then received has been lasting, and "a new vision of sin and holiness remains as a ground of appeal." [1]

There are 12 mission hospitals and 19 doctors in Manchuria, and the number of out-patients in 1913 was about 150,000. At the Moukden Medical College 50 Chinese medical students are being trained.

In Manchuria, to a greater extent than in almost any section of the mission field, the growth of the Church has resulted from the efforts made by the converts to influence their friends and neighbours. As an illustration of this statement we may quote a case described thus by Dr. Christie of the Moukden hospital :—

"A patient came to the Moukden hospital many years ago. When admitted he had never heard the gospel, but before he left he had a clear knowledge of Christian truth and showed an intense desire to make it known to others. For many years he witnessed for Christ, most of the time without salary of any kind and under no control but that of his heavenly Master. The missionary who had charge of the district where he laboured till his martyrdom by the Boxers, tells us that he was a direct means of leading at least 2000 souls into the fold of Christ." [2]

The Report of the U.F.C. of Scotland presented in 1914, referring to the colleges supported by this mission at Moukden, says, these colleges "thrive amazingly and give promise of providing the whole of Manchuria with adequately trained teachers, pastors and doctors."

The R.C. missions in Manchuria date from the seventeenth century. When the first Bishop arrived in 1840 he found a scattered Christian community of over 3000 members, who were for the most part immigrants from China. By 1891 these had increased to 13,000. During the Boxer riots the Bishop of Moukden, his clergy and most of his congregation, 600 in all, were massacred.

[1] *China Mission Year Book*, 1914, p. 421.
[2] *Edinburgh Missionary Conference Report*, i. 334 f.

Mongolia.

Mongolia, the largest dependency of China, is nearly as large as the eighteen provinces of China put together. Its population, however, hardly exceeds 3,000,000, the great majority of whom are Buddhists.

The most extensive work is that done by the *R.C. Church*, which has a chain of stations near the Chinese border, at several of which attempts are made to reach Mongols. At Barin, north of Jehol, and at a station in the Ordos country, there are Mongol congregations under priests who speak Mongolian. The converts number several hundreds in all. The R.C. Church has three bishops and reports 69,000 converts in Mongolia. They have stations at Pakou, Tatzŭk'ou, Hata, and a few other places, and in the far north at Maoshantung. Only a very small proportion of the converts are Mongols, the majority of the remainder being Chinese. In *The Catholic Church in China*, by Father Wolferstan, the Christian community in Mongolia is returned as consisting of " Chinese Christians." J. Hedley, the author of *Tramps in Dark Mongolia*, writes :

The devotion of the R.C. missionaries "is most praise-worthy, and so far as I could learn the conduct of their work of a fine character. . . . They have a practice of insisting on a whole family submitting to baptism, when a man seeks to enter their Church, with the twofold result of swelling numbers much faster than can be done by any Protestant mission, and of having within their Church a large percentage of uninformed adherents."[1]

Referring to the difficulties which confront the Christian missionary in Mongolia the same author writes :

"This colossal system of Lamaism is the most effective obstacle to the Christian missionary. . . . The attempt to evangelize Mongolia presents one of the greatest problems that faces Christian enterprise to-day. . . . Humanly speaking it is impossible, an absolute impossibility, for any

[1] P. 363.

Mongol to avow himself a Christian and remain among his own people and clan. To an extent undreamed of in China the priest terrorizes over the layman, and a profession of adherence to any other faith would inevitably mean a system of persecution that would wear out the unfortunate man's nerves, if he did not sicken and die from some mysterious disease. . . . The only hope for the Mongol who wishes to attach himself to the Christian faith would be to remove far away from the influence and association of the people among whom he has been reared." [1]

Mongolian Bible.—In 1827 two Buriats reached St. Petersburg having been sent from the head Lama of Mongolia to request that part of the N.T. might be translated into Mongolian. They had seen a copy of a N.T. in Kalmuck. The L.M.S. sent two representatives to Irkutsk, and after many years of work the whole Bible was translated into Mongolian. No actual attempt to evangelize the Mongols was, however, made till the coming of James Gilmour in 1870.

James Gilmour.—Of the missionaries who worked in the Far East during the nineteenth century, he was one of the most remarkable. Although his work in Mongolia (1870–91) did not result in a single baptism, his life and labours have been an inspiration to very many. A reviewer of his book, *Among the Mongols*, in the *Spectator* has well expressed the difficulties under which his work was carried on. He wrote:

"Mr. Gilmour . . . quitted Peking for Mongolia on an impulse to teach Christ to Tartars. He could not ride, he did not know Mongolian, he had an objection to carry arms and he had no special fitness . . . for the work. Nevertheless he went and stayed years, living on half-frozen prairies and deserts under open tents on fat mutton, sheeps' tails particularly, tea and boiled millet, eating only once a day because Mongols do, and in all things, except lying, stealing and prurient talk, making himself a lama. As he could not ride, he rode for a month over 600 miles of dangerous desert, where the rats undermine the grass, and at the end found that the difficulty had disappeared

[1] *Tramps in Dark Mongolia*, p. 361 f.

for ever. As he could not talk, he 'boarded out' with a
lama, listened and questioned, and questioned and listened,
till he knew Mongolian as Mongols know it. . . . If ever
on earth there lived a man who kept the law of Christ
and could give proofs of it, and be absolutely unconscious
that he was giving them, it is this man whom the Mongols
he lived among called 'our Gilmour.' He wanted, naturally
enough, sometimes to meditate away from his hosts, and
sometimes to take long walks, and sometimes to geologize,
but he found all these things roused suspicion—for why
should a stranger want to be alone; might it not be 'to
steal away the luck of the land'?—and as a suspected
missionary is a useless missionary, Mr. Gilmour gave them
all up, and sat endlessly in tents, among lamas. And he
says incidentally that his fault is impatience, a dislike to
be kept waiting."[1]

The work of which Gilmour laid the foundation was
not eventually to be developed by the L.M.S., as in 1901
it was handed over to the care of the Irish Presbyterian
Mission. This Mission has mission stations at Sinminfu
and Fakumên in Manchuria, from which some work
amongst Mongols is carried on. The station where
Gilmour worked during the latter part of his life in
Mongolia, Ch'aoyang, has now been handed over to a
mission supported by the "Brethren," who have stations
in N.E. Chihli which are in touch with Mongols. The
Scandinavian Alliance Mission has a small agricultural
mission station at Patsibolong, where 40 or 50 Mongols
are at work, several of whom have been baptized. There
is a small Swedish Mongol mission at Hallong Osso, 85
miles north of Kalgan. The Canadian Pentecostal Movement has sent six missionaries also to this place.

Tibet.

It has often been pointed out that much of the ritual
of the lamas of Tibet, including the use of the cross, the
mitre, censers, the dalmatica, the cope, etc., is so closely

[1] *The Story of the L.M.S.*, p. 384 f.

similar to that which has long been in use in sections of the Catholic Church that it is practically certain that they have come from Christian sources. Father Huc conjectured that these are to be traced to the influence of Franciscan missionaries who were working in China in the fourteenth century. It is not inconceivable that some of the Nestorian missionaries of a much earlier date may have visited Tibet. In 1325 Friar Odoric made a journey from N.W. China through Tibet and resided for some time in Lhasa. In 1661 Fathers Gruber and Dorville, and in 1716 Fathers Desideri and Freyre, made missionary tours in Tibet, and the latter resided in Lhasa for thirteen years. In 1719 a Capuchin Friar named Francisco della Penna, with twelve companions, began a mission in Lhasa which was continued till 1760.[1]

The Tibetans themselves have a tradition that a white lama from the far west visited Tibet long ago and instructed the lamas of Tibet in the doctrines of the West. It is, however, more probable that to some of the missionaries referred to above should be ascribed the resemblances which can be traced to-day between the Tibetan and Christian religious customs.

No success has been attained in establishing mission stations in Tibet despite the many attempts which have been made. The *Moravians* have long had representatives at Leh in Kashmir, and have four stations in the Indian frontier states. The *C. of S. Mission* and the *Scandinavian Alliance* have several similar stations on the Indian side. On the Chinese side, the *Christian and Missionary Alliance* started work at Taochow in Kansu in 1895, the *C.I.M.* started at Tatsienlu in Szechwan in 1897, and later on the Foreign Christian Mission started in the same place. From these centres itinerations have been made, and many thousands of portions of Scripture have been distributed. About twenty Tibetans have been baptized. On the Chinese border there are nine missionaries who speak the Tibetan language.

[1] See *With the Tibetans in Tent and Temple*, by S. C. Rijnhart, p. 108.

The *R.C. Church* has a mission at Tatsienlu at which a Bishop and 22 European priests are stationed. The baptized Christians, who number 2683, include a few Tibetans. The work is supported by the Paris F.M.

There are also mission stations at Batang, Atuntsu, Tseku and Weihsi in the provinces of Szechwan and Yunnan, in connection with which efforts are made to reach Tibetans.

VIII.

JAPAN.

WE have already referred to the influence which Christian teaching probably exerted upon the Buddhism which was introduced into China from India and from which Japanese Buddhism was derived. Professor Lloyd of Tokyo believed that there was so much in common between the Amida sects of Buddhists and Christians that Christian missionaries ought to be encouraged to study their writings, in the hope that a sympathetic understanding of their teaching might enable them to make an effective appeal on behalf of the Christian faith. In considering the rapid spread of Christianity at the time of its first introduction into Japan, it is well to bear in mind the fact that the teachings of the Amida sects had familiarized the Japanese with the doctrine of a divine saviour, through faith in whose name entrance into paradise could alone be obtained. The acceptance of this doctrine may partly account for the rapid spread of the Jesuit missions, and is likely to affect the future history of Christianity in Japan.

The first Christian who is reported to have visited Japan was a Nestorian physician, whose Japanese name was Rimitsu and who was present at the court of the Emperor Shomu, 724–748 A.D. His consort, the Empress Komyo, bore the title "Light and Illumination," which was the official name by which the Christian faith was known in China at that time. She is described by Japanese writers as a great saint and as one by whom miracles of healing were wrought. It is possible to suppose that she had become a Christian under the influence of Rimitsu.

There is no further trace of the existence of Christians in Japan till the day (August 15, 1549) when Francis Xavier and his two companions, Father Cosmo Torres and Brother Juan Fernandez, landed at Kagoshima in the province of Satsuma. The mission to Japan was undertaken at the suggestion of a Japanese named Anjiro, who had been converted to Christianity at Goa and who accompanied the Jesuit missionaries to Japan and acted for awhile as their interpreter. When the missionaries left Kagoshima a year later they left Anjiro in charge of 150 baptized Christians. The methods adopted for effecting the conversion of the Japanese were similar to those adopted by Xavier in India, to which reference has already been made. Baptism was administered as a general rule before those desirous of receiving it had gained any clear appreciation of the meaning of the Christian faith. Thus in a letter written by Xavier from Hirado, where he stayed for ten days after leaving Kagoshima, we read: "The lord of that country received us with much affection and kindness. In a few days about a hundred persons became Christians, thanks to what was preached to them by Brother Juan Fernandez, who already knew how to speak passably well, and to the book translated into the Japanese language, which we read to them."

It is interesting to note, in view of the late Professor Lloyd's investigations, that some of the Buddhist priests belonging to the Shingon sect professed to find a great resemblance between the Jesuit teaching in regard to the Christian Trinity and their own beliefs. The feeling of the Buddhist priests was not, however, reciprocated by Xavier, as Father Froez wrote in 1586: "They should recognize that the teaching of the Shingon sect, like that of the others, was only an invention of devils and a tissue of falsehoods." The visit of the missionaries to Kyoto (in January 1551) where they had hoped to have obtained an audience with the Mikado, proved unsuccessful, and they then retired to Yamaguchi, from which Xavier wrote: "In two months at least 500 persons have become Christians, and the number is daily increasing." After a stay of twenty-seven months in Japan, Xavier sailed on November 20, 1551, for India, whence he sailed again for China, off the coast of which (in the island of Sanchian) he died in November 1552.

Although his name has been completely overshadowed by that of Xavier, to Juan Fernandez is due the chief credit for the initial successes of the Jesuit missionaries in Japan. "No one," says Dr. Otis Cary, "deserves so much as he to be called the founder of the early Japanese Church." Fernandez had been a rich silk merchant in Cordova, and on joining the Society of Jesus had refused the honour of the priesthood and had preferred to labour as a humble layman. Xavier never learned to speak Japanese and had to rely entirely upon interpreters, whereas Fernandez soon learned to speak and preach with fluency. Soon after the departure of Xavier, difficulties arose which tended to become more and more political. The Portuguese Jesuits were followed by Dominicans and Franciscans, who were for the most part Spaniards, and the Dutch and other traders, who began to increase in number and in influence, entertained no good feelings towards any of the missionaries. If the policy of the missionaries had been to establish a Japanese Church which could have been independent of foreign ecclesiastics or princes, all might have gone well and Japan might long since have been a Christian country, but to tell the Japanese that to become Christians was to profess allegiance to an Italian Pope, or to connect Christianity in any way, however indirectly, with the encouragement of European trade, was to build a Church upon foundations which could not endure.

The story of the Roman Catholic Church in Japan affords an object-lesson on the largest scale of the disastrous results which attend the adoption of political methods for spreading the Christian faith. Within thirty years of the departure of Xavier the number of Christians in Japan is said to have risen to 600,000,[1] who were mostly to be

---

[1] In a letter, however, written by Bishop Cerqueira in 1603 he asserts that the total number of Christians prior to 1600 was between 200,000 and 300,000.

found in Nagasaki and the surrounding districts. Nagasaki had become simultaneously a Christian city and the centre of the Portuguese trade with Japan. The spread of Christianity had been in part due to the assistance of Nobunaga, a military dictator in Japan, who did not himself become a Christian, but who supported the Christians against his personal enemies, who were Buddhists. He was killed in battle in 1582. After his death Hideyoshi, who became the real ruler of Japan, began to show disfavour towards the rapidly increasing Christian population, and in 1587 he issued an edict ordering all missionaries to leave Japan within twenty days. The edict was not strictly enforced, but for the next fourteen years the spread of Christianity was checked by intermittent persecutions. In 1596 the captain of a Spanish galleon which had been wrecked at Urado, in explaining to a Japanese official the significance of a map that he produced, said: "The kings of Spain begin by sending out teachers of our religion, and when these have made sufficient progress in gaining the hearts of the people, troops are dispatched who unite with the new Christians in bringing about the conquest of the desired territory." These words were immediately reported to Hideyoshi and did much to confirm him in his hostility towards the missionaries. His dislike of the Christians was, moreover, confirmed by the accusations of perfidy and disloyalty which the Franciscans and Jesuits continued to make against each other. Early in 1597 he commenced to take active measures against the Christians, and on February 5 there were crucified at Nagasaki 6 Franciscans, 3 Japanese who were members of the Jesuit Order, and 17 other converts. Early in 1598, 137 Christian churches were destroyed and a large proportion of the Jesuit missionaries were driven out of the country. Hideyoshi died in September 1598. During the civil war which followed his death three Christian Daimyos, who were leaders of the defeated party, were killed. Ieyasu, who now became the military ruler of Japan, was at first disposed to tolerate the Christians, but in 1603 the persecution of them recommenced. It did not, however, become at all severe till 1613, when three prominent Christians together with their wives and families were burned to death at Arima. As illustrating the superb courage of Japanese Christian children, we may note that one of these who was condemned to be burnt to death as a Christian, when the cords that bound him to the stake had burnt away, went to his mother, who said to him, "Look up to heaven." He died whilst still clinging to his mother. Truly the Japanese Christians of to-day have reason to thank God for their Christian martyrs. To them no less than to their sisters in the West could the words attributed by Browning to St. John be literally applied:

> " What little child,
> What tender woman that had seen no least
> Of all my sights, but barely heard them told,
> Who did not clasp the cross with a light laugh,
> Or wrapt the burning robe round, thanking God!"

In 1614, 300 persons, including a large proportion of the foreign missionaries, were shipped out of Japan, and for the next twenty-four years the Christians were subjected to tortures and persecutions which throw into the shade all the cruelties practised against Christians under the Roman Empire. On the capture of the castle of Shimabara, where the Christians had endeavoured to defend themselves in 1638, 17,000 Christians were put to death.

In the following year an Italian Jesuit (Porro) was burned alive together with all the inhabitants of the village in which he was found. Soon after this all visible signs of Christianity disappeared from Japan. As late as 1666 some Japanese who had escaped to Siam reported that in the previous year 370 Christians had been put to death in Japan. In 1640, 4 Portuguese envoys, together with the 57 other persons who sailed with them in the same ship, were beheaded on their arrival in Japan. A notice-board which was erected near the spot where the heads were exposed bore the inscription:

"Thus is it that hereafter shall be punished with death
all those coming to this Empire from Portugal, whether
they be ambassadors or common sailors, and even though
it be through mistaking the way or because of a tempest
that they come: yea, every such person shall perish, even
though he be the King of Portugal, or Buddha, or a
Japanese god, or the Christians' God Himself, yea all
shall die."[1]

Five Jesuit priests and three other companions who
visited Japan in 1642 were put to death with torture, and
five others who followed them a year later met the same
fate.[2]

In 1708 Father Sidotti landed in Japan. He was
imprisoned for seven years and died in 1715. During the
next century and a half Japan was so closely barred
against foreigners that few tidings reached the outer world.
On two or three occasions Japanese who landed in the
Philippine Islands, or at Macao, described certain Japanese
families as continuing to preserve Christian traditions ; and
in 1821, 17 Japanese who had been shipwrecked on the
Philippine Islands and who were found to possess some
Christian medals, asked for and received baptism.

Modern Missions in Japan.

The resurrection of the Christian Church in Japan dates
from 1859. In the previous year, as the result of treaties
made between America, England, France and Japan,
foreigners were permitted to reside at certain selected
Japanese ports In the very year that these treaties were
signed, 80 Japanese Christians were discovered at Nagasaki,
10 of whom were tortured to death. The honour of sending the first missionaries to take advantage of the sign-
ing of the treaties belongs to America. On May 2, 1859,

---

[1] For the form of this proclamation see *A History of Christianity in
Japan*, by Otis Cary, i. p. 231.

[2] According to Japanese accounts, however, these recanted and became
Buddhists.

before the treaties came into force, the Rev. J. Liggins, of
the Protestant Episcopal Church, and, a month later, the
Rev. C. M. Williams (afterwards Bishop of Yedo) arrived
at Nagasaki. Within a year Dr. Hepburn of the American
Presbyterian Board, Dr. Verbeck of the Dutch Reformed
Church of America, and (in 1860) a representative of the
American Baptists Society were settled at Nagasaki, or at
other treaty ports. In September 1859, M. Girard, a
Roman priest, arrived at Yedo, and two months later M.
Mermet commenced active missionary work at Hakodate.
During the next five years the Roman missionaries got
into touch with a number of Christian communities, whose
numbers were variously estimated at from twenty to fifty
thousand, which still retained the sacrament of baptism
and observed in secret Sundays and other Christian festivals.
Dr. Cary writes:

"The organization of the communities was nearly the
same in all the villages. There were usually two leaders.
When possible the first of these was a man who knew how
to read and write. He presided at the prayers on Sunday
and came to the beds of the dying. The second was the
baptizer. He always had a pupil in training to be his
successor. The baptizer did not hold office for longer than
ten years, and the pupil as a rule studied the formula and
assisted in administering the rite for at least five years
before succeeding to the office. Sometimes the offices of
baptizer and prayer-leader were held by the same person.
The Christians had some books and religious emblems that
had been handed down from generation to generation. One
treatise on Contrition had been composed in 1603."[1]

The open avowal of their Christian faith soon brought
persecution upon the Japanese Christians. Between 1867
and 1870, 4000 who had refused to recant were arrested
in Nagasaki and its neighbourhood. These were deported
from their native villages and were placed in different
provinces, where they were subjected to very harsh treatment, under which many of them died. By the end of
1872 these exiles began to be more kindly treated, and in

[1] *A History of Christianity in Japan*, i. 286.

the following year the persecution of Christians fell into
abeyance.

Dr. H. Nagaoka, who was for a time an attaché at
the Japanese Legation in Paris, and who published in
1905 a book entitled *Histoire des relations du Japan avec
l'Europe aux xvi° et xvii° siècles*, represents the Japanese
official standpoint with reference to the Christian missions.
According to him, the question of encouraging or discouraging the spread of the Christian faith was from first
to last a political and not a religious question.   The
missionaries were encouraged at first by rulers of the
semi-independent provinces of Japan, partly because they
were regarded as the pioneers of profitable trade and partly
because their presence in one district seemed to afford the
ruler of that district moral if not material support in his
disputes with the rulers of adjacent provinces.   The final
extirpation of the Christians was prompted by the conviction that by no other means could Japan retain her
political independence.   Whilst then those who suffered
for their faith have every right to be regarded as martyrs, it
is not possible to ascribe to their persecutors the religious
bigotry or intolerance which in many other countries has
brought about religious persecutions.[1]

The first Japanese unconnected with the Roman
Mission to receive baptism was Yano Riuzan, who had
for three years acted as language teacher to the Rev. J. H.
Ballagh of the Reformed Church Mission, and had helped
Mr. Ballagh to translate the Gospel of St. John into
Japanese.   His baptism took place in November 1864.

In 1868 the revolution occurred in Japan which
restored the supreme power to the Emperor and inaugurated the modern Japanese system of government.
Although the change in the form of government was not
immediately followed by a cessation of persecution, it
facilitated the residence of foreigners in Japan and indirectly paved the way for the spread of Christian missions.
The first English missionary to commence work in Japan

[1] P. 51.

was the Rev. George Ensor of the C.M.S., who reached Nagasaki in 1869. Up to this time the number of baptisms connected with missions other than those of the Roman Church had only amounted to nine. Soon after Mr. Ensor's arrival, a man named Futagawato feigned to be interested in Christianity in order that he might assassinate Mr. Ensor. The story of Christ's love, however, as he heard it from Mr. Ensor, so affected him that he became a Christian, and later on, when imprisoned on account of his faith, he preached Christ to the inmates of his prison, with the result that seventy of them began to study the Bible for themselves. For several years inquirers could only dare to visit Mr. Ensor at night, and interviews had to take place behind barred doors.

Of the pioneer Protestant missionaries Dr. G. F. Verbeck (see p. 225) deserves special mention. He exercised a wide influence, especially amongst the Government officials, and the school which he organized became the first Imperial university. He died in 1898.

The missions that were established in different parts of Japan continued to progress, despite considerable persecution, until the year 1873, when the attitude of the Japanese Government towards Christianity underwent a change. On February 19 the Government ordered the removal of the notice-boards which contained the prohibition of Christianity. At this time some of the recognized leaders of Japanese thought began to suggest that the time had come for Japan to fall into line with the nations of the West by adopting Christianity as its national religion. Had their suggestion been adopted the results from the Christian standpoint would have been disastrous. This danger was happily averted, partly in consequence of the vehement opposition of the official representatives of Buddhism, and partly because the Christians in Japan were not disposed to accept an eclectic form of Christianity and other religions which found favour with the advocates of a new Japanese national religion. In 1873 the number of foreign missionaries in Japan, in addition to those connected with

the R.C. and Greek missions, had risen to 87, of whom 79
hailed from America or Canada.   The only English societies
then represented were the C.M.S. and the S.P.G.   One of
the missionaries wrote—and his words would have been
endorsed by nearly all his fellow-workers—"the avalanche
of opportunities that slides down upon us almost stuns us."

So late as 1886 cases continued to be discovered in
which the Christian faith had been secretly handed down
from generation to generation.   Thus Dr. Cary writes:

"There were sections of the country where even fairly
intelligent men knew nothing of the great changes that were
coming upon their land.   One of these persons, who lived
among the mountains of Yamato, came on business to the
town of Shingu in the province of Kii.   In the evening he
lodged at the house of a friend whom he had not seen for
years.   As the two sat talking together, the master of the
house inquired: 'Have you ever heard anything about
Christianity?'

"His guest, with a frightened air, lowered his voice and
said: 'Be cautious.   If you talk of such things, you will
surely be beheaded.'

"'What makes you think so?'

"'Why, are you so ignorant as not to know that Christianity is strictly prohibited?'

"'Can it be,' said the host, 'that you are unaware of the
great changes that have taken place?   We are now free to
believe in Christianity.   In this city there is a church of
which I am a member, and it is constantly growing larger
and larger.'

"'I never dreamed of such a thing.   I myself am a
Christian.   For ten generations the religion has been handed
down in our family from father to son.   I supposed that
the laws against it were still in force, and so I have never
told others of my faith.   God be praised if I am now at
liberty to speak of it!'

"He was instructed by his friend, and a few months later
became a member of the Shingu Church."

A special characteristic of the work done by Christian
missionaries in Japan up to about 1888 was the successful
appeal which it made to men of culture and education.

In support of this statement we may quote the words of Dr. D. C. Greene, written in 1889:

"Not less than thirty students of the Imperial University are avowed Christians. Among the members of a single Congregational church are a judge of the Supreme Court of Japan, a professor in the Imperial University, three Government secretaries (holding a rank hardly, if any, inferior to Mr. Kaneko himself), members of at least two noble families; while in a Presbyterian church are the three most prominent members of the Liberal party, one of them a count in the new peerage. Two influential members of the legislature of the prefecture of Tokyo, one of them the editor of the *Keizai Zasshi*, the ablest financial journal in Japan, are also members of a Congregational church. In the prefectures of Kyoto and Ehime, the Christians have two representatives in each local legislature. In the prefecture of Guma the president and vice-president and three other members of the legislature are Christians, and in the Executive Committee, out of a total of five, three are Protestant Christians."

The following figures illustrate the progress of Christian missions in Japan other than those connected with the Roman and Greek Churches. The numbers given refer to communicants or baptized members of Christian Churches :—

1879	.	.	.	2,700	1900	.	.	.	42,400
1882	.	.	.	4,300	1908	.	.	.	73,400
1889	.	.	.	31,800	1913	.	.	.	98,000

From these figures it will be seen that a period of rapid advance extending from 1879 to 1889 was followed by a period of retarded growth from 1889 to 1900, and that this has again been followed by a period of steady advance. It is interesting to note that whereas on the accession of the late Emperor in 1868 there were but 4 Christians in Japan connected with Anglican or Protestant missions, at the time of his death in 1912 their number was over 83,000. The least satisfactory point in connection with the numerical progress of the Christians is the large number of persons in Japan who have for a time professed to be Christians and have since abandoned their profession.

The number of self-supporting mission stations in Japan, which formed 14 per cent. of the whole number in 1882, had increased to 40 per cent. in 1913.

Greater progress has been made in Japan than in any other non-Christian land in the formation of churches that are self-governed and are to a large extent independent of help received from foreign missionary societies. The total number of Christians in Japan is about 200,000, of whom half belong to the Roman and Russian missions. Of the other half, at least three-quarters are members of one of the four Japanese Churches which have absorbed the converts connected with the various English and American missionary societies. These are the Nippon Sei Kokwai, the Kumiai Kyokwai, the Nihon Kirisuto Kyokwai and the Nippon *Methodist* Sei Kyokwai. The word *Kokwai* is usually rendered as "Catholic Church" by the members of the first Church and the word *Kyokwai* as "United Church," or "General Assembly," by the members of the other three Churches.

The *Nippon Sei Kokwai* or "Holy Catholic Church of Japan," which was formed in 1887, includes all Christians connected with the missions of the Anglican Church. Its adherents number about 20,000, including 17,500 baptized Christians. In 1903, its baptized Christians numbered 10,500, the increase during the past decade being at the rate of 66 per cent.

The control of the Church is vested in the General Synod, which meets once in three years and in which the Japanese clergy and laity have a predominant share. The appointment of its bishops also rests with the diocesan synods. There are at the present time seven dioceses, all of which are presided over by European or American bishops. The S.P.G. helps to support the Bishops of South Tokyo [originally "Japan"] (1883) and Osaka (1896), the C.M.S. the Bishops of Kyu-shu (1894) and Hokkaido (1894), the American Episcopal Church the dioceses of North Tokyo [originally "Yedo"] (1871) and Kyoto (1900), and the Anglican Church in Canada the diocese of Mid-Japan (1912).

At the end of 1913 the Sei Kokwai contained 7 bishops, 64 European or American and 94 Japanese clergy, and 136 Japanese catechists.

Kumiai Kyokwai (Congregational United Church), which was formed in 1883, includes the Christians connected with the missions established by the A.B.C.F.M. Its total membership is about 20,000. In 1903 its members numbered 18,000, its rate of increase for the decade 1903–13 having been about 11 per cent.

The American Board of Commissioners for Foreign Missions, which is chiefly supported by Congregationalists, began work in 1869. The most famous convert connected with this mission was Dr. Neesima, the founder of the Doshisha College. In 1905 all the churches which were partly supported from America and partly supported by Japanese contributions were handed over to the Kumiai Kyokwai with a gift of money, which was paid in three annual instalments. The groups of Christians who are now ministered to by American missionaries connected with the A.B.C.F.M. are not integral parts of the Kumiai Kyokwai, but the desire of the American missionaries is that they should soon become constituent members of this Church.

The *Nihon Kirisuto Kyokwai* (*i.e.* United Church of Christ in Japan) was formed in 1877, and includes Christians connected with the American Presbyterian missions and with the Dutch and German Reformed Churches in U.S.A. It has a total membership of about 23,000. In 1903 it had 16,500 members; its rate of increase therefore during the decade 1903–13 was about 40 per cent. It supports 146 ordained Japanese ministers. At Tokyo the Presbyterians have a well-equipped series of educational institutions known as the Meiji Gakuin (school of the enlightened rule).

The *Nippon Methodist Kyokwai*, which was formed in 1907, includes the Christians connected with the Methodist Episcopal Church (U.S.A.) (North), the Methodist Episcopal Church (South), and the Methodist Church of

Canada. It has a total membership of about 14,000, and has a Japanese Methodist bishop. At Aoyama in Tokyo the M.E.C. (North) has a college and school with 650 students.

The *Baptists* number about 4000, and there are about 10,000 Christians connected with a large number of small societies, amongst which are two Lutheran societies from America and Finland and the Scandinavian Missionary Alliance, also a Unitarian Mission with 200 members. The Kumiai Kyokwai has made less rapid progress than any other of the Christian Churches in Japan, a fact which is probably to be in part explained by the spread of unitarian teachings amongst its members during recent years and a consequent slackening of their evangelistic zeal.

The Protestant missions, with very few exceptions, have united in a general body called the Federated Missions of Japan, through which a large amount of good work has been done. The object of the Federation is to avoid unnecessary duplication of organization and to arrange joint efforts for the evangelization of Japan. One important piece of work which the Federation has accomplished is the formation of a Christian Literature Society for the production and distribution of Christian literature. A Union hymn-book has already obtained a circulation of 250,000 copies. The Anglican missions have not become a corporate part of this Federation, but many of their representatives have given it their cordial support. A writer on missions in Japan says:

"There is little wonder that the brotherly relationship of the different bodies of Christians becomes a source of surprise to the Japanese, who are accustomed to the contentions and quarrels so common between the different sects of Buddhists and Shintoists. The cordial relations which are maintained between the Christian peoples appear in very great contrast and greatly commend the Christian faith to the approval of the people."[1]

[1] Art. by the Rev. Dr. J. D. Dearing, in *Missions Overseas*, 1914, p. 22.

Special mention should be made of the work that is being done in many parts of Japan by the Y.M.C.A., which has 56 student associations. It arranges lectures for the benefit of the 50,000 "college men"; it supports hostels for business men in Dairen, Kobe and Nagasaki, and exerts a strong influence for good in Tokyo and other towns. The Y.W.C.A. is also doing excellent work amongst Japanese women.

Amongst the philanthropic works which have been inaugurated by Christian Missions mention should be made of the four leper asylums that are supported by Christian Missions in Japan, namely, the Fukusei Kogama at Shizuoka and the Biwasaki Hospital near Kumamoto belonging to the R.C. missions, the Resurrection of Hope Hospital near Kumamoto connected with an Anglican Mission, and one at Tokyo belonging to the Mission to Lepers in India and the East.

Educational Work.—From the time that Japan was re-opened to Christian missionaries, special stress has been laid upon the educational side of mission work. Of the missionary colleges which have been established in Japan, the Doshisha College has perhaps exerted the widest influence. Its founder was Joseph Neesima (or Niishima). In 1864, at a time when Japanese were forbidden under pain of death to leave their country, he made his way to America, where he became a Christian, and ten years later returned to Japan with funds wherewith to establish a Christian college. The site selected was Kyoto, which was the stronghold of Japanese Buddhism. For twenty years this college, which was in part supported by the American Board of Missions, accomplished a great work in training Japanese Christian students. In 1895, however, the character of the college underwent a considerable change. The Japanese trustees refused to co-operate with the American Board, which had been instrumental in building the college and encouraged the teaching of a Unitarian form of Christianity. After a long-protracted dispute the trustees resigned, and the college came again under direct Christian influence. Mr. Kataoka, who was four times chosen as Speaker of the Lower House of Parliament and was a member of the Presbyterian Church, became President of the Doshisha in 1902.

In 1913 its professors and teachers numbered 44, of whom 32 were Japanese and 12 American. There were in addition 29 lecturers, most of whom were attached to the Kyoto Imperial University. In this year the college was raised to university rank. The students number about 700.

In 1912 the Sei Kokwai and the Anglican missionary societies acting together founded a central theological college at Ikebukuro, near Tokyo, for the study of Christian theology. This college is a union of divinity schools which have hitherto been carried on in the different dioceses of Japan. It admits graduates from St. Paul's College (S.P.G.) in the department of philosophy.

At the conference of Christian missionaries in Tokyo, over which Dr. Mott presided on April 7, 1913, it was decided to attempt the formation of a Christian university for Japan.

One of the most serious problems which confront the missionary organizations in Japan is how to develop self-support in the Japanese Church, and to ensure a supply of properly educated clergy and ministers. Bishop Cecil of South Tokyo states the problem thus:

"The conditions of Japan require men of education, and these men must have support for a family as well as for themselves Who is to supply it? Relatively to their degree of education the Japanese, especially the official, professional and student classes, . . . in contrast to the business and farmer classes, are impecunious. Our missions began generally on the theory that a priest or catechist, put down in a station and supported by the mission, would in the course of time raise round him a self-supporting congregation. After a generation this theory is now stultified by general experience, and no one seems to have any other. The number of places in which a foreign mission can support the native pastorate on foreign funds is clearly very limited —if indeed the whole theory be not vicious. Are we to return to the (apparent) New Testament way of a 'tent-making ministry,' of ordaining 'in every city' presbyters who are not set apart from earning their own living?' . . . If so, how is the situation to be combined with their proper educational training?"

The experience of the Kumiai Kyokwai and the Nihon Kirisuto Kyokwai, to which we have already alluded, does not encourage the hope that in the near future the difficulty can be surmounted by the withdrawal of foreign help and by leaving the Japanese to solve the problem for themselves.

Roman Catholic Missions.

The following table illustrates the progress of the R.C. missions to Japan during the last forty years:—

	1870.	1880.	1891.	1900.	1910.	1913.
Christians . .	10,000	23,000	44,505	57,195	63,000	66,000
European priests .	13	28	82	—	150	152
Japanese priests .	—	—	15	—	33	33

It will be noticed that during the decade 1900–10 the rate of increase was only 10 per cent. (as compared with 92 per cent. increase of the Anglican and Protestant missions). During the three following years the rate of progress has been greater. The converts connected with the R.C. missions form about one-third of the Christians now in Japan.

In 1891 Pope Leo XIII. re-established the Catholic hierarchy in Japan, and constituted the archdiocese of Tokyo with three suffragan sees of Nagasaki, Osaka and Hakodate under the care of the Missionary Seminary at Paris. To these have since been added the prefectures of Shikoku and Niigata, under the care of the Dominicans and the Missionary Society of Steyl.

The Jesuit College in Tokyo was recognized by the Japanese Government in 1913 as a university.

The Russian Mission to Japan.

The Mission of the "Orthodox" Church to Japan is one of the most romantic and most successful missions of modern times. Its founder, Père Nicolai, began his work at Hakodate in 1861. For several years he served as a Consular chaplain whilst studying the Japanese language and waiting an opportunity to preach the Christian faith.

"At last the opening came, and in a most dramatic and startling fashion. A certain Japanese knight (Samurai) named Sawabe, who had become the keeper of a Shinto shrine, and had long observed Nicolai with suspicion and horror, burst in upon him as he sat in his quarters and told him to prepare for instant death, rightly deserved by the professor of a corrupt religion, who, moreover, was bent upon handing over Japan to Russia. Nicolai calmly asked him what he knew about Christianity, to which the knight replied that he knew it was an evil teaching, and that was enough. Whereupon Nicolai asked him to hear him for a little while, and then opened his Bible at Genesis and made known the doctrine of creation. Sawabe listened impatiently, but soon became interested, put by his drawn sword, and asked for instruction. Little by little he learned the truth, then brought two friends, and after some months they were baptized. Eight long years had passed since Nicolai had come to Japan before he gained these first-fruits of his vocation. Before he died, early in 1912, over 30,000 Japanese looked up to him as their father-in-God He took away the reproach of sterility from the Church of Russia, for his example in Japan kindled a fresh zeal for missions in that Church, so that all over Siberia little groups of devoted Christians are working for the Master and preaching Christ in all that wide empire."[1]

A special feature of the work of Père Nicolai, or Archbishop Nicolai as he afterwards became, was his reliance upon Japanese workers for the conduct and

[1] *Missions Overseas*, 1914, pp. 16 f.

development of his mission. He never had six Europeans as members of his staff. During the Russo-Japanese War the Archbishop, who had refused to leave Japan, bade the Christians connected with the Russian mission pray for the success of their own countrymen. The mission is represented in many different parts of Japan, especially in the larger towns. Its cathedral at Tokyo occupies the finest site in the city, and its dome and spire can be seen for miles round. Before his death the Archbishop had the help of Bishop Sergius, who has proved a worthy successor to the great founder of the mission. Sawabe, who had desired to murder Archbishop Nicolai, was himself ordained as a priest and survived his master by a year.

A new departure has recently been made by this mission in view of training boys who may hereafter serve as priests in Japan. Several Russian boys are being educated in the theological seminary of the mission along with Japanese boys. The Russian boys share the life of the Japanese boys in every detail. Those who are responsible for the control of the policy of the mission believe that the effect will be to produce Russian priests possessed of a better insight into Japanese character than any which Occidentals have hitherto obtained. The experiment that is being made is one of extraordinary interest.

The total number of adherents of the Russian mission is about 33,000 (1914).

RECENT DEVELOPMENTS.

The year 1889 marked the beginning of a period of reaction, not only against Christianity but against the tendency which had been developed to imitate the customs and actions of Western nations. The reaction was due to political as well as to religious causes. At the time when the edict against Christianity was withdrawn, the Japanese were disposed to look with favour upon almost everything that reached them from the West, or from America, and the suggestion to which we have already referred, was seriously mooted that Japan ought to follow the example of Europe and America and accept Christianity as its national religion. Had it done so it is difficult to say for how long the Christianization of Japan would have been delayed, but happily this was not to be.   As the influence of Christianity continued to spread throughout Japan, those responsible for the government of the country realized that it would be difficult, if not impossible, to maintain the traditional reverence for the Emperor's divinity if the teaching of Christianity were allowed free course.   Moreover, in Japan, as in many other countries, liberal and socialistic movements began to develop which threatened the stability of the Government and of the imperial régime.

Shintoism, which is sometimes called the national religion of the Japanese, had its origin in the primitive nature-worship of the earliest inhabitants of Japan, and an early type of it is found still amongst the Ainu in the north.   It inculcated reverence for deceased ancestors, which developed into a reverence, almost amounting to worship, for the Mikado and the ancestors of his house. The fall of the Shogunate in 1868, and the revolution which accompanied it, were followed by a great revival of Shintoism as distinguished from Buddhism.   The emphasis which was laid upon the cardinal doctrine of Shintoism, that is upon a belief in the Emperor's divine descent, was a chief factor in binding the Japanese nation together and preparing the way for their victory in their war with Russia. The Japanese realized that reverence for the Emperor's divinity was the pivot of the position, and that from a political point of view their best hope of maintaining the popular reverence for the Emperor was to encourage Shintoism as the State religion.   Accordingly official encouragement was given to its supporters and Christianity became correspondingly unpopular.

For twenty years Shintoism and Buddhism, but especially the former, received State patronage, and though Christians were never actively persecuted, it was generally understood that the acceptance of the Christian faith would

retard the advancement of any one employed by the State.
Two causes have been acting within recent years which
have brought about a change of attitude on the part of
the Japanese Government. It has come to be recognized
by the Japanese that whilst Shintoism can suggest noble
ideals, it cannot supply the motive power necessary to the
attainment of these ideals, nor can it become a moral force
which can purify and uplift the life of the nation. For
many years after the re-introduction of Christianity those
who were responsible for the government of Japan believed
that Shintoism, the profession of which involved an acknowledgment of the Emperor's divinity, provided the best
means of inculcating patriotism and loyalty. They have,
however, now come to realize that the belief in the divine
prerogatives of the Emperor can no longer be maintained
in its old form, and that Shintoism can no longer serve
as the national religion of Japan.

At the same time they have realized that Buddhism
cannot take its place, and that the only alternative to
Christianity must be a form of agnosticism, which would
not help the nation either morally or politically. A step,
which marked the beginning of an epoch in the history
of religion in Japan, was taken on January 17, 1912,
when Mr. Tokonami, Vice-Minister of Education, announced
to a meeting of press representatives that the Government
had decided to recognize Christianity as a religion which
they were prepared to encourage. In his speech, which was
in fact a formal declaration of the new Government policy,
he began by saying:—

"In order to bring about an affiliation of the three
religions it is necessary to connect religion with the State
more closely, so as to give it additional dignity, and thus
impress upon the public the necessity of attaching greater
importance to religious matters. In the early years of the
Restoration the nation, too eager to reform all the traditional
institutions, did not judiciously discriminate between what
should be destroyed and what should be preserved intact.
Many Buddhist temples and Shinto shrines were demolished,

and the national sentiment towards religion was thereby greatly impaired. Christianity was then also held in abhorrence and distrust. Since the freedom of religious faith has been arrested, however, Christian teachers have been energetically engaged in the propaganda of their religion. Taking these circumstances into consideration, it is felt necessary to give religion an additional power and dignity. The culture of national ethics can be perfected by education combined with religion. At present moral doctrines are inculcated by education alone, but it is impossible to inculcate firmly, fair and upright ideas in the mind of the nation unless the people are brought into touch with the fundamental conception known as God, Buddha, or Heaven, as taught in religions. It is necessary that education and religion should go hand in hand to build up the basis of the national ethics, and it is therefore desirable that a scheme should be devised to bring education and religion into closer relations to enable them to promote the national welfare. This necessitates binding the State and religion by closer ties."

He then went on to express the hope that Christianity would "step out of the narrow circle within which it is confined, and endeavour to conform to the national polity and adapt itself to the national sentiments and customs, in order to ensure greater achievements."

One result of this action on the part of the Government was that a conference of certain representatives of "the three religions" was held (Feb. 25, 1912) which was attended by several members of the Japanese Cabinet. The resolutions which were subsequently passed began with the following statement (the translation into English is made by a Japanese) :—

"We acknowledge that the will of the Government authorities, which led us to hold the conference of the representatives of *the three religions*, is to respect the authority of religion, which each possesses, to promote national morality, and to improve public discipline, without spoiling our original creeds; and the statesmen, religionists, and educationists, non-interfering with one another, and to maintain the honour of the Imperial Household and to contribute to the progress of the times."

The missionary prospect in Japan has been considerably modified by this change of attitude towards Christianity on the part of the Government of Japan, but whether or no Christian missionaries have reason to be thankful for the change remains yet to be seen.

Count Shigenobu Okuma, who was one of the founders of New Japan and was Prime Minister in 1898, and again in 1914, describes the condition of things in 1909 thus :—

"Japan at present may be likened to a sea into which a hundred currents of Oriental and Occidental thoughts have poured in, and not having yet effected a fusion, are raging wildly, tossing, warring, and roaring." "The old religions and old morals," he writes, "are steadily losing their hold, and nothing has yet arisen to take their place." "A portion of our people go neither by the old code of ethics and etiquette nor by those of modern days, while they are also disinclined to conform to those of foreign countries, and such persons convey the impression of neither possessing or being governed by any ideas about morality, public or private."[1]

We may compare this statement with a later statement by Count Okuma in 1912:

"Although Christianity has enrolled less than 200,000 believers, yet the indirect influence of Christianity has poured into every realm of Japanese life. It has been borne to us on all the currents of European civilization; most of all the English language and literature, so surcharged with Christian ideas, has exerted a wide and deep influence over Japanese thought.

"Christianity has affected us not only in such superficial ways as the legal observance of Sunday, but also in our ideals concerning political institutions, the family, and woman's station. Even our lighter literature, such as fiction and the newspapers, betrays the influence of Anglo-Saxon and German literature and personalities. Not a few ideals in Japan which are supposed to have been derived from Chinese literature are in reality due to European literature."[2]

[1] *Fifty Years of New Japan*, London, vol. ii. p. 568.
[2] See *International Review of Missions*, vol. i. p. 654.

16

In endeavouring to estimate the prospects of Christianity in Japan in the near future, it is necessary to take into account the low standards in regard to purity and truth which the religions of Japan have done little to raise. Polygamy in the ordinary sense of the term is not found, but prostitution and other forms of immorality are sadly common. Moreover, concubinage is sanctioned by custom and divorce is easy. In a country the language of which is said to contain no equivalent for "home," one of the chief tasks confronting those who would interpret Christianity to its people is to place before them the Christian ideal of family life. Until the average conception of home-life is raised far above the level at which it now stands, the opening words of the Lord's Prayer and the fundamental doctrines of the Faith which are inherent in them will wake but a weak response in the hearts of the Japanese nation. In regard to the question of truth, it is hard to convince a Japanese that, unless the telling of a lie involves cowardice or disrespect to authority, there can be anything in it to which objection can be taken. Commercial dishonesty is perhaps less common than it was, the change being partly due to the fact that within recent years the higher and better educated classes of society have taken part in commerce. The greatest of all the obstacles to the spread of the Christian faith is a widespread belief that the Japanese people have a divine descent and a divine mission which differentiate them from all other nations and races. To accept a religion which comes to Japan from Europe or America appears to many Japanese equivalent to the abandonment of this claim. Moreover, to suggest that their Emperor should kneel (albeit in the company of the Kings and Emperors of Europe) and acknowledge himself a "miserable sinner," is to suggest what to the average Japanese appears nothing short of blasphemy. Dr. Cary, in referring to the article published by Professor Inoue Tetsujiro of the Imperial University in 1893, says:

" By quotations from Christ's words and by references to European history, he endeavoured to show that Christianity is destructive of patriotism. He closed by asserting that as Christ Himself had said, 'Every kingdom divided against itself is brought to desolation,' therefore the reception of Christianity would involve national destruction." [1]

A leading monthly periodical published in Japan in 1907, after referring to the progress of Christian missions in Japan, went on to remark:

" Supposing that these movements should be successful, our Empire will be changed into a Christian country, our unique history extending over a period of 2500 years will be trampled on, and the spirit of Japan will be destroyed. Not only is the Christian spirit not sufficient to lead the new generation, but it will make the people weak and hypocritical, and destroy their character." [2]

There is probably no country in the world at the present time in which so large a proportion of the educated section of the population would call themselves " agnostics " as is the case in Japan.

According to a recent analysis of the religious beliefs of the students attending the Imperial University in Tokyo, 3000 were agnostics, 1500 atheists, 450 Shintoists or Buddhists and 60 Christians. We may compare with this statement the fact that out of the 315,000,000 people in India enumerated in the last census, only 50 declared themselves as agnostics, and one as an atheist. Of the former apparently 45 were Chinese.

The Japanese have not the religious instinct developed to anything like the same extent as it is developed amongst the majority of the peoples of India. European civilization and culture burst suddenly upon Japan, with the result that those who began to absorb Western literature and Western science rapidly lost faith in the religious sanctions which had exerted an influence upon

[1] *A History of Christianity in Japan*, vol. ii. p. 243.
[2] Reproduced in *Japan Evangelist*, June 1907.

them in the past, and before they had had time to make any intelligent study of the Christian faith.

We believe that Christianity will one day be the religion of Japan, but the Japanese Christianity of the future may be of a less emotional, and perhaps less devotional, and less dogmatic character than the Christianity of many other countries.

The Bible in Japan.—In the sixteenth century the Jesuits translated the Decalogue, the Lord's Prayer and other extracts from the Bible which occurred in their liturgical services.   They are also said to have printed a translation of the New Testament at Miyako (Kyoto) before 1613, but no copy of this translation appears to have survived.   In 1831 three survivors of a Japanese junk which had been driven by a storm across the Pacific made their way across Canada to London, and eventually assisted the well-known missionary Gutzlaff, of the Netherlands Missionary Society, who was stationed at Macao, to translate into Japanese the Gospel and Epistles of St. John. These were printed at Singapore in 1837.   The earliest complete version of the New Testament was begun by Goble, an American Baptist missionary, in 1871, and was completed in 1879.   In 1887 a complete edition of the Bible was issued, in the translation of which representatives of the principal missionary societies working in Japan had taken part.   In 1895–97 the four Gospels and in 1911 the whole of the N.T. were translated from the Vulgate by Roman Catholic missionaries, and in 1900 a version of the N.T. translated by Bishop Nicolai of the Greek Orthodox Church was issued.   The following story illustrates the influence which a study of the New Testament exerted upon some of the Japanese who first saw it.   In 1855, whilst a British fleet lay at anchor in Nagasaki Bay, Wakasa Murata, who was in command of the Japanese forces which had received orders to prevent any one from the British fleet landing on the shores of Japan, picked up a Dutch New Testament which was floating in the water and had apparently been dropped by one of the Dutch merchantmen which were permitted to trade at Nagasaki. The officer's interpreter, who was a Dutchman, explained that this was the Holy Book of the Christians. The curiosity of Wakasa was aroused, and having learned that a copy of the book could be obtained in classical Chinese, he had a copy sent to him from Shanghai. A study of the book resulted, after eight years, in the baptism of himself, his brother and several other members of his family.

Notwithstanding the large number of missionary societies which are now represented in Japan, and the existence of four self-governed Japanese Churches, Christian missions have hardly yet touched more than the fringe of the country. At the Missionary Conference over which Dr. Mott presided in Japan in 1913, it was stated that whilst 80 per cent. of the Japanese people live in villages, 96 per cent. of the village inhabitants of Japan are as yet unreached by Christian missions, or if we take the town and country population together, 80 per cent. of the entire population of Japan are out of reach of Christian missionaries.

Formosa.

Formosa, which is about half the size of Scotland, has a population of over 3,000,000. The mountains are inhabited by savages, the lower hills by civilized aborigines, and the level plains by Chinese interspersed with Japanese. From 1624 to 1662 the Dutch were in possession of the island, and idolatry was treated as a criminal offence (see p. 47).

Despite the superficial character of the missionary work done by the Dutch in Formosa, some knowledge of the Christian faith lingered on for nearly a century. Long after the Chinese had driven the Dutch from the island (1683) the Jesuit, de Mailla, who was working as surveyor for the Imperial Government in 1715, found indications of the Dutch Mission, and even of the Dutch language. Many natives, abhorring idols, professed belief in one God, Father, Son and Holy Spirit; knew the story

of Adam and Eve's fall; believed that baptism effaced the
"stain" of that fall; knew the baptismal formula; were
reported by the heathen Chinese to have the custom of
pouring cold water on new-born infants.   "Nevertheless,"
de Mailla continues, "we were unable to know certainly if
they were baptized or not. . . . It seemed that they have
no idea of the rewards or punishments of the other life, so
it is probable they do not take great care to baptize their
children.   We tried, as far as we could, to teach them the
most necessary truths of our holy religion . . . and above
all to baptize their children as soon as they were born,
in case there might be some hope of instructing them when
they were capable of receiving it.   What grief for us to
see ourselves in the midst of so fair a harvest, which would
become very abundant if it had apostolic labourers to
cultivate it, and yet to be obliged to abandon it without
hope of help!"

When Formosa became part of the Chinese Empire
in 1683, Christianity, or rather the nominal profession of
Christianity, began to die out.   In 1865 the English
Presbyterian Church began missionary work, having been
preceded by a few years by a R.C. mission.   In 1872 the
Canadian Presbyterian Church started a mission in North
Formosa.   The cession of the island to Japan in 1905
has been followed by its opening up to Western civilization
and has facilitated the extension of missionary enterprise.

In 1912 a union was effected between the Canadian
and English Presbyterian missions.   The united synod
represents a Christian community of over 30,000.

The Japanese Church in Japan in connection with
the Anglican missions started work among the Japanese
residents in Formosa in 1897 at the suggestion of the
Japanese authorities.

IX.

COREA.

THE story of Christian missions in Corea is full of romance and of inspiration. In no other country has the persecution of Christians been so intense, and in no other has Christianity within recent years made such rapid advance. The country is one of which little has been known in Europe until comparatively lately.

Many who are familiar only with its chequered history during recent years are ignorant of its great and, in some respects, glorious past. The Coreans can boast of having been the first people to print from metal type, of having invented an alphabet to take the place of the Chinese ideographs, and of having constructed the first ironclad ship. This last was used by them in their efforts to repel the Japanese invasion in the sixteenth century. At this period, when Corea was starting on her downward career, "she had made great advances in civilization and prosperity. Polite learning, as typified in the knowledge of the Chinese classics, was universal among the higher classes, while among the lower many of her artisans had attained a high degree of technical and artistic skill . . . her people, homogeneous, industrious, intelligent, and tranquil, lived in physical comfort and security."[1] The Japanese invasion of the country resulted in a determination on the part of its rulers rigidly to exclude from Corea all foreigners. By murdering almost every stranger who was shipwrecked on their coasts or who attempted to enter from the north, they succeeded in shutting themselves off from the outside world for three centuries and a half.

[1] *The Story of Corea*, by S. H. Longford, 1911.

Before we describe the introduction of Christianity
into Corea a few words must be said in regard to its earlier
religions

The Religion of Corea.—Corea is a less religious country
than either China or Japan.   The people for the most part
profess to be Confucianists and practise ancestral worship
Buddhism has even less influence than it has in China.
The real religion of the people is a form of Shamanism,
which peoples the world with spirits and demons who are
believed to require constant propitiatory offerings.   •

Hideyoshi, the Japanese commander who invaded
Corea at the end of the sixteenth century, took back to
Japan a number of Coreans, some of whom embraced the
Christian faith and died as martyrs in Japan.   In 1784 a
son of a Corean ambassador to Peking was baptized by the
Franciscan Mission in Peking.   On his return to Corea he
began to preach and to baptize, but persecution almost
immediately broke out and the first convert was induced
to renounce his new faith.   Many, however, of those whom
he had helped to convert were tortured to death rather
than recant, and, despite increasing persecution, the
number of Christians continued to grow.   These elected
from amongst themselves a bishop and priests, who administered the Christian sacraments, and after the lapse
of two or three years they opened communication with the
Roman missionaries in Peking and asked to have a priest
sent to them.   The first sent was a Chinese named Tsiou,
who lived in disguise for seven years, till 1801, when he
was put to death by the authorities.

In this year a systematic attempt was made to
exterminate the Christians, who then numbered nearly
10,000.   Many thousands were put to death, including
all their leaders, their books were destroyed or buried,
and the survivors were scattered among the heathen
without having opportunities for common worship or even
for communication with each other.   Although some
recanted, the vast majority were content to suffer every
form of torture or death rather than abjure their faith.   It

's doubtful whether any Christians in the old Roman Empire suffered as did the Corean Christians during the first seventy years of the nineteenth century. Renewed efforts were made to exterminate the Christians in 1815, 1819 and 1827.

In 1832, Bishop Bruguiere, who had worked in Siam, was sent to Corea by the Society of Foreign Missions at Paris. After a journey which occupied three years he died just as he was reaching the borders of Corea. His place was taken by Maubant, who had previously been a missionary in Tartary, who reached Seoul in safety. In 1837, Bishop Imbert also succeeded in reaching Seoul. At the close of 1838 the number of Christians was reckoned at 6000. In the following year another cruel persecution occurred. Many of the victims belonged to the upper classes in Corea, who sacrificed everything and shared with the common people the death from which their rank should legally have exempted them. Amongst the martyrs were the Bishop and the two European priests at Seoul, who were cruelly tortured before being killed. In 1845, Bishop Ferréol and a priest named Daveluy, both of French nationality, succeeded in crossing in a small boat from Shanghai to Corea, and were joined five years later by another priest named Maistre.

Ferréol died in 1850 and Maistre in 1857, but the number of their successors began to increase rapidly. By 1859 the number of Christians was reckoned at 16,700. In 1865 the anti-Christian party in the State persuaded the Regent to sanction the extermination of the Christians, and the Bishop and seven European missionaries were put to death with cruel tortures. In the course of a few weeks Christianity was well-nigh exterminated. A French fleet made an abortive attempt to obtain redress for the murder of the French missionaries. Between 1866 and 1870 more than 8000 Coreans suffered death as Christian martyrs, apart from the large number of those who perished of cold and hunger on the barren mountains to which they fled.

In 1876 a few Corean ports were opened to Japanese trade, but it was not till 1882 that, by a treaty made with the U.S.A., the country was practically opened to foreigners. Missionary work was commenced by American Presbyterians and by the American Episcopal Methodists in 1884. An Anglican Mission, with Bishop Corfe as its leader, started work in 1890. At this time the number of converts unconnected with the Roman missions did not exceed 100. During the following ten years they multiplied by 10.

Protestant missionary pioneers.—In 1832 Gutzlaff (see p. 244) landed and spent a month in Basil's Bay selling Chinese Bibles and other books. In 1866, Mr. Thomas of the L.M.S. sailed for Corea in an American schooner, but he and all the other members of the crew were apparently murdered by the Coreans. In 1877 the Rev. J. Ross of Moukden (of the U.F.C. of S. Mission) published an English-Corean primer, and he and Mr. M'Intyre translated the whole of the New Testament into Corean, their translation being published by the Presbyterian Press at Shanghai. The conversion of several Coreans is known to have resulted from this work.

So rapidly did Christianity spread that when the annexation of the country was proclaimed by Japan in 1910 there were in all 453 missionaries, of whom 50 were French, 90 British and 306 hailed from America. Although the honour of having started the Christian Church in Corea and of ministering to it during nearly a century of continuous persecution belongs to the Roman missions, these do not at the present time minister to half the Christian population, and the proportion of R.C. converts is rapidly decreasing. As we take note of the rapid change which has come over this ancient land, we cannot but ask with anxiety whether the depth and stability of the work are in any degree proportionate to its speed. On the whole the answer to our question is less unsatisfactory than we might have feared. It is true that some of the missionaries, especially those who come from America, are prepared to baptize converts after a preparation which appears to be dangerously short, but even in these missions baptism has, as a general rule, been preceded by the confession of sins and by efforts to make restitution to those who have been wronged, which have afforded proof of the sincerity of the converts.

General Statistics.—In 1913 the number of baptized Christians connected with the Anglican and Protestant missions numbered 75,000 and the number of Christian adherents 185,000. Connected with these missions there were 10,000 churches and schools containing 13,250 boys and 5800 girls, 20 hospitals and 23 dispensaries. The American and European missionaries (including wives) number about 330. Of these 164 are connected with Presbyterian missions, 95 with Methodist, 32 with Anglican, 16 with the Salvation Army and 24 with other societies.

The number of Christians connected with R.C. missions in 1913 was 80,657. These were ministered to by 58 European and 17 Corean priests.

The statement made by Dr. A. M. Sharrocks with reference to the progress of the American Presbyterian Missions (North) in Corea applies with little modification to the other missions. He writes:

"Those who have been following the missionary enterprise in Corea will have noticed that the phenomenal growth took its start about the year 1904, the year of the Russo-Japanese War. . . . In the years 1904 and 1905 a new life seemed to take hold of the Church. The growth in 1906, 1907 and 1908 became phenomenal. The 30,000 in 1905 suddenly increased to nearly 110,000 in 1911. It seemed as though the whole nation were on the eve of bolting into the Kingdom. . . . In the midst of this rapid growth, that is in the years 1906 and 1907, there broke out in the Church one of the most remarkable revivals that ever swept a mission field. The distinctive feature of the revival was that it was among the professing Christians rather than the non-converted. During the period of rapid growth . . . the year 1907 stands out conspicuously as the only one that shows a falling off in the increasing number of the baptisms. . . . The casual reader of mission reports will pronounce the years 1910–12 as years of decline. In some respects they were. The total adherentage (*sic*), which had been going up by leaps and bounds, not only failed to increase, but actually shrunk about 10 per cent. on its former number. . . . But the year 1912, when so many of the pastors and Church officers were in Seoul on trial in the 'Conspiracy case' turns out to be the banner year in the number of baptisms administered. . . . In 1909 the total adherents numbered about 95,000 and the communicants 25,000. At present (1914) they are 92,600 and 43,000 respectively. . . . There have been far more baptisms administered in the last two years than in any previous two, and more than the total of any seven years prior to 1909."

Referring to the training to which a convert is subjected prior to baptism, Dr. Sharrocks writes:

" Our methods recognize three classifications of Christians; new believers, catechumens and communicants. Any one who attends services and wishes his name recorded, is enrolled as a new believer. If he remains faithful and at the end of six months passes a satisfactory examination, he is received as a catechumen. He is then held on probation for one year, after which time he is again examined to ascertain the progress made, and if his examination and past conduct are satisfactory he is baptized and becomes a communicant. The sum of these three grades constitute what we call the total adherentage." [1]

A similar period of probation is arranged by the other missions. In the case of the Anglican mission, the period is not less than three years.

The *Presbyterian Mission* (American Church, North) began its work in 1884, when Dr. H. N. Allen (afterwards U.S.A. Minister to Corea) was put in charge of a Government hospital. [2] His medical work paved the way for direct evangelistic efforts, which were begun by the Rev. H. G. Underwood in the following year. Since then the work has spread rapidly throughout the central portion of the peninsula, from Kang-kei in the north to Fusan in the south. Sessions, Presbyteries and a General Assembly

[1] *The Christian Movement in Japan*, 1914, p. 378 f.
[2] See p. 31.

have been established, and 43,000 members have been baptized. The doctrine of self-support has been so successfully taught that during the year ending June 30, 1913, the Christians contributed £15,240 towards the support of this Church. A theological college, attended by 200 students, has been established at Pyengyang, from which 101 pastors have already been ordained. The total number of Corean pastors is 219, all of whom are supported by the Corean congregations.

At Phyong An, said to be "the most wicked city in Corea, the Presbyterian Church has a regular Sunday congregation of over 1500 converts, and its mid-week prayer meeting has an average attendance of 1100."

The Severance Hospital at Seoul is supported by several missionary societies; see p. 30.

In 1892 the *Presbyterian Church, South* (U.S.A.), commenced missionary work in the southern part of Corea. In 1907 a united "Corean Presbyterian Church" was constituted, and at the same time 7 Coreans were ordained, being the first ordained ministers of the Presbyterian Corean Church.

The *Australian Presbyterian* and the *Canadian Presbyterian* Churches have also missionaries in Corea; the former began work in 1889 in the south Kyengsang province, the stations of the latter are in North-East Corea and in Manchuria.

The *Methodist Episcopal Mission* (U.S.A.).—The first Protestant missionary to enter Corea was the Rev. R. S. Maclay, who landed in Chemulpo on June 23, 1884. As a result of his favourable report two missionaries were appointed before the close of the year, and reached Corea in April 1885. This mission supports a hospital for women and two dispensaries in Seoul, and has more than 100 churches in the district, which includes Seoul and Chemulpo. It has also a considerable amount of work in the district of Pyengyang. The mission has a joint-college with the Presbyterians in Pyengyang. It has made work among women a special feature of its programme.

In 1895 the *Methodist Episcopal Church, South,* established a mission. It has stations at Seoul, Song Do and Won San.

The Methodist Episcopal Church, North and South, have combined to form one Methodist Episcopal Church in Corea.

Anglican Missions.—Dr. Corfe, who had been a chaplain in the Navy, was consecrated as a Bishop for Corea on All Saints' Day, 1889, and with a small staff of clergy settled at Seoul. At the end of seven years, which were largely occupied in learning the languages required for missionary work in Corea, the first convert was baptized. This convert was ordained in 1914 as the first Corean deacon in connection with the Anglican Church. The missionary who prepared him for baptism is now the Bishop in Corea. The centres of the Anglican Mission are at Seoul, Chemulpo, Kanghwa, Suwon and Chinchun. It also supports work amongst the Japanese at Fusan and Chemulpo, and a mission hospital at Chemulpo, and takes its share in the work of the Severance Hospital at Seoul. The Anglican Mission is supported by the S.P.G.

A small "*Orthodox*" *Mission* has been opened under the auspices of the Russian Archimandrite, who resides on premises adjoining the Russian Consulate. There are in addition several other smaller Protestant missions.

At the Continuation Committee held at Seoul in March 1913, four Presbyterian and two Methodist missions reported 11,700 baptisms as having taken place during the previous year. These four Presbyterian missions have had a united General Council since 1905.

The Y.M.C.A. works in close touch with the various missionary societies. Bishop Turner (of the Anglican Mission) was president of its Board of Directors until his death, and his successor is a member of its Board. Prince Ito took part in laying the foundation-stone of its new buildings in Seoul in 1907.

Medical Missions.—The Presbyterian, Anglican and Methodist Missions have each of them several mission hospitals, which have done much to further the spread of the Christian faith. The Severance Hospital in Seoul (which was founded by Mr. L. H. Severance) in connection with the Presbyterian Mission, North, has a medical training college attached to it. The following missions contribute one or more workers to the teaching staff of the college:—American Presbyterian Missions, N. and S., American Methodist Missions, N. and S., Australian Presbyterian Mission and the S.P.G. Over 30 qualified doctors have already been trained in this college, and the supply is likely to increase during the coming years.

The students, who must be Christians well recommended by their clergy or pastors, take part in Sunday-school teaching and other work connected with the churches to which they are attached.

X.

MALAYSIA.

The Malay Peninsula.

In 1813 the Rev. R. Milne, who was sent out by the L.M.S. to join Morrison in China, was refused permission to land at Macao and eventually settled at Malacca, where he established an Anglo-Chinese college for the training of Chinese and of European students of the Chinese language. Before his death in 1822 Dr. Milne had helped to train several European missionaries and had established schools for Malays and Chinese, besides accomplishing a large amount of translational work and printing. Attempts were also made to start missionary work at Singapore and Penang.

The *Straits Settlements* are situated on the west and south coasts of the Malay Peninsula, and consist of the islands of Singapore, Penang, and Pankor, with the districts of Malacca, Province Wellesley, and the Dindings on the mainland. Besides these there are the protected states of Perak, Selangor, and Negri Sembilan. The total population of this area is about 52,000,000, of whom about 8000 are Europeans. The Straits Settlements were included in the Anglican diocese of Calcutta till 1869, when they became part of the diocese of Labuan and Sarawak. In 1909 they became the diocese of Singapore. On the coast there are a large number of Chinese and Tamil immigrants.

An Anglican mission was established by a local committee in 1857 and was transferred to the S.P.G. in 1861. The Rev. W. H. Gomes, a Singalese who had been trained at Bishop's College, Calcutta, laboured for over fifty years as a missionary, first in Borneo and after 1872 in Singapore. He translated the Prayer Book and several other books into Malay and the colloquial Chinese spoken in Singapore. The S.P.G. started or supported work in Malacca (1860), Penang (1880), Province Wellesley (1879), Perak (1884), and Selangor (1887). Towards the support of the "missionary chaplain," whom the S.P.G. appointed for the Province Wellesley, a Presbyterian Committee formed in Penang contributed £200 per annum from 1879 to 1890.

In these missions, which are still in their infancy, missionary work has been carried on and schools established amongst the Malays, Chinese, and Tamils, with the assistance of Chinese and Tamil missionaries or catechists. There are about 8000 European and 1200 Asiatic members of the Anglican communion in the diocese of Singapore.

Work is also being carried on by the English Presbyterians and by the A.M.E. mission. The Methodist Anglo-Chinese school at Singapore has over 1000 pupils, amongst whom a number of conversions to Christianity have occurred.

The English Presbyterian mission which is represented in Singapore carries on most of its work in China and Formosa. Its work in Singapore is among the Chinese immigrants, many of whom have become Christians in connection with this mission.

The R.C. missions in the Malay Straits are in the diocese of Malacca, which contains 35,000 R.C. Christians, including Europeans. In Singapore there are churches for Europeans, Eurasians, Chinese, and Tamils, also a large Brothers' school with a staff of British and American teachers.

In Malacca the Portuguese Church is over 300 years old, but the descendants of those who originally worshipped in it are Christians only in name.

Siam.—The population of Siam (6,686,000) contains a large intermixture of Chinese, Burmese, and immigrants

17

from the Malay States. The Siamese, or Thai, who are the dominant race, number about 2,000,000, and have been Buddhists for many centuries. Closely related to the Siamese are the Laos, who occupy the tributary states in the north of the country. The Laos-speaking Thai number about 10,000,000, about 2,000,000 of whom live within the kingdom of Siam. The remainder live in Burma, French Indo-China, and Yünnan. A large proportion of them are not Buddhists. The Chinese population in Siam number nearly 2,000,000.

There was apparently a Nestorian bishopric in Siam in early times (see p. 165), but of the Christianity which it represented no trace remains.

The R.C. Church has Apostolic Vicariates of Siam (1662) and of Laos (1899). In the former there are 45 priests and 23,000 Christians; in the latter there are 33 priests and 12,000 Christians. The work is supported by the Paris F.M. Society.

The American Presbyterians, who began missionary work in 1840, have two missions, one to the Siamese and the other to the Laos-speaking people in the north. In Siam they have a station at Bangkok, and at three or four other places, their work being chiefly of an educational character. They have also some medical missions. Their work amongst the Siamese has made very slow progress, and in 1909 the number of communicants was under 1000. The great difficulty which has been experienced in finding native evangelists is attributed by their missionaries to the teaching of Buddhism that religion is a personal matter and that no one is responsible for the religion of his neighbour. The mission to the Laos, which was commenced in 1867, has, after a period of severe persecution, attained considerable success, and what may almost be termed a mass movement towards Christianity has begun amongst them. In 1913 more than 3000 new converts were obtained. The central station of the mission is at Chieng Mai.

French Indo-China, in which many of the Laos live, is

closed by the French Government to the work of Protestant missionaries. Two Swiss "Brethren," who are the only Protestant workers there, report a great desire on the part of the Laos to receive Christian teaching.

Dutch East Indies, etc.

We have already referred to the work of the Dutch missions in the seventeenth and the first half of the eighteenth centuries (see p. 46). At the beginning of the nineteenth century, the total number of Christians throughout the Dutch East Indies was reduced to about 100,000. The great majority of the descendants of the old Christians belong to the Gevestigte Gemeenten, which, with the European congregations, form the Protestant Church, as recognized by the Government in the Dutch East Indies.

The three chief missionary organizations in the Dutch archipelago, which includes Sumatra, Java, the North Celebes and Dutch Borneo, and a few small islands, are (a) The Established Church (Protestantsche Kerk); (b) the Rhenish Mission; and (c) the Dutch missionary societies.

(a) The Established Church includes about 300,000 members, many of whom are the descendants of those who became Christians in the seventeenth and eighteenth centuries.

(b) The Rhenish Mission works amongst the Bataks of Sumatra, in the island of Nias, and in Borneo. It has 72 principal stations and about 100 missionaries.

(c) There are five large and three smaller Dutch missionary societies at work in the islands which form the Dutch East Indies. Of these societies, the Netherlands Missionary Society carries on work in Java, the Celebes, and East Sumatra; the Reformed Church works in Java and Sumba; the Utrecht Association works in Java and Dutch New Guinea. Its staff includes three medical missionaries.

The number of converts from Islam throughout the
Dutch archipelago, chiefly in Java and Sumatra, is about
40,000. Most of these are the result of the work of the
Rhenish Mission.

Sumatra.—Assemani quotes Cosmas (Indicopleustes),
who wrote about A.D. 535, as saying:

" In the island of Taprobana (*i.e.* Sumatra), towards inner
India, where the Indian Ocean is, there is a Church of
Christians where clergy and believers are found. Whether
(there are Christians) beyond (that is in Southern China) I
do not know." [1]

There does not appear to exist any later reference to
this early Christian Church in Sumatra.

In 1861 the Rhenish Missionary Society, working in
conjunction with a Dutch society, started work amongst the
Bataks in the interior of Sumatra. The Batak Christian
community now numbers 30,000, 14,000 having been
baptized during 1913. Thirty Bataks have been ordained,
and work is carried on at 41 centres and 500 out-stations.
There are 55 European missionaries, and 27,500 Batak
children are being educated in 500 schools. A training
school for native evangelists and teachers and a hospital
have been erected in the valley of Si Lidung, and on the
shore of Lake Toba there is a leper asylum and a large
industrial school. The majority of the population of
Sumatra are Moslems, amongst whom the Rhenish Mission
has most encouraging work.

The A.M.E.C. has a missionary in East Sumatra, and
the Rhenish Mission carries on work in Nias and in other
islands along the western coast of Sumatra.

There is a small R C mission manned by 5 priests,
who are Capuchins.

There are over 7000 Christian converts from Islam,
but despite the number of conversions to Christianity
which have taken place, Islam is making rapid progress

[1] Assemani, *Bibliotheca Orientalis*, iii. 2, 487. There is a copy in the
British Museum (see p. 165 n.).

amongst the pagan population. Islam first appeared in Sumatra about A.D. 1200, and in Java about two centuries later. Thousands of pilgrims go annually from Java and Sumatra to Mecca, and on their return become active propagandists of their religion.

Java contains a population of about 30,000,000. The Established Church ministers to the Europeans and to about 5000 native Christians. In addition to that done by the Dutch societies, missionary work is carried on by the German Neukirchen Mission in North Central Java, by the Salvation Army in Central Java, and by the A.M.E.C. in Batavia. The Neukirchen Mission has 11 principal stations.

The principal centre of missionary work in the island is Modjowarno.

The Dutch societies have appointed a joint " missionary consul " in Batavia to look after their common interests.

The Jesuits have a mission in Batavia, connected with which there are 58 priests and 34,000 Christians.

The vast majority of the Javanese are Moslems, but these are more approachable here and in Sumatra than in any other part of the world. A Moslem university has been established in Java, and an edition of the Koran in Javanese has been issued. The Hindu dynasty which formerly ruled in Java was overthrown by the Moslems in the fifteenth century, and the religion which now prevails has absorbed many of the tenets of both Hinduism and Buddhism.

Borneo.

In British North Borneo, the sultanate of Brunei, Labuan, and Sarawak, which have a population of about 550,000, the S.P.G., the A.M.E.C., and the Basel Society are at work.

When James Brooke became Rajah of Sarawak in 1841, he appealed to the English universities to undertake missionary work, and as a result of his appeal the Borneo Church Mission was formed. Its work was taken over by the S.P.G. in 1854 The first missionary, who was also a doctor (Rev. E. T. McDougall), was consecrated as Bishop in 1855. Dr. McDougall, on his arrival in 1848, started work amongst the Europeans and Chinese at Kuching, and in 1851 the work was extended to the Sea Dyaks at Banting. By 1867 the Dyak converts in Sarawak numbered 1000. The Sea Dyaks are an uncivilized people, a whole community living under a single roof and practising cruel and barbarous customs. The acceptance of Christianity has effected marvellous changes in their habits of life and in many cases in their characters. The Anglican mission has always been undermanned, and some stations which had been opened have had to be abandoned through lack of workers. Nevertheless, much encouraging work has been accomplished. The number of baptized Christians is about 7000.

In 1883 a Chinese catechist was sent by the S.P.G. from Kuching to North Borneo to work amongst his fellow-countrymen, and in 1888 the Rev. W. H. Elton opened a mission station at Sandakan as a centre of work among Europeans and natives. There is now a congregation of 100 Chinese Christians at Sandakan, and in 1890 a mission to Chinese was opened at Kudat, where there were 1000 Christians, of whom 600 were converts of the Basel, the Berlin, the Wesleyan, the Baptist, and other missions in China. The two Chinese congregations there are superintended by a Chinese priest. In 1896 a mission station at Kaningan was opened to work amongst the Muruts in the centre of North Borneo, but owing to lack of workers this work has not been developed.

The island of Labuan, off the north coast of Borneo, was ceded to Great Britain in 1846. Its inhabitants are chiefly Malays from Borneo and Chinese. A church was opened in 1866, and some missionary work has been carried on amongst the Chinese.

At Jesselton, on the west coast of Borneo, the missionary chaplain ministers to the East Indian and Chinese Christians as well as to the Europeans.

Roman Catholic Missions.—In 1687, Father Ventimiglia was commissioned by Pope Innocent XI. to preach Christianity in Borneo, but no trace of his labours has survived. In 1857, Father Cuarteron, who had been originally a sea-captain, landed as a missionary in Labuan, but he returned to Rome in 1879 and soon afterwards died. In 1881 a mission was undertaken by the Society for Foreign Missions of Mill Hill, England. The two centres of work are at Labuan and Kuching in Sarawak. There are 22 priests, 2 lay brothers, 15 sisters, and about 3000 baptized Christians connected with this mission.

Dutch Borneo.

In 1835 the Rhenish Mission began work amongst the Dyaks, who were fierce savages and "head-hunters." The missionaries succeeded in establishing eight stations on the rivers, but in 1859, when the Mohammedan Malays rebelled against the Dutch, the Dyaks became involved, and all the inland mission stations were destroyed and seven of the mission staff were murdered. The work was started again in 1866 and is carried on now at nine stations, at which the number of Christians, who include some immigrant Chinese, is already considerable.

The A.M.E.C. has two missionaries in Dutch Borneo, who are stationed at Pontianak.

The R.C. Church has a mission manned by Capuchins which is served by 16 priests and has 876 Christian converts. The chief centres of its work are at Singkawang and Sedijiram.

Celebes.—The majority of the inhabitants in this island are Mohammedans. Amongst the Alifurs in the north-east of the island some remarkable missionary work has been accomplished by the Netherlands Missionary Society. When Hellendoorn, its first representative, began missionary work here in 1826, he found traces of Christianity, the results of some earlier mission. The work has developed in a marvellous way, and has transformed the conditions of life under which the people live. The native Christian Church which has been formed includes over 150,000 Christian Alifurs. Owing to lack of funds the Netherlands Missionary Society has had to transfer this, its most successful mission in the Dutch archipelago, to the Dutch Colonial State Church, which took the missionaries into its service as assistant preachers and now appoints pastors. The Netherlands Missionary Society continues to support a small part of the work.

Near to Celebes are the *Sangir* and *Talaut Islands*, where extensive missionary work has been done. Gossner missionaries from Germany, together with some Dutch assistants, resuscitated the Christian community which had survived from earlier days. The mission, which is now managed by a committee connected with a society in Batavia, reports 44,000 converts. Their moral condition appears to leave much to be desired.

The Netherlands Missionary Society laboured successfully in the Molucca group, especially in *Ceram* and *Ambon*. On the withdrawal of this society in 1865 the congregations became attached to the Netherlands State Church. In the islands of *Buru* and *Almaheira*, where work is carried on by the Utrecht Missionary Union, there are about 2000 Christians. In the *Lower Sunda Islands* there are about 50,000 Christians belonging to the Dutch State Church. Missionary work is carried on in *Sawu* by the Netherlands Missionary Society and in *Sumba* by the Reformed Church, the number of Christians in the two islands being about 6000.

The Philippine Islands number in all about 2500, the largest being Luzon and Mindanao. In the former is situated the town of Manila. The population, about 8,000,000, consists of various Malay tribes who have driven the early population, the Negritos, into the more inaccessible parts of the islands. The non-Christian population, which includes many Chinese and Mohammedans, numbers about 700,000. Most of the non-Christians are to be found in the island of Luzon.

The islands were discovered by Magellan in 1521. In 1565 the Spaniards commenced their conquest and forcible Christianization, but owing to the good influence exerted by the Spanish missionaries, the conquest was effected without the massacres and depopulation of the country which accompanied the Spanish conquests in Mexico and South America.

The first Spanish settlers included an Augustinian friar named Urdaneta, who formed one of the party of Spaniards. The friars soon became a political as well as a religious factor in the development of the islands, and in 1768 Governor Anda addressed to the king a memorial charging the friars with "commercialism, neglect of their spiritual duties, oppression of the natives, opposition to teaching Spanish, and interference with civil officials and affairs." The Augustinians were followed by the Franciscans in 1577, the Jesuits arrived in 1581, the Dominicans in 1587, and the Recolletos in 1606. The Jesuits became the richest of the Orders, and their wealth was in part the cause of their expulsion in 1767. They were, however, allowed to return in 1852 on the condition that they would devote themselves to missions in Mindanao and to the higher education of the Filipinos.

Of the present condition of the R.C. Church in the Philippines the American Bishop Brent writes:

"The parishes are served, except in a few centres, by Filipino priests, many of whom I have met, some of them being worthy of respect as pastors, though the best are incompetent and ignorant according to our mode of reckoning. . . . But there is another less pleasing (aspect of Christian life) to contemplate. No one but a blind partizan, afraid to recognize and face painful facts, seriously denies any longer the grave moral laxity that has grown up and still lives under the shadow of Church and convento (parsonage) in the Philippines. Inch by inch I have been forced back by the pressure of facts from the position I originally held that there was a minimum rather than a maximum of immorality. The cumulative testimony that has come to me has been chiefly incidental and unsought, containing in it the witness of Roman Catholics of good standing. . . . No doubt the Church has in the past spasmodically struggled with this besetting sin of the Filipino.   But in spite of everything, by degrees its filthy stream trickled into the sanctuary, and apathetic acquiescence in a seemingly hopeless situation ensued.   In my judgment the rift in the lute is in the ecclesiastical ordinance, which enforces celibacy upon the priesthood under such racial and climatic conditions as obtain here. . . . Wherever similar climatic and racial conditions obtain, we are confronted with a similar story of shame—Mexico, Central America, South America, and the Azores." [1]

Since the American occupation, an Independent Filipino Church, composed of Catholics who have seceded from Rome, has been formed under the leadership of Gregorio Aglipay, who is styled Obispo Maximo, or chief bishop of the movement.   It claims to have about 3,000,000 adherents.

In 1898, when the Philippine Islands were annexed by the U.S.A., the country was for the first time opened to missionary work other than that connected with the R.C. Church.

In 1901 the Protestant Episcopal Church of America organized missionary work in the islands, and Dr. C. H. Brent was appointed as the first Anglican Bishop.   The mission has started work amongst the Chinese in Manila, but its chief sphere of work is amongst the Bontoc Igorrotes, who number about 70,000 and who are pagans. The centre of the work is at Sagada.   The confidence of many of this tribe has been gained, and there is a prospect of a considerable advance in the near future.

An attempt is also being made to start work amongst the Moros, who number 275,000, and who have been Mohammedan from a date prior to the Spanish occupation of the Philippines.

Work has also been begun amongst the Bagabos in the island of Mindanao.

In 1901 there also arrived representatives of the

[1] *Religious Conditions in the Philippine Islands.*   Published, 1904.

American Methodist Episcopal Church, the Baptists, the
United Brethren, the Congregationalists, and the Disciples
of Christ.   These missions, which work to a large extent
amongst the R.C. Christians, arranged to start in different
areas   Of these, the A.M.E.C., which has the largest
amount of work, has 30 missionaries, about 30,000
members, and 130 churches or chapels.   Its sphere of
work lies in Luzon, to the north and north-east of Manila.

XI

WESTERN AND CENTRAL ASIA.

ASIA MINOR.

WE have not space in which to sketch the gradual spread of Christianity in Asia Minor. Dr. Harnack in his *Expansion of Christianity* suggests four categories in which the countries within or adjacent to the Roman Empire might be placed in the early decades of the fourth century.

"1. Those in which Christianity numbered nearly one-half of the population and represented the most widely spread, or even the standard, religion. 2. Those in which Christianity formed a very material portion of the population, influencing the leading classes and the general culture of the people, and being capable of holding its own with other religions. 3. Those in which Christianity was sparsely scattered. 4. Those in which the spread of Christianity was extremely weak, or where it was hardly to be found at all."[1]

Under 1 is placed the entire province of what is now known as Asia Minor, with the exception of some out-of-the-way districts; also Armenia and the city of Edessa. Under 2: Antioch, Cœlo-Syria, and Cyprus. Under 3: Palestine, Phœnicia, Arabia, parts of Mesopotamia, and perhaps Western Persia. Under 4: the towns of ancient Philistia, Persia, India, and Scythia.

By far the larger number of the Christians were dwellers in towns, and the strongest centre of the Chris-

[1] Vol. ii. p. 457.

tian Church at this time was Antioch, where in A.D. 320, of a population of 200,000 half were Christians.[1] The only known instance in which a whole district had become Christian is Armenia, where at the close of the third century Christianity had so far become the religion of the country that the King of Armenia proposed to make it the State religion. At the beginning of the fourth century the Christian population of the world was probably about 4,000,000.

The capture of Damascus by the Arabs in A.D. 634 was speedily followed by the subjugation of the greater part of Asia Minor. The lot of the Christian population, which was comparatively a mild one under the early Moslem rulers, was much worse when the Ottoman Turks became the dominant power in the eleventh century. Since then the Armenian and other Christians have been subjected to an almost unceasing persecution. We may well hope that the present century will see a great change in their condition, and will witness the final end of the religious persecution which has continued for a thousand years.

As a result of the persecutions suffered by the Christian population of Syria and Palestine, it is probable that at the time of the Crusades the whole Christian population did not exceed half a million in number. Since the wars of the Crusades the Christians have made little effort to convert their Mohammedan conquerors.

In 1820 the American Board of Commissioners for Foreign Missions (A.B.C.F.M.) began to send missionaries to various parts of the Turkish Empire, their primary object being to evangelize Moslems and Jews. In course of time the missionaries came to realize that the unsatisfactory lives of many of the Christians belonging to the Oriental Churches rendered their task of influencing Moslems a hopeless one, and they were led by the force of circumstances to devote a large portion of their time and attention to the education of the Greek and Armenian

[1] See *The Missionary Prospect*, pp. 61 ff.

Christians, amongst whom they were living. The Robert Noble College, which they established in Constantinople, and the schools and colleges at Smyrna, Tarsus, Aintab, and other centres, have had a wide-reaching influence upon the pupils who have attended them, and who have included a considerable number of Moslems. Although the work of the A.B.C.F.M. has not resulted in the conversion of any appreciable number of Moslems, it has indirectly prepared the way for the missionary work which will become possible under the new political conditions that have lately arisen. The pioneers and many of the leaders of this mission have disclaimed any wish to proselytize or to form a Protestant Church in Turkey, and have as a general rule endeavoured to induce those whom they have influenced, or who have been educated in their schools, to continue as members of their own churches. Thus Dr. S. L. Barton, the Secretary of the A.B.C.F.M., writes:

" The missionaries have never had any other purpose or expectation than that the Gregorian, Greek, and Syrian Churches, with their noble histories and splendid services, should be perpetuated . . . they hope to see the churches so reformed from within . . . that they would reach the point where they could present to the Moslems with whom they were in such close contact the beauty and attractiveness of the religion of Jesus Christ and so win them as His followers." [1]

In 1870 the Presbyterians of America organized a separate mission, and the A.B.C.F.M. left to them the work in Syria and in Persia, retaining under their own control the missions which had been started in Macedonia, Asia Minor, Armenia, Kurdistan, and Northern Syria.

The chief educational centre in Syria is the Protestant College at Beyrout (1865), which, though not under the control of the Presbyterian mission, serves as its chief educational centre.

The C.M.S. has stations at Mosul and Bagdad, which are worked in connection with its missionary work in Persia.

[1] *The East and The West*, April 1909.

R.C. missions are carried on in many parts of the Turkish Empire, but the efforts of the various Orders by which they are conducted are almost entirely devoted to winning over other Christians to the Roman Church, and no attempts are made to convert Mohammedans.

There are several missionary organizations, such as the British Syrian Schools and Bible Mission, which carry on good work amongst the Christian population of Asia Minor and Syria, but their work is not of a definitely missionary character.

PALESTINE.

The C.M.S. began work in Palestine in 1851. The chief centres of its work are at Jerusalem, Nazareth, Nablous, Jaffa, Gaza, Haifa, and at Salt on the east of the Jordan. At all the stations special efforts are made by women missionaries to reach Mohammedan women in their homes. The staff includes six medical missionaries. In 1841 a bishopric in Jerusalem in connection with the Anglican Church was founded. The bishop, by the help of his diocesan fund, is endeavouring to develop missionary work amongst Mohammedans.[1]

The U.F.C. of Scotland has a Mission at Tiberias.

Prior to the war the missionaries reported a change of attitude in favour of Christianity on the part of many of the common people, especially in the districts in which medical missions had been stationed. It seems likely that after the war the opportunities of the Christian missionaries will be greatly increased.

ARABIA.

Missionary work in Arabia is still in an initial stage, and there is urgent need of additional missions and missionaries in this long-neglected land.

In 1885 the Hon. Ion Keith-Falconer, who had been

---

[1] See art. "The Anglican Bishopric in Jerusalem" in *The East and The West*, October 1914.

the Reader in Arabic at Cambridge University, made a preliminary visit to Aden, and in 1887 he and his wife and Dr. B. S. Cowan settled at Sheikh-Othman, ten miles from Aden. Four months later Keith-Falconer died. The United Free Church of Scotland has since carried on the mission, and is endeavouring to promote medical and educational work amongst the Arabs and Somalis.

In 1891 Bishop French, who had formerly been Bishop of Lahore, went to live in Muscat in the hope of getting into touch with the Arabs, but after four months' residence there he died. He was a great scholar, and was one of the greatest missionaries connected with the C.M.S. who had worked in India.

In 1889 an undenominational mission was established in America to support work among Mohammedans in Arabia. This mission was taken over by the Reformed (Dutch) Church in America in 1894. In addition to its work at Muscat and Bahrein (an island in the Persian Gulf), it has stations outside the Arabian peninsula at Bussorah and Koweyt. Its staff consists of 14 men and 9 women. Five of its staff are doctors. Dr. S. M. Zwemer, who is one of its staff, is a well-known writer and speaker on missions to Mohammedans.

The population of Arabia is reckoned at about 8,000,000, of whom 6,000,000 are wholly unreached by Christian missions.

PERSIA.

By the end of the third century Christian missions had made considerable progress in Persia, chiefly as the result of efforts made by Syrian and Egyptian missionaries, although the Christians suffered grievous persecution under Shapur II. One of the bishops who attended the Council of Nicæa, A.D. 325, signed as John the Persian. After the separation between the Christians of the East and the West the Persian Church began to display considerable missionary activity in the regions which lay farther to the East. By 641 the Arabs had overrun the country and

had enforced the acceptance of Islam. Christianity,
however, lingered on for a long time. The last of the race
of Christian kings was killed about 1202 by Genghis Khan,
who married a daughter of this king, and was induced by
her to show tolerance towards the Christians. A Nestorian
patriarch ruled the Church during the reigns of seven
Mogul kings, but after this Christianity almost disappeared.
In 1811, Henry Martyn spent ten months in Shiraz and
translated the New Testament into Persian. In 1829 the
Rev. C. G. Pfander of the Basel Mission visited Persia, and
wrote a book entitled *Mizan-el-Hakh* ("The Balance of
Truth"), in which he compared Christianity with Islam, and
which has had a large circulation both in Persia and in
other Mohammedan countries. As a result of the visit of
Dr. Joseph Wolff (a converted Jew) in 1827, the A.B.C.F.M.
opened a mission in 1834 amongst the Nestorian Christians. This mission was transferred in 1871 to the Presbyterian Board, which has also undertaken work amongst
Kurds and Mohammedans in Northern and Western Persia.

In 1869 the Rev. R. Bruce visited Ispahan and Julfa,
and in 1875 the C.M.S. undertook to support and extend
the work which Mr. Bruce had started. A medical
missionary was sent out in 1879, and women were added
to the staff in 1891. Kerman was occupied in 1897,
Yezd in 1898, and Shiraz in 1900. A large proportion
of the work centres in the men and women's hospitals
at Ispahan, Yezd, and Kerman. In 1912 an Anglican
bishop for Persia was appointed. A considerable and
slowly increasing number of converts from Islam have been
obtained, and there is good reason to hope that in the near
future the work of Christian missions will make much more
rapid progress than has been possible in the past.

BALUCHISTAN.

In Baluchistan, missionary work is represented by a
single station belonging to the C.M.S. at Quetta. Connected with the hospital there are two dispensaries in the

18

Kalat State. There are also out-stations in Baluchistan at Sibi and Chaman. According to the last C.M.S. report, "a small mass movement among the same class of people as is being influenced so widely in the Punjab is in progress, and a willingness to learn was displayed such as had not been previously known."

AFGHANISTAN.

The earliest trace of Christianity in what now constitutes Afghanistan is the attendance of a bishop of Herat at the Council of Seleucia in 424. In the thirteenth century there was a Nestorian bishop of Kabul who was subject to the Patriarch, whose seat was successively situated at Seleucia, Ctesiphon, Bagdad, and Alkosh. The Christians at Kabul and other places in Central Asia were exterminated apparently by Timur (1336–1405). There were Armenian Christians who were expelled from Kabul as lately as 1880, but there is no evidence to show that these were descendants of the Afghan Christians of an earlier date.

At the present time no direct missionary work is being attempted. On more than one occasion an Afghan who has become a Christian in India has attempted to preach the Christian faith to his fellow-countrymen, but in each case the missionary has been murdered or has disappeared. Dr. Pennell, whilst working at Bannu near the border of this country, came into touch with many Afghans, and through their instrumentality a knowledge of Christian teaching has penetrated into several parts of Afghanistan.

The story of one of the few who have dared to preach the Gospel in Afghanistan is worth telling, as it illustrates at once the superb courage of an Afghan Christian and the difficulties which lie in the way of those who would undertake missionary work in that country. " Qazi Abdul Karim came of a good Afghan family and was a very learned man. He became a Christian at Quetta. In 1907 he crossed over the frontier with the object of preaching the Gospel to his fellow-countrymen, and was seized by

Afghan soldiers. These brought him before the Governor of Kandahar. He was offered rewards and honours if he would recant and accept Mohammedanism, and when he refused he was cast into prison, loaded with eighty pounds of chains. He was examined by the Amir . . . but remained firm in his confession of Christianity. Finally he was marched off to Kabul. . . . He had to walk loaded with chains and with a bit and bridle in his mouth from Kandahar to Kabul, while any Mohammedan who met him on the way was to smite him on the cheek and pull a hair from his beard. After reaching Kabul . . . (according to a report which purported to be that of an eye-witness) he was set at liberty, and set out alone for India."

Missions of the Greek Church in Central Asia.

Since the rise and spread of Islam very little missionary work has been accomplished by any of the churches of the East, except the Russian Church, and in view of the continuous persecution by the Mohammedan Governments, missionary enterprise in Moslem countries has been practically impossible. By the Russian branch of the Greek Church, however, a large amount of missionary work has been done, though, with two exceptions, this work has been done within the Russian Empire.[1] Russian missions may be said to have begun during the reign of the first Czar, John the Terrible (1533–84), who began to extend the Russian Empire towards the East. The Mohammedan kingdom of Kazan was conquered in 1552, and that of Astrakhan in 1556, and the colonization and conversion of these territories went on together. The subjugation of Siberia, which was begun in 1580, was not completed till 1697. At the present time it has a population of about eight and a half millions, half a million of whom are still heathen. In Tartary and Turkestan the Russian Church is making progress, although

[1] For an account of the missions of the Russian Church see article by R. Eubank in *The East and The West*, April 1904; also *Russian Orthodox Missions*, by E. Smirnoff, published by Rivington.

the majority of their inhabitants are Mohammedans. Special mention should be made of two missionaries of recent times, John Veniaminoff and Macarius. Of the former, Mr. Smirnoff wrote that he was "the most famous missionary of the nineteenth century, and that not only of the Russian Church but of the whole Christian world." He started missions in Siberia, then in Kamtchatka, and afterwards in several different districts of Eastern Siberia. In 1850 he was consecrated as bishop under the name of Innocent, and in 1867, after thirty-three years of work, in the prosecution of which he had endured almost every privation that can fall to the lot of a pioneer missionary, he was made metropolitan of Moscow. In 1870 he founded the Orthodox Missionary Society to assist in the conversion of the non-Christian peoples within the limits of Russia, and in 1879 he died.

The Empress of Russia became patron of the Mission Society, and the metropolitan of Moscow became president. Its work is conducted on the same lines as those of the English Society for the Propagation of the Gospel. Public interest is sustained by sermons and public meetings, and grants are made from its funds to various missions in accordance with their needs. The archimandrite Macarius founded the Altai Mission in Siberia in 1830, and helped to organize mission work, which has since been carried on with a large amount of success.

Mention should also be made of the remarkable missionary work initiated by Nicholay Ivanowitch Ilminsky (1822-91) amongst the tribes in Eastern Russia and in Siberia. During the first half of the nineteenth century Moslem propaganda had made great progress amongst these tribes, but by the labours of Ilminksy, who became Professor of Eastern languages at Kazan University, the Bible was translated into Tartar, and a most hopeful mission has been started amongst tribes who are hovering between Christianity and Islam.[1]

[1] For a detailed account of this mission see article by Professor Alexev Yakovlev in *The East and The West*, July 1913.

XII.

AFRICA.

THE problem with which Christian missions is confronted in the continent of Africa differs materially from that which is presented in any other large section of the mission field. The majority of the inhabitants of this continent are more backward, and from a social and intellectual point of view less developed than are those of any other continent. Whilst it is true to say that many of the South Sea Islanders might vie with the worst of the West African cannibals in savagery and degradation, the campaign which Christian missionaries had there to wage was far less complex, consisting as it did of a series of isolated battles, whereas the missionary campaign in Africa has to be fought on a battle front which reaches for thousands of miles.

If, as we believe, the physical features of the earth have been adapted by God with a view to promote the welfare of its inhabitants, there is no outstanding feature of its configuration for which we have more reason to be grateful than the great Sahara Desert. It is not often realized how important a part has been played by this desert in the evolution of human history. This desert has for decades of centuries prevented the establishment of free intercourse between the peoples of Europe and of Central Africa, and has kept them apart until the time should arrive when the white races had learned to recognize their obligation to bear the black man's burden. By the negative influence exerted by its existence it has affected the religious, moral, and social development of the nations of Europe and indirectly of the whole world.

Had this desert not existed, the African races of the far
interior would long ago have had free access to the shores
of the Mediterranean, and would have been brought into
close contact with the stronger and more virile races which
inhabited its northern shores   The inevitable result would
have been the enslavement of large numbers of the
African races, and a mixed coloured population would
have come into existence, which might have delayed
the progress of European and of the world's civilization
for centuries.   The desert, by interposing an impassable
barrier,[1] deprived the races in the Equatorial regions of
the stimulus which contact with the European races might
have provided, but at the same time saved Europe from
being confronted with a race problem immeasurably more
difficult than that raised by the presence of the negroes in
the United States.

From the missionary standpoint we have reason to be
grateful that the battle between Christianity and paganism
which has now to be joined is not handicapped by the
existence on any large scale of the pagan Christianity
which is to be found in Abyssinia to-day, and which existed
for a time on the Congo and on the Zambesi.   Central
Africa has had long to wait for the advent of Christian
missionaries ; but in view of the past history of Christianity
in Europe, and of the meagre success which attended the
missions of the Dominicans and Jesuits on the west and
east coasts in the sixteenth century, it is doubtful whether,
if free intercourse between Europe and Central Africa had
been established before the beginning of the nineteenth
century, the prospects of Christian missions would be any
brighter than they now are.

The missionary problem in Africa is complicated by
the fact that here, to a greater extent than in any other
continent, Mohammedan missionaries are to be found side
by side with those who represent the Christian faith.   Up
to the present time Islam has hardly penetrated south

[1] The writer of this volume spent the greater part of a year in a vain
effort to cross from Tripoli to Lake Chad.

of the equator, and it rests with the Christian Church to say whether in the near future the wave of Mohammedan propaganda shall be checked in its southward course, as it has been checked in Uganda, or whether the pagan tribes in Central Africa near and to the south of the equator are to become Moslems.

From the Christian standpoint the least hopeful prospect at the present time is in West Central Africa. Here, as will appear in our references to particular missions, partly in consequence of the enervating climate and partly owing to the degradation caused by centuries of intercourse with European slave-traders and gin-importers, the tribes who live on or near the coast are found to be appallingly deficient in moral stamina and strength of character. One result is that Christian missionaries are heavily handicapped when competing with the representatives of Islam, the demands made by which are much less exacting than are those of Christianity. If the Christian faith is ever to become the religion of West Africa and to stay the progress of Islam, this result will be achieved not so much by the development of the Christian communities which are now to be found on the coast, as by the conversion of the Hausas and of one or two other races in the interior, who possess a strength of character which is not to be discovered amongst the peoples in the coastal districts. If, as seems by no means impossible, a Christian Church can be established in Northern Nigeria in the comparatively near future, it may well be that from the members of this Church African missionaries and evangelists will be forthcoming who will spread the knowledge of their new faith amongst the other weaker races, and will be able, by their example and influence, to impart to them the stability and strength of character which they now lack. No part of the world has been more grievously wronged by Europe than has West Africa. To no part of the world, therefore, are the Christians of Europe under a greater obligation to share with its peoples the blessings which their religion can bestow.

In our survey of Christian missions in Africa we shall begin with Egypt, as being the country which was probably first influenced by Christian missionaries, and, travelling in the first instance westwards, shall proceed round the continent.

Before beginning our survey it may be well to give here a rough estimate of the number of Christians throughout the continent of Africa. The following figures are taken from the *Statistical Missionary Atlas*, issued in connection with the Edinburgh Conference (1910), and include all Christian adherents other than Europeans:

North-West Africa (Tripoli to Morocco) . .	224
West Africa	248,702
South-West Africa (Cameroons to German South-West Africa)	103,201
South Africa	1,144,926
South Central Africa	92,583
East Africa	118,107
	1,707,741

To the above should be added about 800,000 Coptic Christians in Egypt.

According to the statistics supplied by this atlas, it appears that the Christian adherents in Africa increased from 576,530 in 1900 to 1,707,741 in 1910, that is at the rate of 196 per cent.

Egypt.

It is probable that Christianity entered Africa by way of Egypt. Eusebius[1] records a tradition that St. Mark preached the gospel in Egypt and founded "churches first of all at Alexandria itself." This tradition apparently existed as early as the beginning of the third century, but there is no other confirmatory evidence. The Christian Church "emerged into daylight" in the episcopate of Demetrius, A.D. 183–231. It was then firmly established and exercised a wide influence. By the end of the second century there were a large number of

[1] *Historica Ecclesiastica*, ii. p. 16.

Christian centres in Egypt and the Thebais. Although in early times Egypt apparently had fewer bishops than other countries in proportion to the number of its Christians, Athanasius is able to state in A.D. 303 that there were nearly one hundred bishops in Egypt, the Thebais, Libya and Pentapolis. The last thirty years of the third century witnessed the development and spread of monasticism for which Egypt afterwards became famous.

One reason why the Church in Egypt increased more rapidly and developed on more stable foundations than it did in many other countries, was the fact that the Bible was translated into at least three Coptic dialects, of which the oldest, the Upper Egyptian, dates from the second half of the third century. The earliest monks in the Nitrian desert probably possessed copies of the Bible in their own language.

It does not lie within the scope of this book to trace the history of Christianity in Egypt down to the time when Islam was introduced and promulgated by force of arms in the seventh century. We pass on to note the efforts which have been made in modern times to convert the Moslems of Egypt to the Christian faith.

The *American United Presbyterian Mission* began work amongst Copts and Moslems in 1854. Although the work lies chiefly among Coptic Christians, the missionaries have by their medical, educational and colportage work exerted a Christian influence upon Moslems, especially in the Delta.

The *Church Missionary Society* began work for Moslems in 1882, the year of the British occupation. The centre of their work is at Cairo, where the Rev. D. Thornton, who died in 1907, did much to interpret Christianity to Moslems, and to pave the way for further work on their behalf. In Old Cairo the C.M.S. has a self-supporting hospital and dispensary with two English and two native doctors. Closely associated with this is Dr. Harpur's itinerating medical mission, which is centred in a floating dispensary on the Nile. In Cairo and three out-stations the C.M.S.

has a staff of clergy whose work lies amongst the more
highly educated Moslems and amongst the students at the
Al Azhar University. The Mission issues a newspaper in
Arabic which has a considerable circulation. It has established friendly relations with the Coptic Church, which it is
the desire of the C.M.S. clergy to strengthen and help.

Other Protestant societies at work are the *N. Africa
Mission*, the *Egypt General Mission* and the *Sudan Pioneer
Mission* (German).

The *Roman Catholic* missions in Egypt contain about
60,000 Christians (including Europeans). The missionaries
are from the Lyons Society for African Missions and the
Minor Franciscans of Rome.

According to the census taken in 1907, there are
10,466,000 Mohammedans and 881,000 Christians in
Egypt.

The Egyptian Sudan.

The Egyptian Sudan, which is under Anglo-Egyptian
rule, contains about 1,000,000 square miles and a population of about 3,500,000. Of these about 2,500,000
are Mohammedans and 990,000 pagans. Of the Christians,
who number about 6000, 3000 belong to the Oriental
Churches, 2000 to the R.C. Church and 1000 are
Anglicans or Protestants.

Connected with the *R.C. missions*, which are supported
by the Algerian Missionary Society and the English Foreign
Missionary Society (Mill Hill), there are 14 priests, 10
schools and 4 orphanages.

In the Northern Sudan, under Bishop Gwynne of
Khartoum, the *C.M.S.* has a medical mission with an
English doctor at Khartoum and schools under women-
workers in and around that city.

As we proceed south from Khartoum, the first mission
station, which is 420 miles south, has recently been opened
by the *Sudan United Mission*; 100 miles farther south,
the *American United Presbyterians* have a station manned
by 7 missionaries at the junction of the Sobat and the

Nile; 200 miles farther south, the *C.M.S.* has a station
with 4 missionaries at Malek.   The next station, which is
300 miles farther south, is the C.M.S. station of Gulu in
Uganda.   West of the Nile, in the Bahr-el-Ghazal province
of the Sudan, are two C.M.S. stations at Zan and Xambio.
On the west bank of the Nile are three Austrian R.C.
missions.

North-West Africa.

Amongst those present in Jerusalem on the Day of
Pentecost were Jews "from the parts of Libya about
Cyrene."   It is possible that some of these acted as the
first Christian missionaries to North-West Africa.   Before
the end of the second century the Church of Carthage was
firmly established and was apparently more vigorous than
the Church of Rome or of Alexandria.   In North-West
Africa, as in Italy, the majority of the early converts were
won from those who had come into contact with Greek or
Roman culture.   Their numerical increase may be roughly
gauged by the increase in the number of Christian bishops.
Harnack reckons the number of bishops in North-West
Africa in A.D. 220 as from 70 to 90, in A.D. 250 as nearly
150, in A.D. 300 as hardly less than 250, and in A.D. 400
as about 600.   When in the seventh century the forces
of Islam spread over North-West Africa, they eventually
swept out of existence this Church which had once been
one of the largest Churches in Christendom.   It has been
suggested that the complete disappearance of this Church
can best be explained by the fact that it had been
conspicuously lacking in missionary zeal, and had failed
to make any serious effort to commend its faith to
the native tribes in the interior.   In support of this
suggestion it may be pointed out that the voluminous
writings of the two great bishops of North-West Africa,
Cyprian of Carthage and Augustine of Hippo, apparently
contain no references to the duty of evangelizing these
races.   Whilst it is dangerous to rely upon negative
evidence, and the traces of ancient Christianity found

in the interior of Tunis and Algeria suggest at least a possibility of the former existence of churches recruited from the native tribes, it is impossible to deny that missionary enthusiasm, especially during the fourth, fifth and sixth centuries, was at a low ebb, or to contest the statement that a Church which makes no effort to do missionary work is itself in danger of its life. Two other reasons which may be alleged to account for the disappearance of this Church are—its failure to translate the Bible into the language spoken by the majority of the inhabitants of the country, and the internecine quarrels that long disgraced the Christians of North-West Africa prior to the destruction of their Church. Harnack writes:

"Rapidly as Christianity struck down its roots into the soil of Africa and spread itself abroad, it was as rapidly swept away by Islam. The native Berber population was but superficially Christianized, so far as it was Christianized at all. The next stratum, that of the Punic inhabitants, appears to have been Christianized for the most part, but as the Punic language never got possession of the Bible, the Christianizing process was not permanent. The third stratum, that of the Greco-Roman population, became in all likelihood entirely Christian by slow degrees. But it was too thin." [1]

There exists no parallel in the history of Christendom to the catastrophe which befel the Church in North Africa. In 411 there met at Carthage a conference of Christian bishops, numbering in all 565, nearly all of whom came from North-West Africa, and each of whom represented a considerable Christian community. The conference was summoned to discuss a dispute relating to details of Church discipline. Impossible as the assembled bishops found it to agree on the subject which they discussed, there was at least one point on which no variety of opinion existed. They all alike believed that the triumph of Christianity in North-West Africa was already assured. What a storm of indignation would have greeted the speaker who should

[1] *Expansion of Christianity*, vol. ii. p. 435.

have dared to forecast the future and to suggest that before many centuries had elapsed the Faith represented by the 565 assembled bishops and by 300 other bishops in North-West Africa who were not present at the conference would have been swept away!

Amid much that is dark and discouraging in the later history of North-West Africa, one story has been preserved which reminds us of the heroic martyrs at Carthage at a still earlier date. An Arab boy named Geronimo, who had been baptized and taught the Christian faith, was captured together with his master and ordered to recant the profession of his faith. On his refusal to do so, twenty-four hours were allowed him in which to change his mind. He was then brought before the Sultan of Algiers, who was engaged in superintending the erection of a fort. In the wall of the fort was a space partly filled with cement. Geronimo was told that unless he would abandon his Christian faith he would be laid in the cement and built up in the wall. He replied that he would not deny his faith. He was accordingly placed face downwards in the cement with his hands and feet tied, and the builders proceeded with their work. The fort in which Geronimo was immured (in 1569) was destroyed by the French in 1853, and at the spot which was identified by tradition, a skeleton of a boy was found embedded in the cement, lying prostrate in the position described.

Towards the end of the thirteenth century Raymond Lull attempted to preach the Christian faith in Tunis and at Bougiah, but without any visible results. He died on board a Genoese ship in 1315 at the age of eighty, from injuries received whilst preaching at Bougiah. See p. 466.

The population of North-West Africa, that is of Tripoli, Tunis, Algeria and Morocco, is about 14,000,000. Protestant missions, which are chiefly represented by the "North Africa Mission," were started about forty years ago, and a few isolated conversions of Moslems have occurred. The attitude of the French Government in Tunis and Algeria has been uniformly hostile alike to Protestant and to Roman Catholic missions. The latter have, however, been allowed to care for and educate a number of Arab orphans and to establish the Order of the White Fathers in Algiers, from which missionaries have been sent out to the hinterland of Algeria and to other parts of Africa. In 1876 three priests who were sent to Timbuctoo were murdered before they reached their destination. In 1881 three more priests were murdered by the Tuaregs at Ghadames. At a later date armed bands of mission-workers were sent by Cardinal Lavigerie, the Head of the Roman Mission in Algeria, with instructions to establish themselves at some of the wells in the interior and to endeavour to preach the Christian faith to those who frequented the wells. On the death of Cardinal Lavigerie this method of work was abandoned.

Morocco.

In Morocco the *North Africa Mission* supports 25 missionaries and 6 mission hospitals or dispensaries. There are 36 *R.C.* priests in Morocco, but these only minister to the resident European population. The Jews number about 150,000.

In the Spanish possession of RIO DE ORO there are no Christian missions. To the south of this come the French possessions. On the SENEGAL RIVER there is a small Protestant mission of the *Paris Society*. In FRENCH GUINEA there is a small Anglican mission called the *Rio Pongo Mission* which is assisted by the *S.P.G.* It was started in 1855 and is manned and organized by the Anglican Church in the West Indies. Connected with the R.C. mission (1897) there are 21 priests and 5680 Christians. In SENEGAMBIA and in the whole of the French territory as far south as Dahomey, which has a population of about 9,000,000, there are 17,000 Christians and 37 priests connected with the R.C. missions. In PORTUGUESE GUINEA, which has a population of about 1,000,000, there is a small *R.C.* mission.

In the British colony of GAMBIA, which lies on both sides of the Gambia River, there is a population of 91,000, of whom 35,000 are Mohammedans and 50,000 pagans. Of the Christians, who number 5600, 3800 are Roman Catholics and 1800 are Protestants. The *W.M.S.* has 9 stations, 2 missionaries and 1500 professed Christians.

Sierra Leone.

Sierra Leone was bought by the African Company in 1790, and was handed over to the British Government in 1808 in order to form a settlement for negro soldiers who had fought on behalf of Great Britain in the War of Independence, and for the African slaves who had been liberated after the legal abolition of the slave-trade had been enacted. As early as 1792 *Methodism* had been introduced into this district by negro converts who came from Nova Scotia. As the result of their work a chapel to hold 400 people was erected, and in response to an appeal which was sent to England some Methodist preachers arrived in 1796. This mission, however, proved unsuccessful and was abandoned. In 1811 a preacher named George Warren, accompanied by three schoolmasters, sailed for Sierra Leone and, despite great loss of life on the part of the early pioneers, the mission was at length firmly established.

In 1804 the *C.M.S.* began work by sending out, in the first instance, some German missionaries, amongst whom the names of Nylander and Jansen are worthy of notice. By 1846, 50,000 liberated slaves had been landed in the colony, who spoke, as it was stated, 117 different dialects. As a result of the multiplicity of African tongues English was adopted as the language of the colony, and most of the inhabitants near the coast speak to-day no other language. The mortality amongst the early missionaries was appalling. In twenty-five years 109 men and women died. In 1852 an Anglican bishopric was established. The first three Bishops (Vidal,

Weeks and Bowen) died at their posts before the end of ten years.

The work of the *English Methodists* has been subject to great fluctuations, but the numbers of converts have steadily increased. The Girls' High School in Freetown, which is superintended by three English Methodist deaconesses, has recently been enlarged. Both the Anglican and Methodist missions have developed into what are practically independent churches. The moral character of the Christians connected with all the missions leaves very much to be desired; the tendency of the Christians is to imitate the dress and the social habits of Europeans, whilst making little attempt to imitate the character which they have acquired as a result of long centuries of Christian education. Their ancestors, who were said to have represented 117 different tribes, were a " confused mass, destitute of the slightest feeling of community, (who) lived in a state of constant conflict among themselves, and were dull, lazy and in the last degree unchaste, besides being in bondage, without exception, to heathenish superstition." [1] It is not, therefore, to be wondered at that the development of Christian character has not kept pace with the material developments of the people.

Until within the last few years no efforts have been made by the Christians of Sierra Leone to evangelize their heathen neighbours, but there is now reason to hope that the recent efforts which have been made to organize and support the Christian missions in the interior of the country will meet with success and will react beneficially upon the Christian population on and near the coast.

Dr. Eugene Stock's reference to the state of the Church in Sierra Leone in 1872 is applicable to the state of the Anglican and Methodist missions at the present time:

" The churches were filled, the Communions well attended, Sunday-schools fairly efficient, the collections large, but . . . while there were many godly and praying people, particularly among the poorer and older members

[1] Warneck's *Protestant Missions*, p. 216.

of the congregations, the younger and more opulent folk manifested for the most part little personal religion. The weaknesses of the African character, too, were very manifest: sensual indulgence and vain display were common, and dislike to hard work crowded the markets for clerks and shopmen, while handicrafts and agriculture were neglected. Together with an almost grotesque aping of the externals of European refinement and luxury, there was a growing spirit of rather petulant independence."

The Fourah Bay College, which is carried on by the C.M.S., is a higher grade school or college at which a large proportion of the African clergy and schoolmasters employed throughout West Africa have been trained.

Other missionary societies which are at work in the colony are the *American United Brethren* (15 of whose missionaries were massacred by the Temné tribe in 1898) and the *International Missionary Alliance.* This latter society works in the Sherbro district, to the south of the colony, and has met with a large measure of success.

The *R.C. missionaries,* who number 22, belong to the Order of the Holy Ghost and the Sacred Heart of Mary. The Christian population numbers about 60,000, of whom about 3250 are African Roman Catholics.

Liberia.

The colony, or state, of Liberia originated with the efforts made by the American Colonization Society (formed in 1817) to transplant free American negroes from America to West Africa. The total number of negroes who have come from America is about 20,000, all of whom were nominally Christian. In 1847 Liberia was declared an independent state, with the result that from a political and social standpoint hardly any progress has since been achieved. Included in its area are various tribes (Kroo, Bassa, Vey, etc.), which number about 2,000,000. The Liberians have not attempted to evangelize their heathen fellow-countrymen, but some good missionary work has been done by the *American Presby-*

19

terians, the *Episcopal Methodists* and the *Protestant Episcopal Church of America*. This last supports work in the Cape Palmas district, which is superintended by Bishop Ferguson, who is himself a Liberian. The total number of professing Christians is about 20,000.

A Lutheran mission has attempted to open some stations in the interior.

A *R.C.* mission was started in 1903, and there are 70 Christians and 7 priests connected with it.

Ivory Coast.

The Ivory Coast, which is a French possession, has a population of about 2,000,000, of whom about 200,000 are Mohammedans. The *R.C. mission* (1895), which is supported by the Lyons Society, has 19 priests and 2400 Christians.

Gold Coast.

The first missionary to the Gold Coast, and perhaps the first Englishman to go as a missionary to any part of Africa, was the Rev. Thomas Thompson (*b.* 1707), who was Fellow and Dean of Christ's College, Cambridge, and resigned his position there (1744) in order to undertake missionary work in New Jersey. After labouring there for five years, he volunteered to the *S.P.G.* to go as a missionary to West Africa, if the Society would support him out of its "Negro Conversion Fund." In offering to go as a missionary, he urged that "if ever a church of Christ is founded among the negroes, somebody must lay the first stone, and should he be prevented in his intention, God only knew how long it might be again before any other person would take the same resolution." He was appointed as Missionary to the Gold Coast on February 15, 1751. On reaching the coast he began at once to learn "the native language." The king frequently attended the services which he conducted, but continued "firm and unshaken in his superstition." He completed a vocabulary of above 1200 words and baptized some adult negroes "as well as others." In 1756, in consequence of a breakdown of health, he returned to England. He had meanwhile sent home three negro boys under twelve years of age to be trained at the Society's expense to become missionaries to their fellow-countrymen. On their arrival in London in 1754 they were placed under the charge of a "very diligent school-master," and after receiving instruction for four years, two of them, Quaque and Cudjo, were baptized (January 7, 1759) in the Church of St. Mary, Islington. The third boy died of consumption in 1758, and Cudjo afterwards died of madness in Guy's Hospital Philip Quaque was ordained as an Anglican clergyman, and in 1765 was appointed by the S.P.G. "missionary, schoolmaster and catechist to the negroes on the Gold Coast."

During his stay in England he had to a large extent forgotten his own language and had, at least for some years, to instruct his fellow-countrymen by the aid of an interpreter. During the first nine years after his return to Africa he baptized 52 persons, some of whom were soldiers or mulattoes.

After his return to England, Thompson published (in 1772) a pamphlet entitled "The African Trade for Negro Slaves shown to be consistent with the principles of humanity and with the laws of revealed religion."[1] He had himself seen much of the operations of the slave-traders on the coast of Africa. The arguments contained in his pamphlet are for the most part drawn from Aristotle and his plea of justification from the Pentateuch.

Quaque continued to work in different parts of the Gold Coast, both as a missionary and as a chaplain to the factory at Cape Coast Castle, till his death at the age of seventy-five in 1816.

The S.P.G. helped to support two chaplains as "missionaries to the natives," but in 1824 their connection with the Gold Coast was interrupted. In 1841 they voted salaries

[1] A copy of this pamphlet exists in the British Museum.

for two clergy to be stationed at Cape Coast Castle, but men were not forthcoming. In 1904 the S.P.G. resumed its work on the Gold Coast and a bishop was appointed, first as a suffragan to the Bishop of W. Equatorial Africa and later on as Bishop of the diocese of Accra. The chief centres of work are at Accra, Cape Coast, Sekondi and Kumasi.

Up to the present the S.P.G. missionaries have been able to do little more than minister to the European and African Christians who belong to the Anglican Church, but the Society hopes to take its share in the evangelization of the large population which has not yet come into touch with any Christian mission.

The greater part of the missionary work in the Gold Coast is carried on by the *English Wesleyans* in the western and the *Basel Mission* in the eastern districts of the colony. The Wesleyans, who work chiefly amongst the Fanti, began their work in 1835.

The climatic difficulties, with which all missionary societies have had to contend in West Africa, may be illustrated by the sacrifice of life which accompanied the start of the Wesleyan mission. The first worker, who landed in 1835, died within six months. His two successors, who arrived in the following year, died within fourteen months. The next two workers died within a month of their arrival. At the present time the mission has 15 European and 27 African ministers and 63,000 baptized Christians.

The *Basel Mission*, which started in 1824, works amongst the Ga, Chi and Fanti peoples. One of its missionaries, Christaller, translated portions of the Bible into the Ga and Chi languages. The mission, which began on the coast, has now penetrated into the interior, and extends from Ashanti to the river Volta. In 1857, after thirty years' work, their converts numbered only 367. In 1867 these had increased to 1500, and the present number of adherents is about 25,000. The mission has organized and developed on a considerable scale industrial missions, which are placed under the charge of a special missionary trading society. It has also devoted special attention to the development both of elementary and secondary schools.

The *R.C. missions* (1879), which are connected with the Lyons Society for African Missions, support 21 missionaries at 8 mission stations, and 13 schools. The Christians connected with this mission number 10,800. The total number in the colony is 41,000.

Togoland.

The *North German (Bremen) Mission* started work among the Evhe people, who number about 2,000,000, in 1847, but owing to constant loss by death of its missionaries and the small permanent staff which it has been able to maintain, its progress has been slow. After twenty-five years' work its church only numbered 93 members. The employment of missionary deaconesses has been a great help in the more recent development of its work. In 1913 the mission reported 1535 baptisms.

The Steyl Fathers of the *R.C. Church* began work in 1894, and the Christian community attached to their mission numbers about 15,000. In 1912 they reported 2000 baptisms. There are 44 priests attached to the mission.

The *English Wesleyans* have a station at Little Popo, and *German Methodists* have also started a mission.

Dahomey.

Dahomey, a French colony, contains a population of about 1,000,000, of whom about 700,000 are pagans and 300,000 Moslems. The *R.C. mission* (1882) is connected with the Lyons Missionary Society. There are about 11,500 converts and 34 priests connected with the missions. The Bishop in Dahomey reports a great opening for evangelistic work.

The *Wesleyan Methodist Missionary Society* has a station at Porto Novo on the coast.

Yorubaland

A number of slaves, who had been set free and had become Christians in Sierra Leone, began, in 1840, to return to the Yoruba country, from which they had been taken by Portuguese slave-raiders. In response to an appeal from these Christians the Rev. H. Townsend, the Rev. C. A. Gollmer and the Rev. Samuel Crowther, who were sent by the C.M S., started work in Badagry and Abeokuta in 1846, and in 1852 work was begun at Lagos and Ibadan, at the latter place by the Rev. D. Hinderer. Within eighteen months of the starting of work at Abeokuta six converts were baptized, one of whom was the mother of Samuel Crowther, whom he had accidentally met in the street of Abeokuta. The mission soon prospered and extended, and by 1860 the number of Christians in the Yoruba mission, including the immigrants from Sierra Leone, numbered 2000. The extension of the work was interrupted by the invasions of the warlike people of Dahomey, and by the state of internal warfare, which continued to distract the country and to endanger the lives of the missionaries. Doherty, an African catechist, was captured by the king of Dahomey, who ordered him to read to him the Christian Scriptures. The king eventually ordered him to be killed, with a portion of Scripture in one hand and a lamp in the other hand, in order that he might be lighted into the spirit world and might read the Scriptures to the last king. The executioner executed another man by mistake and Doherty eventually resumed his work as a catechist.

A state of war existed in the neighbourhood of Abeokuta for five years, 1860–65, during which Mr. Hinderer and his wife were detained as prisoners in Ibadan. Towards the end of 1867 the Egba chiefs suddenly expelled all European missionaries from Abeokuta, and for the next thirteen years the Christians there were left in charge of African pastors.

In 1871, Bishop Cheetham of Sierra Leone ordained

four Yorubas as clergy, and in 1876 he ordained three more. One of the latter was Phillips, who afterwards became assistant bishop.

Soon after the English Government had taken possession of Lagos (1861) it became the centre of the C.M.S. Yoruba Mission; and the interior was left without a resident European missionary, from 1865 to 1883, when the Rev. J. B. Wood became the superintending missionary. In 1888 the C.M.S. obtained the approval of the Archbishop of Canterbury to the appointment of an African as Bishop of the Yoruba country, but owing to the opposition of the African Christians the proposal was abandoned.

In 1864 the Rev. Samuel Crowther was appointed as Bishop of the Niger (see p. 297), and on his death in 1891 Bishop Hill succeeded him in 1893 with the title of "Bishop in West Equatorial Africa," Lagos, which had formerly been supervised by the Bishop of Sierra Leone, being now incorporated in the same diocese as the Niger. At the same time two Africans, Rev. C. Phillips and Rev. I. Oluwole, were consecrated as assistant bishops for the Yoruba country. On the death of Bishop Hill, in the following January, Bishop Tugwell succeeded him. Bishop Phillips died in 1906. In 1900 another African, Rev. James Johnson, was consecrated as an assistant bishop. The Anglican mission has 40,000 adherents and 15,000 school children. On the coast, and specially at Lagos, which is the centre of organization for the various missions, a large proportion of the Christians speak English and tend to imitate English customs.

Many of the churches in Lagos are served by African clergy or pastors. The Anglican church at Breadfruit, which has a congregation of about 1400, and raises nearly £1000 a year for religious objects, is built on the site of the old baracoon, the building in which slaves waiting to be shipped were formerly confined. The Anglican churches in Lagos and district are no longer connected with any missionary society, but are beginning to support missionary work on their own account.

In the "Lagos District," which includes the Yoruba country, the *English Wesleyans* have 11 European and 21 African ministers and 9000 baptized Christians. Missions are also carried on by the *Southern Baptist* and *National Baptist Conventions, U.S.A.*

Belonging to the *R.C. missions*, which are supported by the Lyons Society, there are 27 priests, 24 schools and 16 orphanages.

The Niger Mission.

The *C.M.S. Niger Mission* has a special interest for all students of Missions. It embodied a serious attempt, which was persevered in for nearly half a century, to establish a branch of the Christian Church in tropical Africa through the instrumentality of Africans and with a minimum of European supervision. The attempt was the outcome of the realization that the climate of the river Niger and surrounding districts was so unhealthy that white men could not hope to work there for more than a few months at a time. When the first British expedition, which was accompanied by Dr. Schon and Samuel Crowther, went up the Niger in 1841, 42 white men out of a total of 150 died within two months. After a second and more successful expedition had been made in 1857, Samuel Crowther, who had been originally a slave and had been educated at Fourah Bay and ordained in London in 1843, was commissioned by the C.M.S. to open a Niger Mission to be staffed by Africans from Sierra Leone. In 1859 the C.M.S. sent out five Europeans to join the staff of the mission, but none of them succeeded in reaching Onitsha, which was the first mission station to be occupied. Until the cause of malarial fever was discovered to be the bite of the *Anopheles* mosquito, the river Niger deservedly possessed the reputation of having the most unhealthy climate that the world contained. When the writer of this volume was on the Niger in 1894 the average length of a white man's life was reckoned to be two years. Since the discovery of the cause of malaria the conditions have completely changed. When it was realized that white men could not live for any length of time on the Niger, the C.M.S. decided to apply to the Archbishop of Canterbury to consecrate Crowther as Bishop, and to place the whole of the mission under his charge. Amid scenes of great enthusiasm he was consecrated in Canterbury Cathedral in 1864, and remained as Bishop of the Niger till his death in 1891. The only African who had been consecrated as a bishop before the time of Crowther was the Bishop of the Congo (see p. 302).

The experiment of placing an African bishop to supervise a mission where, as experience seemed to have shown, European missionaries could not work, was fully justified by the circumstances of that time, but it must regretfully be admitted that it proved an almost complete failure. Bishop Crowther was a humble and saintly man, but he lacked the qualities which were essential for the due performance of his duties as a bishop. When, as alas frequently happened, complaints were made to him that one of his missionaries had committed a serious moral offence, he was wont to reply, " I never hear evil spoken against my missionaries." The result was that when he died, after an episcopate of twenty-seven years, little progress had been made, and the reputation of the Christians at some of the mission stations was such that the reconstruction of the mission proved a more difficult task than would have been the founding of a completely new mission.

During his long episcopate Bishop Crowther never learnt any language which could be understood on the Niger, and till his death he was dependent on the help of interpreters, who were in many cases quite incompetent. He habitually spoke English, but could also speak Yoruba, which he had learned as a boy, and which was available in parts of the Lagos district.

Bishop Tugwell in the course of a speech in which he alluded to the jubilee of Bishop Crowther's consecration, referred thus to the failure of Bishop Crowther to infuse his own spirit into his fellow-workers : "He suffered greatly by the hands of others. He suffered greatly because some men who should have been true . . . failed, and failed grievously. Under temptations which were great, cut off from the companionship of their fellow-Christians, some became drunken and immoral, others greedy of gain engaged in trade. In 1885 there was a grievous scandal at Onitsha . . . the blow fell mainly upon Bishop Crowther. The remainder of his life was spent under a cloud, and he carried his burden to the grave." [1]

On the death of Bishop Crowther in 1891 the Archbishop of Canterbury sent out the Rev. J. S. Hill to report to him on the condition of the mission. Mr. Hill was subsequently consecrated as Bishop, but died at Lagos on his return journey in 1894.

Since 1894 much good work has been done and foundations have been laid on which there is every reason to believe that a Christian Church, worthy of the name, may eventually be built up. The two African bishops have given valuable assistance to Bishop Tugwell in the supervision of his widely extended diocese. In this diocese, which includes the Niger and Yoruba Missions, there are now (1915) 89 clergy, of whom 65 are Africans. Of these last 51 are supported by the local Church. Of the 450 African lay agents the local Church supports 225. There are about 70,000 Christian adherents connected with the Anglican Church in the diocese.

In the lower reaches of the Niger missionary work is carried on by the *Niger Delta Pastorate*, which is now practically independent of the C.M.S. Higher up the river, in Southern Nigeria, the chief centres of work are at Onitsha, Obusi and Asaba. There are 9 European clergy in this part of the mission and 2 European doctors.

In 1890 the Rev. J. Alfred Robinson and Mr. G. Wilmot Brooke, accompanied by several others, attempted to start mission work amongst the Hausas in Northern Nigeria. Both the leaders of this mission died, however,

---

[1] Address to his diocesan synod at Lagos, May 1914.

before any station in the Hausa country had been opened.
Dr. Walter Miller, who went out to Nigeria in 1898, has
carried on medical and other missionary work at Zaria
under circumstances of special difficulty, and, besides
gathering round him a number of converts from Islam,
he has seen the building of a Christian village inhabited
by ex-Moslem Christians or Christian inquirers. This
mission has greater promise than perhaps any other in
West Africa, as the Hausas, whose language is the *lingua
franca* of the Western Sudan, and who travel as traders
over the whole of North Africa, are possessed of more
character than those belonging to any other race in West
Africa. The majority of them are nominal Mohammedans,
but there are signs that many are prepared to listen to
Christian teaching. The conversion to the Christian faith
of any large number of the Hausas would be the prelude
to the conversion of a large part of Africa north of the
equator.

By far the greater part of the missionary work on the
Niger is in the hands of the C.M.S., which, in addition to
the stations already referred to, has work amongst the
pagans in the Bauchi district of Northern Nigeria.

The *United Free Church of Scotland* has a mission at
Old Calabar (1846). The success achieved by this mission
is to be attributed to the fact that its work has been
more carefully supervised by European missionaries than
perhaps any other mission in West Africa. The *Sudan
United Mission*, which works on undenominational lines,
and was started in 1904, has several stations amongst the
pagan tribes on the river Benué. Its aim is eventually to
connect with other missions in the Nile basin. The *R.C.
missionaries* belong to the Orders of the Holy Ghost and the
Sacred Heart of Mary. In the Vicariate of Benin (1860)
there are 8500 Christians and 28 priests; in the apostolic
prefecture of Western Nigeria (1884) there are 17 priests
and 2800 Christians; in that of Eastern Nigeria (1911)
there are 5 priests; and in that of Lower Nigeria (1889)
there are 4789 Christians and 18 priests.

The Cameroons.

In 1845, Saker, a representative of the *English Baptists*, coming from Fernando Po, began missionary work, but the visible progress attained was comparatively small. In 1884, when the German Government occupied this territory, the Baptists handed over their work to the *Basel Mission*. Owing to difficulties which arose between the Africans and the European missionaries, several congregations declared themselves independent, while others are now superintended by German Baptist missionaries. The Basel Mission has since made good progress, and has established centres both amongst the Dualla-speaking peoples and in other parts of the territory. In 1913 the Basel Mission reported 1500 baptisms. The Gossner Mission has started work in the eastern districts.

In the southern part of the Cameroons, in Batanga Land, the *American Presbyterians*, who began work in 1875, have a number of stations. They have also stations in French territory on the Gaboon River and Corisco Island.

The *R.C. mission*, which began work in 1890, has been making rapid progress within recent years. During 1913 it reported 6000 baptisms, bringing the total number of baptized Christians up to 20,000. There are 31 priests connected with the mission.

Rio Muni.

Rio Muni, a Spanish possession, which lies to the south of the Cameroons, has a population of about 40,000. Off the coast lie the Spanish islands of Fernando Po, Corisco, and Anno Bon, containing a population of about 34,000. The *R.C. missions*, which are carried on by the Spanish Congregation of the Sacred Heart of Mary, report 6500 converts. Work is carried on at fourteen stations by 24 priests. The *American Presbyterian Church* has five stations and 600 Christians on the mainland. The

Primitive Methodists have four stations and 100 Christians in Fernando Po.

The Congo.

In 1491 a band of Portuguese missionaries, who had come in response to a request sent by the king of the Congo,[1] landed near the mouth of that river. Shortly after their arrival the king of the Congo and many of his principal chiefs were baptized with great state and ceremonial and thousands of persons followed their example. To the capital of the Congo was given the new name of San Salvador. The second Christian king commanded all his subjects to abandon idolatry and receive baptism on pain of being burnt alive, and images of the saints were offered to them to replace their former idols. The European missionaries included representatives of the *Dominicans, Franciscans, Augustinians* and, later on, of the *Jesuits.* Dissensions occurred amongst the representatives of these Orders, and the king sent back some of the priests as prisoners to Portugal. In course of time the kingdom of Congo was declared "wholly Catholic." A large number of the slaves shipped abroad from West Africa were taken from the Congo districts, and a marble chair formerly existed on the pier at St. Paul de Loanda from which the bishops used to give their blessing to the slave-ships which were preparing to sail for the Portuguese possessions in Brazil or the West Indies.

Some of the Jesuit missionaries preached earnestly against polygamy and unchastity, which the African clergy permitted, but they were not supported by the king or the court. After several alternations of revival and retrogression the profession of Christianity began to decrease. In 1640 the Capuchin friars arrived. At first they preached against the practice of polygamy, but

---

[1] For a detailed account of the early Christian missions to the Congo see *A Report of the Kingdom of the Congo,* drawn out of the writings and discourses of the Portuguese Duarte Lopez, by Filippo Pigafetta, 1591. Translated by M. Hutchinson.

they eventually agreed to its retention. In 1698 the missionary Zucchelli wrote, concerning the people amongst whom he was working: "Here is neither knowledge nor conscience, neither Word of God nor faith, neither state nor family, . . . neither discipline nor shame, . . . neither fear of God nor zeal for the welfare of souls. . . . You can say nothing of these people except that they are in fact nothing else than baptized heathen, who have nothing of Christianity about them but the bare name, without any works." A negro, who was a descendant of the royal house, after being educated in Portugal and at Rome, was appointed Bishop of San Salvador, but died before reaching his diocese.

Several subsequent attempts were made by the Capuchins and Benedictines to raise the moral and religious tone of the people, but without success. Captain Tuckey, who was sent by the English Government in 1816 to explore the Congo, could find no trace of Christianity except crucifixes and relics, which were not distinguished by the people from their amulets and fetiches.

It would seem that Christianity had at no time exerted more than a superficial influence upon the inhabitants, and had from the first failed to effect any real change in the characters of those who adopted its profession. It is, indeed, hard to see how a mission which not only condoned but engaged in slave-raiding, and which permitted polygamy in its most repulsive forms, could have obtained better or more permanent results than those which were attained.

The exploration of the Congo by Stanley (1876–77), which was followed by the establishment, under Belgian auspices, of the Congo Free State, prepared the way for the re-establishment of Christian missions. Representatives of the *English Baptists* from the Cameroons began work in 1879, and in the course of a few years established nine stations extending up almost to the Stanley Falls. The eagerness of the missionaries, amongst whom Bentley deserves special notice, to cover too much ground led to the establishment of weak centres at great distances from one another, and the progress attained has been less than might have been expected in view of the number of agents who have been employed. The English Baptists have now opened two stations, Mabondo and Wayika, on the Lualaba River, which are within 300 miles of Uganda.

A little later a mission, entitled the *Congo Inland Mission*, was organized by Grattan Guinness, the founder of the East London Institute. His work was characterized by undue haste, and several stations had to be abandoned after having been opened. Partly in consequence of the lack of due care in the selection of missionaries at home, and partly in consequence of unskilful organization abroad, a large proportion of the missionaries, many of whom were women, died after a very brief period of service. The mission was eventually taken over by the *American Baptist Missionary Union*.

In 1886, Grattan Guinness founded another mission amongst the Balolo tribe, which lives on the basin of the Lulongo, a tributary on the left of the Congo south of its great bend.

In 1886, Arnot, an independent missionary, a member of the *Plymouth Brethren*, started a new mission in Garenganze or Katanga, in the far east of the Congo Free State. This mission, which has now a staff of 15 missionaries, has established fifteen stations between Bihé and Lake Mweru.

The *American Methodist Episcopal Church* (*South*) started a mission among the Batetela, north of the Lobefu River, in November 1913, under the superintendence of Bishop Lambuth. The recently formed *Société Belge de Missions Protestantes au Congo* is starting work at Chofa, on the Lomami.

The *American Presbyterian Church* (*South*), which has a mission on the Kasai and Lulua Rivers, was strengthened in 1914 by the addition of 14 new missionaries, who are to be supported by funds provided as a result of the Laymen's Missionary Movement.

Attempts are being made from three different bases

to evangelize the Niam-Niam or Azandi people, who live
at the meeting-point of the Belgian Congo, the French
Congo and the Anglo-Egyptian Sudan. The C.M.S. are
advancing from Malek on the river Nile, the Africa
Inland Mission is advancing from Mahagi on the western
shore of the Albert Nyanza, and a Roman Catholic mission,
which started from Wau in the Bahr-el-Ghazal, has opened
stations at Mupoi among the Niam-Niam and at Palaro
and Gondokoro.

Many who have had little personal experience of
missionary work and profess to base their theory of
missionary methods simply on the teaching of the New
Testament, have from time to time suggested that a
mission established amongst primitive or backward races
ought to be self-supporting from the outset. The Congo
has been the scene of an experiment based upon this
theory on a large and disastrous scale.

The Rev. William Taylor was appointed by the
American Methodist Episcopal Church in 1884 as "Bishop
of all Africa." He created a great impression in America,
by holding a series of meetings in which he declared that
Africa could be converted to Christianity by the establishment of a chain of self-supporting missions, the members of
which would earn their living as carpenters, agriculturists
and traders. Within twelve years 140 men and women
were sent out to West Africa, and having been deposited
at stations selected by Bishop Taylor, were left to earn
their own living and preach the gospel. At the end of
ten years the vast majority of these had died, and only
17 remained in the Congo district and in Liberia.
A few near Stanley Pool had endeavoured to save themselves from starvation by shooting hippopotami and selling their flesh to the natives. Nothing had been accomplished from a missionary standpoint, and the missionaries
had apparently failed to learn any African language.

It is difficult to insist too strongly upon the fact that
there is to-day little place in the mission field for solitary
missionaries independent of any missionary organization.

Missionaries who have no experience to guide them, and who have no successors, can do little good and may do much harm. The writer came across one such in a lonely spot in Central Africa hundreds of miles from the nearest mission station. He had become impressed, whilst living in America, that it was his duty to attempt the conversion of the people of West Central Africa. Without making an effort to learn any language, or to gain a knowledge of the religion or customs of the people whom he hoped to influence, he and one companion sailed for West Africa. When the writer of this book came across him he was dying of dysentery, and his companion, whom he had left behind at a distant town, subsequently died also, before either of them had got into touch with the people whom they hoped to evangelize.

Hundreds of similar cases have occurred, and it cannot be maintained that these missionaries have by their lives, or even by their deaths, helped forward the cause which they had at heart.

Missionary work needs the very best men and women who can be found, and if there is any place for untrained missionaries it can only be at a mission station, where the untrained recruit can obtain the constant help and guidance of others.

The *R.C. missions* are carried on by the Algerian M. Society, the Belgian F.M. Society and the Order of the Sacred Heart of Jesus (Rome). There are about 100 missionaries and 17,000 converts.

The population of the Congo Free State is about 30,000,000, of whom about 600,000 are Moslems.

French Congo.

In the French Congo the mission work of the *American Presbyterians* in Gaboon was handed over to the *Paris Society* on the establishment of a French Protectorate. There are four missions on the river Ogowe extending to a distance of 250 miles from the coast.

20

The *Swedish Missionary Society* has three stations in the French Congo, one of which is at Brazzaville.

A new and independent mission was begun in 1914 at Lambarene by Dr. Albert Schweitzer, who is widely known in Germany and in England both as a musician and as a learned theologian ; he is the author of *The Quest of the Historical Jesus.*

The *R.C. missions*, which are connected with the Algerian Missionary Society, support 46 missionaries and 26 schools. The total number of Christians connected with the R.C. missions is about 5000.

Angola.

In the Portuguese colony of Angola, which contains 484,800 square miles and a population of about 4,200,000, there are 815,000 R.C. Christians, including Europeans.

The *R.C. missions* are in the diocese of St. Paul de Loanda. The Congregation of the Sacred Heart have their principal station at Huilla, where there is a large industrial institution in which 80 Africans are taught skilled trades, *e.g.* tanning, boot-making, tailoring and wagon-making. The missionaries are specially interested in botany and botanical researches. Of the 36 priests in charge of the missions 2 are Africans.

The *English Baptists* are represented at San Salvador. A mission begun by Bishop Taylor (to whom we have already referred) in Loanda is now under the charge of the *American Methodist Episcopalians*, and industrial and evangelistic work is being carried on in the river region of the Kuansa. In 1881 the *American Board* (*A.B.C.F.M.*) began work in the kingdom of Bibé, where slow but satisfactory progress has been accomplished.

German South-West Africa.

German South-West Africa, which, previous to the war, embraced an area of 322,000 square miles, had a population of about 200,000, of whom 5000 are Europeans. The Herero and Ovambo tribes in the north are Bantus, while the Namaquas in the south are of Hottentot descent. The pagans number about 170,000 and the Christians 30,000. Of the latter 12,000 are Roman Catholics and 18,000 Protestants. Connected with the *R.C. missions*, which form the ecclesiastical prefecture of Cinebabasia, there are 47 priests, 30 schools and 10,600 adherents. The Protestant missions are chiefly conducted by the *Rhenish* and the *Finnish Missionary Societies*. These report 72 missionaries, 58 stations or out-stations and 12,700 professed Christians.

South Africa.[1]

If by South Africa be meant Africa south of the river Zambesi, the honour of sending to it the first Christian missionary and the first Christian martyr belongs to the Portuguese. In 1560, twenty years after the formation of the Society of Jesus, Father Gonzalo da Silveira landed at Sofala, accompanied by two other members of this Order. His first visit was to a chief named Gamba, not far from Inhambane. After a stay of seven weeks with this heathen chief he wrote: "Thanks be to God and to the Holy Virgin, the queen as well as the king's sons and daughters, his household, court and relations—in a word, all the subjects of that kingdom—are now Christians." Leaving this chief and his Christian subjects, Father Silveira made his way up the Zambesi to the Portuguese settlement of Sena. During the two months which he spent here he baptized 500 slaves and servants of the Europeans. He then proceeded to visit the reigning Monomotapa (chief), whose country was probably situated near the modern Mount Darwin, about 150 miles from

[1] I am indebted for a large amount of help in compiling this sketch of missionary work in South Africa to *Christian Missions in South Africa*, by J. Du Plessis. His book is by far the best which has been published dealing with his subject.

Tete on the Zambesi. He was at first well received, and
within a month he baptized the chief and 300 of his
councillors and attendants. He baptized also a number
of others, his custom being to present calico and beads
to all who allowed themselves to be baptized. Soon,
however, the chief became jealous of his influence, and
on March 16, 1561, he was murdered by the chief's
orders.

After a short time, and in obedience to orders received
from Goa, his companions left the country. In 1577 the
Dominicans began work in East Africa, and eventually
established several missions on the river Zambesi, where
they were followed by further representatives of the Jesuits.
The most remarkable among the Dominican missionaries
was Friar Nicolau do Rosario, who began as a missionary
in India and who suffered death as a martyr in 1592. A
son of the succeeding Monomotapa was sent to India and
became a Dominican friar. Despite the fact that two
Monomotapas in succession embraced Christianity, neither
the Dominican nor the Jesuit mission made any real
progress, and complaints, which were apparently not
unfounded, were made to the Portuguese Government concerning the character of the missionaries themselves. At
length, in 1760, the Portuguese Government expelled the
Jesuits from South-East Africa, and in 1775 the Dominicans
also were ordered to leave. Dr. Theal, the chief historian
of South Africa, says that "within 100 years from the
time when European teachers left them, they had lost all
knowledge of what their ancestors had acquired during
nearly two centuries of training." The story of the east
coast is similar to that of the west coast. Missionaries
belonging to different Orders began by quarrelling amongst
themselves, and having lost their purity of aim they
eventually lost their purity of character, and became
incapable of inspiring the Africans to seek after an ideal at
which they themselves had ceased to aim.

Arrival of the Dutch.

Van Riebeek, who was commissioned by the Dutch East India Company to establish a victualling station at Capetown, arrived there on April 6, 1652. He was a religious man, and desired to spread the knowledge of the Christian faith amongst the native population. In 1662 a Hottentot girl who had been servant to a Dutch master was baptized, but the efforts which were made by some of the Dutch settlers to teach the Hottentots were unsuccessful. Soon after the establishment of a settlement at the Cape, slaves who had been captured at sea were brought there, and ere long the slave population became of considerable size. During the first twenty-five years several efforts were made to evangelize these slaves as well as the Hottentots, but ere long these efforts were relaxed, and the irreligious lives of their master or employers rendered missionary work almost impossible.

Reference has already been made to the work of the Moravian, George Schmidt, who reached Capetown as the first Protestant missionary to South Africa in 1737 (see p. 54), but was forced to return to Europe in 1743, after baptizing 5 Hottentots, in consequence of the opposition of the Dutch Ministers.

In 1795 the rule of the Dutch East India Company came to an end and the English took possession of the Cape. In 1802 it was restored by treaty to the Dutch, but in 1806 it was finally annexed by England.

In 1792 three Moravian missionaries arrived in order to take up the work which Schmidt had been forced to leave at Bavianskloof. By 1806 the number of baptized, or candidates for baptism, had reached 464. By 1813 this number had increased to 1157.

(For a further reference to Moravian Missions in South Africa see p. 328.)

We shall now proceed to sketch the development in different parts of South Africa of the missionary work supported by the principal European and American missionary societies.

Anglican Missions.

While the Dutch retained possession of the Cape no Anglican services were allowed to be held, but when in 1819 immigrants from England arrived to settle in the eastern districts, the S.P.G. appointed a clergyman to minister alike to the Europeans and to the African natives. In 1821 the Rev. William Wright landed in Capetown. He opened a school for coloured children at Wynberg, and conducted services for the coloured people on Sundays. In 1822 he started and maintained at his own expense in Capetown a school for free and slave children. In 1835, Captain Allen F. Gardiner of the Royal Navy arrived at Port Natal (Durban) and endeavoured, though without success, to establish a mission station in Dingaan's territory. Later on, having obtained Dingaan's consent, he returned to England and pleaded with the C.M.S. to undertake this mission. In 1837 the Rev. Francis Owen, who was sent by the C.M.S., arrived in Capetown with Captain Gardiner and proceeded to Port Natal. It soon became clear that Dingaan would not allow missionary work to be carried on, and after suffering many hardships, Owen and his family returned to Capetown in 1838. After making another attempt to carry on missionary work at Mosega, he left South Africa in 1841. Captain Gardiner had already left in order to attempt to start a mission in New Guinea, on the failure of which he eventually sailed for South America. This was the only effort made by the C.M.S. to start a mission in South Africa. After the departure of Owen and Captain Gardiner the Anglican Church for several years did nothing towards the evangelization of South Africa beyond sending out a limited number of chaplains, whose primary duty was to minister to the European colonists.

So slowly did the Anglican work develop that in 1847 there were only 14 clergy and 11 churches in the colony.

The first Anglican Bishop, *Robert Gray*, who was

appointed Bishop of Capetown in 1847, was a man full of missionary zeal. He founded Zonnebloem College "for the education of sons of chiefs from all parts of Africa in the Christian faith," an institution which proved an immense help to the cause of Christian missions in South Africa. Before his death in 1872 he had done much to establish Anglican missions in many different parts of South Africa.

The first mission station which he helped to establish was amongst the Xosa people in Kaffraria. His desire was to obtain from Government a series of locations where, under the direction of a missionary, the natives might be taught to become mechanics, carpenters and agriculturists. Between 1855 and 1857 the Home Government granted £40,000 to subsidize educational and industrial work, and the portion of this grant which was entrusted to the Bishop of Grahamstown (Armstrong) was used by him to establish three stations in Kaffraria, in addition to the one that had been already started. These stations were named St. Luke's, situated among the Xosa people, 30 miles east of King William's Town; St. Matthew's, at Keiskama Hoek, among the Fingoes; St. Mark's, among the Galekas; and St. John's, among the Gaihas.

When Dr. Cotterill, the second Bishop of Grahamstown, was appointed Bishop of Edinburgh, he succeeded in inducing the members of the Scotch Episcopal Church to take special interest in Kaffraria, with the result that a Bishop of Kaffraria (Dr. H. Callaway) was appointed in 1873. The first Bishop was a remarkable Bantu scholar and an enthusiastic missionary.

In the *diocese of Capetown* (1847) the Cowley Fathers and the All Saints' Sisters of the Poor carry on work in Capetown amongst Bantus and amongst Malays, *i.e.* Mohammedan immigrants. The S.P.G. has given grants to the college at Zonnebloem, and many of the European clergy whom it helps to support carry on missionary work amongst the African population of the parishes in which they serve.

In the *diocese of Grahamstown* (1853) the S.P.G. helps to support the training and industrial schools at Keiskama Hoek, which have about 350 pupils. In this diocese is found the majority of the members of the Ethiopian Order, under the Rev. J. M. Dwané, who are in communion with the Anglican Church (see p. 338).

In 1911 a new *diocese of George* was constituted to include part of the diocese of Capetown and of Grahamstown.

In the *diocese of St. John's, Kaffraria* (1873), which is almost entirely a missionary diocese, there are 63 clergy, of whom 28 are Africans. The educational establishments include a "Callaway Memorial" College at St. John's, St. Bede's Theological College and an industrial mission at Umtata, and a girls' training school at Engcobo. At the theological college a large number of African clergy have been trained. One of them, Canon Masiza, who was for more than fifty years a missionary, proved conclusively that it is possible for an African to minister to colonial (*i.e.* European) congregations, and to be loved and respected by those not of his own colour.[1]

The first bishop of the *diocese of Natal* (1853) was Dr. J. W. Colenso. Soon after his appointment he caused distress to many missionaries by urging that polygamists should be allowed to be baptized. Later on, the book which he published on higher criticism applied to the O.T. resulted, after a long period of controversy, in his trial and deposition by Bishop Gray, who proceeded to appoint a successor in his place. Bishop Colenso, however, supported by the civil courts and by a section of his clergy, continued in Natal till his death in 1883. The unhappy division which had been created in the diocese was not finally healed till 1901. Despite the long-continued ecclesiastical dispute a good deal of missionary work has been accomplished.

St. Alban's native training college at Estcourt has educated and sent forth a considerable number of clergy,

[1] *South Africa*, by Bishop Baynes, p. 129.

catechists and teachers, who are at work in Natal and Zululand.

Successful mission work has also been carried on amongst the large population of immigrants from India, especially in the neighbourhood of Durban. There is a boarding school for boys at Riverdale and one for girls at Enhlonhlweni, and a home for girls at Maritzburg. There are about 8000 baptized African Christians in the diocese connected with the Anglican missions.

The *diocese of Zululand*, which was formed in 1870, was the outcome of the Memorial Mission which was established in memory of Bishop Charles Mackenzie, who was a missionary in Natal and was afterwards appointed Bishop for the U.M.C.A. The diocese includes Zululand, Tongaland, Swaziland and the districts of Vryheid, Utrecht and Piet Retief. Its African population is about 200,000.

The chief centres of work are at Kwa Magwaza, where there is a training college for African teachers and catechists, also a mission hospital, and St. Augustine's, near Rorke's Drift, where Archdeacon Johnson superintends the work carried on at about seventy different centres. The first Anglican missionary was the Rev. R. Robertson, who entered the country in 1860 and established himself with other workers at Kwa Magwaza in the days of King Panda. Later on a station was opened in Swaziland, near the river Usutu. After the death of Bishop Mackenzie (1862) a Mackenzie Memorial Mission to Zululand was formed.

There are 34 Anglican clergy at work in the diocese, of whom 14 are Africans.

The *diocese of Bloemfontein*, which was formed in 1863, now includes the Orange Free State and Basutoland. It has been suggested that the Anglican Church ought not to have established a mission at Thaba Nchu in Basutoland, inasmuch as the Paris Mission was already represented there, but in view of the fact that this place was the centre of a wide district, the vast majority of the inhabitants of which were still heathens, it cannot be maintained that " effective occupation " had been established by this mission.

The spirit in which the Anglican work was organized may best be described in the words of Canon Widdicombe, its chief organizer, who stated that the desire of the Anglican missionaries was, " to respect the labours of those missionaries already in the country, who, in the present divided state of Christendom, are unhappily not in communion with our branch of the Church catholic : not to receive into the communion of the (Anglican) Church, should they desire to enter it, Christians of other religious bodies under censure for evil conduct, or any whose motives for wishing to unite with us were not, as far as could be judged, pure and above reproach." [1]

The missionary activities in the diocese include St. Mary's Training College for Women Teachers at Thlotse Heights, Basutoland, St. Catherine's Industrial Girls' School at Maseru, the work of the Society of the Sacred Mission at Modderpoort, and of the Sisterhood of St. Michael and All Angels at Bloemfontein.

In 1911 the diocese was divided and a new *diocese of Kimberley and Kuruman* was formed, which includes the whole of Bechuanaland and Griqualand West, with Kimberley as its centre. The missionary work of the Anglican Church is chiefly carried on in South Bechuanaland, the principal centre being Phokoane. The majority of the clergy are Africans.

The *diocese of Pretoria* was formed in 1877, but until after the Boer War comparatively little missionary work could be attempted. The chief centre of work is the Rand, near Johannesburg, which is a series of towns extending for fifty miles. An effort has been made to establish a strong centre at Johannesburg, with a school for catechists. The European missionaries pay sectional visits along the Reef and African catechists are stationed at the large centres, whilst travelling catechists work in the intervening

[1] *Fourteen Years in Basutoland*, p. 75.

country. The contributions received from the Africans are sufficient to pay the salaries of the catechists The work is chiefly carried on by the Community of the Resurrection in connection with the S.P.G. Work amongst women on the Rand is also carried on.

The *diocese of Mashonaland*[1] was formed in 1891, the headquarters of the missionary organization being at Fort Salisbury. The chief mission centres are at Penhalonga, where there are industrial schools for boys and girls (in which 240 boys and 80 girls are being trained), Salisbury, Buluwayo, Bembezi, Francistown, Wreningham, Victoria and Rusape.

The moral and social improvement of the natives, which has been the visible outcome of the missionary work done amongst them, has done much in Mashonaland to enlist the sympathies of the European population, which throughout South Africa has been frequently antagonistic to missionary work. The change of opinion that has been effected in Mashonaland may be illustrated by a recent statement which occurred in the leading newspaper at Buluwayo: "He who scoffs or sneers at missions writes himself down as a fool or something worse."

The baptized Christians connected with the Anglican missions number about 6000.

The *diocese of Lebombo*, which was formed in 1891, and of which the first bishop (Dr. Smyth) was consecrated in 1893, is in Portuguese territory, and includes Delagoa Bay and the country which lies between the Lebombo Mountains and the Indian Ocean. The total population is about 700,000. At St. Christopher's College in the Lebombo Mountains, which was founded in 1901, African clergy and catechists are being trained, their training including a course of manual labour. Other centres of work are at Lourenço Marques, Inhambane East and West, and in Chopiland. The population consists chiefly of Bantu tribes, who speak several different languages.

---

[1] The title of the diocese is about to be changed to *Southern Rhodesia*.

The London Missionary Society.

In 1799, during the first British occupation of the
Cape, the "South African Society for Promoting the Extension of Christ's Kingdom" was formed by Dr. Van der
Kemp and the Rev. M. C. Vos. The former had recently
arrived as a representative of the L.M.S., which was
formed in 1795. The Dutch Government from 1802–6
hindered the extension of their work, but on the restoration of British government it began to expand. Van
der Kemp married a daughter of a slave " of Madagascar
extraction," and three other of the L.M.S. missionaries
married Hottentot wives, a fact which created great
prejudice against them and their work amongst the Dutch
settlers. Work was started amongst the Hottentots in
Griqualand, amongst the Bechuanas, and amongst the
Namaquas, but, partly in consequence of the difficult
character of the peoples amongst whom they worked, and
partly in consequence of the lack of wisdom and missionary
enthusiasm on the part of the early missionaries, the
progress made was slow and discouraging. Van der
Kemp, after an unsuccessful attempt to work in Kafirland,
settled first at Graaff Reinet and afterwards at Bethelsdorp,
near Algoa Bay, where he gathered a small society of
Christian Hottentots. He died in 1811. In this year
the work of the L.M.S. was separated from that of the
"South African Society for Promoting the Extension of
Christ's Kingdom" and was placed under the superintendence of one of the L.M.S. missionaries in South
Africa. From this time onwards the L.M.S. missionaries
had occasion to make frequent complaints, both to the
local authorities and to the Government at home, of the
ill-treatment which the Hottentots and other African
peoples received at the hands of the English and Dutch
colonists. The missionaries were sometimes prejudiced
or ill-informed, but in many cases their complaints were
justified, and the Africans benefited by their interference.

In 1859 the L.M.S. formed the congregations which it

had helped to establish in Cape Colony into a Congregational Union. In 1883 these congregations were received into the fellowship of the " Congregational Union of South Africa," and ceased to have any direct connection with the Society at home.

In 1816, *Robert Moffat* (*b.* 1795), who had been an under-gardener in Scotland, was sent by the L.M.S. as a missionary to South Africa. After a period of waiting at Stellenbosch he reached Afrikaner's Kraal in Namaqualand in 1818. In 1821, at the request of the L.M.S. superintendent in South Africa, he started work amongst the Bechuanas and settled on the banks of the Kuruman River. In 1829 the mission work began to bear visible fruit and the first six converts were baptized. In 1837, Moffat visited England in order to arrange for the printing of his Sechuana version of the New Testament and was received with the greatest enthusiasm.

In 1843 he returned to South Africa, and by 1857 he had completed the translation of the whole of the Bible into Sechuana. In 1870, after nearly fifty years spent in South Africa, he retired from active work and died in 1883, aged eighty-seven. He and Dr. Livingstone, his son-in-law, have left an enduring impress upon missionary work in South Africa.

After his death his son continued for a time in charge of the mission at Kuruman, which included the Moffat institution for the training of African evangelists This institution was subsequently removed to Tiger Kloof, near Vryburg.

David Livingstone, who was born at Blantyre, March 19, 1813, began work in a factory at the age of ten, and worked from 6 a.m. to 8 p.m. Part of his first week's wages were spent on the purchase of a Latin grammar, and by attending a night school after his work in the mill he prepared himself for Glasgow University, where, supporting himself meanwhile, he took his medical degree. He then volunteered to the L.M.S. to go as a missionary to China, but was sent to Africa. When called upon as a student to preach a sermon he gave out a text and then said, "Friends, I have forgotten all I had to say," and forthwith left the chapel. In 1841, at the age of twenty-eight, he sailed for Africa. From 1841 to 1852 he acted as a missionary, and from 1852 to 1873 as a missionary explorer. His first station was at Mabotsa, where he married a daughter of Dr. Moffat. The chief, Sechele, became a Christian, and Christian influence had begun to spread widely when the Boers attacked and plundered the town and carried off 200 of the mission children as slaves, after burning the mission-house and school.[1] It was, to a large extent, Livingstone's horror of slavery as he saw it in South Africa that turned him into an explorer. The ambition which he formed was to open up Central Africa in order that by the establishment of proper trade-routes and by the discovery of satisfactory outlets to the sea, the slave-trade might be rendered unnecessary and eventually be suppressed.

It is not possible to do more than give the briefest outline of his travels. His first long journey of explora- tion was to Loanda on the west coast, in Portuguese Africa. By this journey he established the fact that much country which had been supposed to be desert was fertile land through which ran a magnificent waterway. Return- ing overland from Loanda in order to restore his twenty- seven Makololo companions to their homes, he turned east and, after discovering the Victoria Falls, reached the coast at Quilimane. Thence he returned to England, and at the historic meeting held in the Senate House at Cambridge in 1857, which resulted in the formation of the Universities' Mission to Central Africa, he ended his address with the words, "I know that in a few years I shall be cut off in that country which is now open: do not let it be shut again. I go back to Africa to try and make an open path for commerce and Christianity. Do you carry out the work which I have begun. I leave it with you."

The direct result of this speech was the starting of the

[1] See *Missionary Travels and Researches in South Africa*, by David Livingstone, p. 39. Published 1857.

Universities' Mission to Central Africa, which now works in Zanzibar, German East Africa and Northern Rhodesia. On his return to Africa, Livingstone explored the Zambesi and the Shiré, and discovered Lake Nyasa. Later on, he crossed the Indian Ocean in a small river steamer, navigated by himself, and after his return to Africa spent the last two years of his life searching for the sources of the Nile. Rescued by Stanley when in great distress at Ujiji in 1872, he refused to return to England, and died on his knees in prayer at Ilala to the south of Lake Bangweolo on May 1, 1873.

The annals of missionary enterprise contain no more wonderful illustration of the love wherewith a missionary has inspired his followers than that afforded by the conduct of Susi and Chuma, the two Africans who, after embalming their teacher's body, carried it for hundreds of miles through hostile tribes, at the peril of their own lives, and delivered it at length to English officials on the coast. The inscription which is placed over the spot where the body now rests in Westminster Abbey, reads:

"Brought by faithful hands over land and sea, here rests David Livingstone, missionary, traveller, philanthropist; born March 19, 1813, at Blantyre, Lanarkshire; died May 4,[1] 1873, at Chitambo's village, Ilala. For thirty years his life was spent in an unwearied effort to evangelize the native races, to explore the undiscovered secrets, and abolish the desolating slave-trade of Central Africa, where with his last words he wrote: 'All I can say in my solitude is, may Heaven's rich blessing come down on every one—American, English, Turk—who will help to heal this open sore of the world.'"

Livingstone's claim to fame as an explorer is a unique one. He travelled twenty-nine thousand miles in Africa, and added to the parts of the world known to civilized men nearly one million square miles. Although equipped with but third-rate instruments, he recorded his innumerable observations with scientific accuracy and

[1] This date should probably be May 1.

contributed more towards the construction of the map of Africa than perhaps any three other explorers who could be named. It was not, however, as an explorer that he lived and died. He was primarily and above all else a missionary. He wrote of himself: "I am a missionary, heart and soul. God had an only Son and He was a missionary. A poor, poor imitation of Him I am or wish to be. In this service I hope to live, in it I wish to die." The primary task which he set before him was the abolition of the slave-trade, and his life and death hastened by many long years the accomplishment of this object. The writer of this volume has himself witnessed in West Africa many of the horrors of the slave-trade which Livingstone often described, but here, as well as in the wide districts which Livingstone traversed, slave-raiding is now no more.

The secret of Livingstone's success, as of that of every other great missionary, was his capacity for sympathy. His Christlike sympathy—we can use no other epithet—enabled him to win the confidence of the African chiefs whom he visited, of their peoples amongst whom he stayed, and of the carriers who formed his travelling companions. Apart from the indomitable will and the unfaltering courage which he possessed he could not have attempted the task that he essayed, but without the loving sympathy, which was a divine gift, his task would have remained unaccomplished.

In 1856, on the occasion of Livingstone's visit to England, the L.M.S. arranged to start a mission among the Matabele in Southern Rhodesia. It would be difficult to name any mission field where so much heroic and self-denying labour has been expended with so little visible result. The pioneer, Thomas Sykes, died in 1887 without having baptized a single convert. Coillard, writing in 1878, said: "You ask me what influence the gospel has had up till now on this savage nation? Alas! apparently none whatever. I confess it is the most perplexing problem of modern missions. . . . (the missionaries) have laboured for

twenty years in this country. In spite of all these efforts
and sacrifices there is no school, no church, not a single
convert. In fact, I do not know which ought most to
astonish the Christian world, the barrenness of this mission
field or the courage and perseverance of these noble
servants of Christ, who have for so long ploughed and
sown in tears." After the defeat and exile of Lobengula
in 1894 a little progress was made, but the mission continues to be one of the most discouraging in South Africa.

A much more encouraging mission was established
in 1862 at Shoshong amongst the Bamangwato tribe in
Bechuanaland. Khama, the son of the chief, who had embraced Christianity, established himself after some fighting
as chief at Shoshong. From the first he showed his resolve
to banish heathen customs and to govern according
to Christian principles. His kingdom to-day affords a
unique example of a country governed by an African
chief whose conduct conforms to the teaching of Christianity. His capital was moved later on to Palapye, and
again moved to Serowe.

The L.M.S. stations in Bechuanaland include Kuruman,
Tiger Kloof and Vryburg, and in the Bechuanaland Protectorate Molopolole and Kanye.

The total number of baptized Christians in connection
with the L.M.S. missions in South Africa is about 22,000.

Wesleyan Missions.

In 1816 the Rev. B. Shaw, a Methodist minister who
had been sent by the W.M.S., reached Capetown, and a few
months later settled at Kamiesbergen in Namaqualand.
His work lay chiefly amongst Namaqua Hottentots, with
whom were intermingled representatives of several other
races. After ten years he was removed to Capetown to
work amongst Europeans.

In 1823 work was begun amongst the Kafirs in
Kaffraria, six stations being established, forming a chain
200 miles long In 1822, Samuel Broadbent established

21

a pioneer mission amongst the Baralong in Bechuanaland. In 1833 the people amongst whom the mission was working migrated to Thaba Nchu in Basutoland, accompanied by their missionaries. Since 1832 the Wesleyan Church in South Africa has had an independent organization, and as the Wesleyan Methodist South African Missionary Society it carries on work independently of the W.M.S. in England.

It is difficult to trace the subsequent development of Wesleyan missions, as in their reports work amongst Africans is not distinguished from that amongst Europeans. After making an encouraging start the various Wesleyan missions for many years made but slow progress, a fact which was partly due to the series of native wars, and to the "cattle-killing delusion" which impoverished the people in Kaffraria in 1857. After 1866, when a revival took place, there came a period of steady growth. In 1847 a new mission was started at Edendale in Swaziland which has developed considerably since.

According to the returns of the Government census of the Union of South Africa for 1911, there are 396,797 Wesleyans and 53,100 connected with the American Methodist Episcopal Church. These figures include Europeans.

The *A.M.E.C.* started work at Old Umtali in Southern Rhodesia in 1899 and at Inhambane and Beira on the east coast in 1901. The work in Southern Rhodesia has made some progress and there are about 1200 baptized converts.

The *Free Methodist Church* has a few stations in Natal and one at Germiston, near Johannesburg.

French Missions.

In 1829 three missionaries sent by the Paris Evangelical Missionary Society reached Capetown, one of whom began work amongst Hottentots at Wellington, whilst the other two went north and started work at Motito, near Kuruman. In 1834, at the invitation of Moshesh, the Basuto chief, work was begun near Thaba Bosiu (Bosigo).

In this district the work rapidly developed. From the beginning of the work at Thaba Bosiu the chief Moshesh, accompanied by 400 of his people, attended the Sunday services. By 1850 eleven stations had been occupied and 1200 Christians had been baptized. In 1858 the mission staff was joined by François Coillard, one of the most devoted and successful of the missionaries who have worked in South Africa. During the wars and disputes of the next ten years between the Basutos and the Boers of the Free State the mission suffered considerably, and for a period of three years the 13 French missionaries were kept out of Basutoland by the Boers. In 1869, when Great Britain came to the assistance of the Basutos, the mission was resumed. During the absence of the missionaries a revival had taken place and 436 candidates for baptism were awaiting their return. Since then the mission has steadily progressed.

In 1884 a number of Christians from Basutoland under the leadership of Coillard established a mission amongst the Barotsi people in the neighbourhood of the Zambesi. The Barotsi were a far more backward and degraded race than the Basutos, and, according to Coillard, it took twenty years " to bring the Barotsi up to the social level of the Basuto when mission work began among them in 1833." [1]

The climate proved very unhealthy, and in three years, 1899–1901, 9 missionaries died. The last seven years of Coillard's life (he died in 1904) were clouded with sorrow and anxiety in regard to the future of his mission. In his will he had written: " I solemnly bequeath to the Churches of France, my native land, the responsibility of the Lord's work in Barotsiland, and I adjure them in His Holy name, never to give it up—which would be to despise and renounce the rich harvest reserved to the sowing they have accomplished in suffering and tears."

In 1910 there were in the Basutoland and Barotsiland Missions 15 head stations, with 43 European missionaries and 17,100 baptized members.

[1] *Life of François Coillard*, p. 329.

Scottish Missions.

The Glasgow Missionary Society, which was formed in 1796, and the work of which was eventually taken over by the United Free Church of Scotland, sent out in 1820 the Rev. W. R. Thomson, who joined a representative of the L.M.S. who had settled amongst Gaika's people in Kaffraria. Two further representatives of the Glasgow Society founded the station of Lovedale in 1824.

During the Kafir War, 1834–35, Lovedale and other mission stations were laid in ruins, and at the close of the war Lovedale was rebuilt on a new site on the west bank of the river Chumie. In 1840 the educational and industrial work at Lovedale was greatly enlarged, but in the war of 1846 it was again nearly destroyed. In 1850 another war broke out which caused widespread destruction, but the progress which Christian missions had made was evinced by the fact that in this war 1500 African Christians refused to side with their fellow-countrymen. When the Free Church of Scotland was constituted in 1843 the missionaries in South Africa became members of it, and the Glasgow Missionary Society was placed under the Free Church's Foreign Missions Committee.

After the close of the Kafir War of 1851 the missionaries rebuilt Lovedale with the aid of a Government grant, and it gradually became one of the most important missionary centres in South Africa. The wide influence which it has exerted throughout South Africa has been largely due to the work of Dr. James Stewart, who became Principal in 1867 and continued for nearly forty years. Carpentry, masonry, wagon-making, blacksmithing, and every kind of industrial work in addition to various branches of general education were started. Between 1870 and 1874 the number of students rose from 92 to 480, and the fees paid by them steadily increased. In 1907 the fees received amounted to £5503. There are now (1914) 526 scholars.

In 1877 Blythswood, in the Transkei, was founded in

direct imitation of Lovedale, the Fingoes, for whose benefit it was started, having first contributed £1000 towards its cost. The United Free Church started work on the Emgwali River, and work at several other centres in close co-operation with the United Free Church missionaries has also been carried on by the Free Church of Scotland in East Griqualand, and in the Greytown district of Natal.

"The real value of the Scottish missions in South Africa lies not so much in the extent of territory which they cover —though this is by no means inconsiderable—as in the widespread influence wielded by their educational establishments. Lovedale, Blythswood, Emgwali are names that stand out as landmarks in the history of educational mission work in South Africa. Of Lovedale this is true in an especial degree. Its students are found all over South Africa, filling various positions of trust and responsibility, as native ministers, catechists, teachers, tradesmen, farmers, interpreters, clerks, employees and servants. . . . We may sincerely echo the prayer that, under the hand of God, the promise of its future may be even greater than the performance of its past." [1]

German Missions.

The *Rhenish Missionary Society*, which began to send men to South Africa in 1829, supports work on the west coast between Capetown and the Orange River. Its chief centres are Worcester, Stellenbosch, Wupperthal, Sharon and Steinkop. It has also a station at Carnarvon. Part of its work in Namaqualand and Damaraland lies in German South-West Africa. The total number of baptized converts is about 16,000.

The *Berlin Missionary Society* (Die Gesellschaft zur Beforderung der evangelischen Missionen unter den Heiden), which was established in 1824, sent 5 missionaries to South Africa in 1834. They began work amongst the Koranna between the Orange and Vaal Rivers, and four years later joined with the South African Mission Society

[1] *Christian Missions in South Africa*, by Du Plessis, p. 364 f.

in work which this society had started in Cape Colony, and eventually founded a number of stations in Kaffraria and in Griqualand East. Their work lay both amongst the Hottentots and the Kafirs. Up to 1853 their work was greatly interrupted by the various Kafir wars. In 1860 pioneer missionaries went north to the Transvaal, and in 1865 they established a mission at Botshabelo, near Middelburg, which soon prospered greatly. During the following ten years (1865–75) fourteen new stations were opened in the Transvaal, where the work has so greatly developed that it exceeds that of any other missionary society in the Transvaal.

A mission to Mashonaland was organized in 1892, but after three stations had been opened the Society transferred them in 1907 to the Dutch Reformed Church.

In addition to the centres already mentioned the Society has established missions at Ladysmith (1856), Riversdale (1868), Herbertsdale (1872), Mossel Bay (1879), Laingsburg (1884), Capetown (1907), and has seven centres in Natal. The total number of baptized converts is about 24,000. Amongst its more notable missionaries have been Wuras, who worked at Bethany in Kaffraria for nearly fifty years, and Grutzner, who worked as a missionary at Bethany and elsewhere for forty-nine years. Its staff of European workers is 160, including 67 ordained ministers. It has also 21 ordained African ministers. Its work is carried on at 55 chief stations and nearly 1000 sub-stations.

The Hermannsburg Mission.—In 1854, Pastor Ludwig Harms of Hermannsburg in Hanover dispatched a boat containing 12 missionaries and 8 colonists to found a mission in South Africa. Their first centre was at a place to which they gave the name Hermannsburg, near Greytown, in Natal. The attempts at colonization were not successful, but the mission succeeded in giving a large amount of useful industrial training to the natives amongst whom it was established.

In 1857, on the invitation of Pretorius, President of

the Orange Free State, work was established at Shoshong, where one of the missionaries baptized Khama (see account of L.M.S. mission to the Bechuanas, p. 321).

A few years later several stations were opened in the Western Transvaal.

The baptized Christians connected with the Hermannsburg Mission number about 25,000.

The *Hanoverian Free Church Mission*, which started in 1878 as an offshoot of the Hermannsburg Mission, has 8 stations, with 10 European missionaries and about 6000 converts.

The American Board Missions (A.B.C.F.M.).

In 1834 the American Board of Commissioners for Foreign Missions sent six missionaries to South Africa, hoping to start work amongst the Zulus. The missionaries were allowed by the chief Dingaan to settle at Port Natal, but in consequence of a war between him and the Boers they and the C.M.S. missionary, Owen, were forced to leave the country. One of their number, Lindley, was eventually appointed a minister by the Dutch Volksraad. Two others carried on missionary work at the Umgeni and Umlazi Rivers. By 1850 twelve stations had been established which were occupied by 14 missionaries, and 123 baptized members were reported. By 1870 these had increased to 500. During recent years the mission has been steadily expanding, and after 1894 the American Board was not called upon to make any grant towards the support of African congregations or African preachers in Natal. The majority of the present American staff are engaged in educational work, the most important educational centre being the Amanzimtote seminary and industrial school, which was established in 1853 in the neighbourhood of Durban. Towards the support of the mission's educational work the Natal Government makes a grant of £7000 annually.

The total number of baptized converts is about 5500.

In 1906, as the result of a careful investigation of
the records of the Amanzimtote seminary and industrial
school, it was shown that out of 800 pupils whose record
could be traced, only 11 had been convicted of crime;
10 per cent. had turned out badly, 20 per cent. were
good workmen but not Christians, while 70 per cent.
were living lives which were a credit both to their school
and to their religion.

Members of the American Board of Commissioners for
Foreign Missions have produced the translation of the
Bible into Zulu, which was completed in 1883, and is
used by the other societies working amongst the Zulus.

In 1894, after several unsuccessful attempts, the
Society started work in Eastern Rhodesia at Mount Silinda,
and at Chikore, near the Sabi River. It has also a little
work on the Rand at Johannesburg.

Moravian Missions.

Reference has already been made to the first attempts
on the part of the Moravians to start missionary work
in South Africa (see p. 54). In 1823 they undertook
to minister to the leper settlement near Caledon, and in
1846, when the lepers were moved to Robben Island,
a Moravian missionary accompanied them. In 1826
work construction was started at Shiloh amongst Tembus
and Hottentots. By 1840 the Moravians had seven stations
with a membership of 4500. Since then their work in
the Cape province has largely developed. In South Africa
they have now 65 European or American and 624 African
workers, 23 mission chief stations, 7153 communicants
and 21,133 baptized Christians (1914).

Missions of the Dutch Reformed Church.

It has sometimes been asserted that the Dutch have
been the greatest opponents of Christian missions in South
Africa. This statement has, unfortunately, a measure of

truth in it, inasmuch as the Dutch opposed and interfered with the work of Dr. Moffat and Dr. Livingstone and many other early missionaries; but it is by no means true to-day to say that the Dutch take no interest in missions. In the charter of their East India Company, which was formed in 1602, and which built the first fortress at the Cape in 1652, there was a clause inculcating the duty of instructing the children of the "natives," "in order that the Name of Christ may be extended," and during the next seventy-five years more than 1100 children and 50 adult slaves were baptized. In 1799 was formed "The South African Society for Promoting the Extension of Christ's Kingdom." In 1861 this Society commenced a "foreign" mission in the Transvaal (with the aid of a Scotsman named M'Kidd and a Swiss named Gonin), in 1888 they began work in Nyasaland, and in 1891 in Mashonaland.

The Home Mission work of the Dutch Reformed Church in the Cape province is carried on amongst the coloured population, entirely in the Dutch language. There are at present sixty-seven congregations, with 17,500 members, while during the year 1913 over 1200 were confirmed.

The Foreign Missions of the Dutch Church may be divided into two classes—namely, the older fields, south of the Limpopo River, started about fifty years ago, and the newer fields, north of this boundary, which were entered upon about twenty-five years ago.

The former work is carried on in what are now the Zoutpansberg and Rustenberg districts. At present there are in connection with this older work 7 mission stations, with 8 ordained missionaries (one of whom is an African), and 78 outposts under African evangelists. On these stations and out-stations there are mission schools. The membership is now over 5000, and 300 members were admitted during the past year.

The other two fields of mission work of the Dutch Church lie farther north, in Mashonaland and Nyasaland.

The work in Mashonaland is carried on among the Vakaranga or Banyai, a rather degraded race, who were the slaves of the Matabele, and very much oppressed by them. The headquarters of this mission are at Morgenster, three miles from the Zimbabwe ruins in the Victoria district. The Dutch Church has there 8 chief stations, 20 outposts and 35 mission schools. There are 28 European workers, of whom 12 are ordained missionaries. The total membership is 330, and the communicants are about the same in number.

The largest foreign field of the Dutch Church is in Nyasaland, in a district lying to the south-west of the lake, between the Blantyre Mission of the Established Church of Scotland and the Livingstonia Mission of the United Free Church. The population is about 400,000, and the people call themselves Achewa or Anyanja.

To the west of this field, and adjoining it, in North-East Rhodesia, is the mission sphere of the Dutch Church of the Orange Free State, with 5 stations; while to the south, in Portuguese territory, the Transvaal Dutch Church has started work at 3 stations.

Altogether in these three sections of the work there are 16 chief stations, with about 60 European missionaries, and 600 outposts, under charge of evangelists and teachers trained at an institution at Myera, the present head station.

There has been a great extension in this work during the past ten years. The Church counts over 4000 members, while about 7000 are in the baptism or catechumen classes, and 60,000 children and adults are under daily instruction in the mission schools. There has been a great spiritual awakening among the people; the Christians are earnest and active, about one-fourth of them being workers for the spread of the gospel. The income for Foreign Missions in 1886 was £1700, and in 1913 had risen to £25,000, an average of 4s. per member.

Scandinavian Missionary Societies.

In 1844 the *Norwegian Missionary Society*, which was founded by members of the Church of Norway in 1826, sent Hans Schreuder as a missionary to Zululand. After a preliminary failure and a visit to China he and thirty others started a mission station in 1850 at Umpumulo on the borders of Zululand. After twenty-five years' steady work the number of Christians was 245. In 1913 the Society had 12 chief stations in Natal and Zululand, with 31 European workers and 3842 baptized Christians. Schreuder, its first missionary, founded in 1872 an independent society which is called *The Church of Norway Mission*, of which Bishop Nils Astrup is the present head. There were 5 European and 3 African clergy attached to it in 1910.

The Church of Sweden Mission.

The Lutheran Church of Sweden conducts its missionary work through a Board. Its fields of work are in India and South Africa.

Its first missionary to South Africa arrived in 1876. Work was commenced in Natal, its chief centre being Dundee. Other centres are at Appelsbosch in the Umvoti country, Ekuhuleni in Zululand, and Johannesburg. It has also commenced a mission in Southern Rhodesia. The mission has 8 chief stations, 13 ordained European missionaries, 1 ordained African, and 3408 baptized converts (1910).

In addition to the three Scandinavian societies mentioned, there are several other small societies, *e.g.* the Mission of the Swedish Holiness Union, the Scandinavian Alliance Mission, the Scandinavian Independent Baptist Union.

The *Finnish Missionary Society* sent representatives to Walfisch Bay in South Africa, in 1869, who began to work in Ovamboland. In the Ondonga district their work has specially prospered. The Society has 37 European

and 35 African workers, and 8 chief stations.   The
number of baptized Christians is over 2000.

Undenominational Missions.

The *South Africa General Mission*, or the Cape General
Mission as it was first called, was organized in 1889 to
work amongst both the white and the coloured populations.
Its missionary work is in Swaziland, Kaffraria, Tongaland,
and amongst Indian immigrants in Natal.   It is at present
only a pioneer agency and has no form of Church
government.   It has found it impossible to obtain a supply
of educated or trained workers, and has in some instances
had to rely upon the services of men and women who
were ill-qualified for missionary work of any kind.

The *Salvation Army* started work amongst Africans in
1890 near Eshowe in Zululand.   It has organized agricultural mission centres here, at King William's Town and
other centres in Kaffraria, in the Transkei, on the Rand at
Johannesburg, in Matabeleland and Mashonaland.   The work
has shown considerable advance during the last few years.

Reference ought also to be made to the *South African
Baptist Missionary Society* (1892) and the missions of the
Presbyterian Church of South Africa (1904).

Roman Catholic Missions.

Reference has already been made to the R.C. missions
in East Africa in the sixteenth, seventeenth and eighteenth
centuries.   In 1685 six Jesuit priests paid a visit to
Capetown on their way to Siam, but were not permitted
by the Dutch to celebrate Mass.   In 1805 two priests
obtained the permission of the Dutch authorities to settle
at the Cape in order to minister to their fellow-religionists,
but on the reconquest of the Cape by the English they
were ordered to leave.   In 1820 a R.C. church was
built and a priest was appointed.   It was not, however,
till many years later that any definitely missionary work

was attempted. The missionary work which is now being carried on is so closely identified with the work amongst Europeans that it is difficult to ascertain its extent.

In the eastern and western vicariates of the Cape no missionary work had been attempted before 1879. In that year Bishop Ricards bought a tract of land near Port Elizabeth and stationed on it thirty-one brethren belonging to the Trappist Order, but in 1882 these abandoned this site as unfruitful and built a monastery at Pinetown in Natal, between Durban and Maritzburg. Here have been erected a fine church, a hospital and an industrial school. The work of the Trappists has developed, and there are now 22 chief centres of their work in Natal and East Griqualand. The schools under their charge exceed 100.

In Basutoland, Dr. Allard established a mission station in 1862 near Thaba Bosiu, which is now called Roma. The work, which is carried on at 9 chief stations, is superintended by 25 priests and lay brothers (Oblates of Mary Immaculate). There are 51 European and African nuns, and the African adherents number 11,000.

The Orange River vicariate, which was created in 1898, includes the mission station of Pella, which was occupied in 1870 by the Fathers of the African Mission of Lyons, but was transferred in 1882 to the Oblates of St. Francis of Sales. In the Kimberley and Transvaal vicariates no missionary work is at present being carried on.

In Damaraland and Great Namaqualand the Oblates of St. Francis of Sales occupy 13 stations, but the converts only number about 200.

In Barotsiland the Jesuits commenced mission work in 1879, but eventually withdrew. They have several stations in Matabeleland and Mashonaland, their most important stations being at Empandeni (near Plumtree) and at Chishwasha (near Salisbury). They have also a mission at Shupanga on the Zambesi, and at Chinkoni in North-West Rhodesia.

In German South-West Africa 3 priests made an un-

successful attempt in 1878 to start work amongst the
Omaruru. In 1896 the Oblates of Mary Immaculate
commenced a mission among the Herero. The R.C.
missions in South Africa which minister both to Europeans
and to Africans have 313 European priests, 445 lay
brothers, 1667 sisters, 258 stations and out-stations, 269
churches and chapels, and 58,548 adherents.

General Outlook.

There are over thirty missionary societies now at work
in South Africa, and, according to the Government census
for 1911 (which omits Rhodesia, Basutoland, the
Bechuanaland Protectorate and Swaziland), the total
number of African Christians is 1,053,706; of these the
Anglicans number 170,704, Wesleyans 396,797, Lutherans
113,125, Congregationalists 74,637, Dutch Church 71,422,
Presbyterians 68,211, American Methodist Episcopalians
53,100. The Cape province has the largest number of
African Christians, 472,304; Transvaal has 282,420;
Orange Free State, 158,017; and Natal, 140,965. The
total "native" population, according to the census, is
4,061,082; in British territory outside the Union there
are 1,367,483, and in German and Portuguese territory
3,120,000, making a total "native" population of 8,506,489.

The following statistics are taken from the Government
census of 1911 :—

	Total.	European.	Africans.	Half-castes.
Cape of Good Hope	2,563,024	583,177	1,545,308	434,539
Natal . . .	1,191,958	98,582	951,808	141,568
Transvaal . .	1,676,611	420,831	1,224,155	31,625
Orange Free State .	526,906	175,435	339,811	11,660
Total . . .	5,958,499	1,278,025	4,061,082	619,392

The population of the Union of South Africa, which comprises these four States, increased from 5,175,824 in 1907 to 5,958,490 in 1911. During this period the European population increased at the rate of 14·4 per cent and the population other than European at 15·3 per cent.

It will be seen that the relation between the numbers of Europeans and Africans differs greatly in different districts. In Cape Colony the Africans outnumber the Europeans by nearly 4 to 1; in Basutoland they outnumber them by 380 to 1.

The experience of missionaries in all parts of Africa has been that where they have been enabled to carry on their work apart from the presence of European traders or settlers they have seen the most striking results. Such results are to be seen to-day in Uganda, Kaffraria, Zululand, and several other districts. Their complaints that the kind of civilization which results from the intercourse of Africans with other Europeans is frequently injurious to the African, is borne out by the Report of the Government Commission which was appointed to investigate the condition of the South African "natives." The Report of this Commission may serve as an answer to the suggestion that the effect which Christian missions are producing upon the African races is of doubtful value. The following sentences form part of this official Report:[1]—

"For the moral improvement of the natives there is available no influence equal to that of religious belief. The vague superstitions of the heathen are entirely unconnected with any moral ideas, though upon sensuality, dishonesty and other vices there have always been certain tribal restraints which, while not based upon abstract morality, have been real, and so far as they go, effective. These removed, civilization, particularly in the larger towns, brings the native under the influence of a social system of which he too often sees and assimilates the worst side only.

"The Commission considers that the restraints of the law furnish no adequate check upon this tendency towards

[1] *Report of the South African Native Affairs Commission*, 1903–5, presented to both Houses of Parliament by command of His Majesty, p. 40 f.

demoralization, and that no merely secular system of morality that might be applied would serve to raise the natives' ideals of conduct or to counteract the evil influences which have been alluded to, and is of opinion that hope for the elevation of the native races must depend mainly on their acceptance of Christian faith and morals.

"... To the Churches engaged in mission work must be given the greater measure of credit for placing systematically before the natives these higher standards of belief and conduct. It is true that the conduct of many converts to Christianity is not all that could be desired, and that the native Christian does not appear to escape at once and entirely from certain besetting sins of his nature; but, nevertheless, the weight of evidence is in favour of the improved morality of the Christian section of the population, and to the effect that there appears to be in the native mind no inherent incapacity to apprehend the truths of Christian teaching or to adopt Christian morals as a standard."

The unequivocal testimony in favour of Christian missions contained in these and many other passages throughout this Report is of special interest in view of the opposition to missions which has frequently been displayed by Europeans in South Africa. It cannot be denied that this opposition has sometimes had a measure of justification. The education supplied in some mission schools has not always been adapted to the real needs of the Africans, and, especially in cases in which Africans have received only a smattering of the education provided, they have often brought disgrace upon the mission with which they have been connected. Taught by the experience of the past the missionaries are, as a rule, providing an education which is likely to prove helpful in building up Christian character.

Colour antipathy is a factor in the missionary question in South Africa to a greater extent than it is in any other part of the world. In many parts of South Africa "there is an absolute and almost bitter refusal on the part of white Christians to mingle in any kind of fellowship with black Christians. . . . As regards individual natives, no amount of education or of culture or of that impress which the sacred ministry bestows avails in any appreciable degree to break through this attitude of reserve and aloofness. A native may have passed his Cape matriculation and wear clothes ordered from a London tailor and speak English faultlessly, or he may be a person of considerable wealth, yet there are very few houses where he would run the risk of entering by the front door or sitting down to tea with the hostess." [1]

Many causes combine to account for the existence of this antipathy. Its existence helps to explain why the most successful missionary work has been done where the Africans have not come into contact with Europeans other than missionaries. The contempt with which the African has too often been treated by European colonists in the past, and the sensitiveness and self-assertion which are in part the result of this treatment, greatly complicate the difficulties that lie in the way of the missionaries.

In South Africa, and indeed in all parts of Africa, industrial missions have been of untold use in training Africans and developing their characters on the best lines. The Principal of the largest centre of industrial training in connection with Christian missions in South Africa (at Lovedale) was able to show that out of 2000 Africans who had been trained there, 80 per cent. could be proved to have led industrious and useful lives after leaving. In Central Africa, and in a lesser degree in South Africa, the future of Christian missions is bound up with the successful development of industrial missions.

In South Africa the missionary problem has been made more difficult of solution by the rise of a movement which was more political than religious and which is known as the Ethiopian Movement. This Movement, which had its origin in America, represents an attempt to use the cry, Africa for the Africans, in order to discredit the motives of the European missionaries and to found a national

---

[1] Cf. article on "Colour Antipathies," by R. F. Callaway, in *The East and The West*, January 1910, p. 60.

church in South Africa. Needless to say, it has made no attempt to undertake missionary work amongst the heathen. The more religious section of the Movement under its leader, Dwané, is now a part of the Anglican Church and is known as the Ethiopian Order. It does not appear likely, however, that the Ethiopian Order will greatly increase, or that the time has yet come when the construction of a national church, which is a primary object of Christian missions, can usefully be attempted.

Portuguese East Africa.

Portuguese East Africa contains 301,000 square miles and a population of about 3,120,000, including 100,000 Mohammedans, 3000 Hindus and about 20,000 Christians. Of these latter 4000 are (African) *Roman Catholics.* The R.C. missions are in the ecclesiastical district of Mozambique.

Anglican missions are represented by the U.M.C.A. at Unangu and by the S.P.G. at Lourenço Marques, which is the centre of the diocese of Lebombo. *Protestant missions* are represented by the A M.E.C. and the Free Methodists from the U.S.A., also by the W.M.S. and the Swiss Romande Mission. The A.B.C.F.M. has a station at Beira.

Nyasaland.

Nyasaland, formerly known as British Central Africa, lies on the western shores of Lake Nyasa and in the Shiré country to the south of this lake. It contains an area of 40,000 square miles and a population of about 1,000,000, of whom about 300,000 are Mohammedans and about 20,000 Christians. The *U.M.C.A.* (see p. 343) works amongst the Yao tribes east of the Shiré River, south of Lake Nyasa, on Likoma Island and at several stations on the east shore of the lake, the *U.F.C. of Scotland* on the west shore of the lake, the *S.A. Dutch Reformed Ministers' Union* in the Angoni hills west of the lake, the *Church of*

Scotland at Blantyre in the Shiré district, and the *Zambesi Industrial Mission* west and north-west of Blantyre.

The *Anglican bishopric of Nyasaland,* formerly called Likoma, was founded in 1892, though work had been begun on the shores of Lake Nyasa in 1881. Bishop Maples, who became bishop in 1895, was drowned in the lake the same year. The diocese includes territory belonging to Britain, Germany and Portugal, and extends along the coast for 300 miles. The centre of the mission is the island of Likoma, where there are 3000 baptized Christians. A chain of more than 40 mission stations extends from Amelia Bay in German territory to the south end of the lake. On the west side of the lake is the important station of Kota-Kota, with out-stations extending along a coast-line of twenty miles north and south. There has recently been a large increase of work in the Yao hill country and amongst the Yao and Nyasa tribes along the banks of the Upper Shiré.

The *Livingstonia Mission* of the *Scottish Free Church,* which was organized in 1875, soon after the death of Livingstone, extends along the west shore of Lake Nyasa, the centre of its work being at Bandawe. It has also stations in South Ngoni Land, which lies south of the lake and on the Tanganyika plateau to the north of the lake.

The Livingstonia Institution, which was started in 1895, is situated near Florence Bay, six miles from the lake shore. It provides industrial training on the lines of Lovedale in South Africa. Its first leader and superintendent was Dr. Laws. This mission, which received sympathy and help from the African Lakes Corporation, has exercised a wide influence in behalf of religion and civilization. The number of scholars in the United Free Church schools is very large.

Mr. Donald Fraser, who is a member of this mission, in his book *Winning a Primitive People,* gave an encouraging account of the check which Christian missions have offered to the progress of Islam in the Nyasa district, and specially amongst the Ngoni, Senga and Tembuka peoples. Whilst in 1894 there were no African Christians amongst these peoples, within twenty years the number of Christians has risen to 20,000 and the number of places of worship to 250. Referring to the barrier which Christian missions have raised to the progress of Islam, he writes :

"The Arabs were pressing down from three or four different points, and the whole of the lake regions were in danger of becoming a great Mohammedan slaving empire, threatening disaster to the defenceless tribes, and menacing the progress of civilization. By the timely occupation of strategic points and the final intervention of the British Government with armed forces, these perils were overcome. . . . To-day, Mohammedanism is scarcely a recognizable quantity in any of the tribes among which the Livingstonia Mission is stationed, while Christianity is rapidly becoming the nominal religion, at least, of the people. A large educational system has been developed, and although we have only eight European stations there are 787 schools and 52,000 pupils under our supervision. Thousands of the people are able to read and write.

"A large institute at Livingstonia, under Dr. Laws, is training skilled native artizans, teachers and preachers, and these people, who, a generation ago, were utterly barbarous, to-day send forth scores of builders, carpenters, printers, clerks, and intelligent helpers to the Europeans who are rapidly raising these lands into commercial prosperity."[1]

Other important centres of the U.F.C. Mission are Loudon (11,530), Bandawe (7038) and Ekwendeni (6614). The numbers in brackets represent the size of the Christian community in 1913.

Blantyre Mission.

The Blantyre Mission, founded by the Established Church of Scotland in 1876, is situated on the Shiré highlands south of Lake Nyasa, within the British Protectorate, though close to the Portuguese border. Its church is one of the most striking and dignified in Central

---

[1] *Winning a Primitive People*, p. 9.

Africa. The mission includes a large amount of industrial work, a hospital, in which a course of medical training is provided, and a theological seminary. There are 3 chief centres and 13 schools connected with the mission.

The reunion of the Established Church and the Free Church of Scotland would naturally be followed by the amalgamation of the two Scotch missions which have done such good work in Nyasaland. It has recently been arranged to form a synod of the two Presbyteries of Livingstonia and Blantyre, and to give to the united body the title of "The Church of Central Africa, Presbyterian."

Two other industrial missions have been attempted in the neighbourhood of Blantyre, the Zambesi Industrial Mission and a Baptist Industrial Mission. The Z.I.M. has a staff of 32 European workers, 8 mission stations and 70 schools. It cultivates coffee, cotton and rubber, and teaches various industries. The Christians connected with it number about 1000.

The Christians in Nyasaland connected with the Protestant missions number about 17,000, and those connected with Anglican missions about 8000.

Northern Rhodesia.

The Anglican *diocese of Northern Rhodesia* was founded in 1910 by the U.M.C.A. The bishop resides for the present at Livingstone, Victoria Falls. Other centres of work are Mapanza (where work has been begun among the Baila and Bataliga tribes), Fort Jameson, and in the district south-west of Lake Bangweolo. The work is still in a pioneer stage, the total number of baptized Christians connected with the U.M.C.A. being about 300.

The *L.M.S.* began work near the southern end of Lake Tanganyika in 1877. Its chief stations are at Kawimbe, Kambole, Mbereshi and Mpolokoso.

The *Dutch Reformed Church* has a strong mission near Fort Jameson, the *Paris Missionary Society* has stations at and near Livingstone. The *A.M.E.C.*, the *Primitive Methodists*, the *American Adventists* and the *Brethren* have also missions in Northern Rhodesia. There is also a small R.C. mission superintended by the White Fathers.

The Mohammedan movement coming from the north has not yet begun to exercise much influence.

British East Africa Protectorate.

The B.E.A.P. includes 350,000 square miles and a population of about 4,000,000, of whom 25,000 are Asiatics. About 700,000 are Mohammedans. The chief missionary societies at work are the *C.M.S.*, the *Church of Scotland*, the *U.F.C.M.*, the *Neukirchen Mission Institute*, the *Africa Inland Mission*, the *Scandinavian Alliance* of the U.S.A., and the *American Friends*.

The Christians connected with the Anglican and Protestant missions number about 12,000. The Anglican *diocese of Mombasa*, which was formed in 1899, includes nearly all British East Africa and German East Africa where the Anglican Church is represented, except the area in which the U.M.C.A. is working. The founders of the Anglican missions in British East Africa were Dr. Krapf (1837–56) and John Rebmann (1846–76). In 1875 the C.M.S. undertook to superintend a colony of freed slaves which was established at Frere Town, near Mombasa. In 1883 work was begun among the Wasagalla tribe, and later on work was undertaken in Ukaguru and Ugogo. Within the last few years stations have been established at Nairobi (1906), Weithaga, and other centres in the Kenia province. In the diocese of Mombasa there are about 5000 baptized Christians connected with the Anglican missions and 22 clergy. There are also 3 medical missionaries, who are stationed at Kahia and Embu in the Kenia province.

The *Church of Scotland Mission* includes among its stations Kikuyu in the Kenia province, which has given a name to a recent ecclesiastical controversy. A medical, industrial and evangelistic mission has been established here which is exercising a wide influence in the surrounding districts. Kikuyu lies on the Uganda railway, 340 miles from the coast.

The missions of the *R.C. Church* belong to the Congregations of the Holy Ghost and of the Sacred Heart of Mary. British East Africa, with the exception of a small area near Mount Kenia, is included in the R.C. diocese of Zanzibar. The total number of R.C. Christians in the diocese is 4050.

Zanzibar and the U.M.C.A.

We have already referred to the speech delivered by Dr. Livingstone in the Senate House at Cambridge, December 4, 1857 (p. 318). As a result of this speech and of a visit to Cambridge by the Bishop of Capetown in 1858, committees were formed to promote a Universities' Mission to Central Africa. Charles Frederick Mackenzie, who had been 2nd Wrangler and a tutor of Caius College and for a short time Archdeacon of Natal, was chosen as its leader. He sailed for Capetown with two clergy and three laymen, where he was consecrated as bishop on January 1, 1861. By the advice of Livingstone he settled at Magomero near the river Shiré.

Livingstone did all that was in his power to help forward the work of the mission, and Bishop Mackenzie wrote most gratefully of the help and encouragement afforded by him. Moreover, the fact that he was a Congregationalist did not prevent him from sharing in a common act of worship with the Anglican missionaries. Thus he wrote :

"Livingstone and his party came to our ordinary services. We have on board Morning Prayer and sermon. . . . On Whitsunday I proposed having the Litany, and asked Livingstone whether he thought it would weary the sailors. He said, 'No'; he always used it himself. We have always had it since. They all attend Holy Communion."[1]

[1] *History of the Overseas Mission*, p. 17.

Bishop Mackenzie died on January 31, 1862, and two of his companions died soon afterwards. Bishop Tozer, who succeeded him, moved the mission to the island of Zanzibar, hoping to make this the base for future work on the mainland. Bishop Steere, who became head of the mission in 1874, was one of the most striking and capable missionary bishops whom the Anglican Church has possessed. His attitude towards the problems with which he was confronted may be gathered from his words addressed to one of his ordination candidates. "Let me give you one word of advice. Never say, 'I can't.'"

Under his guidance the mission was re-established on the mainland. At his death in 1882 the mission had 3 stations in Zanzibar, 5 in the Usambara country, 3 in the Rovuma country and 8 in Nyasaland. Under Bishop Smythies, who succeeded him, great progress was made, and in 1892 the diocese of Likoma (subsequently called Nyasaland) was formed. In 1909 a third diocese of Northern Rhodesia was constituted. The mission is staffed by unmarried men and women who receive no stipends beyond an allowance of £20 per annum for clothing and personal necessities. The cathedral at Zanzibar, of which Bishop Steere was the architect, is built on the site of the old slave market, the foundation-stone having been laid on Christmas Day, 1873. The mission in the island of Zanzibar has had to face special difficulties, as a large number of the inhabitants are Moslems and were formerly slave-raiders, whilst a considerable number of those for whom the mission has endeavoured to care have been rescued slaves. Of the people on the mainland amongst whom the mission works, Bishop Steere wrote:

"The East Africans are not idolaters; they all believe in God, but they think of Him as too great and too far-off to care individually for them. Their whole thoughts are full of evil spirits and malicious witchcraft. A man gropes his way through his life, peopling the darkness round him with fearful shapes, and on the continual look-out for some omen, or for some man who, as he supposes, knows more than he does of the invisible world to give him some faltering guidance. His life is dark, his death is darker still. His friends dare not even let it be known where his body is laid, lest some evil use should be made of it No man in the whole world has more need of inward strengthening and comfort, and no man in the whole world has less of it."[1]

Special features of the mission are the Kiungani college for the training of released slaves and up-country boys, hospitals in Zanzibar and on the mainland, and St. Mark's College, Zanzibar, for the training of African candidates for ordination. A cathedral has been built on Likoma, an island in Lake Nyasa, and work is carried on at a large number of stations on the eastern shore of the lake (see p. 339). The Mission works in German East Africa, Portuguese East Africa and in British Central Africa. It has also a station in Pemba Island. For many years after the mission was started the conditions under which the missionaries lived were so unfavourable to health that, on the average, at least half of the men and women sent out died, or were invalided home within a year of their arrival in the mission field. Owing to the improvement in these conditions, and to the advance in medical knowledge, the loss of life has been reduced to a fraction of what it was during the earlier years.

Besides the island of Zanzibar the diocese includes the island of Pemba and the Usambara, Zigua and Rovuma countries on the mainland. In Pemba the work is chiefly amongst released slaves, amongst whom the *Friends* have also a successful mission.

At the end of 1913 the number of baptized Christians in the diocese of Zanzibar was about 9000 and the number of adherents about 20,000. Of the 39 clergy in the diocese 17 were Africans. In the three dioceses supported by the U.M.C.A. there are 71 clergy of whom 24 are Africans.

There is no English or American society other than the U.M.C.A., which supports work in the island of Zanzibar.

[1] *History of the Universities' Missions*, by Morshead, p. 109 f.

The small *R.C. mission* is under the charge of the Brothers of the Congregation of the Holy Ghost, which works both in the island of Zanzibar and in Pemba. Connected with this mission there are about 1400 Goanese Indian Christians and about 500 Swahili-speaking Africans. The mission is in charge of a small Government leper asylum, which is superintended by four " Sisters."

German East Africa.

The population of what was German East Africa, previous to the war, which was bounded by British East Africa on the north and the Portuguese province of Mozambique on the south, is about 10,000,000. According to the " Kolonial Adressbuch" for 1912, published in Berlin, the white population at the beginning of 1911 was 4227, of whom 3113 were Germans.

Two Anglican, five Protestant and three Roman Catholic missions are at work. The Universities' Mission to Central Africa carries on work at sixteen principal stations, most of which are within 150 miles of the coast. The Christians number about 5000.

The *Church Missionary Society* has eight stations in Usagara and Ugogo, the Christians numbering about 1200. The newly-opened railway from Dar-es-Salaam to Lake Tanganyika passes through the district in which these stations are situated.

The *Evangelical Missionary Society*, sometimes called the " Bielefeld Mission," has twelve central stations and a large number of out-stations. Its Christians number about 1700.

The *Berlin Missionary Society* carries on work from three chief centres, Usaramo, Konde and Hehe, and has about 3000 Christians.

The *Moravians* have work at six stations in Unyamwezi and Nyasa. The Christians number about 1500.

The *Evangelical Lutheran Mission in Leipzig* works in four districts (Kilima Njaro, Meru, Pare-gebirge and

Iramba) and has thirteen principal stations and about 2300 Christians.

The three *R.C. societies* working in German East Africa are—

1. The Congregation of the Holy Ghost and the Immaculate Heart of Mary, which carries on work at twenty-three stations in Bagamoyo and Kilima Njaro. The Christians number about 10,000.

2. The St. Benedictine Missionary Association carries on work at fourteen stations near Dar-es-Salaam. The Christians number about 8000.

3. The Missionary Society of the White Fathers carries on work in the vicariates of S. Nyanza, Unyanyembe and Tanganyika. The Christians number about 30,000.

Between 1908 and 1912 the number of baptized Christians connected with the R.C. missions increased from 34,200 to 55,700. During the same period the baptized Christians connected with the Anglican and Protestant missions increased from 8500 to 13,500.

Uganda.

In the annals of missionary enterprise there are few, if any, stories more romantic than that of the founding of the Uganda Christian Church. On April 5, 1875, the traveller Stanley interviewed Mtesa, the king of Uganda, who had made a profession of Islam. A few weeks later Stanley wrote:

"Since the 5th of April I had enjoyed ten interviews with Mtesa, and during all I had taken occasion to introduce topics which would lead up to the subject of Christianity. Nothing occurred in my presence, but I contrived to turn it towards effecting that which had become an object with me, namely, his conversion."

A little later Stanley dispatched a letter addressed to the *Daily Telegraph* which led to the sending out of the first Christian missionaries. In the course of the letter he wrote:

"I have indeed undermined Islamism so much here that

Mtesa has determined henceforth, until he is better informed, to observe the Christian Sabbath as well as the Mohammedan Friday. Oh that some pious, practical missionary would come here! What a field and harvest ripe for the sickle of civilization. . . . Such an one if he can be found would become the saviour of Africa. . . . Here, gentlemen, is your opportunity; embrace it! The people on the shores of the Nyanza call upon you. Obey your own generous instincts and listen to them; and I assure you that in one year you will have more converts to Christianity than all other missionaries united can number."

This letter was entrusted by Stanley to a Belgian named Bellefonds, who was subsequently murdered by members of the Bari tribe. His skeleton was eventually discovered, on the legs of which had been left the high boots for which the Bari had no use. Stanley's letter was found inside these boots and was forwarded to General Gordon, who was at Khartoum. On November 15, 1875, it was published in the *Daily Telegraph,* and within a week of its publication the Church Missionary Society had resolved to send a mission to Uganda. Within two years of their start two of the original party of eight had been massacred, two had died of disease and two had been invalided home. One of the remaining two, Alexander Mackay, an engineer, became the real founder of the Uganda Church. Mtesa at first received the missionaries in a friendly way, but when, two years later, some French R.C. priests arrived and assured him that the religion of the English missionaries was false, he vacillated in his opinions and ended by relapsing into his original heathenism. At his death in 1884 there were 38 African Christians. On January 30, 1885, his successor, Mwanga, began to persecute the Christians with the object of exterminating them. A Celtic cross marks the spot where on this day six Waganda Christians were martyred. Their arms were cut off, and after they had been tied to a rough scaffolding a fire was kindled beneath them. While they were being slowly burnt to death their murderers bade them pray to Jesus Christ to save them. As the flames coiled around them they are reported to have sung the hymn beginning with the words, " Daily, daily, sing the praises."

When the cross which stands upon this spot was erected in 1910, the number of Christians in Uganda had risen to 70,000. A few months after these martyrdoms Mwanga procured the murder of James Hannington, who had been appointed as the first Bishop of Uganda and was approaching Uganda through the Masai territory, by a route which had not previously been travelled by white men. Soon afterwards the king seized 46 more Christians and ordered them to be burnt. Mackay continued to support the Christians by his prayers and exhortations, and, despite the cruel persecutions to which they were subjected, their number continued to increase. The number of adherents of the C.M.S. and R.C. missions who were put to death at this time was at least 200, and many more suffered mutilation or banishment on account of their faith. When news of this persecution reached Tinnevelly, Indian Christians collected £80 and sent it for the relief of their fellow-Christians.

The spirit and language of the letter which Mackay addressed to the Christians of Uganda at the height of the persecution bore a striking resemblance to those which characterized the letters of the Bishops or other Christian leaders during the earliest persecutions to which the Christian Church was subjected. In the course of it he wrote:

"We, your friends and teachers, write to you to send you words of cheer and comfort, which we have taken from the Epistle of Peter the apostle of Christ. Our beloved brothers, do not deny our Lord Jesus, and He will not deny you in that day when He shall come in glory. Remember the words of our Saviour, how He told His disciples not to fear men who are able only to kill the body. . . . Do not cease to pray exceedingly, and to pray for our brethren who are in affliction and for those who do not know God. May God give you His spirit and His blessings. May He deliver you out of all your afflictions. May He give you entrance to eternal life, through Jesus Christ our Lord."

Mackay himself died on February 8, 1890, but by this time the religious crisis had passed and it had become evident that the spread of the Christian faith in Uganda

could not be checked by material force. Bishop
Hannington was succeeded by Bishop Parker, who had been
a missionary in India. He was consecrated in September
1886 and sailed soon afterwards for Africa, but died in
the spring of 1888 before he had reached Uganda. A few
months later Mwanga, having plotted unsuccessfully to
kill all the Christian and Mohammedan teachers in the
country, these combined against him, and having driven
him from his throne, proclaimed religious liberty for all.
On October 12, 1888, the Mohammedans, with the
assistance of some Arab slave-raiders, gained control and
placed Kalema, a son of Mtesa, on the throne, about a
thousand Christians, together with all the Christian
teachers, having been driven out of the country. In 1889,
Mwanga, aided by the Christians whom he had driven away,
regained his throne.

The party supporting Mwanga now appealed for help
to the Imperial East African Company. Their representative, Captain (now General Sir Frederick) Lugard,
entered Uganda, but the Company soon found that the
expense of maintaining their position there was greater
than they could afford. When the Company announced
its intention to withdraw, an appeal was made at a C.M.S.
Meeting in Exeter Hall (October 30, 1891) and £8000
was guaranteed on the spot, the sum being doubled in the
course of a few days and handed over to the Company
on the understanding that their withdrawal would be
postponed for a year.

In January 1892 the R.C. section, which was generally
known as the French party, made an unsuccessful attack
upon the converts connected with the English mission, and
afterwards carried the king Mwanga with them to some
islands in the lake. At Captain Lugard's suggestion, the
province of Budu was then assigned as a sphere of work
for the R.C. mission, and this arrangement proved satisfactory to all concerned.

On January 1, 1894, an English protectorate of Uganda
was declared by Sir Gerald Portal, who had been sent out

as the representative of the British Government. During the years which immediately followed, the number of Christians steadily increased and thousands of persons placed themselves under instruction in order that they might learn to read the Bible. Mr. G. L. Pilkington, who reached Uganda at the end of 1890, was largely instrumental in translating the Bible into Luganda and in preparing catechisms and text-books for the instruction of converts. He was a man "full of the Holy Spirit" and exercised a marvellous influence upon the Baganda. He was killed in the mutiny of the Sudanese soldiers on December 11, 1897. On Trinity Sunday 1893, six Baganda were ordained as deacons and the foundation of an African self-supporting Church was laid. In 1897 Mwanga attempted to revolt, and appealed to the heathen Baganda to aid in exterminating the Christians. As a result he was banished and his infant son Daudi was proclaimed king in his place.

When Bishop Tucker arrived in Uganda in 1890 the number of baptized Christians was scarcely 200. By 1913 this number had risen to 90,000 and the Christian adherents (including the R.C. converts) were little short of half a million. It would be impossible to find a parallel in the history of the Christian Church during the last thousand years for the progress in the establishment and consolidation of a Christian Church in a heathen land to that which has been attained in Uganda in twenty-three years. The present Bishop of Uganda (Dr. Willis) has stated his conviction that the rapid progress must, under God, be largely attributed to the fact that the Church in Uganda has been to a greater extent than almost anywhere else in the mission field a united Church.

The present organization of the Christian Church is thus described by the Bishop:

"Episcopacy in Uganda is not an autocracy; it is the unifying force in an organization scarcely less complex and far more widely extended than the native feudal system.

"The Church in Uganda is self-governing, and its government is at once elastic, capable of adapting itself to a variety of local conditions, and strong, in that it binds the whole Church together in one organization. The unit of government is the 'Parish,' which consists of a central church, with six or eight little village churches which are grouped around it. This 'Parish' has its own parochial Church Council, composed entirely of native members. This local Council conducts all the business of the 'Parish,' interviews candidates for baptism, inquires into cases of discipline, and manages parochial finance. Small and local as it is, it yet has executive power within its own limited area of a few square miles, and more perhaps than anything else, it has trained the native Christians to regard the Church as their own, and its welfare and progress as their own—and not a European responsibility.

"Similarly, but on a larger scale, there is the District Church Council, representative of a pastorate or missionary district, into which a number of 'Parishes' are grouped. This has similar but enlarged powers, and among them the right of hearing an appeal from the smaller parochial Council. An English missionary or a native clergyman presides over this Council, to which every parochial Council within the district elects its representatives. The more important questions, concerning the district as a whole, are submitted to it, and local catechists are sent out by it to take charge of the village churches. This represents the second stage in the development of native self-government."[1]

The final stage in Church government is reached in the synod, composed of 300 representatives, which meets annually and which appoints an executive of 30 members, which is called the Diocesan Council. The Prime Minister of Uganda, Sir Apolo Kagwa, is a member of the synod.

Whether or not we agree with the Bishop of Uganda's suggestion that the phenomenal progress of Christianity in Uganda was chiefly due to the fact that the English missionaries to Uganda were members of a united Church, there can be no doubt that this was one of the most important factors in the situation and one which is deserving of clear recognition by the student of Missions.

[1] "A United Church in Uganda," by the Bishop of Uganda, *The East and The West*, April 1914.

Had the Christian Church not been strong, and perhaps we may add, had it not been united, there can be little doubt that a large proportion of those who are Christians would now be Moslems. The sudden uprising of a Christian Church in the heart of Africa, right across the track of Mohammedan progress southwards, has to an appreciable extent served to stem the tide of the advance of Islam.

Although there has been good reason for encouragement in the rapid development of the Christian Church of Uganda, there is also much cause for anxiety and sorrow. One of the missionaries stationed at Mityana wrote a few years ago, and his description still holds good :

" We are constantly hearing of the sad state of immorality and indifference prevalent. For months past I do not remember a single Church Council meeting here without some case of a breach of the seventh commandment being brought forward. Important chiefs to whom I have spoken tell me that they never knew such widespread immorality in heathen days, as the punishment was too severe. Now there is practically no punishment, and we have to remember that, broadly speaking, the people are still children in self-control, yet men in evil with generations of heathenism behind them." [1]

Educational work has formed a special feature of missionary enterprise in Uganda. The mission schools contain about 50,000 boys and about 40,000 girls. Uganda itself forms but a small part of the Uganda Protectorate, which includes the kingdoms of Toro, Bunyoro and Ankole, and other districts beyond. The country of Busoga had a resident missionary in 1891, Toro was occupied in 1896, Bunyoro in 1899, Kavirondo in 1900, Ankole in 1901, the Acholi country in 1904 and the Teso country in 1908. In 1897 a separate bishopric of Mombasa was established. The missionary evangelistic work has from the first been mainly in the hands of African evangelists superintended by European missionaries. In 1913 the staff of the mission consisted

---

[1] *The Wonderful Story of Uganda,* p. 186.

of a bishop, 33 European clergy, 4 doctors, 61 women missionaries (including wives of missionaries), 35 African clergy and over 3000 African agents. In 1914 the number of persons baptized in the diocese was 7899, of whom 6042 were adults.

The first *Roman Catholic missionaries* to enter Uganda were sent by Cardinal Lavigerie and arrived on February 23, 1879. It was most unfortunate that they were natives of France, the Government of which was at that time eager to extend its influence in Central Africa, as their national aspirations greatly increased the strength of their opposition to those whom on religious grounds they were bound to oppose. When at length the British Government established a protectorate over Uganda, it succeeded in arranging with the authorities of the Roman Church that English missionaries belonging to the Roman Church should be substituted for French missionaries. On Easter Day, 1880, two R.C. catechumens were baptized. During the great persecution which occurred in 1886, 30 newly baptized R.C. converts were burnt to death on May 26th, and 70 others were afterwards murdered. The first R.C. bishop to reach Uganda was Mgr. Hanlon, who arrived in 1895. In 1914 two natives of Uganda were ordained as priests.

It is difficult to form an impartial opinion in regard to the relative condition of the Anglican and Roman converts, who are about equal in number. One significant fact must be recorded. When in March 1893 forty Protestant chiefs voluntarily drew up and signed a petition asking Sir Gerald Portal to abolish slavery and to set free all slaves in Uganda, he was for some time unable to accede to the request owing to the opposition of the R.C. chiefs.

Three R.C. missions are at work in different parts of the Uganda Protectorate. The eastern portion, that is Uganda proper, is occupied by the English mission from Mill Hill, the western by the White Fathers from Algeria, and the northern by the Austrian mission. The complete geographical separation of the Anglican and Roman missions was productive of satisfactory results, but owing to the inevitable intermingling of the Christians the arrangement has now ceased to be operative

In a charge delivered to the missionaries in Uganda in 1913, the Anglican Bishop of Uganda sums up in a few sentences the moral outlook. He says:

"There is something most pathetic in the rushing of a quick, impressionable, intelligent people through all the stages of civilization within the lifetime of a single generation. That momentous decision to build a railway into the heart of this continent has been followed with startling rapidity by consequences, logical, inevitable, necessary, but none the less pathetic. Within thirty years the whole fabric of this country, social and political, has been upheaved; perhaps never in any country has there been seen a more sudden and more complete reversal of the whole national life within so short a time. No people, and certainly no African people, could stand the shock of such an upheaval without serious loss."

Referring to the moral condition of the Christians of Uganda, the Bishop says:

"Apart from the matter of the return to pagan habits of thought and action there are two dominant evils in the field, drunkenness and immorality. These are not new in the country or in the Church. But of late, within the last six years, there has been a recrudescence on an alarming scale . . . there seems no reason to question the statement, all but universally made, that a very large number of the Christians, at one time or another, fall under the power of one or other of those two evils. . . . The passing from a nominal paganism to a nominal Christianity will not at once produce morality, and we must not assume that the establishment of Christianity will, of itself, necessarily regenerate a country."[1]

The reports received relating to the moral condition of the Roman Catholic Christians suggest that the condition

[1] *A Charge to Missionaries of the Uganda Mission*, by the Bishop of Uganda. Published by Longmans, 1914.

of these is not better, if indeed it is not actually worse, than that of the other Christians.

Despite, however, the prevalence of the serious evils to which the Bishop refers, there is solid ground for hope that the Church in Uganda which has had so bright a beginning may yet be purified and strengthened and act as the great missionary Church of Central Africa.

Italian Somaliland.

In Italian Somaliland, which contains about 250,000 Mohammedans and about 50,000 pagans, there are apparently no Christian missions.

British Somaliland.

In British Somaliland, which has an area of about 68,000 square miles, the population is about 500,000, all of whom are Mohammedans.

Eritrea.

Eritrea, an Italian colony on the Red Sea, has a population of about 500,000. Of these 100,000 are Mohammedans and 320,000 are pagans. There are 2000 Europeans. Of the Christians 17,000 are Roman Catholics, 12,000 belong to Eastern churches and 1000 are Protestants. There are 53 *R.C.* priests (Franciscans). The *Swedish National Society* has 34 missionaries, 10 mission stations and about 600 Christians.

Abyssinia.

Abyssinia was converted to the Christian faith in the fourth century, its first bishop being Frumentius, who was consecrated by Athanasius. An Ethiopic translation of the Bible was apparently begun by Frumentius and completed a little later. An Ethiopic king, at the instigation of Justinian, conquered part of Southern Arabia and placed a Christian king on the throne. At the end of the fifteenth century *Jesuit missionaries*, supported by Portuguese soldiers, attempted to win over the Abyssinians to obedience to Rome, but after much fighting they withdrew. Another attempt was made in 1621 and a third in 1750, but without any permanent result. In 1830, Samuel Gobat (afterwards Bishop in Jerusalem) and Mr. Kugler were sent by the *C.M.S.* to Abyssinia, but Mr. Kugler died and Mr. Gobat retired through ill-health. About this time the Jesuits made a further attempt to work amongst the Abyssinians, but in 1859 they were expelled by King Theodore. In 1860 Dr. Stern arrived as a representative of the *London Jews' Society*. The king's suspicions having been excited against Dr. Stern and other Europeans who had been sent by Bishop Gobat, he detained them as prisoners. On his refusal to release them war with England followed in 1868. Abyssinian Christianity is a strange mixture of Christianity, Judaism and Mohammedanism, and it is hard to imagine how it can be reformed from within. It is calculated that 1800 Jews have been baptized in Abyssinia since Dr. Stern began his work.

Of the 3,000,000 nominal Christians 7000 belong to the Roman Catholic Church and all the rest are members of a branch of the Coptic Church. The population of the country includes 50,000 Mohammedans, 60,000 Jews and 300,000 pagans. The *R.C. mission*, supported by the Lazarists of Paris, has 12 European and 18 native priests. The *Swedish National Missionary Society*, which has a mission in Eritrea, supports native evangelists amongst the Gallas.

Madagascar.

Of the Christian missions established during the nineteenth century none have been subjected to so long and severe a persecution as that which befel the mission which the London Missionary Society was instrumental in starting in Madagascar. A larger number of Christians were killed during the Boxer revolution in China, but in this case the trial was brief and none of the Christians were subjected to the long-protracted torments which the Malagasy Christians endured. Their sufferings were worthy to be compared with those of the Japanese Christians in the sixteenth and those of the Corean Christians in the eighteenth and nineteenth centuries.

When the first L M.S. missionaries landed in 1818 the king, Radama, was well disposed to Europeans and desirous of encouraging the education of his subjects. Actual missionary work was begun by Mr. David Jones in 1820, and by 1828 32 schools had been opened containing 4000 scholars. Radama, who died in this year, was succeeded by Queen Ranavalona, one of the twelve wives of Radama. She forbade all teaching and learning and discouraged the spread of the Christian faith. In May 1831 28 converts were baptized, who formed the nucleus of a Malagasy Church. In 1835 the queen began an active persecution, and in 1839 she "issued an order that the soldiers should seize every Christian they could find, and without trial, bind them hand and foot, dig a pit on the spot, and then pour boiling water upon them and bury them." [1]

After a temporary lull the persecutions broke out again in renewed force in 1849, when 18 persons were sentenced to death and over 2000 were condemned to slavery, public floggings and other degradations, and four nobles were burned alive. A spectator of their martyrdom wrote: "They prayed as long as they had life. Then they

[1] *The Story of the L.M.S.*, p. 197.

died, but softly, gently. Indeed, gentle was the going
forth of their life, and astonished were all the people around
that beheld the burning of them."

Meanwhile the missionaries had retired to Mauritius,
as their presence served only to increase the fury of the
persecutors. Though the mission stations were closed for
twenty-six years, the number of the Christians tended steadily
to increase. On the death of the queen in 1861 liberty
of conscience was proclaimed by her successor. Of the
scenes which were then enacted Mr. Silvester Horne wrote :

"Men and women were brought out of the land of exile
who had been banished for many years. There were re-
unions of those who had supposed each other to be dead
long since. Out of the recesses of the forests there came
men and women who had been wanderers and outcasts for
years. They reappeared as if risen from the dead. Some
bore the deep scars of chains and fetters; some, worn
almost to skeletons by prolonged sufferings from hunger or
fever, could scarcely drag themselves along the roads that
led to the capital. Their brethren from the city went out
to meet them, and to help them, and . . . as they saw
their old loved city again, they sang the pilgrim song,
'When the Lord turned again the captivity of Zion we
were like them that dream. . . .'"[1]

In 1836, when the persecution of the Christians began,
the number of Christians in Madagascar was estimated at from
1000 to 2000. During the twenty-six years of persecution
it is reckoned that over 10,000 persons were sentenced to
various punishments as Christians, and that 200 were put
to death. Nevertheless, at the end of this period the
Christians were four times as numerous as they were when
the persecution began. Although the Christians were
deprived of the help of their European teachers, they had
the New Testament in their hands and large numbers of
them had learned to read it. To this fact must to a great
extent be attributed the continuance and extension of the
Church during these years. Queen Ranavalona II. and her

[1] *The Story of the L.M.S.*, p. 353 f.

Prime Minister were publicly baptized by a Malagasy preacher in 1868, and, Christianity having now become popular, the Christians rapidly increased in number. In 1869 they were reckoned at 37,000 and in the following year at 250,000. Many of these were Christians only in name, and their new religion made little perceptible difference in their lives. In 1883 the French bombarded Tamatave and soon afterwards declared a French protectorate over the whole island. One result of the French conquest was that a large number of those who were merely nominal Christians and who had become such because the profession of Christianity had become popular, ceased to call themselves Christians. Thus in 1904 the 250,000 adherents connected with the L.M.S. had sunk to 48,000.

The anti-Christian policy of the French Governor-General, M. Augagneur, who was appointed in 1906, resulted in the closing of four-fifths of all the mission schools in the island. The L.M.S., which in 1888 had 90,000 scholars in its schools, in 1910 had less than 5000. The decree, which was issued in Paris in March 1913, dealing with the regulation of Public Worship has removed some of the obstacles which had been placed by the local authorities in the way of the spread of Christianity, but missionary work is still carried on under exceptional difficulties.

In 1862 the *S.P.G.*, after it "had ascertained that the L.M.S. would gladly see it taking part in the work of evangelizing the Malagasy,"[1] requested the Bishop of Mauritius to visit Madagascar with a view to establishing a mission. In 1864 work was started at Tamatave. In the same year the *C.M.S.* started a mission at Vohimare in the north of the island, but in 1874 this Society withdrew its workers from Madagascar.

Within a year of their arrival the S.P.G. missionaries were able to baptize 81 persons, and in 1866, in response to an invitation from the king, they opened a mission

[1] *Two Hundred Years of the S.P.G.*, p. 374.

station at the capital, Antananarivo (Tananarive). In 1874 the Rev. R. K. Kestell Cornish was consecrated at Edinburgh as the first Bishop in Madagascar.

The first woman to be sent out by the S.P.G. as a missionary was Miss Emily Lawrence, who was sent in 1867 to Mauritius and in 1874 to Madagascar, where she worked indefatigably for over twenty years. Three years after her arrival at Tananarive 43 girls were baptized and 10 confirmed from her own school.

In 1891 the Rev. E. O. (afterwards Archdeacon) McMahon undertook the perilous task of starting a mission amongst the Sakalava in the west of Madagascar. Though the mission had to be abandoned for a time, it has been successfully restarted.

Bishop King reached Madagascar in 1899, and since then the good work which had been accomplished by Bishop Cornish has steadily developed. After the annexation of the island the French Government insisted on French being taught in all mission schools, and by other regulations which they made seriously interfered with the work of all the Christian missions in the island. As the result of remonstrances addressed direct to the Government in Paris these regulations were modified in 1913, but the development of all branches of missionary work is still restricted and liable to be interfered with by the French officials in Madagascar.

Archdeacon McMahon, who has been a missionary in Madagascar for over thirty years, writing of the times which followed the periods of persecution, says:

"The want of catechists and evangelists made it practically impossible to cope with the new state of things, and instead of being an advantage the numbers which professed to be Christians at this time were a decided drawback and set a low standard from which the Malagasy have not yet recovered, . . . the slackness in morality, honesty and truthfulness which troubles us now, is in a large degree owing to the looseness which resulted in the flooding of the churches by half-converted heathens at this time The form of Christianity which they understood was too easy-

going, and there was a great lack of definite teaching. I
think that there are signs of improvement . . . since the
profession of Christianity brings no advantage to anyone,
rather the reverse. . . . It takes generations to make a race
Christian, and the Malagasy have their strong as well as
their weak traits ; for instance, they could give us points in
patience, long-suffering, humility and like virtues." [1]

The R.C. Mission. — French priests accompanied a
French Government expedition to Madagascar in the
seventeenth century and again in 1845, but it was
not till 1861 that a French R.C. mission was established
in Tamatave and in the capital. The mission was for a
time encouraged and subsidized by the French Government,
but in recent years it has been subjected to restrictions
similar to those imposed upon the other missionary
societies. The missionaries include Jesuits, Lazarists and
Brothers of the Congregation of the Holy Ghost. There
are 139 European and 2 Malagasy priests, and about
200,000 baptized Christians.

The *Norwegian Lutheran Mission* sent its first missionaries in 1866, who began work amongst the Betsileo tribe.
With the two affiliated American societies this mission has
worked amongst the Bara, Sakalava and other tribes in the
south, south-east and south-west. In 1913 it had 784
churches and 83,727 baptized members, 5201 of whom
had been baptized during the previous year. Before the
French authorities stopped its schools they numbered 885 ;
these are now reduced to 84. The mission has 96 native
pastors and over 900 catechists. It includes two medical
missions, and a leper asylum at Antsirabe. The work of the
mission is well organized and thorough.

The *Friends Foreign Mission Association* began work
in 1867 and has co-operated with the L.M.S. at Imerina.
It has now started work on the west coast.

After the French occupation of Madagascar representatives of the *Paris Missionary Society* arrived in 1896 to
help the other Protestant missions and to take over part

[1] *Christian Missions in Madagascar,* by E. O. McMahon (1915), pp. 74 f.

of the work of the L.M.S. The help which their missionaries have afforded to the other missions has been specially
welcome in view of the Government's requirement that
all scholars in the mission schools should be taught
French. The French missionaries have helped to get the
Malagasy scholars through their brevet examination and
so to keep open a few of the mission schools. Two of the
French missionaries were assassinated by a band of rebels
in 1897. The Paris Society has undertaken as its special
sphere of work the coast from Tamatave to Diego Suarez.

The total number of baptized Christians connected
with the Anglican and Protestant missions is about
130,000 and of Christian adherents about 250,000. Of
the former, 29,800 belong to the L.M.S. and 14,200 to the
Anglican Mission.

Malagasy missionary societies.—Several attempts have
been made by Malagasy congregations to send out
evangelists to preach to the non-Christian populations in
their districts. No difficulty has been experienced in
raising money for their support, but up to the present the
results have not been encouraging.

The Malagasy version of the Bible, which was issued
in a revised form in 1887, has done much to create a
standard of the written language.

Mohammedan traders and others have effected a considerable number of conversions to Islam in the east of
the island, and the Moslems number about 75,000.
Islam is making rapid progress amongst the Sakalava race.
Nearly all the population on the coast from Soalala to
Mojanja is already Mohammedan. Many Indian Moslems
have settled in the country.

In answer to the question "Has Christianity made
progress in Madagascar during the last twenty years, that
is since the country has been under European rule?"
Archdeacon McMahon writes:

"It is very difficult to say, but I think that there, is not
much doubt that the good Christians have become better,
while there has been a falling off of the nominal Christians,

as was to be expected. In the towns the churches are generally well attended, and there is as much interest taken in all that has to do with religion as was the case formerly. In the country there has been a falling off in the numbers found in Church on Sundays: this is largely due to the difficulty in finding catechists. . . . On the whole I think one may say that the Christian religion has taken deeper and firmer root in the hearts and minds of the Christians in Madagascar, but the difficulties during the last few years show how much there is yet to be done, even more than those who know the country best thought." [1]

Mauritius.

The Dutch, who gave the name to this island, found it uninhabited in 1598. From 1715 to 1810 it belonged to France, and at the latter date it was annexed by England. Of the present population (370,000) about two-thirds are East Indians by birth or descent, the rest are Creoles of various races. At the time of its capture by England there were four *R.C.* priests in the island, and the religion of the whole population was nominally R.C. On the abolition of slavery in 1834 the *S.P.G.* helped to establish schools for some of the 90,000 emancipated slaves. In 1854, when an English Bishop (Ryan) was consecrated for Mauritius, half the population, which was reckoned at 190,000, were "living in a state of heathenism." Since this time a large amount of successful work has been done, especially amongst the Indian coolies, who constitute a majority of the population and are likely to become the permanent inhabitants of the islands.

Work is also being carried on with success amongst the Creoles in the Seychelles Islands.

The *C.M.S.* started work amongst the Indian coolies in 1856. Since then, 7000 converts have been baptized, many of whom have returned to India. The C.M.S. is

[1] *Christian Missions in Madagascar*, p. 104 f.

now withdrawing its grant and handing its work over to the bishop and the diocesan representatives.

The *L.M.S.* supported for many years a mission in Mauritius which was started in 1814.

The *R.C.* clergy, who number about 50, include 6 Jesuits and 11 from the Congregation of the Holy Spirit and the Sacred Heart of Mary. The rest are parish priests.

The population of the island includes 41,000 Mohammedans.

XIII.

AMERICA (U.S.A.).

Spanish Missions in America.

PONCE DE LEON, who sailed for *Florida* about 1520 carried with him instructions from the king which required him to summon the natives to submit themselves to the Catholic faith and to the King of Spain under threat of the sword and slavery. His expedition was driven away by the natives whom he desired to convert. In 1565 Menendez founded the city of St. Augustine. The Floridas were eventually occupied by Dominicans, Jesuits, and Franciscans, and seventy years later the Christians were reckoned at 30,000. For the 115 years during which Spain retained possession of Florida, the number of Christians continued to increase, but when in 1763 Florida was transferred to the British Crown, "no longer sustained by the terror of the Spanish arms and by subsidies from the Spanish treasury, the whole fabric of Spanish civilization and Christianization tumbled at once to complete ruin and extinction." [1]

In *New Mexico* the first permanent occupation of territory took place in 1598, when the Spanish settlers were accompanied by Franciscan friars. In ten years 8000 persons were baptized, and ere long the entire population was nominally Christian. When, however, eighty years later, a revolt occurred against the Spanish Government, within "a few weeks no Spaniard was in New Mexico north of El Paso. Christianity and civilization were swept away at one blow. The measures of compulsion

[1] *A History of American Christianity*, by L. W. Bacon, p. 11.

that had been used to stamp out every vestige of the old religion were put into use against the new." [1]

Although the Spaniards returned, twenty years later, they never again succeeded in producing more than a sullen submission to the religion of their conquerors. In 1845, 20,000 out of a total of 80,000 professed to be Christians. Spanish settlements and missions on the *Pacific Coast* date from 1769. By 1834 these missions had amassed much wealth, but the Indian Christians were in a condition of servitude. In this year the mission property was distributed, and as a result, "in eight years the more than thirty thousand Catholic Christians had dwindled to less than five thousand, the enormous estates of the missions were dissipated, the converts lapsed into savagery and paganism." [2]

Although the Spanish missions in North America produced such small spiritual results and ended so disastrously, it must not be forgotten that the early records of these missions contain many accounts of heroism and devotion which go far to redeem their story from the realm of mere secular history.

Franciscan and Jesuit Missions.

Between 1717 and 1833, 20 Franciscan missionaries laboured among the Indians of *Texas*, and in 1769 a Franciscan monk began a series of missions at San Diego in *California*.

The northern part of what is now the U.S.A., stretching from the Atlantic to the Rocky Mountains, was formerly included in the two French provinces of Canada and Louisiana. As long as the French rule lasted the greater part of the missionary work amongst the Indians was carried on by French Jesuits. The first mission west of Huron county was begun in 1660 amongst the Chippewa and Ottawa Indians. Within the next few years mission stations were established at Sault St. Marie, Mackinaw,

[1] *Ibid.*, p. 12.　　　　　　[2] *Ibid.*, p. 14.

Green Bay, and among the Foxes and Mascoutins.   Père Marquette, one of the greatest of the Jesuit pioneer missionaries, started work amongst the Illinois in 1674, which was carried on with such success that in 1725 the entire Illinois nation was civilized and Christianized. Here, however, as in many other districts, the missionary work was interrupted by wars, and in 1750 the whole Illinois nation was reduced to 1000 persons.

In 1818 work was begun amongst the Chippewas on the Red River inside the U.S.A. boundary.   Missions were also started in East Minnesota in 1837, amongst the Menominees of Wisconsin in 1844, and among the Winnebagos in 1850.

Anglican and Protestant Missions.

The first charter for an English colony, which was granted to Sir Humphrey Gilbert in 1583, contained a reference to the " compassion " of God " for poor infidels, it seeming probable that God hath reserved these Gentiles to be introduced into Christian civility by the English nation."

The first attempt of a missionary character made by the English in North America was made by Thomas Heriot, the scientist and philosopher, who went out as one of a band of colonists to Virginia.   During the stay of the colonists at Roanoke (1585–86), Heriot " many times and in every towne " where he " came," " made declaration of the contents of the Bible " and of the " chiefe points of religion " to the natives according as he " was able."   One of the natives, who was called Manteo, returned to England with the English party in 1586, was appointed by Sir Walter Raleigh as Lord of Roanoke, and was baptized in that island (August 13, 1587). This is the first recorded baptism of a native of Virginia.

In 1588 Sir Walter Raleigh gave £100 to the Virginian Company " for the propagation of the Christian religion in that settlement."

In 1560 John Knox wrote in the first Confession : " This glaid tydingis of the kyngdome sall be precheit through the haill warld for a witness unto all natiouns and then sall the end cum." More than a century later the Scottish General Assembly (1699) enjoined the ministers whom it sent forth with the Darien expedition to labour among the heathen.

Pocahontas, the daughter of the Indian chief Powhatan, who in 1607 persuaded her father to save the life of Captain Smith, the President of Virginia, became a Christian, and having married an Englishman, came to England and was received by King James.

The Pilgrim Fathers, who sailed for Massachusetts in the *Mayflower* (1620), were not unmindful of their obligation to Christianize the American Indians. Their pastor, John Robinson, wrote to the Governor of New Plymouth, " O that you had converted some before you had killed any." One of their number was set apart "to promote the conversion of the Indians." In 1621 one of the Puritan Elders, Robert Cushman, appealed to England on behalf of the Indians, and in 1636 the colony passed legislation in order to promote the "preaching of the gospel among them." In 1628 the charter granted by Charles I. to the colony of Massachusetts stated that " the principal end of the plantation" was that the colonists may "win and invite the natives of the country to the knowledge of the only true God and Saviour of mankind and the Christian faith." In 1646 the Colonial Legislature passed an Act for the propagation of the Gospel among the Indians.

The formation of the Corporation for the Propagation of the Gospel in New England (see p. 56) was indirectly due to the reports which had reached England concerning the labours of *John Eliot* (1604–90), the " Apostle of the Indians." After taking his degree at Jesus College, Cambridge (1623), he acted for a time as an usher in a school near Chelmsford, and, sailing for America in 1631, was appointed as the Presbyterian pastor of Roxbury,

24

near Boston, in 1632. When he began his missionary work there were about twenty tribes of Indians on the plantations adjoining Massachusetts Bay, and for many years Eliot combined the charge of the church at Roxbury with pioneer evangelistic work amongst the Indians. His biographer remarks of him that his name written backwards spells "toile," and few missionaries have toiled harder than he. His first attempt to evangelize the Indians was made at the Falls of the Grand River in 1646. His great desire was to establish Indian settlements which should realize the Jewish theocracy described in Exodus. His first baptisms were at Natick, near Boston, where a settlement of Indians was organized in 1651, in accordance with the directions given to the Israelites in Exodus xviii. His work was imitated by Mayhews, "a pious colonist," and others, and ere long there had arisen in New England fourteen "praying Indian villages," containing 3600 Christians. Everything went well till 1675, when the war between the English and the Indians brought about the destruction of nearly all their settlements and put back the work amongst Indians for many years. He was an indefatigable student and translator, and in 1661 he published the New Testament in the Indian (Mohican) language, and two years later the Old Testament was also issued. He published in addition Indian grammars and primers, and translations of several English theological books. He died at Roxbury at the age of eighty-six in 1690. After witnessing the destruction of his Christian settlements and the apparent ruin of his work, he wrote to Robert Boyle, shortly before his death, "My understanding leaves me, my memory fails me, my utterance fails me, but I thank God my charity holds out still." His dying words were, "Welcome joy."

The Scottish Society for the Propagation of Christian Knowledge, which was founded in Edinburgh in 1701, gave some occasional assistance to missionary work. It helped to support *David Brainerd*, who was born in

Connecticut in 1718. For nearly four years he worked amongst Indians in Pennsylvania and New Jersey, and gathered some converted Indians at a settlement which he named Bethel, where he attempted to teach them husbandry. He died before he was thirty in 1747. His *Journal*, which was published in 1746, and his *Life*, which was afterwards written by his friend President Edwards, influenced many in later times to give their lives to the work of Christian missions.

Anglican Missions to Indians and Negroes.

New York.—In 1704 Mr. Elias Neau, a Frenchman, was appointed by the S.P.G. as a catechist to work amongst negroes and in charge of a "catechising school," having received a licence from the Governor of New York "to catechize the negroes and Indians and the children of the town." In exercising his office he found reason to complain that "the generality" of the "inhabitants" were "strangely prejudiced with a horrid notion, thinking the Christian knowledge" would be "a means to make their slaves more cunning and apter to wickedness." Later on the Rev. S. Auchmuty (1747–64) reported that "not one single Black" who had been "admitted by him to the Holy Communion" had "turned out bad, or been in any shape a disgrace to our holy profession," and that the masters of the negroes had become "more desirous than they used to be of having them instructed." In 1707 the Rev. W. Barclay became minister at Albany and helped to prepare for publication in the Iroquois language translations of the Gospels and of the Book of Common Prayer which had been made by Mr. Freeman, "a devout minister of the Dutch Church." He and his successors started work amongst the Mohawks. Towards the furnishing of the first chapel for the Mohawks, Queen Anne contributed "altar plate and linen."

In 1727 the S.P.G. appointed the Rev. J. Miln to minister to the Indians at Fort Hunter near Albany. The result of his labours was thus described by the officer commanding the Fort Hunter garrison in 1735 :

"I have found the Mohawk Indians very much civilized, which I take to be owing to the industry and pains taken by the Rev. Mr. John Miln in teaching and instructing them in the Christian religion. The number of communicants increases daily. . . . The said Indians express the greatest satisfaction with Mr. Miln. . . . They are become as perempter in observing their rules as any society of Christians commonly are. . . . They are very observing of the Sabbath, conveneing by themselves and singing Psalms on that day, and frequently applying to me that Mr. Miln may be oftener among them." [1]

By 1742 a missionary was able to report that only two or three of the tribe remained unbaptized.

A mission to the Oneidas was opened in 1816 which made good progress, but in 1823 the U.S.A. Government transferred the Indians to a new reserve in Wisconsin. All the Indians on this new settlement are now baptized Christians.

South Carolina.—The first missionary sent out by the S.P.G. for work amongst the heathen was the Rev. S. Thomas. He was designed for a mission to the Yammonsees and on his appointment £10 was voted by the society "to be laid out in stuffs for the use of the wild Indians." Mr. Thomas was so ill during his voyage down the Channel that his life was despaired of at Plymouth, but after a voyage of three months he reached Charlestown on Christmas Day, 1702. As the Yammonsees were engaged in fighting at the time of his arrival, he devoted his attention to the negro and Indian slaves in the Cooper River district, and at the same time ministered to the English settlers, who "were making near approach to that heathenism which is to be found among negroes and Indians." Returning to England in 1705 in the hope of securing additional fellow-workers, he died in 1706.

[1] See *Reports and Letters of the Society's Missionaries in Wisconsin*, vol. A., 26, p. 4.

In 1713 the Rev. G. Johnston of Charlestown brought to England a Yammonsee prince, at the request of his father and of the "Emperor of the Indians," in order that he might be instructed in the Christian religion and in English manners. He was "put to school and instructed at the charge of the society," and was baptized by the Bishop of London in the Royal Chapel of Somerset House on Quinquagesima Sunday, 1715, at the age of nineteen, Lord Carteret, one of the proprietors of South Carolina, being one of his sponsors. After his baptism he was presented to the King. On his return to America he continued his education under Mr. Johnston, to whose care the eldest son of the "Emperor of the Cherequois" was also entrusted. A few months later a war broke out in which the missionaries and the Indian Christians suffered grievously.

In 1743, two negroes having been purchased and trained as teachers at the cost of the S.P.G., a school was opened at Charleston by Commissary Garden, with the object of training the negroes as instructors of their countrymen. The school was continued with success for more than twenty years, many adult slaves also attending in the evening for instruction. This school was maintained in the face of many difficulties and at a time when the Government had not one institution for the education of the 50,000 slaves in the colony.[1]

North Carolina. — Attempts were made in several districts by missionaries of the S.P.G. to evangelize the negro slaves, but in many cases their efforts were frustrated by the opposition of the slave-owners.

Mr. Rainsford, who was stationed at Chowan in 1712, baptized "upwards of forty negroes" in one year. As the prejudices of the masters were overcome a missionary would baptize sometimes fifteen to twenty-four negroes in a month and as many as seventy in a year. The Rev. C. Hall reported having baptized 355 in eight years. Some of the missionaries received very little support from

[1] *Two Hundred Years of the S.P.G.*, p. 18.

the colonists, and suffered severe hardships in consequence.
Thus the Rev. J. Urmston reported in 1711 that he and
his family were " in manifest danger of perishing for want
of food." " We have," he said, " liv'd many a day only on
a dry crust and a draught of water out of the Sound."

Georgia was established as a colony in 1733. On the
return of Mr. Quincy, the society's first missionary in
Georgia, the Rev. *John Wesley* was appointed as his
successor. The meeting of the S.P.G. committee at which
he was appointed was held on January 16, 1736.
Amongst those who were present were the Bishops of
London, Lichfield, Rochester, and Gloucester. Wesley
sailed for Georgia in the hope that he might be able to
evangelize the heathen, but the claims of the settlers at
Savannah left him little time to preach to the Indians,
though he made several attempts to do so. He returned
to England after an absence of two years. During his
stay in Georgia he got into trouble with some of the
settlers owing to his refusal to read the Burial Service
over a Nonconformist, and by others he was accused of
being a Papist. The actual difficulty which caused his
abrupt departure from the colony arose in connection with
his refusal to admit to Holy Communion a member of his
congregation. A little later missionary work was started
amongst the Chickasaw Indians and negroes.

There appears to be no account of missionary work
amongst the Indians and negroes in *Pennsylvania* supported by the S.P.G. until 1756, when the society granted
£100 per annum for the training of native teachers in the
college at Philadelphia under the Rev. Dr. Smith.

In *New England* the efforts of the missionaries to
evangelize the Indians and negroes were bitterly opposed
by the colonists. In 1730 the Rev. J. Usher reported
from Bristol that " sundry negroes " had made " application for baptism that were able to render a very good
account of the hope that was in them," but he was
" not permitted to comply with their requests . . . being
forbid by their masters." In the same year, however, he

succeeded in baptizing three adult Indians, and later on the Bristol congregation included "about thirty negroes and Indians," most of whom joined "in the public service very decently."

At Stratford Dr. Johnson "always had a catechetical lecture during the summer months, attended by many negroes and some Indians, as well as the whites, about 70 or 80 in all." At Naragansett, Dr. Macsparran had a class of 70 Indians and negroes, whom he frequently catechised and instructed before Divine Service, and the Rev. S. Honyman of Newport, Rhode Island, besides baptizing some Indians, numbered among his congregation "above 100 negroes who constantly attended the Publick Worship." Among the Naragansett tribe in Rhode Island Catechist Bennet of the Mohawk Mission, New York Province, laboured for a short time on the invitation of their king.[1]

New Jersey.—Attempts were made in several parts of this province to do missionary work amongst negroes between 1701 and 1750. Towards the end of this period (1746-51) the Rev. Thomas Thompson laboured in New Jersey. In 1751 he left America in order to go as a missionary to the Gold Coast, being the first S.P.G. missionary and probably the first Englishman to work as a missionary in Africa.

The difficulties which the missionaries connected with the S.P.G. had to face in America were the same as those which confronted John Eliot and the Moravian missionaries. These were created by the attitude of the colonists towards the Indians and by the reluctance of slave-owners to allow their slaves to receive any kind of education. Again and again a promising community of Christian Indians was established, only to be scattered or massacred in one of the intermittent wars which were waged between the non-Christian Indians and the colonists. Had these Christian communities been allowed to develop, it is inconceivable that the American people could have

[1] See *Two Hundred Years of the S.P.G.*, p. 47.

incurred the disgrace of allowing the twentieth century to dawn upon their country whilst a large proportion of its Indian subjects still remained heathen. The difficulties raised by the slave-owners in regard to the evangelization of the negroes retarded but have not prevented the nominal Christianization of the race. In many cases these difficulties were not removed until the emancipation of the negroes in 1863.

After the Declaration of Independence the Anglican Christians in the U.S.A. were comparatively few in number and were not in a position to develop mission work amongst the Indians, but by the middle of the nineteenth century the Protestant Episcopal Church began to organize such work.

The first of a chain of Anglican missions was opened at Gull Lake, *Minnesota,* for the Chippewas in 1852. In 1859 Henry Benjamin Whipple, who became the great champion of the Indians in their dealings with the U.S.A. Government, was consecrated as the first Bishop of Minnesota. In 1860 Bishop Whipple opened a mission amongst the Santee Sioux Indians. In 1872 William Hobart Hare was consecrated as a missionary bishop to the Indians. The Sioux Indians who lived in South Dakota were his special charge. For thirty-seven years Bishop Hare, who eventually became known throughout the U.S.A. as the Apostle to the Indians, shared the life and the privations of his beloved Indians, and before his death in 1909 he had the satisfaction of seeing a large Indian community which was Christian in something more than name. He was "God's chief human instrument in the transformation of a tribe of murderous savages into gentle, worshipful citizens of the Kingdom of Christ."[1]   Of the 25,000 Christians in South Dakota 10,000 are baptized members of the Anglican Church. At the present time the Anglican Church has missions to Indians in twelve states and supports 23 white and 25 Indian clergy.

[1] *Handbook of the Church's Mission to Indians,* p. 139.

In the state of Oklahoma, which contains the largest number of Indians, there are about 120,000 Indians or people with Indian blood.

The greater part of the missionary work in this state is carried on by the Roman Catholics and the Presbyterians.

We have already referred to the attempts made by the Moravians to work amongst Indians in Georgia and New York during the first half of the eighteenth century. Later on they started missions among the Delawares and associated tribes in Ohio, and still later, in Ontario and Kansas. Early in the nineteenth century the Friends established missions in Indiana, and, at a later period, in Oklahoma.

"The Presbyterians began their work among the Wyandottes about the same time as the Friends, and later among the Cherokees, Osages, and Pawnees. To the Congregational missionaries we owe most of our knowledge of the Sioux language, their work being almost entirely in the Santee or Eastern dialect. . . . The Methodists were the first to minister to the Flatheads in the mountains at the head of the Missouri River; they also had missions among the Chippewas. The Baptists laboured for the Weas, a sub-tribe of the Miamis, in 1818–21. Later on missions were established for the Pottawatomie, near South Bend, Indiana, and among the Ottawas on Grand River, Michigan. This is but passing mention of work divinely inspired and nobly done; lack of space prevents more detailed description of these the earliest missions among the Indians of the Mississippi River region."[1]

The American Board of Commissioners for Foreign Missions, which was organized in 1810 and is the oldest missionary society having its origin in the U.S.A., worked for many years amongst the Indians. Up to 1890 it had supported 1600 missionaries, of whom 512 had been sent to work amongst the Indians. The first missionary, the Rev. Cyrus Kingsbury, was sent in 1815 to start work

[1] *A Handbook of the Church's Mission to the Indians* (Christian Missions Publishing Co., U.S.A.), p. 103.

amongst the Cherokees of Georgia. In 1818 a second
station was opened amongst the Choctaws on the Yazoo
River. In 1825 a half-breed Cherokee invented the
Cherokee alphabet, with the result that within four years
half his nation had learned to read. The work of the
A.B.C.F.M. made rapid progress for several years, but was
eventually checked and interrupted by the ill-treatment
of the Cherokee, Sioux, and other Indians by American
settlers who took possession of their land.

In 1834 the Dutch Reformed Church handed over to
the A.B.C.F.M. their mission stations west of the Rocky
Mountains, and this work was extended amongst the
Spokanes and Cayuses. In 1848, in consequence of a
massacre, the missionaries had to be withdrawn, but seven
years later, when they were able to return, they found
that a large proportion of their converts had " lived consistent Christian lives, having continued the reading of the
Scriptures in their own languages and also kept up regular
family worship." The Cayuses have now become extinct.

In 1846 the American Missionary Association for the
promotion of missionary work amongst the Indians was
established, and in 1883 the A.B.C.F.M. transferred to
this society the care of all its missions to American
Indians.

The Women's National Indian Association has done
much to influence public opinion in favour of the Indians,
and has started several missions amongst them which it
afterwards transferred to the charge of various missionary
societies.

The American Baptist Home Missionary Society, which
began its work in 1807, and the A.M.E.C. have work
amongst several different tribes. A missionary of the
latter body, John Stewart, who was called the "Apostle
to the Wyandottes," died in 1823.

The total number of Anglican and Protestant missionaries now at work amongst the American Indians is
about 200.

The societies which report the largest amount of

work amongst American Indians are the following (the figures indicate the number of Christian adherents):—

The Presbyterian Church Board of Home Missions, 18,108; the Protestant Episcopal Church, 12,900; American Baptist Home Mission Society, 8156; the Methodist Episcopal Church, 5000; the Methodist Episcopal Church, South, 5000. Twenty-five American societies report a total of 66,928 adherents and 28,092 baptized Christians. These figures do not include the Indian Christians belonging to the R.C. Church.

R.C. Missions to Indians. — Of the Indians in the U.S.A. and Alaska 64,741 are attached to the R.C. missions. Of these 3200 are in the diocese of Alaska, 9633 in the diocese of Santa Fé, 7344 in the diocese of Lead, 3664 in the diocese of Crookstone, 3643 in the diocese of Seattle, 4380 in the diocese of Helena, and 3890 in the diocese of Great Falls. During 1912 the number of adults baptized was 1017. The number of priests attached to the R.C. missions is 163. In 1874 the Bureau of Catholic Indian Missions, of which the R.C. Archbishop of Baltimore was president, was established. This Bureau helps to support the mission schools and to maintain and develop the various missions. The Society for the Preservation of the Faith among Indian children, established in 1901, collects from each of its members, who number about 50,000, an annual subscription of 25 cents for the benefit of the missions.

The number of Indians in the U.S.A., according to the census of 1910, was 265,683, and in Alaska, 25,331. The largest number of Indians is found in Oklahoma, namely, 74,825; while Arizona has 29,201; New Mexico, 20,573; South Dakota, 19,137; California, 16,371; Washington, 10,997; Montana, 10,745; Wisconsin, 10,142, etc. Indians are found in every state and territory, but their number in Delaware, Vermont, New Hampshire, and West Virginia is less than 50.

It is satisfactory to note that, after several fluctuations, their number appears to be definitely increasing. Their total number was 278,000 in 1870, 244,000 in 1880, 248,253 in 1890, and 237,196 in 1900. Thus, their number decreased from 1870 to 1900, but it increased considerably (28,487) during the decade between 1900 and 1910. The number of Indians in Alaska is on the decrease, namely, from 32,996 in 1880 and 29,536 in 1900 to 25,331 in 1910.

The number of Indian tribes is large, but some have very few members, six tribes being represented by a single member each, and 30 having a membership under 10. The Cherokees have 31,489 members; the Navajo, 32,455; the Chippewa, 20,214; the Choctaw, 15,917; and the Teton Sioux, 14,284. Of the remaining continental United States tribes none has as many as 7000 members, but there are 74 tribes represented by not less than 500 individuals. In Alaska the Kuswogmiut have 1480 members and the Aleutt 1451, but none of the other tribes in the territory has as many as a thousand members.

Alaska.

Alaska contains a population of 65,000, which includes about 15,000 Eskimo, 2000 Aleutians, 25,231 Indians, 2000 Chinese, and a steadily increasing number of white immigrants and half-breeds. It was bought from Russia by the U.S.A. in 1867.

A mission was founded by the Russian Orthodox Church in the Aleutian Islands between Kamtchatka and Alaska in 1793. We have referred elsewhere (see p. 276) to the good work accomplished here by John Veniaminoff, afterwards Archbishop Innocent. The mission was extended to Alaska in 1834, and is now superintended by a bishop whose diocese is called "The Aleutian Islands and North America" and whose cathedral is at San Francisco. The members of the "orthodox" Church in his diocese number between 40,000 and 50,000 and include over 10,000 Indians, Aleutians, Creoles, and Eskimos.

The U.S.A. Presbyterians started a mission at Fort

Wrangel in 1877. This mission has now 8 stations and 4000 Christians. The Moravians, who started in 1885 amongst the Eskimos in the south-west, have about 1400 baptized Christians attached to the mission.

Missionary work in Alaska was begun by the Protestant Episcopal Church U.S.A. at Anvik in 1887, and Bishop Rowe was consecrated as its first bishop in 1895. In addition to the bishop there are 12 clergy and 6 lay readers. There are 2 industrial schools, 6 mission hospitals, 20 churches, and 20 mission rooms. At Point Hope there are 3 Eskimos who conduct services for their own people whom the bishop hopes to be able to ordain.

Mr. Duncan, who founded the C.M.S. Mission of Metlakahtla, after separating from the C.M.S., migrated with a large number of Indians to Annetta Island, which is within the territory of Alaska.

Orientals in the U.S.A.

The Chinese number about 75,000, of whom the greater part are on the Pacific Slope, most of the remainder being in the Rocky Mountain districts. The number and location of the Japanese are about the same. The immigrants from India are probably fewer in number and are widely scattered. Attempts to evangelize these immigrants are being made by many local churches, and organized missionary work is being carried on on a small scale on the Pacific coast and in a few large cities in the east. It is estimated that about 7000 Chinese and about 5000 Japanese have been baptized. Very few attempts are being made to reach the Indians except by the agents of the American Bible Society.

XIV.

CANADA.

Canadian Indians.

THE first missionary to set foot in Canada was Father Fléché, who in 1610 joined Champlain's settlement in the Bay of Fundy, Nova Scotia. Within a year of his arrival the chief Membertou and all his tribe had become Christians. In the following year two Jesuit priests arrived to assist in the missionary work which had been begun.

In 1633 Jesuit missionaries started work amongst the Indian tribes in the neighbourhood of Quebec, but despite the devotion and activity of the missionaries the progress made during the first few years was slow. "On one occasion Brebeuf appeared before the chiefs and elders at a solemn national assembly council, described heaven and hell with images suited to their comprehension, asked to which they preferred to go after death, and then, in accordance with the invariable Huron custom in affairs of importance, presented a large and valuable belt of wampum, as an invitation to take the path to Paradise." [1]

For forty years the Jesuits laboured hard, but in vain, to reclaim the Indians from their wandering life and to induce them to abandon their cruel customs. In individual cases they attained some success, but, partly as a result of fighting between them and the French, and partly as the result of quarrels among themselves, their efforts proved unavailing, and in 1675 the mission came to an end.

Of the deeds of heroism accomplished by these Jesuit missionaries many instances might be given, but a single

[1] *The Jesuits in North America*, by F. Parkman, p. 151.

illustration must suffice. In 1660 Father René, who was then an old man, in response to an invitation brought by a party of Ottawas, left the St. Lawrence and travelled with them to their own district. After a while they left him to starve on the shores of a lake, but eventually they relented and carried him to the home of their tribe, a hundred miles west of Sault Ste. Marie, where, living in a miserable dug-out under a hollow tree, he began his missionary work. Driven out of this, he was compelled to spend his first winter in a little cabin built of fir-tree branches. The following summer, while trying to reach another Indian settlement, he was either murdered by hostile Indians, or died of exposure. This story aptly illustrates the difficulties under which the work of the Jesuit missionaries was carried on. Many of the missionaries and of their Indian converts suffered martyrdom, which was inflicted with the most barbarous cruelty.

After the recall of the Jesuit missionaries in 1773 the care of the Indians fell upon the Sulpicians and upon those of the secular clergy who were able to assist them. Sporadic attempts were made to evangelize the Indians in different parts of Eastern Canada, and in 1842 Father Thibault began to preach to the Crees and Blackfeet in Alberta. In 1844 Jesuit missionaries inaugurated work on Walpole Island in Lake Superior, and at several other centres.

In 1860 Mr. J. G. Kohl, in a book describing his travels on the shores of Lake Superior, refers thus to the work of the R.C. missionaries :

"Everything I heard here daily of the pious courage, patience, and self-devoting zeal of these missionaries on Lake Superior caused me to feel intense admiration. They live isolated and scattered in little log huts round the lake, often no better off than the natives." [1]

Between 1850 and 1870 Oblates and other missionaries started work amongst several tribes in the north-

[1] *Wanderings round Lake Superior*, xix. 306.

west. In 1847 work was started in Vancouver Island. In 1875 Brother Alexis was killed and eaten by an Iroquois Indian. Within recent years the work has been developed and has been carried on with a fair amount of visible success.

Anglican Missions.

In 1820 the Rev. S. West, the first chaplain of the Hudson Bay Company, began work in the Red River Colony near the site of the present town of Winnipeg. He received a grant from the C.M.S. towards the education of Indian boys, and two of his earliest pupils, H. Budd and J. Settee, were eventually ordained. In 1831 an Indian settlement was attempted and an effort was made to reclaim the Indians from their wandering life; but out of an encampment of 200 Indians only seven could be induced to take part in cultivating the ground, and when the first harvest was reaped, four of these consumed the whole produce at a single feast, reserving nothing for the coming winter. One of those who helped to establish the settlement had previously eaten seven of his own relations. Notwithstanding, however, the initial difficulties which were experienced, the settlement proved a success, and a well-ordered Christian community eventually came into existence. A series of other stations were established, and in 1872 it was reported that no heathen Indians were to be found in this whole district. The work gradually spread towards the west and towards the north. Budd was ordained by the first Bishop of Rupertsland in 1850. In 1865 there were in Rupertsland and the North-West Territories 5000 Indian Christians and 1000 communicants.

In 1851 work amongst Indians was begun in what is now the diocese of Moosonee, which includes the whole coast-line of Hudson Bay. In this year a schoolmaster named John Horden was sent out by the C.M.S. to Moose Fort. In the following year he was ordained, and in 1872 he became the first Bishop of Moosonee. Before his death

in 1893 he had seen successful missions established
amongst all the Indian tribes within the limits of his vast
diocese, and the beginnings of a Christian literature in the
Cree, Ojibbeway, Chipewyan, and Eskimo languages. All
the Crees, three-fourths of the Ojibbeways, and many of the
Chipewyans in the diocese have now been baptized. There
are several missionaries at work in connection with the
Indian reserves in Saskatchewan and Alberta, but the
results have not been as encouraging as they have been
farther north. It seems well-nigh impossible to induce
the Indians to work for more than a few weeks at a time,
or to acquire habits of thrift. The most hopeful features
of the work are the Indian boarding schools—*e.g.* the school
at Lytton, supported by the New England Company
(see p. 56), or the school at Battleford, which is supported
by the Government but is carried on under missionary
supervision.

In 1858 the C.M.S. began work amongst the Tukudh
Indians at Fort Simpson and a little later at Fort
MacPherson and across the Rocky Mountains at Fort Yukon.
Archdeacon M'Donald began his work amongst the Tukudh
Indians in 1862 and laboured for fifty years on their
behalf. In 1865 he was joined by the Rev. W. C. Bompas,
who afterwards became Bishop of Athabasca, and later on
Bishop of Selkirk (Yukon). Within a few years of the
opening of the mission these two missionaries baptized
over 1000 Indians.

In British Columbia and the islands on the Pacific
coast are found Indians belonging to several distinct tribes.
In 1856 William Duncan, a schoolmaster, was sent out by
the C.M.S. to Fort Simpson on the Pacific coast, and in
1862 he founded a settlement at Metlakahtla, seventeen
miles south of Fort Simpson, which rapidly developed into
a flourishing community. Difficulties arose between the
C.M.S. and Mr. Duncan, who refused to allow the Holy
Communion to be administered to Indians, and eventually,
in consequence of a dispute between him and the Canadian
Government, Mr. Duncan withdrew to American territory

25

in Alaska.   Metlakahtla became, under Bishop Ridley, the
centre of a series of mission stations for work amongst
Indians.   Other stations have been opened on the Skeena
River, on Queen Charlotte's Island, and in Vancouver Island.

The Anglican missions to Indians and to the Eskimos,
most of which were inaugurated and supported by the help
of the C.M.S., are now supported by organizations belonging
to the various dioceses in which they are situated, though
the C.M.S. still provides some financial assistance.

Distribution of the Indian population.

The Indian population of the Dominion of Canada in
1909 was 111,043, which represented an increase of
3406 on the return for 1905.   Their distribution according to provinces is as follows: Nova Scotia, 2103; New
Brunswick, 1871; Prince Edward Island, 274; Quebec,
11,523; Ontario, 23,898; Manitoba, 8327; Saskatchewan,
7971; Alberta, 5541; North-West Territories, 21,362,
British   Columbia,   24,871;   Yukon   territory,   3302.
The religious census was as follows: Roman Catholics,
40,820; Anglicans, 16,590; Methodists, 16,776; other
denominations, 3460; pagans, 9622.

The largest number of converts connected with the R.C.
missions are found in British Columbia (11,470), Ontario
(6319), and Saskatchewan (2939).

The Anglican missions are strongest in Ontario, British
Columbia, Manitoba, Saskatchewan, the North-West, and
in the Yukon territories; the Methodists work chiefly
in Alberta, Ontario, British Columbia, and Manitoba; the
Presbyterians in British Columbia, Saskatchewan, and
Ontario; and the Baptists in Ontario.

The missions receive a considerable amount of help
from the Canadian Government, especially in the upkeep
of their schools.   There are altogether 20 industrial
schools, 57 boarding schools, and 231 day schools.   Of
the total number of schools 109 are Roman Catholic,
86 Anglican, 44 Methodist, 16 Presbyterian, 51 un-

denominational, and 2 belong to the Salvation Army.
There are 5323 boys and 5156 girls in these schools,
which contain about half the total number of Indian
children of school age.

The Eskimos.

The word Eskimo is a corruption of an Indian word
which means " eaters of raw meat." They number about
40,000 and are scattered over 3200 miles. They live on
the seacoast and are seldom found more than 20 miles
inland. Their language has but few dialectical variations.
Of the total number, 11,000 are found in Greenland and
13,000 in Alaska and the Behring Straits.

Greenland was discovered by Red Erck and his Norsemen in A D. 986. Soon after the Norsemen had effected a
settlement, mention is made of twelve churches, several
cloisters, and one nunnery. We have already referred to
the good work done by the Moravians, which ended in
1900, when they handed over the care of their converts to
the Danish Government Mission. The Danish missionaries
have a seminary for the training of mission workers, and
the number of non-Christians is now small.

In *Labrador* the Eskimos number about 2000, and
mission work amongst them is chiefly carried on by the
Moravians, who, in addition to their spiritual work,
endeavour to organize trade. Dr. Grenfell's Labrador
Medical Mission work, both amongst the white fishermen
and amongst the Eskimos, and the hospitals which he has
established, have been a great help to the latter.

The first regular mission to *Eskimos in the Canadian
Dominion* was undertaken by Edmund Peck, formerly a
seaman in the Navy, who began at Little Whale River on
the south-east shore of Hudson's Bay in 1876. After
fourteen years he started another mission among the
Eskimos on Blacklead Island in Cumberland Bay. The
church which he built at this station, and which was
made of whale-bone and seal-skins, was eaten by

dogs. His work, which was carried on under great difficulties, has been most encouraging. In 1892 he started work amongst Eskimos within the Arctic Circle to the north of Cumberland Sound. In 1882 the Rev. T. H. Canham started work in the Mackenzie River district, and Archdeacon Lofthouse made extensive missionary journeys among the Eskimos on the western shores of Hudson Bay. In the far north-west the names of Bishop Bompas, Archdeacon Macdonald, and Bishop Stringer are associated with successful work which has been established amongst the widely scattered groups of Eskimos to be found between Alaska and the Hudson Bay districts.

Orientals in Canada.—Of those living in Canada in 1909, who numbered in all 36,591, there were 21,122 Chinese, 12,003 Japanese, and 3466 from India. Most of these are in British Columbia. A limited amount of missionary work is carried on by the Anglican, Methodist, and Presbyterian Churches. In Winnipeg, where there are 1000 Chinese, the Presbyterians and Methodists have a joint mission.

XV.

THE WEST INDIES.

THE spread of the Christian faith in the West Indies has been conditioned by their political history. The islands which have been long under the control of Spain or France have been chiefly influenced by R.C. missionaries, whilst those which have been under the control of England or Holland have been influenced by Anglican and Protestant missionaries.

Spain secured Cuba, Porto Rico, the eastern part of Hispaniola (San Domingo), and Trinidad. The French secured the western part of Hispaniola (Hayti) and other smaller islands, *e.g.* Martinique, Guadeloupe, Grenada, St. Vincent, and St. Lucia. Great Britain at first occupied Barbados, Antigua, St. Kitts, and Nevis, to which Cromwell added Jamaica, which was captured from Spain. By the close of the eighteenth century Great Britain had taken Trinidad from Spain, and Grenada, St. Vincent, St. Lucia, and Dominica from France. St. Vincent and Grenada, which were acquired earlier than the others, are more anglicized, but in Trinidad, Dominica, and St. Lucia Spanish and French patois prevail and most of the inhabitants belong to the R.C. Church.

The Spaniards made little effort to evangelize the Caribs or other original inhabitants, and the massacres and deportation of these peoples to work on the mainland forms one of the blackest pages in history. The responsibility for their disappearance rests chiefly with the Spaniards, though the French and English are not free from blame. In a few islands some of their descendants are still to be found. Thus in St. Vincent there are about 200, in

Dominica about 300, and there are a few in the Virgin Islands. In other islands there are a certain number of inhabitants of mixed Carib and negro descent.

Practically the whole population of the West Indies, with the exception of the Chinese and East Indian labourers, is, and has for a long time been, nominally Christian.

The work of evangelizing the negro slaves was slow. It was left almost entirely during the eighteenth century to the Anglican clergy, who were not as a rule conspicuous for missionary zeal: the Wesleyans and others who desired to share in the work were in many cases prevented from doing so by the opposition of the English colonists. Despite, however, the hindrances which were placed in the way of missionary enterprise, by the time that the emancipation of the negroes took place a large proportion of them had been deeply influenced by Christian teaching. Professor Caldecott writes:

"It stands out as one of the most signal triumphs of religion in human history that Emancipation was regarded by the freed slaves themselves as a religious boon to be received with pious gratitude and celebrated with religious rites. The last hours of slavery and the first hours of freedom were spent in churches and chapels. And the new centres round which the emancipated rallied were neither ignorant agitators nor firebrand orators holding out plunder and rapine as now within reach, but the missionaries, pastors, deacons, and class-leaders of Christian congregations." [1]

It is difficult to prevent contrasting what happened in the islands in which English missionaries had been working with the occurrences which took place in Hayti, when in 1791 the French Revolutionary Assembly decreed the emancipation of the slaves. When the news reached Hayti, 1000 plantations were wrecked by the slaves, and in the conflict which ensued 2000 whites and 10,000 negroes were killed.

[1] *The Church in the West Indies*, p. 98.

Reference has already been made to the work of the Moravians in the West Indies during the first half of the eighteenth century. Between 1732 and 1739 twenty-two Brethren died in St. Thomas and St. Croix. In 1754 they occupied St. Jan, and soon extended their work over the Danish islands. From 1764 onwards they opened stations in Jamaica, Antigua, St. Kitt's, Barbados, Tobago, and Trinidad. They are now also represented in the Leeward and Windward Islands.

The Methodists began work in 1786, and by the time of Dr. Coke's death in 1813 they had obtained 11,000 negro converts.

English Baptists began work in Jamaica in 1831, and by 1842 their church members numbered 24,000. They have also missions in Trinidad, the Turk's Islands, San Domingo, and the Bahamas.

The Scotch United Presbyterians took over in 1847 a mission which had been started in Jamaica in 1824. They have also work in Trinidad.

The relative strength of the chief denominations in the islands belonging to Great Britain may be gathered from the following estimate, which was made in 1897 but which may be taken as representing the relative numbers to-day (the figures given represent communicants or full members): Anglicans, 127,000; Wesleyans, 52,000; Baptists, 42,000; Presbyterians, 19,000; Moravians, 19,000.

It is not possible to do more than touch briefly upon the missionary work which has been done in a few of the more important islands. The story of one, however, is with a few exceptions the story of all.

Jamaica was discovered by Columbus in 1494. During the 150 years in which it remained in the possession of the Spaniards they exterminated its native population, destroying altogether 1,200,000 Arawaks in it and the adjacent islands. When in 1655 it became a British possession it contained about 1500 whites and the same number of African negro slaves. That the R.C. Church had endeavoured to minister to the slave population is evidenced by the fact that when the English captured the island they found there several negro priests belonging to the R.C. Communion. By the end of the eighteenth century the slaves had increased in number to 300,000, and when slavery was abolished in 1833 the number of slaves who were set free in Jamaica was 309,338.

The Jamaica Expedition organized by Cromwell was provided with seven chaplains, whose instructions were drawn up by John Milton. The Slave Code of Jamaica (1696) contained the following injunctions, which, however, were seldom carried into effect: "All masters, mistresses, owners, and employers are to endeavour as much as possible the instruction of their slaves in the principles of the Christian religion, and to facilitate their conversion, and do their utmost to fit them for baptism, and as soon as convenient cause all such to be baptized as they can make sensible of a Deity and the Christian faith."

In 1664 five parishes were constituted which were served by five ministers, two of whom were Swiss. In 1703 the S.P.G. began to vote money for the support of clergy, and in 1825 Dr. C. Lipscomb was appointed as the first bishop. Prior to his appointment, the Anglican clergy, both in Jamaica and in other parts of the West Indies, had in many instances been men of unsatisfactory character, who had but little influence with the white settlers and were not interested in missionary work.[1] Until the negroes were set free obstacles were frequently placed in the way of their becoming Christians, but their emancipation was followed by the conversion of a large number. In 1840 the bishop confirmed nearly 9000. For many years the S.P.G. continued to support missionary work in Jamaica, and it did not withdraw till 1865, when practically the whole of the population had become nominally Christian.

In 1825 the C.M.S. sent out two catechists and their wives, and by 1840 it had work at 21 stations with a staff

[1] See *The Church in the West Indies*, by Professor Caldecott, ch. iii.

of 7 clerical and 11 lay missionaries. It finally withdrew about 1848.

Moravian missionaries were sent to Jamaica in 1754 at the instigation of two absentee proprietors of estates, who desired to benefit their slaves. At the outset some success was attained, but during the first fifty years not more than 1000 persons were baptized. The Moravian missionaries themselves became the owners of slaves and supported themselves in part by their labours.

The Wesleyan Methodists started work in 1789, but were bitterly opposed by the Planters. At the close of the eighteenth century they had 600 converts.

Baptists from Virginia began work in Kingston in 1814. This was transferred to the English Baptists in 1831. A Jamaican Baptist missionary society has stations in Central America and in several of the West Indian Islands. The unjust disabilities under which the Nonconformist missionaries worked may be gathered from the Ordinance passed in 1807 by the Corporation of Kingston which provided that they were to conduct no services except in open daylight and that no persons were to lend their houses for worship. An Act passed at the same time forbidding them to instruct slaves was disallowed at home.

The Bahama Islands are 500 in number and extend over a line 700 miles in length, but of the whole number only about 20 are inhabited. These include *St. Salvador*, the first land in the New World sighted by Columbus in 1492. Nearly the whole of the original inhabitants, *i.e.* about 40,000, were transported by the Spaniards to Hayti or to the mines of Mexico and Peru, and the islands became depopulated. They were annexed by England in 1578, but were not settled by English immigrants till 1666. During the two following centuries missionary work was carried on amongst the negro slaves by the clergy who were sent out to minister to the English population. In 1843 the Colonial Church Society (now the Colonial and Continental Church Society) sent a lay-agent to work in the Bahamas. It subsequently gave some assistance here and in Jamaica. In 1861 a bishop was appointed, the centre of the diocese being fixed at *Nassau* in the island of *New Providence*. The diocese includes the Bahama Islands, together with the *Turk's* and *Caicos* group. The other chief islands are *Andros, Harbour Islands*, and *Long Cay*.

The Wesleyan Methodists began work in 1825 and eventually occupied five islands. The Baptists opened a mission in 1833.

The Leeward Islands, which include Antigua, Montserrat, St. Kitt's (or St. Christopher's), Nevis, Dominica, Barbuda, Redonda, and certain of the Virgin Islands, were constituted a Federal Colony in 1871. The Leeward Islands also include several islands belonging to France, Holland, and Denmark. The islands contain a number of Creoles, but 85 per cent. of the population are descendants of the negro slaves. The description of the inhabitants of the Leeward Islands given by Bishop Mather, who was formerly Bishop of Antigua, is true of nearly all the islands in the West Indies. After referring to the people as intensely impulsive, easily moved by religious emotions, devoted to singing hymns, but deficient in their sense of the meaning of morality, truth, and honesty, he wrote :

"This is only what their history leads us to expect . . . the heritage and taint of slavery will not be eradicated for many a generation yet to come. Marriage as a rule was forbidden to the slave; what wonder then that his grandchildren think lightly of that holy ordinance? (Two-thirds of the children in this diocese were of illegitimate birth.) . . . It is a sad thought for Englishmen to remember that the vices and faults of the negro are the direct product of the slave trade. . . . We brought the negro to the West Indies, we ill-treated him and ground him down. Surely we have a long debt to make up to him if we do not wish him to rise up in the Judgment against us."

The first serious attempts to evangelize the negroes in *Antigua* were made by the Methodists. The Speaker of the Assembly in Antigua having come into personal contact with John Wesley in England, on his return to Antigua began reading Wesley's sermons to his slaves. In 1789 Dr. Coke visited Antigua, and by 1793 there were 6570 Methodist members, most of whom were slaves.

The Moravians began work in 1756, and by 1812 had reported 8994 members. The Anglican Church had chaplains in Antigua as early as 1634, but comparatively little was done by way of ministering to the spiritual wants of the slaves. Mr. W. Dawes, formerly Governor of Sierra Leone, acted as a catechist in connection with the C.M.S. from 1813.

By the beginning of the nineteenth century efforts were being made by several bodies to reach and benefit the negroes. Thus between 1803 and 1815 the number of persons baptized by the parochial clergy was 2700; by Methodists, 2000; and by the Moravians, 1300.

The Anglican diocese of Antigua (Leeward Islands) was formed in 1842. In 1844 a lay writer in Antigua spoke of there being then in the island "an enlightened and evangelical clergy."

Barbados.—The first batch of settlers in Barbados (1625) were of "such a temper" that their first chaplain is reported to have left them in despair. Later on it was reported that the clergy who endeavoured to instruct their negroes were exposed to "most barbarous usage" and the slaves to worse treatment than before. That the opposition to teaching Christianity to the slaves was not universal is shown by the wording of one of the earliest Ordinances relating to the island, which reads: "That Almighty God be served and glorified, and that He give a blessing to our labours, it is hereby enacted that all masters and overseers of families have prayers openly every morning and evening with his family upon penalty of 40 lb. of sugar, the one half to the informer, the other to the public treasury of the island." It is needless to say that the enactment of this Ordinance did not result in the spread of genuine religion in the island. An important date in the missionary history of Barbados, and in that of the greater

part of the West Indies, is 1710, when, by the will of
General Codrington, the S.P.G. was enabled to establish a
missionary training college for the West Indies.   The will,
which was dated 1703, reads:

"I give and bequeath my two plantations in the Island
of Barbados to the Society for the Propagation of the
Christian Religion in foreign parts, erected and established
by my late good master King William the third, and my
desire is to have the plantations continued intire and 300
negroes at least always kept thereon and a convenient
number of Professors and scholars maintained there . . .
who shall be obliged to study and practise Phisick and
Chirurgery as well as Divinity, that by the apparent usefulness of the former to all mankind they may both endeavour
themselves to the people and have the better opportunities
of doing good to men's souls whilst they are taking care of
their bodys, but the particulars of the constitutions I leave
to the Society composed of wise and good men."

"The design of the Bequest," as explained in the
funeral sermon preached on the death of General Codrington,
"was the maintenance of . . . missionaries to be employed
in the conversion of negroes and Indians."

Owing to insufficiency of funds, the first building to
serve the purpose of a college was not erected till 1742.

Meanwhile the society began a mission to the negroes
in Barbados, and in 1712 they sent out the Rev. Joseph
Holt, "who, being well approved of as to life and morals,
and appearing with due testimonials of his skill in Physic
and Surgery," was instructed to perform "the ordinary
duties of a missionary" and "to instruct in the Christian
religion the negroes and their children within the Society's
plantations in Barbados and to supervise the sick and
maimed negroes and servants."

These instructions were so far carried out by Mr. Holt
and his successors that the Report for 1740 states that
through their labours "some hundreds of negroes have been
brought to our Holy Religion, and there are now not less
than seventy Christian negroes on those Plantations."
These last words imply that missionary work was by no

means confined to the negroes who were employed on the Codrington Plantations. In the same year, 1740, the society ordered that some of the negroes should be trained to act as schoolmasters.

The college subsequently became a most important centre for the training of missionaries, catechists, and schoolmasters for work throughout the West Indies. It has recently been expanded, and should exercise an increasing influence for good in the years to come.

In 1824 William Hart Coleridge was consecrated as the first Bishop of Barbados, and the seventeen years of his episcopate witnessed a great advance of missionary work amongst the negroes. Referring to the service which he conducted on the day of the emancipation of the slaves in Barbados (1838), he wrote:

"It was my peculiar happiness on that memorable day to address a congregation of nearly 4000 persons of whom more than 3000 were negroes just emancipated. And such were the order, deep attention, and perfect silence, that you might have heard a pin drop. Among this mass were thousands of my African brethren joining with their European brothers in offering up their prayers and thanksgivings to the Father, Redeemer, and Sanctifier of all."

Referring to the work of the S.P.G. in Barbados and elsewhere in the West Indies, he added:

"It was chiefly owing to the Society for the Propagation of the Gospel that that day not only passed in peace, but was distinguished for the proper feeling that prevailed and its perfect order."

The Moravians began work in Barbados in 1765, but after thirty years' work they had only 40 communicant members. Later on their work developed largely.

The Wesleyan Methodists have also done good work amongst the negroes. According to the census return of 1901 the members of the different Churches were as follows: Anglicans, 156,000; Wesleyans, 14,400; Moravians, 7000; Roman Catholics, 800; others, 4182.

The Windward Islands include St. Lucia, St. Vincent, Grenada, and the chain of islands which lie between St. Vincent and Grenada called the Grenadines. The total population is about 200,000. In *St. Vincent* and the *Grenadines* the majority of the population belong to the Anglican Church, whilst in *St. Lucia* and *Grenada*, where the population is largely French in descent and language, the majority are Roman Catholics. The S.P.G. has supported missionary work in these islands since 1712.

The Wesleyans have also worked amongst the negroes since the early part of the nineteenth century. The Anglican diocese of the Windward Islands is under the charge of the Bishop of Barbados.

Trinidad, which was in the possession of Spain for 300 years prior to its capture by England in 1797, contains the descendants of many Spanish and French settlers, and a large proportion of its inhabitants are members of the R.C. Church. The S.P.G. began work in 1836, and a diocese of Trinidad was formed in 1872. The Moravians, the United Free Church of Scotland, and the Presbyterian Church of Canada have also work in the island.

A new missionary problem has been created within recent years by the immigration of about 100,000 Hindus and other non-Christians to work on the cocoa and sugar plantations. In the Port of Spain and several other centres missionary work is being carried on amongst these immigrants with considerable success. The Anglican work amongst the Hindus is superintended by the Rev. C. Ragbir, himself a Hindu, who is assisted by others of his fellow-countrymen.

Tobago, which is included in the diocese of Trinidad, was the scene of Robinson Crusoe's adventures, and his cave is shown in the island. His man "Friday" was an Arawak, and his cannibal enemies were Caribs. Half the inhabitants are members of the Anglican Church and a large number of the remainder are Roman Catholics. The population (20,000) includes East Indians, Chinese, French-Creoles, and Spaniards.

Apart from that of the S.P.G., the principal missionary work in the island is carried on by the Moravians, who began work in 1790. The Wesleyans and Baptists are also represented.

Hayti (or *Haiti*), as it was called by its original inhabitants, was renamed Hispaniola by Columbus. Of its two republics the western is now called Hayti and the eastern *San Domingo*. At the time of its discovery it had a population of about 2,000,000, but few of their descendants remain, the population consisting chiefly of negroes. Of the total population of about 700,000, about 525,000 are of African descent. Of the mixed races about 125,000 are of Spanish and 50,000 of French descent. The Spaniards made little effort to convert either the original inhabitants or their own African slaves to the Christian faith and were content with a superficial profession of religion, the result being that the greater part of the population remains practically heathen. In 1861 an American negro, the Rev. J. T. Holly, went to Haiti with a colony of 111 persons and established a centre of missionary work. A few years later Mr. Holly was consecrated as an Anglican bishop, and the work was placed under the Board of Missions of the American Episcopal Church. In connection with this mission there are 13 clergy and 22 organized mission stations.

Cuba, at the time of its discovery by Columbus in 1492, contained a population of about 350,000. By 1560 the whole of this population had been killed or had disappeared. The negro slaves who were introduced became nominal Christians, but their Christianity has never been more than nominal.

Bishop Whipple, who visited Havana in 1871, raised money for the support of an American clergyman whose primary duty was to hold services for Europeans. He, however, succeeded during the nine years in which he was in Cuba in establishing some missions to the negroes on the plantations. Other centres of work were established by refugees who had visited the U.S.A., and the American

Bible Society soon began to send colporteurs through the island. In 1885 Bishop Young of Florida confirmed 325 candidates at six mission centres. In 1904, after the Spanish government of the island had been overthrown, Bishop Knight was consecrated as Anglican Bishop of Cuba. The work which he superintends is carried on at 57 mission centres, and the work is gradually becoming self-supporting. A new bishop was consecrated in 1915.

Several other American missionary societies are beginning to organize work in the island.

The original inhabitants of *Porto Rico*, which was discovered by Columbus in 1493, were soon exterminated by the Spaniards. Of the negroes who were introduced in their place, and who became nominal Christians, very many are still virtually pagans. In 1899, when the island was annexed by the U.S.A., a mission was started by the American Episcopal Church, and a bishop was consecrated in 1902. Work has already been started in thirteen centres. Several other American missionary societies have also begun to organize work in this island.

XVI.

CENTRAL AMERICA.

AMONG the missionaries who have laboured in the West Indies and in Central America the Spanish missionary Las Casas stands pre-eminent. His English biographer [1] writes of him:

"At a period when brute force was universally appealed to in all matters, but more especially in those that pertained to religion, he contended before Juntas and royal Councils that missionary enterprise is a thing that should stand independent of all military support, that a missionary should go forth with his life in his hand, relying only on the protection that God will vouchsafe him, and depending neither upon civil nor military assistance."

The one great mistake of his life, which he acknowledged afterwards with tears of repentance, was the advice which he gave to the Spanish Government to introduce African negroes into the West Indies as slaves. His primary object was to secure the enfranchisement of the native populations in the West Indies, which were being reduced to slavery by the Spaniards; but he soon realized that in order to redress one evil he had countenanced the perpetration of a far greater.

Born in 1474, he sailed under Columbus to the West Indies in 1498.

He was the first priest ordained in the West Indies, and worked at first amongst the Indians in the island of Hispaniola (Haiti). He accompanied the Spanish troops in their conquest of Cuba and laboured hard to protect

[1] See *The Life of Las Casas*, by Sir Arthur Helps, p. vi.

the Indians from their cruelty. After the conquest he himself settled in Cuba with a friend, and became the possessor of Indians, whom he sent to work in the mines for his advantage. After a while he came to realize that the employment of Indians as slaves was wholly inconsistent with the principles of the Christian faith, and having set free his own Indians, he sailed for Spain in the hope of persuading King Ferdinand to alter the policy which he had adopted towards the Indians in the West Indies. As a result of his mission he was appointed "Protector of the Indians," and returned again to Cuba. After vain attempts to secure the enfranchisement of the Indians, he suggested, as a solution of what appeared to be the insuperable difficulties with which he was confronted, that each Spanish colonist should be allowed to have twelve negro slaves. Such slaves had already been imported by the Portuguese, but the suggestion of Las Casas resulted in a great extension of the slave trade. Owing to the incapacity of his fellow-workers, his efforts to organize a Spanish colony on Christian lines met with poor success. In 1522 he became a Dominican monk, and devoted his time for eight years to the study of literature in St. Domingo.

In 1536 Las Casas arrived in Guatemala, after spending some time in Nicaragua. He was invited by the Spanish Governor of Guatemala to attempt the Christianization of the neighbouring province of Tuzulutlan, the conquest of which had been thrice unsuccessfully attempted by Spanish troops. He agreed to do so on condition that no Spaniard should be allowed to enter the province for five years. As this missionary enterprise proved eminently successful, and as a trustworthy account of the methods which were followed has been preserved, it is worth while describing it in some detail. Sir A. Helps writes:

"After the manner of pious men of those times, Las Casas and his monks did not fail to commence their undertaking by having recourse to the most fervent prayers, severe fasts, and other mortifications. . . . The first thing they did was to translate into verse in the Quiché language the great doctrines of the Church. In these verses they described the creation of the world, the fall of man, his banishment from Paradise, and the mediation prepared for him."[1]

As it appeared to be certain death for a Spaniard to enter Tuzulutlan, which was popularly known as the Land of War, they taught the poem which they had composed to four Indian merchants who were in the habit of trading in the country. Three months were spent in teaching the Indian merchants to chant their poem to the accompaniment of Indian musical instruments. When at length the merchants were received by the chief of the country, they were hailed by the assemblage to whom they chanted the poem as ambassadors from new gods. When asked to explain the meaning of the poem, they referred the chief to the Dominican monks, whereupon he sent an embassage to invite them to come to his country, having first made large sacrifices to his idols in the hope of securing their presence. The final result was that within a year the chief and a large portion of his people embraced the Christian faith. The story illustrates well the spirit in which Las Casas pursued his missionary task and the methods by which, when he could free himself from Government interference, he loved to attempt its accomplishment.

Returning again to Spain, Las Casas wrote, and eventually published, a treatise entitled *The Destruction of the Indies*, in which he denounced in vigorous language the treatment of the Indians by their Spanish conquerors. In 1544, much against his own wish, he was consecrated as Bishop of Chiapa, a province between Mexico and Honduras. His efforts to secure the enforcement of the new laws which had been promulgated in Spain in favour of the Indians made him so unpopular in his own diocese and in Mexico that in 1547 he returned to Spain, believing that his influence with the king would help the Indians

[1] *Life of Las Casas*, p. 195 f.

more than his actual presence in their midst. Though residing in Spain, he continued to act as the protector of the Indians, and at the age of ninety-two he pleaded the cause of the people of Guatemala before the Ministers of Philip II. There were others, both statesmen and missionaries, who made repeated efforts to improve the lot of the Indians and to mitigate their oppression by the Spaniards, but the name of Las Casas occupies an unique position amongst them. He did and suffered more on their behalf than any others of his contemporaries, and his life helps to light up one of the darkest pages of history, which is filled with records of cruelty and crime.

Indians in Central America.

The population of the seven Central American States —*i.e.* British Honduras, and the six republics: Honduras, Costa Rica, Guatemala, Nicaragua, Panama, and Salvador— is estimated at 4,270,000, and of these 1,700,000 are said to be Indians. The R.C. Church claims three-fourths of these as Christians, but this is apparently an overestimate. There are probably nearly 500,000 Indians who have not been touched by Christian missions. These include whole tribes amongst whom the R.C. Church has no priests.

The Central American Mission—which in 1910 had 28 missionaries, about 70 churches, and 1100 members —is endeavouring to send two missionaries to each non-Christian tribe. The Moravians are working in Nicaragua and in the Moskito Reservation. They have 32 missionaries and about 1300 communicants.

The Wesleyan Methodist Missionary Society has work, chiefly amongst Roman Catholics, in all the Central American States.

The greater part of the missionary work which has been done in the past amongst the Indians in Central America other than that done by the early R.C. missionaries has been done by the S.P.G., but the total amount is exceedingly small.

The *Moskito Shore*, on the Bay of Honduras, which was discovered by Columbus in 1502, was first settled by British adventurers in company with Belize. In 1741 George II. appointed English Commissioners for this district, but in 1786 England relinquished it to Spain. Before this latter event missionary work had been started by members of the Anglican Church amongst the Indians who lived on the Moskito Shore, and in 1742 the S.P.G. contributed towards establishing a mission in response to an appeal received from some of the Indians. The English Governor of Jamaica, in supporting their appeal, urged that "those Indians, besides the claim they have in common with other savages to the charity of the society, have a demand in justice upon the nation. As they have learned most of their vices, particularly cheating and drinking, from the English, they ought in recompense to receive some good and learn some virtue and religion too." In 1747 Nathan Price, a former Fellow of Harvard College, New England, having been ordained by the Bishop of London, began work amongst them, but he died in the following year. Mr. Warren, who began work in 1769, baptized about 100 Indians and Mestizos, who included the Moskito king and queen and three or four of their sons.

Mr. Stanford, a few years later, baptized 120 Indians and negroes. The Spaniards eventually ousted the missionaries and put an end to their work. In 1840 an application for missionaries was received by the S.P.G., but it proved impossible to make any response. In 1848 the young king of the Moskitos was confirmed by the Bishop of Jamaica. A large portion of the Moskito territory has now been absorbed in the republic of Nicaragua, and some missionary work has been done at Rama. The Anglican Church is also represented at Greytown.

In *British Honduras* British adventurers from Jamaica settled about 1638. In 1862 Belize, as the settlement had hitherto been called, became the colony of British Honduras. In 1776 the Rev. R. Shaw, a representative of the S.P.G., started work amongst the English settlers, but very little was done for the Indians till 1836, when a school for their children was erected at Belize.   In 1891 an Anglican Bishop of Honduras was appointed.   In 1894 a mission to the Caribs was started at Stann Creek.

In *Panama* a large number of West Indian labourers have been employed, who are all nominal Christians.

Guatemala was annexed to the Crown of Spain in 1523. In 1536 Las Casas reached Guatemala from Nicaragua and helped to organize missionary work amongst the Indians.

Its subsequent religious history has been similar to that of Mexico and of Central America.   Protestant Missions are carried on by American Presbyterians, by the Central American Mission, and by the Pentecost Bands.

In *Costa Rica* Protestant Missions are represented by the Wesleyan Methodist Missionary Society, the Central America Missionary Society, and the Jamaica Baptist Missionary Society.

Mexico.

When Cortés, the conqueror of Mexico, interviewed the Mexican ruler Montezuma, he declared that his object, and that of his fellow-countrymen, was to spread the light of Christianity far abroad and to open to the people a full participation in the blessings which it would bring. Referring to the siege of the city of Mexico, which took place in 1521, his biographer writes:

"There can be no doubt that Cortés, with every other man in his army, felt he was engaged in a holy crusade, and that, independently of personal considerations, he could not serve Heaven better than by planting the Cross on the blood-stained towers of the heathen metropolis."[1]

This belief, whilst it does not excuse the countless atrocities and massacres which accompanied the conquest and settlement of Mexico, enables us to acquit the conquerors of conscious hypocrisy.

[1] *Conquest of Mexico*, by W. H. Prescott, bk. vi. ch. iii.

The judgment which Prescott passes upon Cortés might be passed upon many of the conquerors of South America and the West Indies. He writes:

"When we see the hand red with the blood of the wretched native raised to invoke the blessing of Heaven on the cause which it maintains, we experience something like a sensation of disgust at the act, and a doubt of its sincerity. But this is unjust. We should throw ourselves back into the age—the age of the Crusades. . . . Whoever has read the correspondence of Cortés . . . will hardly doubt that he would have been among the first to lay down his life for the faith. He more than once perilled life and fortune and the success of his whole enterprise by the premature and most impolitic manner in which he would have forced conversion on the natives. To the more rational spirit of the present day it may seem difficult to reconcile gross deviations from morals with such devotion to the cause of religion. But the religion taught in that day was one of form and elaborate ceremony."[1]

Throughout Mexico the work of conversion was as rapid as it was superficial. Twelve Franciscan friars arrived in 1524. Nine years later one of their number declared that nine million converts had been received into the Christian fold, a number which was probably in excess of the total population.

Helps, referring to the success attained by the Franciscan missionaries as described by the Bishop of Mexico in 1531, wrote:

"Five hundred temples have been thrown down, and 20,000 idols broken in pieces or burnt. In place of these temples have arisen churches, oratories, and hermitages. But as the good bishop says, that which causes more admiration is that whereas they were accustomed each year in this city of Mexico to sacrifice to idols more than 20,000 hearts of young men and young women, now all those hearts are offered up, with innumerable sacrifices of praise, not to the Devil but to the Most High God."[2]

[1] Ibid. bk. vii. ch. v.
[2] The Spanish Conquests in America, vol. iii. p. 300.

The lapse of centuries has brought little or no improvement in the religious ideals or practices of the Mexicans. Abbé Dominic, chaplain to the Emperor Maximilian, said that Mexican Christianity was, and had been from the beginning of the Spanish conquest, a baptized heathenism.

The Presbyterian Church U.S.A. North, the A.M.E.C., the A.B.C.F.M., and several smaller missionary bodies support work amongst people all of whom are nominally Christian.

In 1869 the Rev. H. A. Riley of the American Protestant Episcopal Church arrived in Mexico. About this time several Roman priests had seceded or been driven out from their Church, and these, with the help of Mr. Riley, formed a congregation and began to organize missionary work in different parts of Mexico. Mr. Riley was consecrated as Bishop in 1879, but resigned in 1884. The Rev. H. D. Aves was consecrated in 1904. Work is carried on at about 60 different centres, and the number of baptized Christians is about 3500. The work is carried on amongst English, Mexicans, and Indians.

XVII.

SOUTH AMERICA.

THE population of South America to-day is reckoned at about 50,000,000, of whom 30,000,000 are aboriginals or of mixed descent. The population of the several states is as follows: Brazil, 20,515,000; Argentine, 6,989,023; Peru, 4,500,000; Colombia, 4,320,000; Chili, 3,500,000; Venezuela, 2,685,606; Bolivia, 2,267,935; Ecuador, 1,500,000; Uruguay, 1,112,000, and Paraguay, 800,000.

It is not possible within the limits of our space to provide even an outline sketch of the conquest of South America by Spain and Portugal in the sixteenth century, nor to give in any detail an account of the nominal spread of the Christian faith throughout the continent. A few outstanding events connected with the latter will be found under the different provinces.

To the student of missions the missionary work which was attempted in South America during the sixteenth century makes sad reading. Apart from that which was done by the Jesuits, who were expelled in 1760, it was, with few exceptions, founded upon physical force and of a wholly superficial character, the result being that after three centuries of nominal Christianity any conversion of its peoples which will involve the practice of the elementary teaching of Christianity lies still in the seemingly distant future. The religious conditions which prevail in the different states of South and Central America differ to a certain degree, but what is true of one state is as a general rule true of the country as a whole.

We realize and we thank God for the good work which R.C. missions have done and are doing in many parts of the world, but our appreciation of this cannot blind our eyes to the fact that in Central and South America the missions of the R.C. Church have proved an almost complete failure. We will quote the words of a few R.C. writers, all of whom would presumably be prejudiced in favour of the work which is now being carried on by their Church.

Cardinal Vaughan, after visiting South America, wrote thus of what he saw in New Granada:

" The monks are in the lowest state of degradation, and the suppression of them would be an act of Divine favour. . . . Priests scandalize the people much by cock-fighting. I have been several times told of priests taking their cocks into the sacristy, hurrying disrespectfully through their mass, and going straight off from the altar to the cock-pit. They are great gamblers." [1]

The Archbishop of Caracas and Venezuela, in a pastoral letter published in a leading newspaper of Caracas, writes:

" The clergy have fallen into profound contempt because of events which have placed them on the declivity which leads to all manner of failure. There are no calls for the clergy, and this contempt for them, so general, is one cause for this lack. Impotence, sterility, decadence, moral and spiritual . . . these form the true and striking picture presented to all who deign for a moment to contemplate it. . . . Why does ignorance of religion continue to brutalize and degrade more and more these people? Why exist so many parishes which are true cemeteries of souls dead to God?" [2]

Father Sherman, a R.C. priest, son of the famous General Sherman of the U.S.A., said, after visiting Porto Rico:

" Religion is dead on the island. Whether it can be revived as a living influence is highly problematical. . . . The non-observance of the sanctity of Sunday, the number of illegitimate children exceeding that of the legitimate, the fact

[1] *Life of Cardinal Herbert Vaughan*, by Cox. p. 125.
[2] " El Constitucional," December 7, 1908, quoted in *South American Problems*, by Speer, p. 162.

that concubinage is said to be common and is not sufficiently discountenanced, either legally or socially . . the prevailing distrust of the priesthood, among whom concubinage is the rule and not the exception, the decreasing influence of religion, the ethical status of the Roman Church, sunk lower oftentimes than the atheism which surrounds it, such are the dark lines which portray the condition of that portion of America which is under undisputed Roman sway."[1]

To the above witnesses we will add one more, whose name will carry equal weight in England and America. Sir James (now Lord) Bryce writes of South America as a whole:

"Another fact strikes the traveller with surprise. Both the intellectual and the ethical standards of conduct of these countries seem to be entirely divorced from religion. The women are almost universally the 'practising' Catholics, and so are the peasantry, though the Christianity of the Indians bears only a distant resemblance to that of Europe. But men of the upper or educated class appear wholly indifferent to theology and to Christian worship. It has no interest for them. They are seldom actively hostile to Christianity, much less are they offensive when they speak of it, but they think it does not concern them, and may be left to women and peasants. . . . In the more advanced parts of South America it seems to be regarded merely as a harmless Old World affair which belongs to a past order of things just as much as does the rule of Spain, but which may, so long as it does not interfere with politics, be treated with the respect which its antiquity commands. In both cases the undue stress laid upon the dogmatic side of theology and the formal or external side of worship has resulted in the loss of spiritual influence. In all the Spanish countries the Church had trodden down the laity and had taken freedom and responsibility from them more than befell anywhere else in Christendom, making devotion consist in absolute submission. Thus when at last her sway vanished, her moral influence vanished with it. This absence of a religious foundation for thought and conduct is a grave misfortune for Latin America."[2]

[1] Quoted by Bishop Kinsolving in *The East and The West*, April 1903.
[2] *South America, Observations and Impressions*, by Sir James Bryce, p. 582 f.

It would be easy to quote many similar testimonies, but these will serve to indicate, what few who know South America would attempt to deny, that the R.C. Church is less worthily represented there than it is in any other part of the world. Even in cases—and thank God there are many such—in which the priests are men of unblemished character, the teaching which they are authorized by their superiors to give to the people is far removed from the teaching of the early Christian Church. It has been said, and the statement is by no means unfounded, that Mariolatry is the practical religion of South America. In the wall of the ancient Jesuit church in Cuzco are cut the words, " Come unto Mary, all ye who are burdened and weary with your sins, and she will give you rest "

Bishop Kinsolving of the American Episcopal Church in Brazil writes :

" In the interests of Mariolatry, or at least without the protest of the dominant Church, there is in South America an ethical status more detrimental to pure morals and more dishonouring to Christ than is found in open paganism." [1]

Our object in referring to the failure of the R.C. Church in South America is in no sense controversial. We do so partly in order to appraise the missionary methods which were adopted three centuries ago and which to a large extent are still followed, and partly in order to justify the attempts which have been made within recent years by Anglican (i.e. American Episcopal) and Protestant missions to appeal to those who are already Christians in name. It is distressing to note how largely the European immigrants have drifted away from the R.C. Church of which they were at least nominal members before leaving Europe. The R.C. Church, moreover, appears to make but little effort to minister to their spiritual wants. In the whole of the Argentine there were in 1909 less than 1000 priests for a population of 5,000,000. In Buenos Ayres one parish with a population of 130,000 had but one priest and two assistants.

[1] *Missionary Review of the World*, February 1914.

Brazil.

The state of Bahia was first sighted by the Portuguese explorer P. A. Cabral in 1500, but for thirty years afterwards no attempt at settlement was made. In 1549 John III. of Portugal dispatched six Jesuit missionaries who were the forerunners of the great army of Jesuits that were to follow. The early missionaries had to contend as much with the wickedness and immorality of the Portuguese adventurers in Brazil as with the ignorance and ferocity of the Indians. Amongst the hundreds, or rather thousands, of Jesuit missionaries who have laboured in Brazil have been very many who have lived heroic and apostolic lives and who were privileged to see as the results of their labours large tracts of country the degraded or even cannibal inhabitants of which had adopted the customs of civilized society and whose lives had been transformed by the Christian faith.

Missionaries belonging to the Dominican and Franciscan Orders arrived later and shared in the difficulties and perils which accompanied the prosecution of the Church's work in Brazil, but the chief credit for the good work which was accomplished belongs to the Jesuit Order. One of the greatest of these missionaries was Joseph Anchieta, who reached Brazil in 1553, and laboured for forty-four years as a pioneer missionary amidst difficulties and hardships which have seldom been surpassed. At his death in 1597 there were in Brazil alone 120 Jesuit missionaries. The Jesuits were the only missionaries who uniformly opposed the tyranny of the Portuguese and strove to protect the Indians from their cruelty. They became in consequence extremely unpopular with the governing class, and after being twice previously expelled from Brazil, were in 1760 finally deported. 428 members of the Order were deported with every form of insult and indignity. The number expelled from all the Spanish Indies was 5677. This expulsion of the Jesuits was a blow to the well-being of the native population of Brazil from which it never recovered. Mr. Robert Southey, in his *History of Brazil,* published in 1817, says: "Decay and desolation succeeded the prosperity which had prevailed in the time of the missionaries; houses falling to pieces; fields overgrown with wood; grass in the market-places; the limekilns, the potteries, the manufactories of calico introduced by the Jesuits in ruins." It was charged against the Jesuits in South America generally that they had been mining precious metals by slave labour without giving the Government its share. "In the neighbourhood of Lima alone, they owned 5000 negro slaves and property to the value of 2,000,000 dollars." [1]

The number of Indians now left in Brazil is between one and two million. A large number of these live in remote parts of Brazil which have never been explored by Europeans. The methods adopted by the Jesuits in Brazil and in other parts of South America, and the results which these methods produced, are well summarized by the writer from whom we have just quoted:

"The Indians were easily induced to conform to the externals of the Christian cult. Wherever the Jesuits penetrated the aborigines soon adopted Christianity; but to hold the Indians to Christianity, the Fathers were obliged to fix them to the soil. As soon as a tribe was converted, a rude church building was erected, and a Jesuit installed, who remained to teach agriculture and the arts as well as ritual and morals. His moral and intellectual superiority made him perforce an absolute ruler in miniature. Thus that strange theocracy came into being which, starting on the Brazilian coast, spread over most of Central South America. In the early part of the seventeenth century the theocratic seemed likely to become the dominant form of government south of the Amazon and east of the Andes. . . . The Jesuits gave the South American Indian the greatest measure of peace and justice he ever enjoyed, but they reduced him to blind obedience and made him a tenant and a servant." [2]

---

[1] *South American Republics,* by T. C. Dawson, ii. 71.
[2] *Ibid.* i. 326.

Missionary work is now carried on amongst the Bororos, the most widely distributed tribe in Brazil, by R.C. Salesian priests. Remnants of the Jesuit missions are found at Villa Rica and elsewhere in North-West Parana.

During the last century and a half the moral and religious conditions prevailing generally in Brazil have become worse and worse. A recent writer on Brazil says :

"Of the . . . educated only the smallest proportion adhere to any form of religion whatever. Statesmen, lawyers, physicians, army and navy officials, have almost to a man rejected the historic Christ, and have turned to infidelity and Positivism. In one city with a population of 35,000, after careful investigation less than 200 could be found in full communion with the Roman Church."

He quotes the R.C. Bishop of Sao Paulo as saying in an official paper :

"Brazil has no longer any faith. Religion is almost extinct here." [1]

Father Currier, writing in the *American Catholic Quarterly Review*, after admitting the desolate condition into which religion had fallen in Brazil, expresses the belief that a revival of religion has already commenced.[2]

It is impossible to express in words how great is the need of such a revival.

Protestant Missions in Brazil.

An unsuccessful attempt was made from Geneva to start missionary work in Brazil in the middle of the sixteenth century. The Protestant missionaries were at first welcomed by a French adventurer, Nicholas Durand de Villegagnon, who, however, turned against them after their work had been begun. The missionaries were eventually expelled by the Portuguese in 1567 (see p. 44).

[1] "Rome in Many Lands," by Isaacson, p. 160. Quoted by R. E. Speer in *South American Problems*, p. 185.
[2] July 1910.

In 1624 the Dutch conquered Bahia and Dutch ministers commenced to do missionary work, which was interrupted by the capture of the Dutch settlement by the Portuguese in 1654.

In 1835 the A.M.E.C. sent a representative to Rio de Janeiro and later on started a mission in the Amazon valley.

The Presbyterian Church (North) of the U.S.A. sent a representative to Brazil in 1859. Its work is now carried on in seven of the Brazilian states, the most important centre being M'Kenzie College at Sao Paulo, which has 500 students. The Presbyterian Church (South) of the U.S.A. started work in 1869. These two bodies amalgamated in 1888, and there are now about 7000 communicants attached to the United Mission.

The A.M.E.C. South and the Southern Baptist Convention are also represented.

The Protestant Episcopal Church of America began work in Rio Grande do Sul in 1889, and one of their first missionaries (the Rev. L. Kinsolving) was consecrated as Bishop in Brazil in 1898.

The Church of England supports chaplains in several cities, but their chief duty is to minister to the English-speaking inhabitants of these cities.

The total number of "Protestant communicants" in Brazil is about 30,000.

Peru.

In 1532 Francisco Pizarro, a Spanish adventurer, after several experimental expeditions, seized and eventually murdered the Inca of Peru, and in the six following years overran the whole country, seeking for gold and other treasures. No women came with the early Spanish settlers to South America, and a people of mixed blood soon arose who now constitute the greater part of the South American population. Priests accompanied and followed the Spanish conquerors, and the acceptance of Christianity was soon forced upon the inhabitants and towns were baptized *en masse*. The description given by the Mexican historian, General Vicente Riva Palacio, of the introduction of Christianity into Mexico applies exactly to its establishment in Peru, and, with but little modification, to its establishment in several other states of South America. He wrote:

"The people conquered by the Spaniards in the Indies did not have even a remote idea of Christian doctrine or Catholic worship, but they looked upon their conversion to that doctrine and worship as a necessary consequence of their defeat in battle, as an indispensable requisite which affirmed their vassalage and slavery to the Spanish monarch." [1]

There is but little cause for wonder that countries which were thus evangelized should remain, after the lapse of more than three centuries, in a state of paganism which is but partly concealed by a thin veneer of Christian profession.

The Inca population in Peru at the time of its conquest by the Spaniards has been reckoned at from 20 to 40 millions. Fifty years after its conquest its population had been reduced to 8 millions. According to the last census taken before the declaration of independence by Peru in 1821, the Inca population was 608,999. The decrease of population affords some indication of the cruelties practised by the Spaniards on the native population during the long centuries of their misrule. One name which shines out in the dark background of the conquest and subjugation of Peru is that of St. Francis Solano, who laboured as a missionary from 1589 to 1610. He is said by his biographer (Courtot) to have converted 9000 persons in a single day, and was greatly beloved by the Peruvians. More than half the population of Peru is of pure aboriginal descent and retains the superstitions connected with its ancient sun-worship.

The A.M.E.C. has work amongst the R.C. population of Peru and a few stations amongst the aboriginal Indians,

[1] Quoted in *South American Problems*, by Speer, p. 123.

27

but there are few states in which so little missionary work is being attempted.

The Regions Beyond Missionary Union supports work amongst Indians at Cuzco and an industrial farm in the same district.

Until 1914 the Peruvian Government discountenanced the starting of any Protestant mission. When the news of the atrocities committed upon the Putumayo Indians on the borders of Peru and Brazil reached England in 1912, an attempt was made by the Evangelical Union of South America to start a mission amongst them, but the attempt did not prove successful. A Franciscan mission has also been attempted. As a result of the barbarous treatment of the Putumayo Indians their numbers have decreased during the past century from 100,000 to 10,000.

Chili.

Chili was subjugated to Spanish rule and Spanish Christianity by Valdivia, one of Pizarro's lieutenants, 1540–45. Spanish priests accompanied Valdivia in his campaign of conquest, one of whom was appointed Vicar of Chili in 1546.

Its former population of Araucanian Indians has almost become extinct, chiefly as a result of alcoholism, which is also the curse of the whole population, especially in the towns of Santiago and Valparaiso.

The total number of the Indians is about 100,000. The American Presbyterian Church (North) and the A.M.E.C. have organized missions amongst the people of Chili, and the S.A.M.S. has stations at Cholchol and Quepe amongst the Araucanian Indians. The well-known Mapuche chief, Ambrosio Paillalef, is a strong supporter of the S.A.M.S. Mission. This society has also a medical mission at Temuco. At Quepe, which was opened as a mission station in 1898, the Indians have been successfully taught farming and carpentering.

Bolivia.

Bolivia was conquered by Pizarro and placed in charge of his brother Hernando. According to the last census, 903,126 of its inhabitants are indigenous, or Indians; 485,293 Mestizos, or of mixed Indian and white blood; and 231,088 white. The Jesuits established a mission to the Indians on Lake Titicaca in 1577. They introduced the printing press in order to provide their converts with grammars and catechisms in their own language, and did much to civilize and raise the Indians. They were expelled from Bolivia, as from other parts of South America, in 1760. Of the Indians in Bolivia to-day, 9 per cent. are "in a full state of barbarism," and cannibalism is reported as prevailing amongst them. The Indian population is steadily on the increase.

Of the total population rather more than half profess to be Roman Catholics. The rest are pagans, with the exception of about 4000 Protestants. The Baptist Convention of Ontario and the Plymouth Brethren have small educational missions.

Paraguay.

The first Spanish settlement which was made in 1536 was on the site of Asuncion, which is the present capital. Its people were regarded by the Spaniards as the most "irreclaimable" in South America. The most remarkable among the earliest missionaries was the Jesuit Manuel de Ortega, who died in 1622, after thirty years of laborious and self-denying toil. Another missionary, Christoval de Mendoza, who was martyred in 1632, was said to have himself baptized 95,000 Indians. Yet another martyr, Cyprian Baraza, is reported to have established fifteen colonies of Christian Moxos and to have baptized with his own hand 110,000 converts. To an Englishman, Father Falconer, belongs a share in the honour which is due to the pioneer missionaries in Paraguay. He was a Jesuit "of great skill in medicine," and founded a mission in the Pampas.

The Franciscans shared with the Jesuits the perilous task of endeavouring to convert the Indians. Seldom did a year pass for many decades after the work had been begun without adding to the list of martyrdoms. One instance may suffice to illustrate the heroic courage and faith of these missionaries.

"Gaspard de Monroy, baffled in one of his journeys by the obstinate ferocity of an Omagua chief, who not only rejected the gospel himself but threatened the most horrible death to the missionaries and to all who should embrace their doctrine, . . . set out alone and entered the hut of the savage. 'You may kill me,' said the Father, with a tranquil air, as soon as he stood in the presence of the barbarian, 'but you will gain little honour by slaying an unarmed man. If, contrary to my expectation, you give me a hearing, all the advantage will be for yourself. If I die by your hand, an immortal crown awaits me in heaven.' Astonishment disarmed the savage, and admiration kept him silent. Then, with a kind of reluctant awe, he offered to his unmoved visitor a drink from his own cup. A little later he and his whole tribe were converted." [1]

The ruins of the buildings erected by the Jesuits and their converts are still to be seen in Paraguay.

The Chaco Indians, amongst whom Anglican and Protestant missionaries are now working, have maintained their virtual independence ever since the first arrival of the Spaniards.

The total Indian population of Paraguay is computed at 100,000.

The Chaco Mission.

The most successful mission now being carried on in South America is that to the Chaco Indians in Paraguay. In the region known as the Grand Chaco, which is situated in the republics of Argentina, Bolivia, and

[1] *Christian Missions*, by T. W. Marshall (1863), p. 196.

Paraguay, there are a large number of Indians who have hardly as yet come into contact with Europeans. Captain Gardiner travelled in their country, but was not himself able to start a mission. In 1888 the South American Missionary Society undertook work amongst the Chaco Indians in Paraguay, and in the following year Mr. W. B. Grubb, who was one of the first missionaries, commenced a work amongst them which has been fruitful of marvellous results. After twenty-one years' work he wrote:

"During these twenty-one years the average mission staff has not numbered five men actually in the field. Only four men have exceeded ten years' service, and yet, in spite of small numbers and limited means, and the immense and varied difficulties which had to be overcome, I leave the reader to judge, from the results which I give, whether or no we have laboured in vain, whether we were justified in our belief that this degraded people could be elevated and developed; and (most important of all in our eyes) whether the Lenguas are not only capable of receiving Christianity, but of forming a Church which shall be self-supporting and, in its turn, missionary.

"Where formerly it was dangerous for the white man to go without an armed party, anyone can now wander alone and unarmed, so far as any risk from the Indians may be apprehended, over a district rather larger than Ireland. In a country where fifteen years ago there were no tracks other than Indian footpaths, resembling sheep-tracks at home, now about four hundred and fifty miles of cart-track have been made in order that the mission bullock-carts might readily traverse the country. Where formerly tribal war was common, peace has reigned for many years over a district as large as Ireland and Scotland combined. . . .

"Lastly I come to the Christian Church as the crowning effort of all our work. From out of a chaotic mass of savage heathenism we have now, by the aid of the Divine power, the satisfaction of having admitted by baptism into the Church of Christ 149 Lenguas, and of this number there are no fewer than 38 communicants. There are, in addition, at least an equal number of probationers or inquirers. But these figures do not represent the total extent of Christian progress. Over a large area the whole tone of the people has been changed for a better, the gospel message

has been clearly delivered, and we can afford to wait in
patience until the Spirit of God moves them, as He has
done others. Our business is to plant and water diligently
and faithfully; it is God who gives the increase.   The
Church of England Prayer Book almost complete, together
with the four Gospels, portions of the Epistles and Genesis,
have been translated and printed in Lengua, and also a
small Hymnal set to familiar tunes."[1]

This mission is now advancing westwards and north-
wards from the river Paraguay and is starting work on
the western frontier in the Argentine republic among the
Tobas, Matacos, Chiriguanos, and other tribes who are
employed on the sugar plantations.

Uruguay.

Upper Uruguay and the far interior of Southern
Brazil were the scene of the best work accomplished by
the Jesuit missionaries.   Their work was of a less arduous
nature than that which was accomplished in Paraguay, to
which reference has already been made.

The total population of the province is 1,112,000, of
whom one-fifth are foreigners. In 1900 there were
73,000 Italians and 38,000 Spaniards.

The Anglican Church, the A.M.E.C., and the Lutheran
Church minister to Europeans in Uruguay.

Argentina.

In the eighteenth century Argentina formed part of
the Spanish viceroyalty which also included Paraguay and
Bolivia. Its present population of nearly 7,000,000
includes a large and increasing number of European
immigrants. Argentina was the first of the Spanish
colonies in South America to vindicate its independence.

The A.M.E.C., in addition to its work amongst English-
speaking people, has missions up the river Parana and in
several other districts.   There are about 30,000 Indians,

[1] See *An Unknown People in an Unknown Land*, by W. B. Grubb, 1911.

most of whom have come from Bolivia and the Paraguayan Chaco to work in the sugar factories. The South American Evangelical Mission and the Christian and Missionary Alliance of New York are also represented.

A new mission has been started by the S.A.M.S. in the Argentine Chaco with its headquarters at San Pedro de Jujuy, a large sugar estate to which several thousands of Indians come annually for the sugar harvest.

Tierra del Fuego, which lies at the extreme south of Argentina, was the scene of the most romantic mission which has been established on the continent of South America. Captain Allen Gardiner, an English naval officer, in the course of a voyage in 1822 came into contact with some of the aborigines of South America, and after attempting missionary work in Zululand and New Guinea (see p. 310) he succeeded in establishing, in 1844, the "Patagonian Missionary Society," which afterwards became the South American Missionary Society. His two first attempts in Chili and Paraguay ended in failure, but, undeterred by the hardships which he had suffered, he and six companions sailed for Tierra del Fuego in 1850. The whole party were left to die of starvation by the hostile aborigines in the following year, and their bodies were found in Spaniard Harbour in a cavern, the search party having been directed to the spot by a hand painted on the rocks on which Ps. lxii. 5–8 was written: "My soul, wait thou only upon God, for my expectation is from him." Almost immediately on the reception of the news in England a new missionary expedition started which established a station in the Falkland Islands. In 1860, when the mission ship attempted to get into touch with the Tierra del Fuegians, the whole crew with one exception were murdered.

In 1868 Bishop Stirling, who was in charge of the mission, succeeded in establishing a station at Ushuwaia on the mainland, and in 1872 36 Tierra del Fuegians were baptized. The station Tekenika, which was established in 1888, was for many years the centre of the mainland mission. This has now been moved to Douglas River, Navarin Island. Charles Darwin, who had visited Tierra del Fuego and had tried to get into touch with its inhabitants, had expressed the confident opinion that its people were incapable of becoming civilized or of being Christianized. After interviewing some of the Christian converts, he wrote to the S.A.M.S.: "The success of the Tierra del Fuego Mission is most wonderful, and charms me, as I always prophesied utter failure. It is a grand success. I shall feel proud if your committee think fit to elect me an honorary member of your society."

British Guiana.

British Guiana was first colonized by the Dutch in 1580, the first English settlement taking place in 1663. After being held in turn by Holland, France, and England, it was finally ceded to England in 1814. In 1831 the three counties named after the three rivers which traverse them—Demerara, Essequibo, and Berbice—were united into the present British Guiana. Its total population is about 300,000. In this total are included about 100,000 Hindus, 10,000 Mohammedans, 40,000 pagans, and 130,000 Christians, of whom about 40,000 are Roman Catholics. The coast districts are inhabited chiefly by negroes, the descendants of slaves who were imported from Africa. There are also a large number of Indian and Chinese immigrants.

In 1735 the Moravians began work amongst the negroes in Berbice, and later on amongst the Arawaks. Their mission was totally destroyed by revolted negroes in 1763. Another mission amongst the Arawaks, begun in 1757, was finally abandoned in 1812.

In 1807 the L.M.S. began work among the plantation slaves on the invitation of a Dutch planter. The work rapidly spread, but the antagonism of the slave owners, which was accentuated by a rising of slaves that took place in 1823, greatly interfered with its progress. Nevertheless, by 1829 there had been established seven stations in Demerara and nine in Berbice, and in 1838 the number of the Christians was reckoned at 18,000. The L.M.S. eventually withdrew, and some of the Christians joined the Anglican Church, whilst others formed themselves into a Congregational Union.

In 1815 the Wesleyans started work amongst the slaves and later on amongst the East Indian immigrants. The "Brethren" have also a mission amongst both negroes and East Indians which is carried on from Georgetown.

In 1829 the C.M.S. began work amongst the Indians on the Essequibo and Potaro rivers. This work, which attained considerable success, was, however, given up in 1856.

In 1835 the S.P.G. began work amongst the negroes, and the Colonial Government contributed towards the extension of the work, which was superintended by Dr. Coleridge, the first Bishop of Barbados. In 1840 Mr. W. H. Brett, a young layman who had been sent out by the S.P.G., began work amongst the Arawaks at the junction of the rivers Pomeroon and Arapiaco. He was ordained in 1842. His work, which was carried on under great difficulties, proved at length most encouraging. Mr. Brett acted as a pioneer missionary, and drew up a grammar and vocabulary for four different languages— Arawak, Acawaio, Caribi, and Warau. Owing to ill-health, he was compelled to return to England for awhile, but on his recovery he went back to Guiana, and after a long service, extending altogether over forty years, he died in 1886. He was in a true sense the Apostle to the aboriginals of British Guiana.

Bishop Austin, who was consecrated as the first Bishop of British Guiana in 1842, was Bishop for fifty years.

The centres of work amongst the aboriginal Indians belonging to the Anglican Mission are at Mahaica Creek and Demerara River in Demerara, Cabacaburi on the Pomeroon River, Bartica and Rupununi in Essequibo, and Orealla in Berbice.

The R.C. missions are in charge of the Jesuits. The number of "Catholics," including Europeans, is 22,000.

Work amongst the Chinese has been carried on with such success that nearly all the Chinese immigrants have become Christians. The work is chiefly supported by the S.P.G. The Baptists have also two or three stations.

Archdeacon Josa writes:

"Ninety out of every hundred of our Chinese in British Guiana are now Christians. What kind of Christians do they make? Not rice Christians. On the contrary, they are most liberal contributors to all Church funds. They are upright in their dealings, and a Chinese man's word is his bond."

French Guiana.

In 1560 the Spanish missionary Sala, together with another Dominican Father, entered French Guiana, but both were immediately martyred. In 1643 French Capuchins repeated the attempt, with a similar result. In 1639 the Jesuits entered the country at a different point and evangelized the Galibis tribe. In 1674, the tribes on the coast having been evangelized, three Jesuit missionaries started from Cayenne for the interior, and fifteen years later they erected a church on the river Kourou. In 1711 it was stated that five other tribes had become Christian. When, however, the Jesuits were banished from South America these missions collapsed. In 1852 the Jesuits returned and recommenced their work near Cayenne.

The population, which is about 35,000, includes 10,000 French convicts.

Dutch Guiana.

In Dutch Guiana or Surinam there are about 17,000 "bush negroes," or aboriginal Indians, about 50,000 negroes of African descent, and a number of imported Indian coolies. Dutch Guiana was acquired by the Netherlands in 1667 and its present population is about 86,000. The

Moravians [1] began a mission in 1738 at the mouth of the river Berbice in what was then Dutch but is now British Guiana. By 1748, 41 Indians had been baptized; four years later, chiefly as the result of the labours of T. S. Schumann, "the Apostle of the Arawaks," the number had risen to 266. Several mission stations were opened, but, partly owing to the nomadic tendencies of the Indians, the work failed to progress. In 1754 the Moravians started work amongst the negro slaves in Paramaribo, which has since made slow, but steady, progress. In 1765 two missionaries left Paramaribo to start a mission in the interior amongst the Saramaccas. By 1818, 9 missionaries and 6 wives of missionaries had died at this station, and the mission was eventually abandoned.

The Moravian Church at the present time has missions amongst the bush negroes along the Coppename, the Saramacca, the Surinam, and the Marowyne rivers. Work is carried on at 31 stations and 25 out-stations. There are 27 ordained European brethren, and 16 unordained, in addition to 8 ordained and 10 unordained native brethren. The Christian adherents number 30,000.

Venezuela, Colombia, and Ecuador.

In 1545 the Spaniards began to establish permanent settlements in the interior of Venezuela. Ecuador was conquered by one of Pizarro's officers, Benalcazar, in 1534, soon after which Pizarro's brother Gonzalo was appointed Governor of the province of Quito. In the eighteenth century Venezuela formed part of the viceroyalty of New Granada, which included also Colombia and Ecuador. These three states were the first to assert their independence of Spain in 1819. In these states there has been less immigration from Europe than in most of the other states, and their peoples are more backward and more irreligious than any others. A former American Minister to Colombia thus describes the attitude of the R.C. Church

[1] See p. 53.

throughout South America generally during the eighteenth
century:

"It had prohibited the teaching of the arts and sciences,
restricted education to the Latin grammar and the catechism,
and limited the public libraries to the writings of the Fathers
and to works on civil and ecclesiastical jurisprudence.   It
had even prohibited the study of modern geography and
astronomy and forbade the reading of books on travel . . .
it had placed under the ban *Robinson Crusoe*, and there had
never been a book or a magazine or a newspaper in the
whole country that was not conformed to the strictest rule
of the Roman Index."[1]

There is no state in which the R.C. Church to-day
has exercised, and still exercises, a more complete control
than it does in Colombia.   In the Inquisition at Carthagena
it is stated that 400,000 have been condemned to death.

"The moral conditions are the same as elsewhere in
South America.   The control of marriage by the R.C. Church,
and the use of this control by the priests as a source of
income to the Church, have resulted, as the priests themselves
admit, in the failure on the part of great masses of the
population to get married.   Men and women live together
with no marriage ceremony."[2]

In Colombia there are about 250,000 Indians.   There
is a small R.C. mission amongst the Indians on the Goajira
peninsula between Colombia and Venezuela, which is under
the charge of the Capuchin Fathers in Barranquilla.   In
Ecuador, the population of which is about 1,400,000, there
are about 400,000 of mixed blood and about 200,000
"civilized Indians."   Amongst the remaining 800,000
Indians the R.C. Church has a few missions, but the
results are far from being encouraging.

"The Blessed Peter Claver" is regarded by the R.C.
Church as the Apostle of Carthagena and Colombia.   He
left Seville in 1610 and laboured in South America for

[1] *The Colombian and Venezuela Republics*, by W. L. Scruggs, p. 128.
[2] *South American Problems*, by Speer, p. 58.

thirty-nine years. According to his biographers, his life was a constant succession of miracles. One of his reputed labours was the conversion of 600 Englishmen who were captured at sea and brought to Carthagena.[1]

American Presbyterians have started work amongst the R.C. population at Barranquilla at the mouth of the Magdalena River and several other centres.

In Venezuela the U.S.A. Presbyterians and the "Brethren" have preaching centres and other work at Caracas. The Christian and Missionary Alliance and the South American Evangelical Mission are also represented. Of the total population of Venezuela, which is reckoned at 2,685,606, 90,000 are returned as pagans.

[1] *Christian Missions, their Agents and their Results,* by T. W. Marshall (1863), pp. 169-71.

XVIII

AUSTRALIA.

The Australian Aborigines.

THE total number of Australian aborigines is reckoned by the Government authorities at 74,000. Of these, 20,000 are found in Queensland, 27,000 in West Australia, 16,000 in the Northern Territory, 7370 in New South Wales, 3500 in South Australia, and 250 in Victoria. The appalling rate at which they have decreased may be gathered from the fact that less than one hundred years ago the number in Queensland alone was 200,000. In 1837 the number in Victoria was reckoned at 15,000. The total number of those who are "living in contiguity to the settlements of whites," according to the census of 1911, is 19,939. Hardly more than 6000 have as yet been reached by Christian missionaries. Efforts are now being made by the various states to safeguard the interests of the aboriginals, but it is doubtful whether a further decrease in their number can be prevented. In 1911 the Government grants amounted to £68,120, and in addition a distribution of 5000 blankets was made to the aboriginals in Queensland.

Early in the nineteenth century, Samuel Marsden, a chaplain at Sydney, helped by Governor Macquarie, endeavoured to protect the aboriginals from the cruelties that were being practised upon them by the early settlers and convicts.

In 1823 the S.P.G. signified to Mr. Hill, a chaplain at Sydney, its willingness to assist in establishing a mission to the aboriginals in New South Wales, but nothing was actually accomplished. In 1829 Archdeacon (afterwards Bishop) Broughton put before the clergy in Australia the "appalling consideration that after an intercourse of nearly half a century with a Christian people, these hapless human beings continue . . . in their original benighted and degraded state."

In 1825 some L.M.S. missionaries who came from Tahiti made several unsuccessful efforts to establish work amongst the aboriginals in the neighbourhood of Sydney. Mr. L. E. Threlkeld printed a spelling-book and translations of some selections from Scripture for some tribes near Lake Macquarie, but no permanent work resulted.

In 1830, in response to a request from the Home Government, the C.M.S. sent out two clergy and a farmer, and a mission station was opened at Wellington Bay, a Government station 200 miles from Sydney. Some good work was done, though apparently no aborigines were baptized, and in 1842, in consequence of difficulties which arose between the C.M.S. and the Government authorities, the mission was discontinued.

The first successful attempt to start mission work for their benefit was made, in connection with the S.P.G., by Archdeacon Hale of South Australia, who started an aboriginal settlement in 1851 at Poonindie near Port Lincoln on the Spencer Gulf. Two years later, when Bishop Short visited it, the settlement consisted of 54 natives, including 11 married couples. The Bishop during his visit baptized 10 men and 1 woman. A period of sickness (1856–58), during which 21 deaths occurred, was followed by financial difficulties, which for several years interfered with the development of the mission. By 1863 two natives were able to conduct the Sunday morning service. In 1872 Bishop Short reported that there was there "a well-ordered community of more than 80 aboriginals and half-castes . . . living in quietness, sobriety, and godliness, employed in the various labours of a sheep station and a cultivated farm of 260 acres."

Many efforts were made from time to time by Anglican, Presbyterian, and Wesleyan ministers working amongst white people to get into touch with the aboriginals, with varying success. Thus the Rev. G. King, whom the S.P.G. sent out to Fremantle in West Australia, reported the baptism of ten aboriginal children whom he had been teaching for some years. Later on four of his aboriginal girls were married by the Bishop of Adelaide to four aboriginals who had been trained in the Wesleyan school at Wonneroo. In 1850 the S.P.G. helped to establish an aboriginal school near Albany which was removed to Perth in 1859 and to the Swan River in 1876.

In 1859 the Moravians started a mission to aboriginals at Ebenezer in the Wimmera district of Victoria. The mission received encouragement and financial support from Bishop Perry of Melbourne, and in 1860 the first convert was baptized. Encouraged by the success of the mission, the Presbyterian Assembly of Australia offered to supply funds for another station, if the Moravians would supply the missionaries. A station was accordingly opened at Ramahyuk, on a native reserve near Lake Wellington. The first convert was baptized in 1866. Much good work was done at this station, which, in consequence of the steady decrease in the aboriginal population in Victoria, was eventually abandoned.

The following are the principal mission stations now in existence :—

Yarrabah, 15 miles south of Cairns in North Queensland, founded in 1892 ; *Trubanaman*, or the *Mitchell River Mission*, on the Gulf of Carpentaria, founded in 1905 ; the *Roper River Mission*, on the west coast of the Gulf of Carpentaria, founded in 1907 ; the *Forrest River Mission*, in North-West Australia, founded in 1913. These four missions belong to the Anglican Church. The *New Norcia Mission* in West Australia, 170 miles north-east of Perth, is managed by Trappists belonging to the R.C. Church. The *Mapoon Mission*, founded in 1891, is a joint station of the Moravians and the Presbyterians ; and the *Cape Bedford Mission*, north of Cooktown, is supported by the Lutherans.

In Victoria the Presbyterians have a station at *Coranderok*.

The German Neuendettelsau Society has a station at *Elim-Hope* in Queensland and another at *Bethesda* in South Australia. The Australian Immanuel Synod (German) has also a station in South Australia at *New Hermannsburg*.

To the above list should be added the *Moa Island Mission* in the Torres Straits, belonging to the Anglican Church, which was founded in 1907.

The inhabitants of Moa Island are of mixed aboriginal and South Sea Island origin. Another Anglican mission is in course of being established at *Groot Island* in the Gulf of Carpentaria.

The mission at *Yarrabah*, which is in the diocese of North Queensland, was started by the Rev. J. R. Gribble, who had previously interested himself in the welfare of the natives in West Australia. When he had been three months at Yarrabah his health gave way, and his son undertook the charge of the mission. After passing through several vicissitudes, the mission is now firmly established. The Bishop of Carpentaria, after visiting the Mitchell River Mission in 1913, wrote concerning it and the Yarrabah Mission:

"There are practically no able-bodied men at the head station, which consists of the children of school age, the sick, and the aged. The rest are all living in one of the eight or nine settlements, from 2 to 12 miles distant, under the charge of a native teacher who holds daily service and superintends the life of the community. Each family cultivates an area of land of its own, planted with fruit trees or vegetables, or has a share in a fishing-boat provided by the mission on terms by which it becomes his own property. The superintendent reports that the amount of work done by the natives had enormously increased since they have been working for themselves; while the cost of the mission has proportionally decreased. The same plan has

28

been followed with even greater success at the Presbyterian mission at Mapoon, which was founded about the same time as Yarrabah; and the two form an encouraging ideal towards which to work. Such results, however, are only possible when a whole generation has been trained up under mission influence; and that it should be possible even in a generation to convert the aboriginal savage into a working, self-supporting tiller of the soil is no small tribute to the missions.

"If one who was a sceptic in the aboriginal capacity for regeneration really desired to be enlightened, a visit to Yarrabah would remove the scales from his eyes. Standing near a large tree quite close to the beach, he would see a rough wooden cross to mark the spot where more than twenty-one years ago the Rev. J. R. Gribble landed with three Christian blacks. To-day he would find a community of about 300 Christian blacks, under the direction of six white missionaries. He could not remain many hours in the place without discovering that savage devil-worshipping nomads had been converted into industrious, intelligent, and reverent Christians. He would not find that one side of their nature had been developed to the exclusion of the others. He would acknowledge that the savage had been taught to work as he surveyed the crops of maize, taro, bananas, casava, and pineapple which he would see at the settlements, where neat matting and grass cottages, with bright gardens, well-swept paths, and decorated inside with gay pictures, show that they have learnt to care for their homes." [1]

"Work on the plantations," says the Report for 1912, "has gone on steadily throughout the year. Bananas have been sent to Sydney and Brisbane, while sweet potatoes, mangrove bark, and fish were sold in Cairns. Quite an industry in native weapons and curios has been developed. An effort is being made to make the adult natives materially independent. Plots of land have been taken up by some, others are working on boats. Full market price is given to them for produce and fish. Only a few natives in Yarrabah itself are now paid wages and given rations. The remainder buy their rations and other necessaries by their own exertions."

This description of the Yarrabah Mission applies with-

[1] *Australia's Great Need*, by C. Tomlin, p. 220 f.

out any modification to that at *Mapoon*. This mission, which was started in 1890, was staffed by Moravian missionaries but is supported financially by the Federated Presbyterian Churches of Australia. It is situated on the west shore of the Cape York Peninsula in North Queensland. James Ward, the first missionary, went alone among the natives, knowing that during the previous two months they had killed and eaten two white men. Again and again he quelled fierce quarrels and restored peace in the native camp by fearlessly placing himself between the infuriated combatants, taking the spears from their hands, and reasoning with them in such English as they could understand. Before Ward died, in 1895, the mission had been securely established, and is now as successful as any aboriginal mission in Australia. The number of aboriginals reached by the mission is about 400. In the year 1905–6 the aboriginals at Mapoon contributed £4 towards the support of foreign missions. The Presbyterian Church also supports stations at *Weipa* (1898) and *Aurukun* (1903), which are chiefly staffed by Moravian missionaries, and are situated in the same native reserve as Mapoon. There are 3 "ordained brethren," 3 missionaries' wives, and 3 native helpers connected with the 3 stations.[1]

In the last annual report (1914) issued by the Moravian Church the writer deplores, in common with other authorities, the decrease in the aboriginal population. He writes:

" In spite of all the care and medical aid of their missionaries, the sad fact remains that the blacks of North Queensland are a dying race. At our stations too the deaths outnumbered the births last year. Consumption is among the diseases formerly unknown but now brought in by contact with the whites. This has taken several of our most promising young people."

The missions on the *Mitchell River* and the *Roper River*,

[1] For an account of the Mapoon Mission see *The Romantic Story of Mapoon*, by A. Ward.

which were founded in 1905 and 1907, are still in the pioneer stage, but there seems every prospect that they will develop satisfactorily. A church has been built in the Mitchell River Mission district and one aboriginal has been confirmed. The mission boat *Francis Pritt* is worked by a crew of Mitchell River natives. The influence of the mission on the people is steadily growing. They are learning the dignity of work and learning also that Christianity means character and righteousness of life.

The Archbishop of Brisbane, after visiting the Mitchell River Mission in 1906, wrote—and his words are applicable to nearly all the missions to the Australian aboriginals:

"These missions are refuting in fact and experience the oft-repeated formula that it is impossible to raise the Australian aboriginal. The moral of Yarrabah, of Mapoon, of Mitchell River is that, given favourable circumstances (especially isolation from contact with the whites), the Queensland aboriginal is docile, law-abiding, and even quick to learn. . . . We wonder whether, if their natural habits and characteristics are wisely dealt with, and they are preserved from the contamination of the white man's drink and the white man's lust, the extermination of the race is after all so near."[1]

The *Forrest River Mission*, which is situated 70 miles down the west shore of Cambridge Gulf in the diocese of North-West Australia, was established in 1913. It was the renewal of an attempt made twelve years earlier to start a mission at this place. The staff consists of one clergyman and three laymen. It is hoped that it may prove possible to open several other stations in this part of North-West Australia.

The mission on *Moa Island*, which is in the Torres Straits, 30 miles north of Thursday Island, was superintended and developed (1908–11) by the late Deaconess Buchanan, who, though crippled with illness, did a wonder-

[1] "A New Mission to Australian Aboriginals," *The East and The West*, April 1907.

ful work both amongst the aboriginals and amongst the Japanese immigrants.

"'Teassher,' as the Moa natives called her, was the only white person in the South Sea Island community at Moa. There, in her two-roomed grass house, she carried on all her work as teacher, priestess, doctor, councillor, and friend. The Moa Island Mission will always remain the chief monument of her devoted life. In 1910 the Government showed their appreciation of the work which she initiated by giving a grant of £120 towards the educational work of the mission, and by extending the reserve in acknowledgment of the industry shown by the mission 'boys' in planting gardens. A year or two ago a church, largely subscribed for by the contributions of the islanders, was opened, and the mission still flourishes under the able direction of the present superintendent."[1]

The R.C. Church has a mission to aboriginals the centre of which is *New Norcia*, 82 miles from Perth. The Benedictine abbey of New Norcia was founded in 1846 by a Spaniard, Rudesindus Salvado, for the purpose of evangelizing the Australian natives. For three years its founder lived a nomadic life and ate the same food as the savages whom he hoped to influence. In 1849 he started for Rome, where he was consecrated as Bishop of Port Victoria in North Australia; but his destination was eventually altered, and having obtained forty volunteers in Spain, he reached New Norcia again in 1852. With their help he built a monastery, a school, and a village, in which many of the aboriginals were induced to live, some of whom became Christians. Bishop Salvado died in 1900, in the eighty-seventh year of his age and the fifty-first of his episcopate. His successor, Abbot Torres, brought out many priests to minister both to the aboriginals and to the white settlers who had begun to settle in the neighbourhood. In 1908 he opened a branch mission 2000 miles away in the extreme north-west of Australia, which is called the *Drysdale River Aborigines Mission*. This mission was

[1] See *Australia's Greatest Need*, p. 219 f.

opened with a party of 15 in charge of 2 priests. In 1910 Abbot Torres was consecrated as a bishop.

An inter-denominational society called "The New South Wales Aborigines' Mission" employs 27 workers who labour chiefly in New South Wales but also work in West Australia and in the north-west.

Other non-Christian peoples in Australia include, according to the census of 1911 : Chinese, 23,000 ; Hindus, 3000 ; Japanese, 3000 ; Malays, 1000 ; and South Sea Islanders, 2500. As these are widely scattered throughout the different states, missionary work amongst them is difficult to organize. Good work has been done amongst the Chinese immigrants by the Anglicans, Presbyterians, and Wesleyans. The writer of this volume was present on one occasion when eight Chinese who had been prepared by a Chinese catechist were baptized in Sydney Cathedral. As a result of the Immigration Restriction Act of 1901, the number of coloured aliens in Australia fell in the course of a decade from 55,000 to 38,000.

A large amount of good work had been done amongst the Kanakas—*i.e.* the immigrant labourers from the South Sea Islands—before they were excluded by law from Australia. Many who have become Christians in Australia have returned as supporters of Christian missions to the islands from which they came. At the mission which the S.P.G. helped to support at Bundaberg in Queensland there were in 1891 10,000 men from fifty different islands under Christian instruction.

TASMANIA.

It is a disgrace to the Christian Church that the aboriginal population of Tasmania was exterminated, or allowed to die out, before any missionary work had been started amongst them. After their numbers had been greatly reduced by fighting with the English immigrants, they were removed to Flinders Island in the Bass Straits in 1835. Here, despite the fact that they were kindly treated, they rapidly dwindled in numbers. When Bishop Nixon visited them in 1843 there were only 54, and four years later they were reduced to 16. The last died in 1876.

XIX

NEW ZEALAND.

THE first missionary to set foot on New Zealand was Mr. Wilson of the L.M.S., who spent one night on shore there, in 1800, on his way to the Society Islands. The Rev. Samuel Marsden, the senior Anglican chaplain at Sydney, having made friends with two chiefs who had come from New Zealand, appealed to the C.M.S. to start a mission there. In 1809 this society sent out a schoolmaster, a carpenter, and a shoemaker; but such was the evil reputation for cannibalism of the New Zealanders that they had to wait two years before they could get a boat to take them there. After a preliminary visit to the coast had been made, Mr. Marsden, accompanied by the C.M.S. missionaries and the New Zealand chiefs, sailed from Port Jackson in 1814, and on Christmas Day of this year the first Christian service was held at Rangihona (Bay of Islands). Mr. Marsden returned to his work in Sydney in the following March. In 1822 the C.M.S. sent out the Rev. Henry Williams, and in 1825 his brother William, who became the first Bishop of Waiapu. These two brothers did much to promote the evangelization of the Maoris in the early days of the mission. In 1825 the first convert was baptized. Nearly five years passed before a second baptism took place. In 1830 an industrial mission was started at Waimate, and from this date the mission made rapid progress. In 1837 Mr. Marsden paid his seventh and last visit to New Zealand, and in 1838 he died. During this year the New Testament and the Prayer Book were printed in Maori, and the mission was visited for the first time by Bishop Broughton of Sydney. In 1839 the New

Zealand Land Company, which had been formed in England, having bought large tracts of land from the local chiefs, founded the town of Wellington. In 1840 the islands became a British colony.

In 1842 Bishop George Selwyn, the first Bishop of New Zealand, was able to say in a sermon preached at Paihia : " We see here a whole nation of pagans converted to the faith."

Charles Darwin, after visiting the Anglican mission station at Waimate in 1835, wrote : " All this is very surprising when it is considered that five years ago nothing but the fern flourished here. . . . The lesson of the missionary is the enchanter's wand."

In the course, and as a result, of the second Maori war, which lasted with short intermissions from 1860 to 1870, a great apostasy occurred. In 1864 the Pai Marire, or Hau Hau fanaticism, swept over the country. It originated in the delusions of a half-witted man who declared that the angel Gabriel and the Virgin Mary had appeared to him and had promised that the Maoris uttering a dog-like cry (Hau Hau) should drive the white man into the sea. The new religion was a strange medley of Christianity and paganism and contained many contradictions.

" The abiding presence of the Virgin Mary was promised, and the religion of England as taught by Scripture was declared to be false and the Scriptures were to be burnt. Yet the creed and form of worship adopted included not only Romanism but articles from Judaism and the Old Testament, to which were added a mixture of Mormonism, mesmerism, spiritualism, ventriloquism, and some of the worst features of the old Maori usage and the days of cannibalism. The rites which accompanied these doctrines were bloody, sensual, foul, and devilish." [1]

During one of the outbreaks which accompanied the establishment of this new religion the Rev. C. S. Volkner, a C.M.S. missionary, was martyred in 1865. Two-thirds

[1] See *Two Hundred Years of the S.P.G.*, p. 441 f.

of the Maori Christians abandoned their faith and adopted
the Hau Hau religion, but their number did not include
any of the Maori clergy.

In 1882 the C.M.S. began to withdraw from New
Zealand and to hand over its work to a special Maori
Board appointed by the Church of the Province of New
Zealand. Its grants in support of the work ceased
altogether in 1903.

Wesleyan Missions.

In 1822 the first Wesleyan missionary, the Rev.
S. Leigh, arrived and started work at Kaeo in the Auckland
district. Mr. Leigh had previously visited New Zealand
in 1818 at the request of Mr. Marsden, who desired to
interest him in missionary work amongst the Maoris. In
1827 this mission station was destroyed by the chief
Hongi Hika, and the missionaries retired to Australia.
Returning in the course of a few months, they established
a new station at Hokianga. In 1831 they obtained their
first converts, and in 1834 81 converts were baptized in
the mission chapel at Mangungu. By 1838 the worshippers at Mangungu had increased to 1000. In 1844
a training college was established at Auckland. In 1855,
when the Australian Wesleyan Conference undertook the
charge of the mission, the Maori "members" numbered
3070 and the adherents 7590. The churches used by
the Maoris numbered 74. When the Hau Hau fanaticism
spread, the Rev. John Whiteley, who had come out as a
missionary in 1833, was murdered in 1869 by men on
behalf of whom he had laboured for so many years. In
1874 a New Zealand Conference was formed. The work
amongst the Maoris, which had been seriously interrupted
by the spread of the Hau Hau superstition, has gradually
recovered, but the number of Maori Christians connected
with the missions never attained to its former totals.
There are now a considerable number of Maoris connected
with Wesleyan congregations in different parts of New

Zealand, but there appear to be no definite mission stations.

In 1844 the Rev. J. Duncan of the Reformed Church of Scotland started a *Presbyterian Mission* in the Manawatu district in the North Island. He lived to be ninety-four, and died in 1908. Since 1871 the Presbyterian Church of New Zealand has been carrying on this work amongst the Maoris. At its principal station, Turakina, in North Island, it had in 1910 53 Christian adherents and 13 communicants.

The total number of Maoris in New Zealand is about 47,000. About half of these live in the north-west part of the North Island, which forms the diocese of Auckland. In this diocese there are 51 Maori churches and 221 Maori lay-readers. Of the Maoris living in this area about 8000 belong to the Anglican Church, about 3000 are Roman Catholics, 2000 or 3000 are Presbyterians or Wesleyans, and the rest are heathen or apostates.

In the diocese of Waiapu, which occupies the eastern part of North Island and contains a population of 17,000 Maoris, there is an Anglican college for Maoris at Gisborne. In this diocese there are 27 Maori and 4 English clergy working amongst Maoris. The Maori clergy receive stipends from funds which have been raised by their own people supplemented by grants from the Waiapu Maori Mission. The Maoris in this diocese belonging to the Anglican Church number about 8000. In the diocese of Wellington, which contains 6000 Maoris, 3500 belong to the Anglican Church. In the South Island there are 2500 Maoris, the majority of whom belong to the Anglican Church. In the South Island the work amongst Maoris is carried on as a rule by the European clergy in conjunction with their ordinary parochial work amongst white people. There are 43 Maori clergy, who are members of the General Synod and have the same status as European clergy.

The Mormons claim 5000 Maori adherents.

Roman Catholic Missions to the Maoris.

In 1836 seven members of the Marist Brothers landed in the north-west part of the North Island, and they and their successors began work both amongst the colonists and the Maoris. By 1850 the number of Maori "neophytes" had risen to 5044. In 1853 there were about 1000 native Christians in the diocese of Wellington. When the Hau Hau fanaticism spread in 1860 and the following years the R.C. missions were almost completely obliterated. The work has been re-started, and steady progress has been made within the last thirty years. In the dioceses of Wellington and Christchurch there are 19 churches served by 7 priests and the number of Christians is about 2000. In the diocese of Auckland there are about 4000 Christians, 22 churches, and 16 priests.

One of the most successful missions to the Maoris in New Zealand is that of the R.C. Church on the Wanganui River.

The following figures will show the fluctuations of the Maori population (the figures include about 3000 half-caste Maoris):—

1891	.	.	.	.	.	.	41,993
1896	.	.	.	.	.	.	39,854
1901	.	.	.	.	.	.	43,143
1906	.	.	.	.	.	.	47,731
1911	.	.	.	.	.	.	49,844

The Government spends about £32,000 per annum on the education of the Maoris and its 99 schools are attended by 4735 children.

XX

ISLES OF THE PACIFIC.

THE *Islands of the Pacific* may be classified under three heads: *Polynesia, Melanesia,* and *Micronesia.*[1] Polynesia includes the islands south of the Sandwich Islands and east of 170° W.; Melanesia includes most of the western islands of the South Pacific west of Fiji; Micronesia lies to the north and north-east of Melanesia. The population of the South Pacific Islands is probably under 2,000,000. The total Christian population is about 400,000, of whom about 80,000 are connected with the R.C. Church.

Ninety years ago the South Pacific Islands were almost entirely heathen and were the home of cannibalism and every form of cruelty. To-day, more than 350 are professedly Christian.

POLYNESIA.

The *Hawaii* or *Sandwich Islands,* which were the scene of Captain Cook's murder in 1779, contain a population of about 170,000.

The capital of the islands is *Honolulu,* which is in Oahu, one of the four largest islands of the group. In 1794 the king, Kamehameha, sent a request to England begging for Christian teachers, but no response was made. The A.B.C.F.M. began work in 1820, which received support from the local chiefs and attained such rapid success that within fifty years the Christianization of the islands was completed. This society, having helped

---

[1] The three words respectively denote many islands, black islands, and small islands.

to constitute a local Church, withdrew its supervision prematurely, with the result that many of the converts lapsed and the moral tone of the Christians became very unsatisfactory. In 1827 some French R.C. priests endeavoured to start a mission, but they were banished in 1831. In 1839 a R.C. mission was established. A large number of the Christians connected with the Hawaiian Evangelical Association, which the A.B.C.F.M. had established, eventually joined this mission.

In 1861, as the result of a direct appeal of Kamehameha IV. to Queen Victoria, an Anglican bishop and two missionaries supported by the S.P.G. were sent to Honolulu. The first person to receive baptism from the Anglican missionaries was the queen, who was baptized in 1862. At the time when the request for an Anglican mission was made by the king, there were 25,000 persons in the islands "unconnected with any creed." Work was also undertaken by this mission amongst the Chinese immigrants.

In 1902 the charge of the diocese and the mission was transferred to the American Protestant Episcopal Church.

The Hawaiian group includes the island of *Molokai*, where the R.C. missionary Damien and a Protestant minister Hanaloa, after ministering to the lepers, both died of leprosy.

The mixed character of the population of the Hawaiian Islands adds greatly to the difficulties with which the Christian missionary has to contend. The population includes 21,666 Chinese, 79,520 Japanese, 4500 Coreans, 22,701 Portuguese, 2031 Spaniards, 4896 Porto Ricans, 14,409 of American, British, and German birth, 26,108 pure Hawaiians and 11,912 part Hawaiians. There are 5000 Mormons and 44,000 Buddhists.

The American Episcopal Mission, besides carrying on work amongst the Hawaiians in several of the islands, has missions to the Chinese, Japanese, and Corean immigrants. The mission to the Chinese, which was begun in 1887, has resulted in the ordination of several Chinese clergy, one of whom now ministers to the Chinese immigrants in Tonga. Japanese work is carried on at Hilo, and is superintended by a Japanese missionary who has been ordained. As a result of work amongst the Coreans, over 100 have been baptized during the last few years. There are 20 clergy belonging to the American Episcopal Mission who work at 27 centres.

The missionary enthusiasm of the Hawaiian people may be illustrated by the fact that 30 per cent. of its native ministry are foreign missionaries and 22 per cent. of the Christian contributions in the islands are devoted to foreign missions.

In the *Marquesas* and *Paumotu* islands, which lie to the south-east of Hawaii, Protestant missions are represented by the Paris Missionary Society and by the Hawaiian Evangelical Association. The R.C. mission, which began work in 1848, has 9 priests and about 2500 Christians.

The *Society Islands* —The Tahiti Archipelago, or Society Islands, consists of eleven islands, of which Tahiti is the largest. The total population is about 30,000.

When the discovery of Tahiti by Captain Cook became known, the Viceroy of Peru sent two R.C. priests to start a mission there. They remained only ten months, and returned to South America in the ship which brought them. In 1777, when Captain Cook revisited Tahiti, he saw the house which had been erected for them, with a cross bearing this inscription, " Christus vincit, et Carolus imperat. 1776." After seeing this, he wrote in his journal:

"It is very unlikely that any measure of this kind should ever be seriously thought of, as it can neither serve the purpose of public ambition nor private avarice, and without such inducements I may pronounce that it will never be undertaken."

Despite the pessimistic attitude of Captain Cook, the reading of his *Voyages* inspired several Englishmen to attempt missionary work in Polynesia and elsewhere.

The first successful attempt to introduce Christianity was made in 1796 by the L.M.S. In this year the mission ship *Duff* landed 18 missionaries, most of whom were artisans or mechanics. After enduring many hardships, the majority of them retired to Sydney in 1798. Later on, when King Pomare, who favoured the Christians, gained a victory over his opponents, several of these returned, and rapid progress began to be made.

In the early decades of the nineteenth century many of the supporters of missionary enterprise believed that it would be difficult, if not impossible, to evangelize savages until they had become to a considerable extent civilized. In accordance with this belief, the majority of the mission workers first sent out by the L.M.S. were mechanics. When the L.M.S. ship *Duff* sailed from London on its first voyage the mission party included 4 ministers, 6 carpenters, 2 shoemakers, 2 bricklayers, 2 tailors, 2 smiths, 2 weavers, a surgeon, a hatter, a shopkeeper, a cotton manufacturer, a cabinetmaker, a draper, a harness maker, a gentleman's servant who had become a tinworker, a cooper, and a butcher. There were also 3 children. When the *Duff* first visited Tongatabu in the Friendly Islands, it disembarked 10 mechanics, to begin a "mission of civilization," and so prepare the way for missionary work. The C.M.S. also began their work in New Zealand by sending out 3 mechanics (at the suggestion of Mr. Marsden), and several years were allowed to elapse before a missionary teacher was sent. Subsequent experience has shown that the Christian teacher is the best pioneer of civilization, and that civilization which is not the outcome of the acceptance of Christian teaching will seldom prepare the way for the latter.

James Chalmers, who possessed unique experience of the influence exerted by the advent of Western civilization apart from religious teaching and of the influence exerted by Christian missionaries in the South Sea Islands and afterwards in New Guinea, once said: "Nowhere have I seen our boasted civilization civilizing, but everywhere have I seen Christianity acting as the true civilizer."

How great was the civilizing influence which was exerted by the L.M.S. missionaries in the early years of the nineteenth century may be gathered from the statement made by Commander Duperry, who wrote in 1823 :

" The missionaries of the Society of London have entirely changed the manners and customs of the inhabitants. Idolatry no longer exists . . . the bloody wars in which the people engaged and human sacrifices have entirely ceased since 1816. All the natives can read and write."

The most renowned missionary in the South Seas was John Williams, who began work at *Raiatea* and made this island the starting-point for his extensive missionary journeys.

The R.C. Church started a mission in 1837, and partly in consequence of the difficulties which resulted from this mission the French Government proclaimed a protectorate over the islands in 1842, and finally annexed them in 1880. After the annexation the L.M.S. handed over its missionary work to the Paris Missionary Society.

In *French Polynesia, i.e.* in the Society Islands, the Leeward Islands, the Paumotu Islands, the Austral Islands, the Gambier Islands, and the Marquesas, the total population of which is about 30,000, there are about 20,000 Roman Catholics and about 10,000 Protestants. The R.C. missionaries, who belong to the Order of the Sacred Heart of Jesus and Mary, number 18 and have 52 schools. The Protestant missions are supported by the Paris Society, which has 58 stations, 10 European and 44 local workers. The Mormons are active in these islands.

The *Cook Islands* lie midway between Tahiti and Samoa. The largest, Raratonga, has a population of 7000. *Niué*, or Savage Island, which lies a little to the west, has a population of 4000. John Williams, helped by some Tahitian teachers, acted as a pioneer missionary in *Raratonga.* The whole group has been evangelized by L.M.S. missionaries and many converts from these islands have acted as

29

evangelists to other islands.   One instance, which is typical of many, deserves special mention.   Pao, who was born in Raratonga, became a Christian as a result of his association with a sailor on an American whaler.   Leaving Raratonga, he landed at *Lifu* in the Loyalty Islands, 3000 miles distant, and springing ashore from a canoe amidst a crowd of cannibal savages he called out to them, " Go tell the king I am a friend, and have brought him a message from the Great Spirit." [1]   When brought before the king, he was asked, " Have you seen the Great Spirit ? "   " No," replied Pao, " you cannot see a spirit."   " Then how did you get the message ? " inquired the king.   " By letter," said Pao, " and here it is "—producing his New Testament.   The king received him kindly, but later on Pao was forced to flee from the island.   However, he was eventually recalled by the people, and in the course of a few years the inhabitants of Lifu had become Christians.

The population of the Cook Islands and Niué is 12,000.   In 1909 there were 4407 Church members, 6885 other adherents, and 32 ordained teachers.   Much, however, remains to be done, as the moral stamina of the population is low even by comparison with that of the inhabitants of other islands.   Since 1823 the population of these islands has decreased by half.

Tonga.—The Tongan group, or Friendly Islands, consists of about 150 islands, most of which are very small. The population forty years ago was about 50,000, to-day it is about 22,000.   In 1797 the L.M.S. ship *Duff* visited Tongatabu.   The efforts of the mechanics which it disembarked proved unsuccessful, and in 1800 they withdrew to Sydney.   In 1822 the Wesleyan Methodists established a mission which after several vicissitudes became firmly established.   A great revival in 1834 resulted in the general acceptance of Christianity and led to the attempt to send the gospel to Fiji.   The spread of the Christian faith was largely due to the support of the chief Taufaahau (afterwards known as King George), who died in 1893,

[1] " Pao, the Apostle of Lifu," *The Pacific Islanders*, pp. 29–54.

aged 100. Eventually, however, a " Free Church of Tonga " under the patronage of the king was established as a rival to the Wesleyan Church, and the majority of the people now belong to this Church.

The R.C. Mission, which was established in 1851, has about 2000 members.

There is also a small Anglican mission which is under the charge of Bishop Willis, formerly Bishop of Honolulu.

Of the *Samoan group*, three small islands, including Tutuila, form a protectorate of the U.S.A.; the rest belonged to Germany until the war of 1914, when they were taken over by Great Britain. The population, which is now about 35,000, has been steadily decreasing. Christianity was first preached in the islands by some converted Tongans who had married into Samoan families. The first European missionary to visit the islands was the Rev. John Williams of the L.M.S., who in 1830 left 8 Tahitian teachers. In 1836 European missionaries were introduced by the L.M.S., and the work rapidly developed. In 1835 the first Wesleyan missionaries arrived. For some years there was a certain amount of misunderstanding between the converts connected with the two missions, but the rivalry and disputes have practically died out. Samoa is now nominally Christian. The L.M.S. returns 8861 members and 28,000 attendants; the Wesleyans return 2359 members and 6500 "hearers."

At the Malua school, which is under the charge of the L.M.S. Mission, 1300 men have been trained as preachers who have acted as mission agents over a wide area. The mission industrial schools are exerting a beneficial influence throughout the island. There are a large number of Chinese coolies, for whom but little has as yet been done by the Christian missionaries. Robert Louis Stevenson is buried at Vailima in Samoa. " Since he died, the chiefs of the district have forbidden the use of firearms on the hillside, that the birds may sing undisturbed the songs he so loved in life." [1]

[1] *The Call of the Pacific*, by J. W. Burton, p. 48.

The R.C. Mission, which was begun in 1845 and is under the charge of the Marist Fathers, returns 7500 Catholics. There are 21 priests, of whom several are natives. The Mormons number 300.

The *Fiji Islands*, 230 in number, have rapidly decreased in population since the people came in contact with Europeans. In 1850 the population, which is now about 87,000, was reckoned at 200,000. The people "are of a lower grade than the Tongans, Samoans, Tahitians, and Maoris. They have not nearly the same intellectual development and their civilization is of a coarser order. They are in turn superior to the western peoples of New Hebrides, New Britain, and New Guinea. . . . Cannibalism was an integral part of Fijian life, and the worst forms of barbarity found constant expression. This has affected not only the mental and moral development of the people, but it has weakened and poisoned their physical strength."[1]

Christianity was first introduced into Fiji by two islanders sent by John Williams from Tahiti. In 1834 two English Wesleyan ministers from Tonga, together with a number of Tongan preachers, arrived. At first all went well, but "bloodshed, cannibalism, licentiousness, and cruelty were entrenched behind stubborn customs," and a series of persecutions followed. One of the first missionaries who set foot in Fiji began his work by burying the hands, feet, and heads of eighty victims whose bodies had been roasted and eaten at a cannibal feast. Gradually, however, the new faith spread from island to island, and before 1850 at least a third of the population had been influenced by the teaching of the missionaries.

At this period the work progressed so rapidly that it became almost necessarily superficial. Whole tribes renounced idolatry in a day, and so great was the number of those who became nominal Christians that it was impossible to give them any adequate instruction. Churches and mission schools have now been built all over the islands, and the vast majority of the people attend church

[1] *The Call of the Pacific*, p. 8.

on Sundays and have family worship in their own houses. The people are with few exceptions adherents of the Wesleyan or of the R.C. Church. The adherents of the latter number 10,824, but this includes many Europeans, Indians, and other South Sea Islanders.

The R.C. Mission, which was begun in 1863, is staffed by 33 priests.

Many of the Fijian converts connected with the Wesleyan Mission have gone as Christian evangelists to New Guinea, New Britain, and the Solomon Islands.

Indians in Fiji.—The rapid increase of Indian coolies in Fiji, combined with the steady decrease in the native population, threatens to result in re-establishing heathenism in these islands. The Indians number over 40,000, and increase year by year. The immorality and drunkenness which in many instances prevail among these coolies render it most difficult to prosecute successful missionary work on their behalf. In 1897 the Wesleyans made a first attempt to work amongst the Indians in Suva, and the Methodist Missionary Society of Australasia now supports three missionaries amongst them. In 1902 the Rev. H. Lateward, who had worked for many years in India in connection with the S.P.G., began work amongst the Indians at Labasa. In 1908 an Anglican bishop was appointed to superintend work amongst the English settlers in Polynesia and to develop the mission to the Indian coolies in Fiji. This mission is supported by the S.P.G., and work is carried on at Labasa and Suva.

The R.C. Church reaches some of the Indians who have settled in Fiji through its schools.

The *Tokelau* or *Union Islands*, which lie north-west of Samoa, were evangelized by L.M.S. missionaries. They include the islands of Fakaafo, Nukunono, and Atafu.

MELANESIA.

Melanesia, which lies to the west of Polynesia and south and west of Micronesia, includes about 250 islands, of which the largest are in the Bismarck Archipelago and a the Solomon group. The population is reckoned at ⸗75,000, of whom 141,000 are Christians. Of these atter about 30,000 are Roman Catholics.

The Anglican *Melanesian Mission* has as its sphere of work the western islands of the South Pacific from the northern New Hebrides to the Solomon Islands inclusive.

Bishop Selwyn of New Zealand, having visited in 1848 the islands which now form the diocese of Melanesia, decided to open a training school at Auckland, N.Z., and to bring to it boys from the various islands which he desired to evangelize, who after being taught the Christian faith might go back to their homes as evangelists and teachers. The method inaugurated by Selwyn has been followed by the mission ever since. The first five native scholars reached Auckland in 1849, and their number rapidly increased. By 1852 the bishop had visited fifty islands and had collected forty scholars who spoke ten different languages. The island of Mai in the New Hebrides sent its chief as one of the scholars. The school was for some years held at Auckland during the summer and at one of the Melanesian islands during the winter. In 1861 John Coleridge Patteson, a Fellow of Merton College, Oxford, who had joined the mission in 1855, was consecrated as Bishop of Melanesia. In 1867 the school and the centre of the mission were transferred to *Norfolk Island*, its situation rendering it possible to maintain the school throughout the whole year. In 1868 George Sarawia was ordained as the first native deacon and stationed on *Mota Island*. In 1871 the mission suffered a serious loss by the murder of Bishop Patteson at *Nukapu Island*, one of the Santa Cruz group. The bishop had visited the island before and had been well received, but previous to his last visit a " labour ship " had visited the island and had apparently carried off forcibly five of the inhabitants. When the bishop landed he was murdered and several islanders who accompanied him were wounded in revenge for the wrong which had been done by the "labour ship." When his body was recovered, a palm frond with five knots tied in its foliage lay across the breast.[1]

On the reception of the news in England, great enthusiasm on behalf of the mission was called forth. The mission was referred to in the Queen's Speech at the opening of Parliament in 1872. Max Müller, writing to the *Times*, said: "To have known such a man is one of life's greatest blessings"; the name of Patteson will "live in every cottage, in every school and church in Melanesia, not as the name of a fabulous saint or martyr, but as the never-to-be-forgotten name of a good, brave, God-fearing, and God-loving man. His bones will not work childish miracles, but his spirit will work signs and wonders by revealing even among the lowest of Melanesian savages the indelible God-like stamp of human nature, and by upholding among future generations a true faith in God, founded on a true faith in man."

Amongst other qualifications which Bishop Patteson possessed was a marvellous capacity for learning the Melanesian dialects. He was credited with being able to speak forty. The multiplicity of these dialects adds greatly to the difficulties with which the missionaries working in these islands are confronted.

The S.P.G. issued an appeal for a memorial to Bishop Patteson which should endow the bishopric, build a church at Norfolk Island, and provide a new mission ship, in response to which more than £6000 was subscribed.

In 1877 John Selwyn, a son of the first Bishop of New Zealand, was consecrated as successor to Patteson. In 1880 Bishop Selwyn was able to visit Santa Cruz, and eventually mission work was established at Nukapu. In consequence of ill-health, brought on by his arduous work, he was compelled to resign in 1890.

In 1895, when Bishop Montgomery (then Bishop of Tasmania) visited the mission, there were 12 European and

[1] This palm frond is now preserved in the chapel of the S.P.G. Mission House.

9 native clergy, 8929 baptized Christians, 12,183 scholars, 122 schools, and 381 teachers.

In 1912 one of the European missionaries, the Rev. C. C. Godden, was murdered by a native at Opa in the New Hebrides.

In addition to the school on Norfolk Island the Melanesian Mission has opened a training centre in the Solomon Islands. It is endeavouring to place a resident missionary on each of the islands within its sphere of influence.

The three islands in the *Northern Hebrides* which are under the charge of the mission have in them 2286 baptized Christians and about 1000 more in the schools. In the *Banks Islands*, where there are but few heathen left, there are 3135 baptized and 600 hearers. The last of the four Torres Islands has lately accepted Christianity. In these islands there are 470 baptized and 100 hearers. In *Santa Cruz* and the *Reef Islands* there are only 106 baptized and 106 hearers. In the *Solomon Islands* great progress has been made, and there are 8415 baptized and 3000 hearers.

The present staff of the mission includes 20 European and 16 local clergy, 6 laymen and 12 women missionaries. There are 350 schools and 760 teachers.

The population of English-speaking people in the islands which are included in the diocese is about 700, and the islanders number about 300,000.

We have so far only referred to the work of the Anglican Mission to Melanesia, but the work done by other missions has been at least equally productive of results. In 1839 John Williams, the well-known L.M.S. missionary, to whose work we have already referred, landed in *Erromanga* in the New Hebrides, but he and his companion were almost immediately murdered. For many years the task of evangelizing these islands proved exceptionally difficult, and up to 1856 over 50 missionaries white or coloured had died or had been murdered by their inhabitants. In 1848 a Presbyterian missionary, the

Rev. J. Geddie, succeeded in starting work at *Aneityum*, and within ten years this island had not only become Christian but had begun to send out native evangelists to other islands farther to the north. In 1858 the Rev. J. G. Paton of the United Presbyterian Mission started work at Tanna, from which he shortly afterwards moved to Aniwa, which he lived to see completely evangelized.

His name is connected with some of the noblest and most heroic work that has been accomplished in the South Seas, and the record of his life's work has been an inspiration to many. In 1906 he wrote:

"As the results of the missionary work in the New Hebrides our dear Lord has given our missionaries about 20,000 converts, and the blessed work is extending among the other cannibals. . . . In one year 1120 savages renounced idolatry and embraced the worship and service of Christ. . . . We never baptize and teach afterward, but educate and wait till they give real evidence of consecration to Jesus Christ, and then, at their desire, baptize and continue teaching them to observe in their life and conduct all things Jesus has commanded. . . . All of the converts attend church regularly. They contributed last year over £1300 in money and arrowroot, and a number of the islands now support their own native teachers." [1]

In addition to the islands in the New Hebrides to which we have already referred, *Erromanga*, *Efate Nguna*, and *Tongoa* have now become entirely Christian, while *Futuna*, *Epi*, and *Paama* are fast becoming Christian. In *Tanna*, *Ambrim*, *Malekula*, and *Santo* the majority of the inhabitants are still heathen.

A Roman Catholic mission was begun in the French New Hebrides in 1887, and a bishop resides at Port-Vila. The staff of the mission consists of 26 priests and 3 lay brothers of the Lyons Society of Mary. The number of converts is about 1000.

The *Solomon Islands* include several islands of considerable size, namely, Malaita, Guadalcanar, San Cristoval,

[1] *The Pacific Islanders*, p. 138 f.

Bougainville, and Bugotu.   The first attempt to evangelize
their inhabitants, who were notorious " head-hunters," was
made by R.C. missionaries belonging to the Society of Mary.

In 1845 eighteen missionaries under Bishop Epalle
tried to evangelize the Solomon group.   On December 12,
the bishop, three priests, and some sailors landed on
Ysabel, but were suddenly attacked.   The bishop was
killed and one priest and one seaman were dangerously
wounded.   Soon afterwards three priests were killed and
eaten in San Cristoval, and the work was eventually
abandoned.   It was resumed in 1898, when three priests
landed at Rua Sura, near Guadalcanar.   There are now
17 priests and 10 sisters at work in the Solomon group.

Later on the Solomon Islands became one of the chief
spheres of work of the Anglican Melanesian Mission.   The
proposed transfer of the centre of this mission from Norfolk
Island to the Solomon group should do much to strengthen
and   develop   its   work.   The   Methodist   Missionary
Society has had work in the island of *New Georgia* since
1902, and the South Sea Evangelical Mission, which is
chiefly supported by the " Brethren," has work amongst
the Kanakas who have been repatriated from Australia.
Comparatively little work, however, has been done in
the Solomon group, and of the total population of about
180,000   only   10,000   have   as   yet   been   influenced
by Christian missionaries.   In *Mala*, the most populous
island, the majority of the inhabitants are still cannibals.
Guadalcanar and *San Cristoval* are also heathen.   *Bugotu*
is mainly Christian and *Gela* is at least nominally Christian.
Many of the Kanaka labourers who had been evangelized
whilst working in Queensland have helped to spread the
Christian faith in the islands to which they have returned.

MICRONESIA.

The principal groups of islands which are included in
Micronesia are the *Gilbert, Ellice, Marshall, Caroline*, and
Ladrone or *Marianne Islands*.   The first two groups are

British and the last three were German prior to 1914. *Guam*, in the last group, belongs to the U.S.A.

The Protestant missions throughout Micronesia are carried on by the A.B.C.F.M. at 67 stations. This society employs 25 American and 200 native missionaries. There are altogether about 20,000 professed Christians, rather less than half being communicants. The L.M.S. has a station in the Ellice Islands.

The R.C. missions are carried on by the Order of the Sacred Heart.

Of the 30,000 Christians in Micronesia about 18,000 are Protestants and 12,000 Roman Catholics.

Since 1852 missionary work has been carried on throughout a great part of Micronesia (with the exception of the Ladrones) by the Hawaiian Evangelical Association, which is under the superintendence of the American Board. The work is mainly conducted by local teachers, of whom about 30 are ordained. They are superintended by 9 American missionaries.

The *Gilbert Islands*, which lie across the Equator, contain a population of 25,000. The islands north of the Equator were evangelized by the A.B.C.F.M., the first of whose missionaries began work in 1857. Christianity was first preached in the *Ellice Islands*, which lie to the south of the Gilbert Islands, by a native, Elikana, in the employ of the L.M.S., who, after drifting in a canoe for eight weeks a distance of 1800 miles from the Cook Islands, landed with four others at Nukulaelae. He was kindly received by the inhabitants, to whom he preached the Christian faith with great success.

All the islands in these two groups have now been evangelized. On *Ocean Island* the A.B.C.F.M. has started a training school for native teachers. The *Marshall Islands* include 24 lagoon islands, of which the most important are *Ebon* and *Jalut*, and have a population of about 15,000. The centre from which the missionary work in the Gilbert and Marshall Islands is superintended is *Kusaie* in the Carolines.

The *Caroline Islands* number about 500 and contain a

population of about 140,000. They were annexed by Spain in 1686, but practically abandoned by her until 1885, when Protestant missionary work had been established in them. The first Protestant missionaries sent by the A.B.C.F.M. arrived in 1852. A large amount of good work had been accomplished in *Kusaie*, *Ponape*, and other islands, but on the arrival of the representatives of the Spanish Government the mission schools were closed, the church services were discontinued, and the people were encouraged to manufacture intoxicating drinks. In 1890 the mission buildings were destroyed and the missionaries were banished. In 1900, when the islands were ceded to Germany, the Protestant missionaries were allowed to return, and since then the work has made good progress.

In the *Ladrone Islands*, which contain a population of about 2000, the only missions are those of the R.C. Church, except in the island of Guam.

In 1668 the Queen Regent of Spain sent missionaries to evangelize the Ladrones. The seven missionaries who reached *Guam* in 1669 "taught and baptized 6000 persons during the first year." Their leader was killed after three years for baptizing the chief's child without his consent. The Ladrone Islands eventually became nominally Christian, but the conversion of its peoples was of a superficial character, and many heathen superstitions survived. Moreover, the acceptance of Christianity failed to effect any great improvement in the moral character of the people. On June 24, 1908, the U.S.A. took possession of Guam, and in 1900 missionaries sent by the A.B.C.F.M. arrived. The work which they have initiated has already met with considerable success, and although it has been bitterly opposed by the representatives of the R.C. Church, it has reacted beneficially upon the R.C. Mission. More instruction is now being given to the people by the R.C. missionaries and a higher standard of conduct is being inculcated. The population of Guam is about 10,000, of whom 7000 live in the capital, Agana. A large number of the inhabitants are of mixed Spanish descent.

New Caledonia, which is the largest island in the South Seas, with the exception of New Guinea, has for many years been used by the French as a convict settlement. Its population includes 16,000 aboriginal inhabitants and about 3000 Japanese. The French R.C. Mission is under the charge of the Marist Fathers. There are 48 missionary priests who minister to 11,500 non-European Catholics.

There are also a French Protestant mission and a small Baptist mission.

The *Bismarck Archipelago*, which lies to the east of New Guinea, became a German protectorate in 1884. The largest island in the archipelago is New Britain (re-named by the Germans New Pomerania), which has a population of about 190,000, of whom about 500 are Europeans. Since 1875 the Australian Wesleyans have carried on missions, chiefly staffed by evangelists from Fiji and Tonga, in the islands of *New Pomerania*, *New Lauenburg*, and *New Mecklenburg*. The pioneer of the mission was Dr. George Brown, who, with his band of Christians, landed on the *Duke of York Island*, which was inhabited by cannibals. Three of the Fiji Christians were killed and eaten, but their places were immediately filled by eager volunteers. After less than forty years' work the mission was able to report 189 churches, 200 catechists and teachers, 3600 full members, and 21,000 adherents or hearers. The Christians, who are extremely poor, contribute nearly £2000 per annum towards the support of the mission work. At the George Brown College at Ulu 80 students are being trained to become preachers or teachers. In the mission schools instruction is also given in various forms of industrial work.

A R.C. mission was started in 1889 and entrusted to the missionaries of the Sacred Heart of Issoudun. There are 28 missionaries, 40 brothers, 27 sisters, and about 15,000 Roman Catholics.

Of the total population of the archipelago, about

210,000, only 40,000 are at present reached by the Wesleyan and R.C. missions.

R.C. Missions.—The following table shows the number of R.C. dioceses or bishoprics in the South Seas :—

	Year.	Priests.	Christians.
Marianne and Caroline Islands .	1886	16	4,730
Guam	1911	6	12,000
New Pomerania . . .	1889	37	20,417
North Soloman Islands . .	1898	12	480
South Solomon Islands . .	1897	16	3,000
New Hebrides . . .	1901	26	1,500
New Caledonia . . .	1847	57	10,783
Marshall Islands . . .	1905	6	730
Gilbert Islands . . .	1897	23	14,037
Fiji	1863	33	12,000
Oceania, Central . . .	1842	28 [1]	9,940
Samoa	1851	24 [1]	7,854
Sandwich Islands . . .	1848	37	15,000
Marquesas Islands . . .	1848	9	2,488
Tahiti	1833	30	5,800

[1] Including four native priests.

NEW GUINEA.

New Guinea, or *Papua,* as it is now commonly called, was discovered by the Dutch in the fourteenth century. In 1848 they took possession of its western half.   In 1884 the eastern part was divided between Great Britain and Germany, and in 1906 the British portion was transferred to the Commonwealth of Australia.

In British New Guinea missionary work was begun by the L.M.S. in 1871.   In the first instance, native Christians who had volunteered for this hazardous enterprise from Lifu, Samoa, Niué, and Raratonga were stationed at selected points.

The heroic deeds done by the native Christians would take long to recount.   When an invitation was given to the Christians in Lifu to take part in the mission, every student in the missionary college and every teacher in the island volunteered. During the first twenty years of the mission 120 Polynesian teachers died of fever, or were poisoned, or murdered. It would be hard to find a parallel to their self-sacrifice in the whole history of Christian missions.

In 1874 the Rev. W. G. Lawes, the pioneer of the L.M.S. Mission, settled at Port Moresby, where he was joined by the Rev. James Chalmers in 1877. Chalmers, or "Tamate," as the islanders called him, had already worked for ten years on Raratonga Island before coming to New Guinea. Here he acted as a pioneer and organizer, and soon gained a marvellous influence over the fiercest and least approachable of the local tribes. "No white man had ever had a more wide and varied knowledge of the mainland of New Guinea, or visited more tribes, or made more friends, or endured more hardships, or faced more perils." [1]

On April 7, 1901, he landed at the Aird River with a colleague, the Rev. Oliver Tomkins, and twelve students, when the whole party were killed and eaten by the inhabitants. R. L. Stevenson had written to Chalmers' mother: "I shall meet Tamate once more before he disappears up the Fly River, perhaps to be one of the unreturned brave: he is a man nobody can see and not love. He has plenty of faults like the rest of us, but he is as big as a church."

In 1881 the first converts of the L.M.S. Mission were baptized, and since then steady progress has been maintained. The sphere of the L.M.S. Mission is the south coast of British New Guinea. There are 15 English missionaries and 148 local preachers, 1355 church members, and about 7000 adherents. At Kwato a successful industrial mission has been established.

An Anglican mission was established on the north coast in 1881, the pioneer missionaries being the Rev. A. A. Maclaren and the Rev. Copland King. The first

[1] "James Chalmers, the 'Greatheart' of New Guinea," by George Robson, *The Pacific Islanders*, p. 292.

station occupied was at Dogura in Bartle Bay.   In 1891
Maclaren died, worn out by his hard and unremitting
labours.   A bishop was appointed in 1897, and the work
has since steadily expanded.   There are 22 European
missionaries and 29 Papuan teachers, 650 persons have
been baptized, and there are about 5000 hearers or
adherents.   Two Papuans have been ordained.

A Wesleyan mission was commenced in 1881 on the
islands off the south-east coast, the first island to be
occupied being Dobu.   Several of the missionaries had
already had experience of missionary work in Polynesia.
The work has made steady progress, and there are now
6 missionaries, 7 lay missionaries, 74 Papuan preachers,
909 church members, and 22,000 attendants at public
worship.

A R.C. mission was begun in New Guinea in
1889, when a Vicar Apostolic was appointed.   He was
assisted by priests, brothers, and sisters belonging to the
Order of the Sacred Heart of Issoudun.   In British New
Guinea there are 26 missionaries, 21 brothers, 38 sisters,
and 1500 Catholics.

In *German New Guinea* a mission which was started
by the Lutheran Church in 1880 has a staff of 18 clergy
and one medical missionary.   It reports 850 members
and 300 scholars in its nine schools

In *Dutch New Guinea*, the R.C. Mission, which was
started in 1889, became a separate vicariate in 1902.   Its
staff consists of 20 Fathers and 15 lay brothers belonging
to the Order of the Sacred Heart, and 10 sisters belonging
to Our Lady of the Sacred Heart.   The Roman Catholics
number about 3500.

Some Dutch Protestant ministers have endeavoured to
evangelize the inhabitants at three or four places on the
coast.

XXI.

MISSIONS TO MOSLEMS.

REFERENCE has already been made to the missions to Moslems which are being carried on in different parts of the mission field, but it may be well to add a few notes dealing with these missions as a whole.

Distribution of the Moslem population.

According to the latest estimates made by Dr. S. M. Zwemer and Professor D. Westermann, the total population of the Moslem world is about 200,000,000, and is distributed as follows:

In Europe there are 2,373,676, most of whom are to be found in Turkey, Austria-Hungary, and the Balkan States.

In the Russian Empire there are about 20,000.

In South America there are 159,511, principally in Brazil, British and Dutch Guiana, and Trinidad.

In Africa there are 42,000,000. About half of these are north of the twentieth parallel of latitude, but Islam is encroaching upon the pagan tribes, and in South Africa has already 53,000 adherents.

In Asia the following countries are wholly Mohammedan: Arabia, Persia, Afghanistan, Bokhara, Khiva, Baluchistan.

The number in China is uncertain, and is somewhere between 5,000,000 and 8,500,000.

In India there are 66,577,247; in Malaysia, 35,308,996.

30

In Australia there are 19,500; and in the Philippine Islands, 277,547.

Of the total Moslem population over 167,000,000 were under Christian rule at the outbreak of the European War. The estimated total (200,000,000) is nearly 30,000,000 less than that given at the Cairo Conference, and is 100,000,000 less than that given by the Moslem press of Cairo, but it is based for the most part on official government statistics, and is a more accurate estimate than either of the latter.[1]

Early missionaries to Moslems.

John Damascene (d. 754), who held office under the Caliph of Damascus, wrote a book entitled *The Superstition of the Ishmaelites*. Al Kindi wrote (*circ.* 830) an *Apology for Christianity*, which has often been translated and circulated by Christian missionaries. Petrus Venerabilis, a Benedictine abbot of Clugny (d. 1157), translated the Koran and pleaded for a translation of the Bible into Arabic. He condemned the Crusades, and wrote : " I come to win the Moslem, not as people oft do with arms, but with words; not by force, but by reason; not in hatred, but in love." [2]   St. Francis d'Assisi (d. 1226) sailed to Egypt in 1219 and endeavoured to preach the Gospel to the Sultan, El Kamil, but with no apparent success. Raymond Lull, who was born in Majorca in 1235, was inspired by the example of Francis d'Assisi to become a missionary to Moslems. For many years he laboured in vain to persuade the representatives of the Church, the Pope included, that the policy of the Crusades was anti-Christian, and to interest them in schemes for developing missions to Moslems. Having purchased a Moslem slave, he studied Arabic with his assistance for nine years. He afterwards preached for two years in Tunis, where he was imprisoned, sentenced to death, and finally banished.

---

[1] See *The Moslem World*, April 1914.
[2] See *The Reproach of Islam*, by W. H. T. Gairdner, p. 224.

Later on he spent a year and a half at Bugia in Algeria, where he made several converts. Here he was again imprisoned, and eventually deported to Italy. Returning again to Bugia when eighty years of age, he encouraged his converts for a year, but was eventually stoned to death by a mob in 1315.[1]

We have already referred to the attempt made by Ignatius Loyola to preach to Moslems in Jerusalem (p. 69), and to the work of Geronimo Xavier at the court of Akbar in North India at the beginning of the seventeenth century (p. 77).

Modern Missions to Moslems.

Early in the nineteenth century Henry Martyn endeavoured to preach to Moslems in India and in Persia (p. 84). His work in Persia was eventually taken up and continued by Pfander and others (p 273).

References to the missions to Moslems which are being carried on in Persia, Asia Minor, North, East, and West Africa, India, Arabia, and Malaysia will be found under these several countries. Judged by visible results, the missions in Java and Sumatra, where there are now over 40,000 converts from Islam, have been the most successful. The most important mission from a strategic standpoint is perhaps the C.M.S. mission at Cairo. The missionaries here are brought into touch with Moslem students, who come from many lands to attend the great Al Azhar University. "There," writes Mr. Gairdner, "you see black Sudanese from Hausaland or the Gambia river, browny-yellow skinned Maghrabis from Morocco, fair pink-and-white Turks from Stamboul, almond-eyed Mongoloids from far Russian Siberia and Turkestan, and many more. In the memory of living men no Christian could do so much as enter that place; now they enter unmolested. Students

---

[1] For a sketch of his life and writings see *Raymond Lull, First Missionary to the Moslems*, by S. M. Zwemer, 1902, and *Raymond Lull, the Illuminated Doctor*, by W. T. Barber, 1903.

and ex-students have been converted to Christ, and not a few students have, as they paced or sat apart, studied there, not the Koran, but the Injil Yasu' al Masih." [1]

The American United Presbyterian Mission has for some time past been trying to promote the establishment of a Christian university in Cairo, the establishment of which would be a great boon to the Christian community in Egypt and eventually to the cause of missions.

An American professor who has made a special study of the religion of the Egyptian dervishes has maintained that Sufi mysticism, by which many of them have been deeply influenced, "has come to be really the ultimate, the final basis for all thoughtful religion in Islam." [2]   Even if this statement be correct, it does not indicate that the task of the Christian missionary is likely on this account to become less arduous than it has been in the past.

It has, indeed, been suggested that inasmuch as love occupies the central place in Sufi mysticism, this form of Mohammedan teaching may eventually serve as a bridge between Islam and Christianity.   This might be the case were it not for the pantheistic tendencies of Sufi mysticism. The Sufi mystic seeks God within himself and finds Him everywhere, and God ceases to be a personality.   Although he acknowledges an obligation to love his neighbour because God is present in him, he loves himself because he, too, is part of the divine being.   The most unsatisfactory outcome of the teaching of Sufi mysticism is that the mystic regards himself as not only above all ceremonial but above all moral law.   It is obvious, therefore, that although in individual cases the constant contemplation of the love of God may help to render intelligible the doctrine of the love of God revealed in Christ, it is not likely that the spread of Sufi doctrines, whether in Egypt or India, will pave the way for the spread of Christian missions.

In view of the close connection between politics and religion which exists in the minds of Moslems, the loss of

---

[1] *The Reproach of Islam*, p. 268 f.

[2] *Aspects of Islam*, by D. B. Macdonald, 1911, p. 149.

political power by Moslem rulers which has recently occurred is likely to have a profound influence upon the prestige of Islam. The French occupation of Morocco, the Italian conquest of Tripoli, the Anglo-Russian agreement in regard to Persia, the defeat of Turkey by the Balkan States, and, lastly, its suicidal participation in the European War, followed by the dethronement of the Khedive, constitute a series of events without parallel in the history of Islam. The Amir of Afghanistan is now the only really independent Moslem ruler in the world, and the population over which he rules is probably less than 5,000,000.

During the greater part of the time which has elapsed since the establishment of modern Christian missions, India and the Dutch East Indies have been practically the only countries in which it has been possible for a Moslem to acknowledge himself a Christian without facing the almost certain prospect of being murdered. Even in India the converts from Islam have, as a general rule, had to submit to the loss of all their property and of their wives and children. The mere fact, therefore, that it is not possible to point to the conversion of large numbers of Moslems affords no argument that the contest between Christianity and Islam has been decided and that Christianity has sustained a defeat. We should have much less respect for the Mohammedan faith than we now have if, with the slight knowledge of Christianity which most of its adherents at present possess, any number of them were prepared to forsake their ancestral faith in order to embrace its rival. That which is calculated to create surprise is the measure of success which Christian missionaries have attained in India, and the encouraging prospect which is opened before them both there and elsewhere.

Referring to the prospects of Moslem missions in India, Dr. Wherry writes:

"The accessions from Islam, especially in Northern India, have been continuous during all the years since the death of Henry Martyn. One here and another there has been added to the Christian Church, so that now, as one looks over the rolls of Church membership, he is surprised to find so many converts from Islam, or the children and children's children of such converts. In the North, especially in the Punjab and the North-West Province, every congregation has a representative from the Moslem ranks. Some of the Churches have a majority of their membership gathered from amongst the Mussulmans. In a few cases there has been something like a movement towards Christianity, and a considerable number have come out at one time. But perhaps the fact which tells most clearly the story of the advance of Christianity among Moslems in India, is this, that among the native pastors and Christian preachers and teachers in North India there are at least two hundred who were once followers of Islam."[1]

From the returns of the last Indian census it appears that the increase in the Mohammedan population throughout the Indian Empire during the decade 1901–11 did not quite keep pace with the ordinary increase of the whole population.

Dr. Imad-ud-din, in the course of a paper sent to be read at the religious conference held at Chicago, wrote : "There was a time when the conversion of a Mohammedan to Christianity was looked on as a wonder. Now they have come and are coming in their thousands." At the end of his paper he appended a list of 117 converts from Islam to Christianity who at that time were occupying influential positions in the State or in the Church in India.[2]

The prospect of commending the Christian faith to Moslems was never so bright as it is at the present time. Dr. Zwemer, one of the best known missionaries to Moslems, who is in touch with work amongst them in all parts of the world, recently wrote:

"Without in any way underestimating the new anti-Christian attitude of some educated Moslems and the pan-

---

[1] *India and Christianity in India and the Far East*, by E. M. Wherry, p. 145 f.

[2] A reprint of this paper and of its appendix is given in the *C.M.S. Intelligencer* for August 1893. The author himself belonged to one of the ꞏꞏꞏ

Islamic efforts of others to oppose Christian missions by every modern method of attack or defence, it yet remains true that the whole situation is hopeful to the last degree. The light is breaking everywhere. There never was so much friendliness, such willingness to discuss the question at issue, such a large attendance of Moslems at Christian schools, hospitals, public meetings, and even preaching services as there is to-day. . . . What is true of Egypt is true, *mutatis mutandis*, of Turkey, Persia, India, Algeria, and Java, as abundant testimony and recent missionary correspondence could show. And what does it all mean? It means that we should press forward with all our might plans for the immediate evangelization of these educated classes. They are adrift, and the Gospel alone can give them new anchorage. . . . They have lost faith in the old Islam and reach out to new ideals in ethics. Who can satisfy them but Christ? This is the missionary's supreme opportunity. If we can win the leaders of Moslem thought now, ' reformed Islam will be Islam no longer,' but an open door into Christianity."[1]

In support of the above statement, we may note that during the year preceding the outbreak of the European War, the increase in the number of Moslems attending American missionary colleges was 20 per cent. and of those attending high schools 40 per cent.

If it be true, as Dr. Zwemer asserts, that the religious influence of Mohammedanism is on the decline, the inference is obvious. The declining power of Islam involves the increasing responsibility of Christendom. God forbid that any one should regard with satisfaction the waning power of Islam as a religious factor in the world, or should do anything to weaken the faith of a single Moslem in his Prophet, who is not himself prepared to offer him what he believes to be a truer faith in its place. The task of converting the Mohammedan world to Christ is indeed a hard task but it is not an impossible one. Eight centuries have passed since Pope Urban II. stood in the market-place at Clermont and explained to the vast assemblage there collected the proposal which was then under consideration

[1] See *International Review of Missions*, October 1914.

for attempting to crush by force of arms the Mohammedan power of the East. As those present listened to his impassioned appeal and to his demand to sacrifice, if need be, their lives in the campaign to which he invited them, the whole assemblage exclaimed with one voice, " It is the will of God." " It is indeed the will of God," said the Pope ; " take, then, this word as your battle-cry, and go forth to victory in the name of Christ." To those who have ears to hear, a call comes not unsimilar to that which shook Christendom eight centuries ago, but it is a call to a nobler and more difficult crusade than any which the Middle Ages conceived, to one, too, which requires no less courage and no less perseverance than those which the Crusaders displayed, but in the prosecution of which we too may take as our watchword with unfailing confidence, " It is the will of God."

In responding to this call and in trying to preach the Gospel to Moslems and to explain the half truths of Islam in the light of the Christian revelation, we may claim to be following in the steps of their own Prophet and to be acting in accordance with the spirit by which, at any rate, the earlier part of his life was inspired. Voiced by the unconscious needs of the Moslem world comes to the Christian Church the appeal to impart to it the knowledge of the Christian faith, which Mohammed himself never possessed, but which, had he possessed it, he would have spent his life in proclaiming.

XXII.

MISSIONS TO THE JEWS.

THE Jewish population of the world is approximately 12,000,000. Of these over 9,000,000 live in Europe (5,000,000 in Russia, 250,000 in Great Britain) and 2,211,000 in America. Palestine contains 100,000, New York City 1,000,000, London 140,000, Berlin 100,000, Chicago 185,000. There are a certain number of Jews who are Jews by faith but not by race. The Beni-Israel who settled in India in the first century A.D. gained a number of converts the descendants of whom are the "Black Jews" of Cochin. There are 3000 Karaite Jews in the Crimea who are of Tartar origin and a number of negro Jews at Loango in West Africa.

It has often been asserted that no missionary work has been less fruitful in result than that which has been carried on amongst the Jews. This statement is not, however, supported by statistics. Dr. E. Stock writes:

"Relatively to the numbers of the Jewish race the converts are as numerous as those from the heathen and much more than those from the Mohammedans. It is estimated that quite 250 Anglican clergymen are converted Jews or the sons of converted Jews. The London Jews Society alone has 93 on its missionary staff. . . . Professor Delitzsch estimated that 100,000 Jews had been baptized in the first three-quarters of the nineteenth century, and Dr. Dalman of Leipsic has remarked that 'if all the Jews who have embraced Christianity had remained a distinct people, instead of being absorbed by the nations among whom they dwelt, their descendants would now be counted by millions.'"[1]

The chief British societies working amongst Jews are the *London Society for promoting Christianity among the Jews* (1809), which supports work in Great Britain, the continent of Europe, North Africa, Turkey, Syria, Palestine, and Persia; the *Parochial Mission to the Jews* (1875) and the *Barbican Mission*, working in East London; the *Mildmay Mission to the Jews* (1876), which works in London and abroad; and the *Jerusalem and the East Mission Fund* (1890), which helps to support the work which is superintended by the Anglican Bishop in Jerusalem. The above are connected with the Anglican Church. The *British Society for the Propagation of the Gospel among the Jews* (1842) is undenominational. There are also four societies supported by English, Scotch, and Irish Presbyterians, besides a number of very small societies. Some of the most fruitful work which is being done amongst Jews in England is that carried on as part of the ordinary parochial machinery of the many parishes in East London which contain a large Jewish population. In the parish of Spitalfields, for example, which contains a population of 19,000, 14,000 are Jews. In this parish and in a number of other parishes which contain a similar proportion of Jews, the "East London Fund for the Jews" supports assistant curates, lay workers, both men and women, and nurses, many of whom are converted Jews. Although the number of conversions is small, the agents employed in these parishes can point to a change of attitude towards Christianity and a willingness to read the New Testament and to attempts to practise its teaching which afford solid grounds for encouragement. In the U.S.A. and Canada there are 44 societies, but these only support 51 stations between them. There are 16 small continental societies. The total number of missionaries supported by 95 societies throughout the world are about 500 men and 350 women.

---

[1] *A Short Handbook of Missions*, p. 155.

The work accomplished cannot be gauged by statistics. Very many Jews on the continent of Europe become convinced of the truth of Christianity after studying the New Testament or as the result of personal intercourse with Christian missionaries, but are not baptized until they have left their neighbourhood or country. Thus in six years (1895–1901) 582 Jews were baptized in various American churches who stated that they had been brought to believe in Christ as their Saviour as the result of their intercourse with Christian missionaries in Europe.

Missionary work amongst the Jews is in urgent need of expansion. In Russia and other countries there are millions of Jews for whom nothing has been done by Christian missionaries.

Amongst the number of Christian Jews whose names have become more or less famous, we may notice Neander, the German theologian and historian (his original name was Mende, but on the occasion of his baptism he adopted the name Neander, *i.e.* new man); Dr. Edersheim, the author of the *Life and Times of the Messiah*; Bishop Schereschewsky, Bishop of Shanghai, a great missionary and translator of the Bible into Chinese; Hellmuth, Bishop of Huron; Alexander, Bishop in Jerusalem (1841–45); Felix Mendelssohn; Sir William Herschel, the astronomer; Sir Francis Palgrave, a poet; Benjamin Disraeli; Sir Arthur Sullivan.[1]

How sadly the Christian Church has failed to recognize its responsibility towards the Jews may be inferred from the fact that nearly eighteen hundred years were allowed to pass before the New Testament was translated into their language. It was first published in Hebrew by the London Jews Society in 1817.

Baptisms during the Nineteenth Century.—During the nineteenth century the number of recorded baptisms was as follows: by the Russian and Oriental Churches, 74,500; by the Roman Church, 57,300; by the Anglican Church, 28,830; and by other Christian Churches, 72,740.

[1] See *Some Great Christian Jews*, by Dr. Jas. Littell, Keene, U.S.A.

The following figures are quoted in *Missions to Jews*,[1] by W. T. Gidney. They relate to baptisms in connection with Anglican or Protestant Churches · *Germany*, Jewish population, 560,000—baptisms, 17,520. *Great Britain*, population in 1800, 14,000; in 1900, 250,000—baptisms, 28,830. *Holland*, 98,000—baptisms, 1800. *France*, 72,000 — baptisms, 600. *Austria* and *Hungary*, 1,800,000 — baptisms, about 9000. *Russia*, baptisms, 4136. *North America*: the Jewish population increased from 1000 in 1812 to 2,211,000 at the present time —baptisms, 12,000.

Converts to the R.C. Church.—In *Germany*, 5000; *Austria* and *Hungary*, 36,200, apart from children of mixed marriages; *Russia*, 12,000; *Italy*, 300: estimated total number of converts, 57,300.

Converts to the Greek Church.—In *Russia*, 69,400; *Austria* and *Hungary*, 200; *Roumania*, 1500; *Turkey*, 3300: total number of converts received into the Greek Church, 74,500. Of this total a very large proportion of the conversions were due to political and social pressure rather than to any direct religious influences.

The number of conversions which have taken place as a result of Anglican and Protestant missions is much smaller, but nearly all have taken place as a result of deep religious conviction and in most instances the converts have been exposed to serious persecution at the hands of their fellow-countrymen. In connection with the work of the L.J.S. 2150 baptisms have taken place in London between 1809 and 1910. Over 700 Jews have been baptized in the L.J.S. church in Jerusalem. In Persia the rate of conversion has been steadily increasing: 13 baptisms occurred between 1880 and 1889, 31 between 1890 and 1899, 55 between 1900 and 1909. In Teheran 56 were prepared for baptism in 1910, of whom 12 were actually baptized.

[1] Tenth edition, pp. 143-46.

XXIII.

MISSIONARY SOCIETIES.

In the sketch that has been given of the missionary work which is being carried on in different countries, attention has been drawn to the work and organization of the chief missionary societies. In the present chapter we shall endeavour to give a list of the largest societies, together with a few notes relating to their origin and activities. For a further account of the work of any particular society, reference must be made to the index under the headings relating to the various societies.

References to societies whose work is confined to a particular country, *e.g.* The China Inland Mission or The Universities' Mission to Central Africa, will be found in the chapters dealing with the countries in which they are at work. An account of the Moravian Missionary Society, the New England Company, and the early Danish and Dutch Missions is given in the chapter on the "Dawn of Modern Missions" (p. 42 ff).

The *Society for the Propagation of the Gospel in Foreign Parts* was founded by Royal Charter in 1701 with the twofold object of ministering to English colonists and of converting the heathen to the Christian faith (see p. 58). The following are some of its chief centres of work amongst non-Christian populations: West Indies (1710), West Africa (1751), British Guiana (1835), South Africa (1819), India (1820), Borneo (1848), Burma (1859), Madagascar (1864), Japan (1873), North China (1880).

There are (1914) 1291 missionaries on the Society's list, of whom 941 (750 Europeans and 241 natives) are ordained. Of the ordained missionaries about 300 are engaged wholly or in part in ministering to Europeans. Its annual income is about £250,000.

The *Church Missionary Society*, formerly called The Society for Missions to Africa and the East, was formed on April 12, 1799. Its first missionaries were sent to Rio Pongas in West Africa, the headquarters of this mission being subsequently moved to Sierra Leone. The following have been the chief centres of the society's work: New Zealand (1814), India (1814), Ceylon (1817), Mid-China (1844), South China (1862), Japan (1869), Persia (1875), West Africa (1845), Uganda (1876), Palestine (1851), Egypt (1882), North-West Canada (1822).

Its medical missions are more extensive than those of any other society. Its staff includes 407 English and 454 other ordained missionaries. Its income is about £400,000. It has 65 men and 21 women medical missionaries.

The *Baptist Missionary Society*, which was founded on October 2, 1792, was the outcome of appeals made to his fellow Baptists by William Carey, the converted Northamptonshire cobbler, who became its first missionary. The twelve ministers who were present at its first meeting subscribed £13 and drew up its constitution. In his account of a subsequent meeting called to consider the question of starting missionary work in India, Andrew Fuller, its secretary, wrote: "We saw plainly that there was a gold mine in India, but it was as deep as the centre of the earth. Who would venture to explore it? 'I will go down,' said Carey, 'but you must hold the ropes.'" The chief centres of work are in India (1793), Ceylon (1812), China (1877), the Belgian Congo (1877), and the West Indies (1813).

Its staff includes 191 European and 41 other ordained missionaries. Its annual income is about £90,000. To this should be added the income of the Baptist Zenana Society (£18,000).

The *London Missionary Society* was founded in 1795.

Amongst its founders and early supporters were many Anglican and Presbyterian clergy, but it is now, and has for a long time been, chiefly supported by members of Congregational or Independent Churches. One of its earliest and best known missionaries was the Rev. Robert Morrison, who sailed for Canton in January 1807, and was the inaugurator of modern missions in China. Its first sphere of work was in the islands of the South Seas (1797). Its other chief centres of work are in India (1798), South Africa (1799), Central Africa (1877), Madagascar (1818), and New Guinea (1871).

Its staff includes 167 European and 966 other ordained missionaries. Its annual income (1914) is £121,000.

The *Wesleyan Methodist Missionary Society* was founded in 1813. As early as 1760, Gilbert, a slave-owner in Antigua, had formed a Methodist society of West Indian slaves, which by 1786 had increased to 2000. The Rev. Thomas Coke, an Anglican clergyman who had joined the Methodists, organized and carried on missionary work in the West Indies, and helped to send missionaries to West Africa for thirty years before the formation of a missionary society. At the age of seventy-six he left England with 7 missionaries—3 for Ceylon, 2 for India, 1 for Java, and 1 for South Africa. He died, and was buried at sea on June 1, 1814. On October 6, 1813, the missionary society was organized at Leeds. In 1817 work was begun in Madras, in 1821 in Mysore, in 1860 in Bengal, in 1822 in New Zealand, and in the Friendly Islands. In 1836 was begun the work in Fiji which, after the conversion of King Thakombau, transformed the whole character and appearance of these islands (see p. 452). A number of missions have been originated by this society in different parts of the world which are now under the direction of local or colonial Methodist Conferences. In its missions in India and other countries where Europeans reside, the attention of its missionaries is divided between the inhabitants of the country and the European population. The chief

fields in which the society labours or has laboured are the
West Indies, India (1817), Ceylon (1813), New Zealand
(1818), South Sea Islands (1822), South Africa (1815),
West Africa (1845), China (1852), and America. The
affiliated Women's Auxiliary supports women missionaries
in many of these fields.

The society has 385 British missionaries (not including
wives) and 94 unmarried women workers. The number of
"members" is 129,000, and of baptized adults, 287,000.
Its staff includes 319 European and 336 other ministers.
Its annual income is about £160,000, to which should
be added the income raised by the Women's Auxiliary,
£22,000. It has recently raised a centenary fund of
£250,000.

Amongst other smaller British Societies the following
should be mentioned. (In each case the income given in
brackets is for 1913) :—

Presbyterian Church of England (£43,025), *Presbyterian
Church in Ireland* (£31,782), *Welsh Calvinistic Methodists*
(£18,283), *Primitive Methodist Missionary Society* (£26,610),
United Methodist Church Missionary Society (£13,519),
Friends' Foreign Missionary Association (£33,000), *Sudan
United Mission* (£12,223), and the *North Africa Mission*
(£7068).

The total raised by British and Irish Societies in 1913
was £2,046,126. Of this amount, £1,041,543 was
contributed by the Church of England, £834,509 by
the Free Churches, £29,205 by the Church of Scotland,
and £140,869 by the supporters of interdenominational
societies.

In considering the development of missionary work in
recent times, special reference should be made to the help
which has been afforded to nearly all missionary societies
by the Student Volunteer Missionary Union. The British
branch of this Union was founded in 1892, and afterwards
became a department of the Student Christian Movement,
the membership of which consists of about 10,000 students.
The S.V.M.U. is not a missionary society, but aims at

creating interest in missions amongst college and university students. Its members, who sign a declaration, "It is my purpose, if God permit, to become a foreign missionary," are encouraged to connect themselves with some existing society and to go abroad as its representatives.

It is hard to estimate the help which this organization has afforded in promoting intelligent interest in Christian missions at home and in recruiting for the work abroad. The number of members of the British section of the S.V.M.U. who have already (December 1914) sailed for work abroad is 2048.

The missionary societies in connection with which they are working are as follows: Anglican, 487; Wesleyan Methodist, 367; London Missionary Society, 181; United Free Church of Scotland, 174; Baptist, 148; Irish Presbyterian, 53; Church of Scotland, 55; other societies, 583. A recent publication of the Student Christian Movement states:

"The Movement is seeking to interest in foreign missions those who intend to work at home, as, *e.g.*, clergy and ministers, business men, doctors, lawyers, engineers, schoolmasters, schoolmistresses, etc. This it does by having missionary addresses frequently delivered at its conferences and meetings of the Christian Unions, and also by the promotion of missionary study. The Movement was the pioneer of missionary study in Great Britain, being the first organization to appoint a missionary study secretary and to publish a missionary study text-book. Its example has now been followed by most of the larger missionary societies.

"Last year there were over 356 missionary study circles in the colleges, with a membership of about 2345 students."

Work of a similar character and on a still larger scale is being carried on by the same movement in America.

Scottish Missionary Societies.

We have already referred (p. 369) to the Confession of John Knox, in which he declared his belief that the

3I

gospel should be preached throughout the whole world.   No
missionary enterprise, however, was attempted for upwards
of a century.   In 1647 the Scottish General Assembly
recorded a desire for "a more firm consociation for propagating it (the Gospel) to those who are without, especially
the Jews," and in 1699 it counselled the ministers who
went with the expedition to Darien to labour among the
heathen.   In 1796 the Scottish (afterwards called the
Edinburgh) and the Glasgow Societies were organized.
The former society sent out Peter Greig, a gardener, and a
member of the Secession Church of Donibristle, who was
murdered in the Fulah country in West Africa, and was
perhaps the first Protestant missionary martyr.   This society
started missions in India and the West Indies.   The Glasgow
Society started a mission in Kaffraria in 1821.

In 1825 the *Church of Scotland Foreign Missions
Committee* was formed, which in 1829 sent Dr. Duff to
India.   In 1835 this Committee took over the mission
in India which had been organized by the Edinburgh
Society.   Its chief centres of work are India (1829),
Blantyre (1874), and China (1878).   Its annual income
is about £30,000.   Its staff includes 32 foreign and 15
other ordained missionaries.

The *Foreign Missions Committee of the United Free
Church* dates from 1843.   At the Disruption, Dr. Duff and
the other missionaries in India became members of the
Free Church.   The Disruption movement served to increase
interest in foreign missions to such an extent, that in the
year which followed it the contributions of the members of
the Free Church alone exceeded those of the entire Church
before the Disruption by £3600.   The chief centres of work
of this Church at the present time are India, Manchuria
(1873), Calabar (1846), Kaffraria (1821), Livingstonia
(1875), New Hebrides (1876), and West Indies.   The
work in the West Indies was taken over from the Edinburgh
Society in 1847, and that in Kaffraria from the Glasgow
Society in the same year.   (For an account of the Lovedale
Institution which forms part of this mission, see p. 324.)

The annual income of this society is about £125,000. Its staff includes 117 foreign and 68 other ordained missionaries.

The *Episcopal Church in Scotland* supports missions in Kaffraria, and at Chanda in the diocese of Nagpur, North Central India. The work in Kaffraria was undertaken at the instigation of Bishop Cotterill, who was Bishop of St. John's, Kaffraria, and afterwards became Bishop of Edinburgh in 1872.

Other Scottish societies include the *Edinburgh Medical Missionary Society* (1841), which supports work in India and Syria, and the *Mission to Lepers in India and the East* (1874), which endeavours to support missions in all lands where leprosy is found.

American Missionary Societies.

Missions supported in America may be said to date back to 1806, when three students—Mills, Hall, and Richards—held the "Haystack prayer-meeting," and resolved to form a society the object of which should be "to effect a mission to the heathen in the person of its members."[1] Their desire to be sent out as missionaries led to the formation of the American Board of Commissioners for Foreign Missions in 1810, and, later on, to the American Baptist Missionary Union in 1814.

The *American Board of Commissioners for Foreign Missions* (A.B.C.F.M.) was organized in 1810 by the General Association of Congregational Churches of Massachusetts. In the following year Judson was sent to England to confer with the L.M.S. with regard to mutual co-operation, but this was not found to be feasible. In 1812 its first five missionaries, of whom Judson was one, sailed for Calcutta. In 1812 the Presbyterians decided to support the A.B.C.F.M., and in 1826 they entrusted to the Board their work amongst American Indians. In 1837, however, they formed a separate organization for work

[1] See p. 377.

amongst the Indians, but in 1870 a Board of Foreign Missions of the re-united Presbyterian Churches was formed, and the Board since then has represented Congregationalists alone.

Its chief centres of work are: The Marathi Mission (1812), the Mission to Tamils in Ceylon (1813), and Madura (1834), Micronesia (1852), Asiatic Turkey (1831), China (1847), Zululand (1835), Portuguese West Africa (1880), Japan (1869). It also supports a number of missionaries who work amongst those who are nominally Christians in South America, Mexico, Spain, and Austria.

Its staff of ordained missionaries includes 165 Americans and 322 others. Its annual income is about £200,000.

The *American Baptist Missionary Union* dates from May 18, 1814, and was founded in order to support Judson, who had sailed for India as a Congregationalist, but prior to starting work in Burma had become a Baptist. It received the general support of Baptists in America till 1845, when, in consequence of the refusal of the Northern Baptists to allow the appointment of slave-owning missionaries, the Southern Baptist Convention was formed.

Its chief centres of work are Burma (1813), Assam (1836), the Telugu country (1836), China (1842), Japan (1860), Congo (1878).

Its annual income is about £220,000, and its staff of ordained missionaries includes 211 American missionaries. The society also carries on work amongst Christians in Europe and in the Philippine Islands.

The *Southern Baptist Convention* supports work in China, Africa, and Japan. Its income is about £117,000, and its staff of ordained missionaries includes 109 Americans and 112 others.

The missionary organization of the *Methodist Episcopal Church in the United States* dates from 1819, but its foreign work was only started in 1833. In all countries in which there is a Christian population its work is carried on simultaneously amongst the white and coloured population, and in its returns the two kinds of work are not distinguished. Its principal work amongst non-Christians is in Liberia (1833), Angola and the Congo district (1885), East Central Africa (1901), China (1847), India (1856), Japan (1873), Corea (1884).

A women's auxiliary was formed as early as 1819, but did not take any active part in the work of the society till 1869. Its annual income is about £540,000, but this includes a large number of contributions towards the support of work amongst European Christians.

A Board of Missions connected with the *Methodist Episcopal Church* (South) was organized in 1846. It started work in China in 1848. One of its missionaries has been Dr. A. P. Parker, afterwards President of the Anglo-Chinese College in Shanghai. It began work in Japan in 1886 and in Corea in 1895. Its annual income is about £150,000.

The *Protestant Episcopal Church in the U.S.A.* in 1817 offered, through Bishop Griswold, to co-operate with the C.M.S. of England in sending out missionaries to the foreign field, but was urged by this society to organize independent work. In 1820 the Domestic and Foreign Missionary Society was formed, and in 1835 the Protestant Episcopal Church took over the work and became its own missionary society. In 1830 work was started in Liberia, and in 1850 a bishop of Cape Palmas was appointed. Its work was extended to Batavia in 1835, and to China in 1837, to Japan in 1859, and to the Philippines in 1901.

Its annual expenditure on work outside the United States is about £130,000. It helps to support 11 bishops (Cape Palmas, Shanghai, Hankow, Anking, Tokyo, Kyoto, Brazil, Cuba, Mexico, Philippine Islands, and Porto Rico).

Its missionary staff includes 60 American and 114 other clergy. In its mission hospitals 250,000 cases were treated in 1913.

The *Presbyterian Board of Foreign Missions* (North) was constituted in 1837, but missionary work had been supported by Presbyterians in America at a much earlier date. Thus in 1741 the Rev. Azariah Horton was appointed by the Presbytery of New York to labour among Indians in Long Island, and in 1744 David Brainerd was ordained by the same Presbytery (see p. 370). Several other efforts were also made to organize work amongst the Indians. In 1818 the United Foreign Missionary Society was formed, the work of which was transferred to the A.B.C.F.M. in 1826. When the Board was formed in 1837 it received support from the Presbyterians who belonged to the "old school," whilst the "new school" continued to support the A.B.C.F.M. till 1870, when the Board received the united support of both sections. The Board is a permanent committee of the General Assembly, which supervises and controls the missions. It began its work in India, where it took over a mission at Ludhiana which had been started in 1833. Its chief centres of work at the present time are in the Punjab (1846), the United Provinces (1836), Western India (1870), Central China (1844), Canton (1845), Peking (1863), Shantung (1861), Siam (1847), Japan (1859), West Africa (1850), Persia (1870), and Corea (1884).

Its annual income is about £470,000, and its staff of ordained missionaries includes 365 foreign and 277 others. These figures include the support of work carried on amongst Christians in South America, Syria, etc.

The *Presbyterian Church* in the Southern States formed a separate missionary organization on the outbreak of the war (1861). Its chief centres of work are in China (1867), Japan (1885), Congo (1890), and Corea (1892). Its annual income is about £100,000, and its staff of ordained missionaries includes 100 Americans and 35 others.

Amongst other smaller American societies should be mentioned the *Dutch Reformed Church* (1832), which supports work in China, Japan, India, and Arabia; the

American Friends' Board of Foreign Missions (1871), which supports work in Japan and China; the *General Missionary Board of the Church of the Brethren* (1884), which supports work in China and India; the *United Brethren in Christ* (1853), which supports work in West Africa, China, and Japan; the *Swedish Missionary Covenant* (1885), which supports work in China and Alaska; and the *Christian and Missionary Alliance*, which supports work in West Africa, India, China, and Japan.

Missionary Societies on the Continent of Europe.

The *Berlin Missionary Society*, which was founded in 1824, was the outcome of a missionary training school founded by Janicke in 1800. The appeal for funds wherewith to found the society was signed by Neander, Tholuck, and other well-known writers. It began by supporting the Moravian and Basel Missions, but in 1834 sent out missionaries on its own account. This society has kept constantly in view the design of making its missions self-supporting by the opening of stores, mills, and other enterprises in connection with its mission stations. Its chief centres of work are South Africa (1834), German East Africa (1891), and China (1846).

The *Leipzig Evangelical Lutheran Mission Society* was founded in Dresden in 1836, but its centre of organization was removed to Leipzig in 1846. Its chief centres of work are in India (1840) and East Africa (1902).

The *Rhenish Missionary Society* was the outcome of a missionary union organized by twelve laymen in Elberfeld in 1799. It was formed in 1828 at Barmen. Its chief centres of work are South Africa (1829), Dutch East Indies (1842), China (1846), and German New Guinea (1887).

The *Hermannsburg Missionary Society* was founded by Louis Harms as a private society in 1849, but after his death in 1865 it came under the direction of the Lutheran "Free Church of Hanover." In the early days of this mission efforts were made to establish self-supporting farms in connection with the mission stations, but this policy has been gradually abandoned. Its chief centres of work are in South Africa (1857) and the Telugu country in India (1866).

The *Basel Evangelical Missionary Society*. In 1730 the German Christian Society was founded at Basel in order "to collect and impart information concerning the kingdom of God." Later on it corresponded with the L.M.S. In 1815 members of this society and others founded a missionary training home in Basel with the intention of supplying missionaries to some of the English missionary societies. In 1821 it sent out its first missionaries. The society is undenominational and has relations with nearly all the Protestant Churches of Central Europe. Its chief centres of work are West Africa (1827), Western India (1834), and China (1846).

The *Paris Evangelical Mission Society* was founded in November 1822. After the Revolution in 1848 the support which it received became so small that it had for a time to close its missionary training institution, but soon afterwards its work greatly expanded. Its chief centres of work are Basutoland (1833), Senegal (1862), the Zambesi (1877), French Congo (1887), Tahiti and French Polynesia (1845), and Madagascar (1902).

Some particulars in regard to the above missions and in regard to the chief missionary societies supported in the Netherlands, Scandinavia, and Finland are given in the table on the opposite page:—

[TABLE

	Organized.	Home Income.	Ordained Missionaries.		Communi- cants.	Field of Labour.
			Foreign	Native		
Germany—						
Berlin	1824	£76,000	118	31	39,000	China, East and South Africa
Rhenish	1828	62,000	171	40	102,000	South Africa, Dutch East Indies, China
Gossner	1836	19,000	47	43	34,000	India
Leipsic	1836	45,000	56	28	11,000	India, East Africa
Hermannsburg	1849	26,000	61	4	34,000	South Africa, India, Persia
France—						
Paris Society	1822	40,000	58	106	10,000	Africa, Melanesia, Polynesia
Switzerland—						
Basel Society	1815	96,000	214	57	41,000	India, China, West Africa
Mission Romande	1875	18,000	18	...	2,500	South Africa, East Africa
Netherlands—						
Neth. Society	1797	16,000	19	..	17,000	Dutch East Indies
Utrecht Union	1859	10,000	18	..	...	Dutch East Indies, Dutch N. Guinea
Scandinavia—						
Danish Society	1821	24,000	32	7	1,000	India, China
Norwegian Mis- sionary Society	1842	19,000	68	101	30,000	South Africa, Mada- gascar, China
Swedish Mission- ary Union	1878	24,000	56	...	3,000	Congo, China, Chin- ese Turkestan
Church of Sweden Mission	1874	17,000	24	5	3,000	South Africa, India, Ceylon
Swedish Evangeli- cal National Society	1856	10,000	29	5	1,700	East Africa, India
Finnish Mission- ary Society	1859	15,000	27	...	1,800	German South-West Africa, China
Total for all Continental Protestant Societies [1]		£900,000	1508	488	371,000	

[1] 1914 Reports

Roman Catholic Missionary Societies and Associations.

A considerable extension of the missions connected with the R.C. Church dates from the early years of the nineteenth century, the missionary activities of the Church having been practically dormant during a great part of the eighteenth century. The revival of interest in missions was greatly assisted by the formation of the Lyons Missionary Society. In 1822 "a few humble and obscure

Catholics " (as they described themselves) founded at Lyons an Institution for the Propagation of the Faith, their object being not to send out missionaries but to collect money to hand to various religious Orders and societies. The earliest members of this society were some of the women engaged in the silk factories at Lyons. At its first meeting twelve persons were present, when a priest proposed a resolution to found an association to help Roman Catholic missions all over the world. In the recent report of the society it is stated: "that the root-idea of the organization is due to Pauline Marie Jaricot, who formed the girls working in the silk factories of that city into groups of apostolic workers for the missionary cause. Each group of ten was headed by a promoter who collected the halfpenny subscribed by each associate per week and in return circulated the news that came from the missionaries in response to their zeal and generosity.

The society was founded by laity, and the administration of its funds is almost entirely in their hands. The Pope blessed the society in 1823, and by 1843 its income had reached £141,000. It then claimed to be assisting 130 bishops and 4000 priests. The receipts of the society in 1914 were £324,000. Of the sum received £30,000 was contributed towards the support of Jesuit missions.

As the other societies and Orders which support foreign missions do not publish statements of accounts, it is difficult to form any estimate of the whole amount contributed annually by Roman Catholics towards the support of missionary work.

At the beginning of the nineteenth century the number of the Roman Catholic missionaries hardly amounted to 1000. To-day there are in non-Christian countries 6000 European priests, 2400 teaching brothers, and about 8500 sisters, apart from native workers.[1] The Roman Catholic missions are carried on partly by missionary societies and partly by religious Orders, and have been,

[1] From these figures at least 10 per cent. ought apparently to be deducted (see p. 492).

to a greater or less extent, under the supervision of the Congregation de propaganda Fide at Rome since its foundation in 1622. The congregation of Lazarists was founded by St. Vincent de Paul in 1632 and the Société des Missions Étrangères in 1663. This latter, which is one of the most important of the R.C. missionary societies, supports work in Japan, Corea, Indo-China, Burma, and South India. The headquarters of both are at Paris. Other smaller societies have their headquarters in Italy, Belgium, England, and Ireland. Of the religious Orders the Anglican Benedictines work in several of the English colonies or dominions; the Capuchins in the Levant, Western Asia, North Africa, and South America; the Carmelites in India; the Dominicans in Turkey and Indo-China; the Lazarists in China, the Levant, Persia, Madagascar, and South America; the Franciscans in China, in the Philippines, the Pacific Islands, Egypt, and North Africa, and the Jesuits in all parts of the mission field. An English organization entitled St. Joseph's Foreign Missionary Society, established in 1870, works in Uganda, India, and Borneo.

The Jesuit Order numbers altogether (1914) 16,735, of whom 3619 are serving in foreign missions Of the 720 members in the "English Provinces" 110 are serving in British Guiana and Zambesiland.

Among other smaller societies or associations should be mentioned the Congregation of the Holy Ghost and the Immaculate Heart of Mary, the Oblates of Mary Immaculate, the Society of Mary, the Oratorians and Oblates of St. Francis de Sales, the Redemptionists, the Paulists, and the Congregation of the Sacred Hearts of Jesus and Mary.

Roman Catholic Missionary Statistics.

The following statistics relating to Roman Catholic missions in non-Christian countries have been condensed from the *Atlas Hierarchichus* issued in 1913:—

COUNTRIES	MISSIONARY FORCE.				NATIVE MEMBERSHIP	
	European Priests	Native Priests	European Lay Brothers.	European Sisters	Baptized	Catechumens
Japan	182	38	99	100	66,134	16,452[1]
Corea	40	15	7	10	78,850	8,220[1]
Chinese Empire . .	1,305	721	247	1,429	1,406,659	613,402
Further India . .	517	689	130[1]	120	986,597	22,576[1]
East India Islands . .	101	2	41	200[1]	37,707	815
Oceania . . .	427	8	227	418	181,436	11,598
India and Ceylon[2] .	1,268	1,280	400[1]	2,000[1]	2,146,854[3]	55,443[1]
North Africa (East)[4]	266	80	300[1]	900	30,000	1,500
North Africa (West)	497	5	141	339	120,000	43,245
South Africa . .	387	4	360	1,672	50,000[1]	5,866
Central Africa . .	810	3	311	466	332,676	352,763
African Islands . .	188	2	128[1]	467[1]	223,504	253,015
United States (Indians) .	163	..	55[1]	391[1]	64,741	
Totals . .	6,131	2,792	2,446	8,512	5,675,158	1,384,995

[1] These figures are not given in the *Atlas Hierarchicus*, but are estimates taken from other sources.

[2] The Christians in Ceylon connected with Roman Catholic missions number about 350,000.

[3] According to Indian Census Returns.

[4] Including work amongst Europeans in Egypt and Tripoli.

The figures given above include many priests and other workers who are engaged in ministering to Europeans or Eurasians in India, South and North Africa, and Oceania. These workers constitute from 10 to 15 per cent. of the totals given. In the R.C. returns no distinction is made between these workers and those who are working amongst non-Christians.

The amount contributed towards the support of R.C. missions in the U.S.A. has increased during the last ten years from £9000 to £88,000. During the same period the amount contributed in France has fallen from £163,000 to £118,000.

XXIV.

THE OUTLOOK.

In the preceding pages we have tried to avoid giving any missionary statistics which were not necessary in order to elucidate the progress of Christian missions. Students of missions have learnt by experience how easily statistics can mislead, and how poor a test they afford of the depth or stability of the work in any given place. Whilst, however, the student has need to sift the missionary statistics which are available with the utmost care, he cannot afford to neglect them altogether, as in many cases they afford the only means of estimating the progress of missions over a wide area and within any given period. In order that we may form some estimate of the missionary prospect throughout the world at the present moment, it will be well to take note of the latest available statistics which relate to the mission field as a whole. Surveying the whole field of Anglican and Protestant missions, we note that the total sum raised by missionary societies in 1914 was about £7,000,000. Of this amount, roughly speaking, £3,200,000 was contributed in the United States, £2,400,000 in Great Britain and Ireland, £900,000 on the continent of Europe, £250,000 in Canada, £100,000 in Australia, and the rest in Africa and Asia. To this total should be added about £1,500,000 raised in the mission field for the support of Christian Churches or for the evangelization of non-Christians. The most encouraging fact revealed by the statistics is the rapid expansion of Christian missionary organizations. During the twelve years between 1901 and 1913 the contributions more than doubled. The increase in the American contributions was greater than it has been in England, but in both countries it has been remarkable. Moreover, the increase during the five years 1909–14 has been much more rapid than during the earlier years of this period. During these five years the total increase was roughly from £5,100,000 to £7,000,000, *i.e.* 37·2 per cent., or 7·4 per cent. per annum.

If we extend our survey of Protestant and Anglican missions and take in the whole of the century ending in 1910, we should find that the contributions towards the support of foreign missions increased during this period three-hundredfold.

During the period 1900-14 the number of European and American missionaries connected with the various societies increased from 16,218 to 24,871, and the number of local missionaries and mission helpers from 62,366 to 129,527. Although the contributions raised in America exceed those raised in Great Britain by nearly 50 per cent., the number of European missionaries supported by British societies is greater than the number of American (U.S.A.) missionaries, *i.e.* 10,871 as compared with 9000, the expenditure in connection with each missionary being considerably greater in America than it is in England. The following statistics relating to Foreign Missions supported in the United States and Canada were issued in January 1915 by the Committee on Home Base representing the Foreign Missions Conference of North America. The total income of American (U.S.A.) Foreign Mission Boards during 1914 was $15,449,990, and of Canadian missionary organizations $1,250,075. To these totals should be added $468,545 contributed for educational and medical work in America, and $4,243,967 contributed in the foreign mission field. In connection with the missions supported in the United States and Canada, 159,286 persons were baptized during 1914 as compared with 121,811 during 1913; there are 606 colleges, theological seminaries, and training schools, and 12,969 other schools, with a total attendance of 547,730.

The foregoing statistics make it clear that, whatever criticism may be passed upon the work which is now being done by Christian missionaries, it can no longer be said that it is being carried on on such a small scale that the student of modern history can afford to pass it by. To the Christian who contemplates his obligations in the spirit of Christ's teaching, the work which is being done will appear pitifully minute, but if the influence which it is exerting be compared with the other influences which are shaping the destinies of nations, it will be seen to be both large and intense.

If we include the missionaries of the Roman and Greek communions, the number of European and American workers in the mission field to-day exceeds 50,000 ; whilst the number of communicants, or full members of the Christian Church, exceeds 7,000,000. Each year, moreover, sees the addition by baptism of more than half a million members, whilst the number of Christian adherents in the non-Christian countries which constitute the mission field is not far short of 10,000,000. We should be the first to deprecate the thought that the work of Christian missions can be estimated by figures, but in view of the comparative neglect with which such work has often been treated, it is helpful to recall the fact that if they are gauged by the standards of business life they cannot justly be described as devoid of visible results.

It would be impossible to name any subject other than that of foreign missions which so few persons have carefully studied, but on which, nevertheless, so many are prepared to pass judgment. Careful study may be defined as study continued for a space of at least ten years. If it be objected that this is a long period to expect a student of foreign missions to devote to his subject before we are prepared to listen with respect to the conclusions which he has to report, we have only to consider the length of time which is regarded as necessary to qualify one who aspires to be an expert in any other branch of knowledge in order to establish the justice of our demand. We should listen with undisguised impatience to anyone who presumed to criticize and reject the conclusions of his predecessors if the subject with which he was dealing were the cure of disease, the motions of the stars, or the results of historical investigation, or metaphysical speculation, if he had spent any shorter period in preparing himself for his task; but the globe-trotter, who has spent a few days or weeks in examining the methods and results of Christian missions, is usually sure of a sympathetic audience when, on returning from his travels, he communicates his discoveries to the world.   With what a different reception would he meet if, after spending the same number of days in examining hospitals, in visiting observatories, in skimming historical works, or in studying metaphysics, he were to presume to speak with authority on the results of his investigations!

The majority of the missionaries who are in the field to-day would welcome an examination of their work at the hands of intelligent investigators who possessed some knowledge of the history of missions, but, conscious of the fact that their methods are the outcome of eighteen centuries of experience and that the task on which they are engaged, whether viewed from a spiritual, a moral, or an educational standpoint, is the greatest which men have ever essayed to undertake, they find it hard to be patient when the superficial critic presumes to pass judgment upon their methods or their results.

What may be termed the sociological results which have been achieved by missionaries in non-Christian lands have been well summarized by Dr. Capen, a well-known student of missions in America.   He writes:

"Missionaries have done much to remove the evil of ignorance.   They have introduced into the East modern medicine, and are treating yearly millions of patients who would otherwise be beyond the possibility of relief.   Where the need is the greatest, they have undertaken to increase the industrial efficiency of the Christian community, and to prepare Christian leaders for the new industry.   In various ways they have raised the standard of living among the native Christians and those who are under Christian influence. Under the impulse of Christianity, woman has been coming to her own. Education has provided for her, and in Christian homes the wife is becoming the companion and helpmeet of her husband, and the intelligent guide and teacher of her children. Christianity has emphasized the infinite worth of the individual before God, and the Christian has come to have a new sense of self-respect, and he stands before the community as a free man in Christ. The missionary has ever preached and exemplified new standards of justice, honour, truthfulness, and purity, and thus personally, and through those whom he has influenced and trained, he has helped to solve both the political and the ethical problems of the people among whom he has lived."[1]

In the course of this volume we have referred to and endeavoured to illustrate many different methods of missionary enterprise, but we can never allow ourselves to forget that the supremely important method of missionary work is the method of the Incarnation. As Jesus Christ revealed God by being what He was, so in a true sense the aim of the Christian missionary must be to reveal God made manifest in Christ by living over again the Christ-life. The secret of St. Paul's missionary success was contained in the statement, "To me to live is Christ."

For the successful prosecution of the missionary campaign character is of greater importance than method. Many a missionary whose intellectual and other qualifications have been small, has exerted what to onlookers has appeared to be a miraculous influence by the life which he has lived in a non-Christian land. Many a mission which has adopted physical methods of propagating Christianity which appear to be wholly inconsistent with the Spirit of Christ, has achieved spiritual results which other missions that have been conducted upon the most approved lines have failed to accomplish. In both instances the influence exerted by the personal character of the individual missionary has been so strong that the wisdom or un-

[1] *Sociological Progress in Mission Lands*, by E. W. Capen, p. 397 f.

32

wisdom of the methods which he has adopted has become a matter of secondary importance. It is St. Paul's character even more than his missionary methods which the missionary of to-day needs to imitate and to make his own.

The task of compiling this sketch of Christian missions has been completed in the midst of the greatest war which this earth has witnessed, and the issues of which must profoundly affect the influence which Christian principles will hereafter exert both in Europe and in the remotest part of the mission field. It is impossible to forecast what the future has in store, or to predict the effects which the war will have upon the future of Christianity at home and abroad. But though all else be enshrouded in uncertainty, which nothing but the march of time can dispel, there is one occurrence which we can predict with completest confidence. Though upon the earth there be now distress of nations with perplexity, the sea and the waves roaring, men's hearts failing them for fear and for looking after those things which are coming upon the earth, though the powers of heaven be shaken and the stars fall from heaven, one thing in the future is certain. Of its details we may not be sure, but of the fact itself there can be no doubt, the fact which all history demands and which all revelation asserts. Earth's greatest kingdoms may have their day and cease to be, but the establishment of the kingdom of heaven is drawing nigh, and of this kingdom there shall be no end. Other suns may fail to rise or fade for ever from our view, but the Sun of Righteousness shall eventually arise and the day which it will usher in will know no evening. For it is no mere possibility, no considerable probability, but a glorious and complete certainty, independent of human belief and unalterable by human incredulity that the petition which has formed the age-long prayer of the Christian Church—"Thy kingdom come"—will receive its fulfilment, and that this fulfilment will exceed the highest hopes which any who have offered it have dared to entertain.

APPENDIX.

CHRISTIAN REUNION IN THE MISSION FIELD.

AMONGST the many subjects with which a history of Christian missions would naturally deal, but which it has been necessary to leave untouched through lack of space, one of the most important is the development of Christian Unity in the Mission Field. On this the writer of this volume would like to say a very few words. If, or rather when, Christian unity is achieved throughout Christendom it will probably be a direct result of foreign missions. From the point of view, therefore, of the Church at home, no less than from that of the Church in the mission field, the subject is one of the greatest importance.

On the need for unity, or at least for some form of combined action in the mission field, there is no need to dwell.

Dr. Mott, in presenting the Report of the Commission for Carrying the Gospel to all the non-Christian World at the Edinburgh Conference, said:

"It is our deep conviction that a well-considered plan of co-operation in the missionary work of the societies represented in this hall, entered into and carried out with a sense of our oneness in Christ, would be more than equivalent to doubling the present missionary staff."

The need for securing united action in the mission field which the Edinburgh Conference emphasized, must not, however, blind our eyes to the fact that any union which might conceivably be secured by a willingness on the part of Christian Churches to sink their differences and to insist only on the few doctrinal points on which they were all agreed, would not be worth securing and could not endure. Any action is to be deprecated which will tend to obliterate the distinctive message which the various representatives of the Christian Churches in the mission field have to give. We believe that the distinctive doctrines, or the distinctive emphasis which is laid upon the same doctrine by different Churches, or by different missionary societies acting as the agents of these Churches, is of priceless value, if the mind of Christ is to be fully made known to the peoples to whom they are trying to appeal.

The Roman Catholic missionary, in the conscientious carrying out of his missionary obligation, lays emphasis upon the importance of submitting his will and his judgment to an external authority which for him is embodied in Christ's "Vicar on earth." He believes, too, that by confession to and absolution received from a human priest, man's character can best be strengthened and purified, and that by the reception of sacraments ministered by a duly ordained priest, vital union with God can be established and maintained. On the other hand, the Protestant (as distinguished from the Roman, Greek and Anglican) Churches emphasize in the presence of the non-Christian world the reality of man's individual responsibility alike for his opinions and his actions and the possibility of his enjoying close communion with God apart from the practice of specified religious rites, and without the help which might be afforded by a priesthood that claimed a direct succession from the Apostles.

Lastly, the representatives of Anglican missions, who hold a position intermediate between the Roman Catholics and the Protestants, endeavour to combine the teaching of both, and, whilst emphasizing the value of external authority and of sacramental grace, strive to inculcate man's complete responsibility as an individual. It is in the mission field that the representatives of the Churches can least afford to lose sight of the distinctive doctrines to which their branch of the Christian Church has borne witness in the past. Unity, therefore, when it comes, can involve no compromise of principles, but it will involve the thankful recognition that God has worked in the past and will work in the future through men and women whose instincts and environment have led them to interpret the Divine Revelation in very different ways, but who are united by a true devotion to their common Lord. It is not compromise, but comprehension, on which our eyes are fixed.

The difficulty which, more than any other, at the present time stands in the way of any progress in the direction of reunion as between the Anglican and Protestant Churches, is the insistence which is laid by the former on the " historic episcopate."

As this difficulty has within recent years been much discussed in India, it may be well to refer in further detail to the questions which have there been raised.

As far as the Anglican Church throughout the world is concerned, the successful carrying out of any scheme of reunion depends upon the willingness of other churches to accept as the basis of reunion what is popularly known as the Lambeth Quadrilateral, which was adopted by the Lambeth Conference in 1888, and which reads as follows:

" 1. The Holy Scriptures of the Old and New Testaments, as containing all things necessary to salvation, and being the rule and ultimate standard of faith.

" 2. The Apostles' Creed as the Baptismal symbol, and the Nicene Creed as the sufficient statement of the Christian faith.

" 3. The two Sacraments ordained by Christ Himself— Baptism and the Supper of the Lord—ministered with unfailing use of Christ's words of institution, and of the elements ordained by Him.

" 4. The historic episcopate, locally adapted in the methods of its administration to the varying needs of the nations and peoples called of God into the Unity of His Church."

Whilst nearly all the Churches now at work in the

mission field would be prepared to accept the first three of these conditions, the acceptance of the fourth by any of the representatives of the Free Churches in Great Britain or the non-Episcopal Churches in America, will depend upon their interpretation of the words "the historic episcopate." If by these words be implied the doctrine of apostolical succession, the validity of which is to depend upon the uninterrupted and mechanical transmission of grace by the laying on of hands, it is most unlikely that any large scheme of reunion will ever be accomplished. There are, however, many representatives of Anglican Churchmen both at home and abroad who place upon these words a meaning which would render the acceptance of this clause acceptable to very many who are at present outside the Anglican Church.

The Bishop of Madras (Dr. Whitehead) in a speech on the subject of Christian reunion delivered to the members of the National Conference of Missionaries at Calcutta on December 20, 1912, quoted and endorsed the article by Dr. A. Headlam in *The Prayer-Book Dictionary* (p. 42). In the course of which he wrote :

"The idea of apostolic succession . . . is really a deduction from the right theory of Orders, and the mistake has been to make Orders depend upon apostolic succession and transmission. . . . The authority to consecrate and ordain, or to perform all spiritual offices, resides in and comes from the Church to which God gives His Holy Spirit. . . . The idea of transmission is an additional and late conception which, instead of expressing the idea of succession, has by its exaggeration of it led to a rigid and mechanical theory of the ministry. . . . As the grace of Orders depends upon the authority of the Church and not upon a mechanical transmission, all objections from supposed irregularities of ordination are beside the point, and the opinions of Churchmen and others who have maintained that in certain circumstances a presbyter may ordain, are explained. Ordination depends upon the authority of the Church, and not the Church upon ordination."

As the views which have been expressed by the Bishop

of Madras form a distinct contribution to the discussion of the question of reunion in the mission field, it is worth while giving in his own words his plea for the acceptance of the doctrine of episcopacy as defined by Dr. Headlam. Speaking in Calcutta, the Bishop of Madras said:

"I believe myself that whatever the reason for its adoption, the ultimate ground for the principle (of episcopacy) lay in the fact that it was imperatively needed as a safeguard to unity; and I believe also that it is as much needed for that purpose to-day as it was then, and that it is far more needed in India than it was in the early Church. When I ask, 'If I give up this, what principle should I adopt?' I find it can only be this, that any body of Christian men and women are at liberty to make their own arrangements for their own ministry. Now I have often thought of this alternative principle, and it seems to me that not only does it everywhere throw open the door to division and schism, but, if we were to proclaim it in India, the necessary and inevitable result would be the creation of caste churches. When the Indian community is freed from the restraints of foreign missionary societies, if it accepts this principle, it will necessarily and inevitably take the line of least resistance, and then we shall see in India divisions based on caste, far more numerous and infinitely worse than anything that the Church has yet seen in East or West."[1]

The words of the Bishop of Madras may help to explain to those who are not members of the Anglican Church why the representatives of this Church in India and elsewhere, in their anxiety to "safeguard unity," lay what appears to them to be undue emphasis upon the necessity of the historic episcopate. The plea which they put forward does not unchurch other Churches, but represents an attempt to secure an increase of mutual fellowship, without sacrifice of principle on either side. If this were not so, or if the proposals put forward by the Bishop of Madras were equivalent to a proposal to absorb and remould on Anglican lines all other Churches, the prospect of reunion would be far less bright than it now is.

[1] *The next Step towards Unity*, p. 6.

One scheme for practical co-operation and federation which was drawn up by the representatives of a number of missionary societies working in East Africa has attracted special attention, as it appears to some to indicate the lines on which co-operation in other parts of the mission field might be attained. The scheme was drawn up at a conference of missionaries which was held at Kikuyu, in British East Africa, in June 1913, and which was attended by representatives of all missionary societies in that district other than those connected with the Roman Church. The basis of the federation was to be the acceptance of the Bible and of the Apostles' and Nicene Creeds. The same rules relating to the admission of catechumens were to be adopted by all missions and Baptism was to be administered, whether by sprinkling or immersion, in the name of the Holy Trinity. It was further suggested that any minister recognized by his own Church might be allowed to preach, but not to administer the sacraments in a mission Church belonging to other churches. The proposed scheme has since been ratified by the Church of Scotland Foreign Mission Committee. The conference was followed by a Service of Holy Communion, at which the Bishop of Uganda administered the Holy Communion to the missionaries of various denominations who were present.

No proposals for reunion in the mission field can be regarded otherwise than as sadly incomplete which do not include reunion with the branches of the Church established by the Roman Catholic missions. What answer, then, can be given to the question—Is there any prospect that the Church of Rome can ever be included in any scheme of reunion which could commend itself to other Christian Churches ? Whilst on the one hand it would be unwise to under-estimate the difficulties which will have to be surmounted before such a reunion could be effected,[1]

[1] How great these difficulties are, may be gathered from a quotation from a catechism expressly authorized by Pope Pius x. in 1906 and published by the Vatican Press. On page 119 we read: "Can anyone outside the

on the other hand, it would imply a lack of faith in the destiny of the Christian Church and in the power of the Divine Spirit to guide and direct its members if we could bring ourselves to believe that the prospect is hopeless and that the attitude of the Church of Rome will ever remain what it is to-day. Bishop Brent, the Bishop of the Philippines, who was one of the delegates to the Edinburgh Missionary Conference in 1910, referring to the letter of sympathy which was read to the Conference from the Roman Bishop of Cremona, wrote:

" The letter of the Italian ecclesiastic which was written for the Conference was the little cloud not larger than a man's hand to-day, destined to-morrow to cover the Roman heavens. A major law may temporarily be held in suspense by a minor law. When this happens we need not be over-anxious. The issue is certain. Already the true greatness, that is to say the catholicism, of the Roman Catholic Church is busy at her heart, and the secondary power of the Roman curia can do no more than delay its triumph. The Bishop of Cremona did not speak of himself or for himself, but consciously, or unconsciously, voiced the mind of a growing minority who are the soul of his communion. It may not be to-morrow, or a century hence—Christianity, be it remembered, is very young—but ultimate victory is as sure as Christ is real."

The need to promote reunion in the mission field has become increasingly urgent in recent years in view of the fact that in India, China, and elsewhere local Churches are beginning to spring up, the members of which know nothing of the past history of the Christian Church. The danger

Catholic Apostolic Roman Church be saved?—A. No." On page 180: "Who are they who do not belong to the Communion of Saints?—A. The damned, and those who belong neither to the soul nor to the body of the Church—that is, those in mortal sin and those outside the true Church." On page 131: "Who are outside the true Church?—A. Infidels, Jews, Heretics, Apostates, Schismatics, and the Excommunicate." "Who are Heretics?—A. . . . The various sects of Protestants." On page 398: "Protestantism . . . is the sum of all Heresies. . . . The most monstrous congeries of errors, both private and individual, and enfolds all Heresies."

which is involved in the creation of such local Churches is well described by Dr. Mott, who writes :

"Everything practicable should be done to strengthen the bonds of union between the new Churches in non-Christian lands and the Church Universal. This point is one of cardinal importance just now, when independent Churches are springing up on every hand, and when, owing to the growing national spirit, there is danger of the development of Churches in the East which will be separate in aims and sympathies, as well as in activities, from the Church in the West. In this connection the importance of the study of Church history should be emphasized among both the missionaries and the native leaders, as well as among the students in theological colleges and Bible schools . . . The fact that many of the native Christian leaders have such a poor historical sense makes it all the more important and necessary that in this and other ways we seek to keep the growing native Churches in closer touch with the great consensus of the continuous Church of all the ages. There could be no greater danger than for native Christianity to become separate from historical, credal, œcumenical, living Christianity."[1]

In the course of this volume we have referred to efforts which have been made in particular sections of the mission field to promote union or reunion between different churches or organizations (see pp. 142, 203, 232, 504). The success which has already been achieved justifies the hope that schemes of a bolder and more far-reaching character may meet hereafter with a like success.

The Continuation Committee Conferences, presided over by Dr. Mott, which were held in India, China, and Japan, 1912–13, and which were an outcome of the Edinburgh Missionary Conference (1910), helped to focus the attention of missionaries in the field upon their common needs and problems, and by facilitating joint counsels and joint action prepared the way for a closer union than is at the present moment within sight.

[1] *The Present World Situation*, by J. R. Mott, p. 193 f.

INDEX.

References to missionary societies and organisations are given under the word " Societies."

34

Lightning Source UK Ltd.
Milton Keynes UK
UKHW021828170722
405991UK00003B/11